# The Atlas of
# Breeding Birds of Connecticut

STATE GEOLOGICAL AND NATURAL HISTORY SURVEY OF CONNECTICUT

DEPARTMENT OF ENVIRONMENTAL PROTECTION

# The Atlas of Breeding Birds of Connecticut

EDITED BY LOUIS R. BEVIER

Illustrated by Michael DiGiorgio

Contributing editors:
George A. Clark, Jr., Marshal T. Case, David Rosgen, Christopher S. Wood, and George W. Zepko

Contributing authors:

Robert A. Askins
Robert I. Bertin
Louis R. Bevier
Anthony H. Bledsoe
Winifred B. Burkett
Elizabeth Bushnell
George A. Clark, Jr.

Robert K. Colwell
Michael R. Conover
Arnold Devine
Phillip F. Elliott
Walter G. Ellison
George Gale

Donald A. Hopkins
Gordon Loery
Donald E. McIvor
Paul R. Merola
Kenneth E. Petit
Alan F. Poole

Noble S. Proctor
Frederick Purnell, Jr.
Fred C. Sibley
Dwight G. Smith
Jeffrey A. Spendelow
Mark S. Szantyr

Sponsored by the National Audubon Society and the Audubon Council of Connecticut

BULLETIN 113
1994
ISBN 0–942081–05–6

STATE GEOLOGICAL AND NATURAL HISTORY SURVEY OF CONNECTICUT

DEPARTMENT OF ENVIRONMENTAL PROTECTION

The Honorable Lowell P. Weicker, Jr.
*Governor of Connecticut*

Timothy R. E. Keeney
*Commissioner of the Department of Environmental Protection*

Hugo F. Thomas
*Chief of the Bureau of Environmental Services*

Richard Hyde
*Director of the Natural Resources Center*

Leslie J. Mehrhoff
*Supervising Biologist,*
*State Geological and Natural History Survey*

William P. Delaney
*Director of Education and Publications Division*

Allan N. Williams
*Publisher, Technical Publications Program*

Additional copies may be purchased from:
DEP Maps and Publications Office
79 Elm Street
Hartford, Connecticut 06106
(203) 566–7719

ISBN 0–942081–05–6

Printed in the United States

Dedicated to the memory of

Aretas A. Saunders

(1884–1970)

# CONTENTS

# TABLES

# FIGURES

# *Foreword*

This book is really for the birds! I don't mean this in the sense that it is not to be taken seriously but rather in the very literal sense of the expression. Although people will benefit from its publication, the real benefits will accrue to the birds themselves through better understanding of their ways and concomitant increase in their preservation.

People have been interested in birds since the time in our own evolutionary history that we began to look around our environment expanding our search for what there was to eat. This first interest was purely utilitarian, that of obtaining food. As our species moved into cooler areas, birds were of interest as a source of feathers for insulation. At times, other parts of birds were of interest for ceremonial ornamentation. This interest eventually gave rise to the economic interests in birds we see in the seventeenth, eighteenth, and nineteenth centuries. Later, interests branched to sports, either through hunting or falconry, both of which have their roots in food gathering as well. Still later came an interest in birds as a recreation, through birdwatching, and as a source of scientific information through observation and data gathering.

In the latter half of the present century people have had another interest in birds, an increasingly important one. We are becoming more aware of the value of birds as indicators of environmental quality—the almost proverbial use of the miner's canary. This was best brought to the world's attention by Rachel Carson in her 1962 book *Silent Spring*. It was the paucity of American Robins that she observed in areas where before they had been prevalent that caused her concern. The rest is well known. Persistent pesticides such as DDT had accumulated within the invertebrates that make up the robin's food and eventually caused the numbers of robin eggs that successfully hatched to drop precipitously. Fortunately for both people and birds, many scientists and environmentalists rallied behind her. As a result, the use of persistent pesticides, at least in this country, was curtailed. There are other less well known stories involving DDT, such as the pioneering work of Joe Hickey on eggshell thinning in many species of raptors.

In the 1980s and 1990s, declining bird populations have illuminated the severity of another global environmental problem—the increasing loss of tropical forests. Destruction of rain forests, cloud forests, and even tropical dry forests has contributed to serious declines in the numbers of certain bird species returning each year to their nesting grounds. At the same time, the loss of large, undissected tracts of deciduous forests in the Northeast has put additional pressures on some of our breeding species.

It is exciting for the State Geological and Natural History Survey of Connecticut to join with the National Audubon Society and the Audubon Council of Connecticut in publishing *The Atlas of Breeding Birds of Connecticut*. This atlas represents countless hours spent by volunteers, both professional and amateur, gathering information on the birds which breed in Connecticut. It is fitting, too, that the survey publish this atlas; since its inception in 1903, the primary function of the survey has been to gather and disseminate data on our state's geology and biota.

The importance of preserving our state's natural diversity has become increasingly clear to the citizens of Connecticut. Beginning to understand distribution patterns and population trends of our state's birds is a very necessary first step in their preservation. Rachel Carson was a pioneer in using birds as indicators of a healthy environment. But before we can use any living organism as a good indicator of environmental quality, we must know something of its abundance and distribution. Scientists no longer take specimens to voucher the existence of breeding birds. Neither are eggs collected for this reason. The use of documented sightings gives us valuable data on the birds which breed in our state. We can then attempt to understand their biology. *The Atlas of Breeding Birds of Connecticut* is one of these important first steps. We are all better off for its publication.

People should not look at this atlas as an end point but rather a beginning. All too frequently people see lists of organisms, be they of birds, butterflies, or flowers, as final products. To conservationists, these lists are just begin-

nings. *The Atlas of Breeding Birds of Connecticut* should be viewed in this light. I am hopeful that those involved in this project will continue to gather information. More exciting, however, is the prospect of this work's encouraging others to take binoculars in hand and to experience for themselves the joys that come from serious observation of our avifauna. If people gain familiarity with an organism, there is a better chance that they will understand the importance of preserving the species in its natural habitat. Habitat protection should be the ultimate goal of preservation because only in this way can we truly preserve a species and all its natural interactions.

The synergism of a project in which both a state agency and a private conservation organization contribute their skills and capabilities may be the way to get through these austere financial times. The information presented in this atlas reveals the level of commitment of those who have worked in one way or another to bring this project to fruition. On behalf of those of us who care for our state's rich biota, I am deeply appreciative of their time and efforts.

*Leslie J. Mehrhoff*

# *Acknowledgments*

This project has drawn on the resources of many organizations, agencies, and hundreds of individuals across Connecticut. As Editor, I wish to thank everyone involved in the completion of this atlas, especially the individuals who contributed their time as observers, for without them this project would never have come to fruition.

Special recognition should be given to the staff at the Natural Resources Center and Technical Publications Program of the Connecticut Department of Environmental Protection for providing the means to publish this atlas. I wish to thank Nancy Murray, Dawn McKay, and Allan Williams for much useful advice and support. Jon Scull's expertise with geographical information systems allowed the first maps to be produced; without his help, interpretation of the data would have been impossible. Stacey Kingsbury expertly refined the symbols for the maps and assisted with the transfer of computer files. My greatest appreciation and thanks go to Richard Hyde and Les Mehrhoff both of whom stepped forward to offer the assistance of the Natural Resources Center and applied the much needed encouragement and urging for completion of the task.

The graphic design and layout of the atlas was accomplished by Mary Crombie at Acorn Studio. Michael K. Oliver proofed the entire manuscript and helped enormously to dig out those misplaced references and pernicious bits of inconsistent usage. Julie Tamarkin made a final check of the manuscript before printing. Many thanks to you all.

During the entire course of preparing this atlas publication, I was kindly and generously offered the use of facilities, computers, and assistance by the Department of Ecology and Evolutionary Biology at the University of Connecticut in Storrs. I am deeply indebted to that institution and its faculty and staff. Special thanks are due Greg Anderson, Carol Blow, Alan Brush, Janine Caira, Robin Chazdon (whose then speedy Macintosh computer aided development of the first maps), George Clark, Robert Colwell, William Crepet (now at Cornell University), Elna DeCarli, Robert Dubos, Charles Henry, Carl Rettenmeyer, James Slater, Kelly Steele (now at Appalachian State University), and Burma Stelmak.

Numerous individuals were consulted for information on birds or the history of the atlas project. Foremost among these were Robert Askins, Thomas Baptist, Eirik Blöm, John Bull, Milan G. Bull, Thomas Burke, Winifred Burkett, Marshal Case, Roger Clapp, Robert J. Craig, Walter G. Ellison, Charles Hills, Betty Kleiner, the late Ruth Löf, John Löf, Nancy Martin, Raymond A. Paynter, Jr., Fred Purnell, David Rosgen, Fred C. Sibley, Eleanor Stickney, George Zepko, and Joseph Zeranski. Their assistance is greatly appreciated. When it became imperative to complete this publication, several individuals were asked to write species accounts in rather short order. Every contributing author whose name appears at the beginning of this publication deserves my deepest regard for making this atlas a reality.

Marshal Case raised and managed nearly all the funds for this project; he kept the project on a steady course through many difficult times. I offer my deepest appreciation to him for putting this project together and enduring the seemingly endless process until completion. Thank you for patience, understanding, and an abiding commitment to bird conservation.

For moral support and valued insights on all aspects of this process I thank Winifred Burkett, Julio de la Torre, Walter G. Ellison, Frank Mantlik, Kelly Steele, Catherine Robb, and Connie Wood. For sustenance, humor, and above all a shared belief in acting strongly to protect the beauty and free spirit of all birds, Fred and Susan Purnell deserve my warmest thanks.

To George Clark, whose encyclopedic knowledge of birds, fair and objective advice, and wonderful wit have inspired me, I must express my deepest gratitude, for this atlas could not have been completed without him.

*Louis R. Bevier*

## THE CONNECTICUT BREEDING BIRD ATLAS PROJECT (1982–1986)

### Participating bird clubs and sponsors

Major organization was directed under the sponsorship of the Audubon Council of Connecticut and the National Audubon Society. Funding and support for the project was donated by the following organizations, in addition to the National Audubon Society and the Aretas A. Saunders memorial fund of the Audubon Council of Connecticut.

### Participating chapters

*Aretas Saunders Audubon Society*
*Audubon Society of Northeast Connecticut*
*Darien Audubon Society*
*Greenwich Audubon Society*
*Housatonic Audubon Society*
*Lillinonah Audubon Society*
*Litchfield Hills Audubon Society*

*Mattabeseck Audubon Society*
*Menunkatuck Audubon Society*
*Naugatuck Valley Audubon Society*
*New Canaan Audubon Society*
*Pequot Audubon Society*
*Potapaug Audubon Society*
*Quinnipiac Valley Audubon Society*
*Saugatuck Valley Audubon Society*

### Affiliated and participating organizations

*Connecticut Ornithological Association*
*Hartford Audubon Society*
*Natchaug Ornithological Society*
*New Haven Bird Club*
*Western Connecticut Bird Club*

ACKNOWLEDGMENTS

## Atlas Staff

*Project Coordinator:*
Marshal T. Case

*Chairman:*
Christopher S. Wood

*Computer Programming:*
George W. Zepko

*Statewide Field Coordinator:*
David Rosgen
Elsa Bumstead (1982 only)

*Regional Coordinators:*
Marshal T. Case, Harold F. Crandall,
Robert J. Craig, Robert C. Dewire,
Betty S. Kleiner, Frank Mantlik,
Thomas Rochovansky, David Rosgen,
Raymond Schwartz, Clayton Taylor, James Zipp

*Publication Coordinator:*
Gary Haber

*Office assistant:*
Patricia Creswell

## PUBLICATION CONTRIBUTORS

*Editor:*
Louis R. Bevier

*Artist:*
Michael DiGiorgio

*Review Editor:*
George A. Clark, Jr.

*Contributing Authors:*
Robert A. Askins
Robert I. Bertin
Louis R. Bevier
Anthony H. Bledsoe
Winifred B. Burkett
Elizabeth Bushnell
George A. Clark, Jr.
Robert K. Colwell
Michael R. Conover
Arnold Devine
Phillip F. Elliott
Walter G. Ellison
George Gale
Donald A. Hopkins
Gordon Loery
Donald E. McIvor
Paul R. Merola
Kenneth E. Petit
Alan F. Poole
Noble S. Proctor
Frederick Purnell, Jr.
Fred C. Sibley
Dwight G. Smith
Jeffrey A. Spendelow
Mark S. Szantyr

*Map Production:*
Jonathan Scull
Stacey Kingsbury
Louis R. Bevier

## List of Atlas Participants

The following 515 (plus) people contributed their time to the Connecticut Breeding Bird Atlas Project. Without the generous efforts of these individuals, the atlas could not have been completed. Every effort was made to list all participants; however, the file containing the original lists of names was unfortunately lost during renovation of the Audubon Center in Sharon, Connecticut. If the names of some individuals do not appear here, please know that your contribution is valued no less and that everyone involved in the compilation of this list offers their sincerest apologies.

George Adams, Chris Aiello, Nancy Aiello, Constance Alexios, Florence C. Allain, Donald Alston, William Altmann, Janet Amalavage, Lorraine Amalavage, David Anderson, Roger Anstett, Margaret Ardwin, Robert Askins, Ann Augustien, Michael Aurelia, Sally Austin, Jay Bacca, James Bair, Rev. Kenneth Ballas, Thomas R. Baptist, John Barclay, Cheryl Barker, Leon Barkman, Charles Barnard, John Barry, Dan Barvir, Fred Bashour, Chris Bates, Peter Begley, Raymond Belding, George Bent, Rev. Thomas E. Berberich, Ben Berliner, Richard Bernard, Louis R. Bevier, Mark Biercevicz, A. Billings, Gene Billings, Ginger Bladen, Anthony H. Bledsoe, Jim Blever, Susan Bohlin, Betty Bond, Peter Bono, Judy Bothwell, Doris Bova, John Bova, George Boynton, Ella Bradbury, Joseph Bradbury, Rob Braunfield, Mary Brescia, Ed Briggs, Lysle Brinker, Polly Brody, Stephen Broker, Pam Brundage, Alan Brush, Milan Bull, Thomas W. Burke, Winifred Burkett, Lisa Burns, Greg Butcher, Eldridge Camp, Jane Camp, Nelson Camp, Paul Carrier, Marshal T. Case, Suzanne Caturano, Pedro Cavanna, Richard Cech, Dexter Chafee, Walter Charsky, Carol Charter, Greg Chasko, Dean Christianson, Canfield C. Clark, Ellen Clark, George A. Clark, Jr., Roland C. Clement, Barbara Cole, Albert Collins, Elizabeth Cooling, Les Corey, Paula Coughlin, Maury D. Covington, Jill Coyle, Chris Craig, Robert J. Craig, Harold Crandall, Dan Crosby, Winifred Crosby, Thomas I. Crossman, Neil Currie, Ed Czlapinski, Mary Czlapinski, Mark Dall, Tom Damiani, Holly Darr, Andrew Dasinger, Bruce Dasinger, Ann Davenport, Douglas Davenport, Shirley Davis, Steve Davis, Jane Day, Jim Day, Pat DeBonte, Robert DeBroisse, Julio de la Torre, Ayreslea Denny, Duncan Denny, Robin Denny, Rowland Denny, Paul Desjardins, Arnold Devine, Robert C. Dewire, Townsend Dickenson, Michael DiGiorgio, Angela Dimmitt, Ron Dodson, Rita M. Duclos, Mike Dudek, Adele Duffy, William Duffy, Frank Dunstan, Lucia Eastman, Meada Ebinger, John Egan, Sharon Egan, Robert Ehrlich, Carl Ekroth, Joseph Elias, Phillip Elliott, Adelaide Emory, Ostrom Enders, Richard L. English, Steve Faccio, Andrew Farnsworth, John Farrand, Cameron Faustman, Jeff Fengler, Roger Ferguson, Virginia Ferguson, Larry Fischer, Susan

Fitch, Robert Fletcher, Robert Foley, Ruth Fowler, Sam Fried, Elise Friend, Merion Frolich, Roxanne Frosceno, Frank Gallo, Alexander Gardner, William Gaunya, Shirley Gay, Jon Gibbs, Ray Gilbert, Sybil Gilbert, Ellen Gillard, Robert Gillard, Ted Gilman, Art Gingert, Lex Glover, Raelene Gold, John Gradowich, Steve Grant, Stuart Grant, John Granton, Gerda Grasso, Leroy Allen Green, Jeff Greenwood, Paul Gros, Hank Gruner, John Guarnaccia, Hazel Guest, Dave Gumbart, Tom Gumbart, Kevin Gunther, Paul Gurn, Marjorie Hackbarth, Ed Hagen, Marjorie Haley, Don Hall, Jim Hammer, Jay Hand, Kenneth Hannan, Rick Hannon, Fred Hargan, Caroline Hartel, Michael Harwood, Donald Hastings, Donald Havelka, Dave Havens, George Haydock, David Hayes, Julia Hayes, Michael Hayes, William Hegener, Richard Helprin, Scott Heth, Thomas Hewes, Ed Hiestand, Isabel Higgins, John Higgins, Marilynn Higgins, Dolores Hilding, David O. Hill, Charles Hills, Ellen J. Hobby, Tom Hoehn, Donald A. Hopkins, Frances Hottin, John Hudson, Ron Hummel, Robert Humphries, Jean Hurlbut, Judy Hyde, Steve Jackson, Linda Jacobsen, Ann Jambriska, Joe Jambriska, Alice Jansen, Buck Jenks, Elsa Jennings, Hazel Jockheck, Elsbeth Johnson, Loretta Johnson, Jay Kaplan, Jeanne Kauffman, Seth Kellogg, Leonard Kendall, Terry Kennen, Jeff Kirk, Phyllis Kitchin, Marcia Klattenberg, Ronald Klattenberg, Betty Kleiner, Gilbert Kleiner, Gayle Kochan, Douglas Konopaske, Meriam Kursawe, Bill Lafley, Jim Lafley, Jill Lamoureaux, David Lapham, Beth Lapin, Roy E. Larsen, Vima LeJuene,

Jim Lee, Rebecca Lehmann, George Letis, Mildred Letis, Stan Lincoln, Denise Lindsey, Les Line, Fred Lipshultz, Phyllis Lodder, Gordon Loery, John Löf, Ruth Löf, Eleanor Loft, John Longstreth, Bill Low, Jane Low, Joanne Luppi, Marion Lyga, Linda Macaulay, William Macaulay, Florence McBride, Jim McBride, Rea King McCarty, Ed McDonald, John McDonald, Joan E. McGill, Todd McGrath, John McIlwaine, Ann MacLachlan, Bruce MacLachlan, Timothy W. McNally, Glenn McNamara, John McNeely, Pamela McVay, Vicki Magaraci, Arthur Manthorne, Frank Mantlik, Joseph Marks, Peter Marra, Tim Marsh, Joyce Marshall, Bill Martha, Patsy Mason, Tom Mason, John Mathews, Dianne Mayerfield, John Maynard, Steve Mayo, Leslie J. Mehrhoff, Agnes Melia, Mort Melia, Larry Mencuccini, Gerald S. Mersereau, Paul Merola, Debra Miller, Phoebe H. Milliken, Alberta Mirer, Robert Mirer, Jan Mitchell, Stuart Mitchell, Jim Mockalis, Robert Moeller, Jim Moore, Ruth Moore, Thomas Morck, Valerie Morck, Betty Moylon, Jason Mullins, Betty Murphy, Kathleen Murphy, Nancy Murray, Russ Naylor, Lydia Nelson, Richard Nelson, Pamela Newman, Kris Norling, Dave Norris, Nancy Norton, Robert L. Norton, Patricia Noyes, Grissies Oliver, Thomas Oliver, Ann Orsillo, Joan Osterling, Ray Packard, Dolores Page, Marilyn Paley, Gary Palmer, Lauren Parmalee, David Parsons, Stu Parsons, Peter Paull, Claire Pelletier, Badger Perrin, Christine Perrin, Dave Perry, Chuck Peterson, Peggy Peterson, Roger T. Peterson, Susan Peterson, Virginia Peterson, Bill Phillips, Carol Phillips, Hazel Phillips, Lyda

Phillips, Richard Philpitt, Dan Pokras, Joel Popowitz, Karl Porgas, Rosa Porgas, Stephen Potter, Ross Powell, Jr., Joseph D. Pratt, Thomas Prescher, Roger Preston, Ruth Price, Cindy Prior, Noble S. Proctor, Bob Proverb, Dana Pumphrey, Frederick Purnell, Jr., Grace Quick, John Rakoczy, Sharon Rakoczy, Krbtin Ranhosky, Julia Rankin, Linda Rapp, Daryll Rathburn, Mike Redmond, Courtney Reed, William Reid, Jeanne Rivenburg, Jim Rivenburg, Belle Robinson, Betty Rochovansky, Dave Rochovansky, Tom Rochovansky, Pat Rogers, George Romano, Bill Root, Mike Root, David Rosgen, Jane Rosgen, Joseph Rosgen, Stanley Rosgen, Nancy Ross, William Ross, Jane Rossman, Paul Rothbart, Ron Rozsa, J. Ruoff, Penny Rusch, Phil Rusch, Todd Russo, Gilbert Salk, Juan Sanchez, Leland Sanders, Joan-Marie Schaeffer, Phil Schaeffer, Lee Schlesinger, George Schneider, Karen Schnitzer, Wilford Schultz, Jonathan Schwartz, Ray Schwartz, Edith Scott, Helen Sebastian, Henry Sefton, Patricia Sellars, Shari Sellars, Mary Sharkey, Ed Shove, David Sibley, Fred C. Sibley, Steven Sibley, Laurie Siegal, James Slater, Jim Smith, Richard Soffer, Avo Somer, John Souther, Jeffrey A. Spendelow, Jim Spignesi, Elaine Staiger, John Stake, Paul Stake, Roxanne Steinman, John Stepney, Will Stoddard,

Doris Stroh, Aimee Suhie, Richard Suhie, Donald Suojamen, Carol Sutton, Robert Sutton, Elizabeth Swanson, Jonathon Swartz, Lynn Sweeney, Joseph Sworin, Eileen Synott, Mark Szantyr, Dot Szczesnick, Richard Tapp, Larry Tauro, Jr., Clay Taylor, Donald Taylor, Nellie Teale, Lucille Tegg, Gerard Therrien, Barbara Thomas, Ed Thomas, Michael Thomas, Robert Thomas, David H. Thomson, Eric Thum, Dotty Tischler, Art Titus, David Titus, Carl Trichka, David Tripp, Jr., Jonathan Trouern-Trend, Beatrice Tyrrell, Charles Tyrrell, Chris Vann, Dennis Varza, Arthur Vavoudis, Barbara Vavrek, Diane Vendola, Tom Vendola, Julie Victoria, Charles Vinsonhaler, Nancy A. Voldstad, Betty Walker, Margaret Warner, Lorraine Washburn, Richard Washburn, Bill Watson, Terry Weaver, Cora Webb, Tom Wehtje, Todd Weintz, Berna Weissman, Mary Beth Wheeler, Elinor Whitaker, Judy Whittlesley, Lyle Whittlesley, Dominick Wilcinkas, Leonard Wilcinkas, Andrew Wolfson, Christopher Wood, Constance Wood, Ray Woodbridge, Thelma Woodbridge, Diane Worden, Scott Wright, V. P. Wystrach, Jeffrey Young, George W. Zepko, Joseph D. Zeranski, Julie Zickefoose, Jim Zipp, Francis Zygmont, students of Deer Spring School 1982–1986.

# Project Purpose

This special publication, *The Atlas of Breeding Birds of Connecticut*, is dedicated as a memorial to a great Connecticut ornithologist, Aretas Andrews Saunders (1884–1970). It would be difficult to name a more appropriate individual for this dedication, even with the long list of distinguished Connecticut ornithologists, for Aretas Saunders was a pioneer in the area of recording bird song as well as author of more than 100 published articles and books on birds.

On the cover of Saunders' book *The Lives of Wild Birds* is the caption "How to study wildbirds and learn more about them." That is precisely the path that this atlas publication has followed—to learn more about the birds of Connecticut. More than five hundred individuals have gone into the field over a designated five year period (1982–1986) to study breeding birds to learn how many species there are and in what locations they are found in Connecticut. The purpose of this study is to set a benchmark of scientific data on breeding birds in Connecticut in order to allow a reasonable approach to decisions on when not to allow destruction of critical habitat as we continue to face encroachment by highways and roads, housing and mall development, radio towers and transmission lines, and "simple" filling of wetland. This atlas also provides data to judge better which natural areas not currently set aside need to be moved to the top of the preservation list.

During the 1970s, with the first Earth Day and the creation of federal government's Environmental Protection Agency and the Connecticut Department of Environmental Protection, early public hearings that involved potential and planned habitat destruction drew a reasonable number of environmental "extremists." The movement was still young, the number of organized environmentalists was quite small, and field data on natural history were most often pulled from small pockets of well meaning citizens who spoke out against habitat destruction with a passion; rarely were these data in any scientific or organized form. Public hearings often turned into shouting matches in high school auditoriums and town offices where development interests most often won simply because they knew what they wanted and hired the "right" people as consultants to argue their case, persuading others that business interest or land ownership had higher priority than protection of birds (and other plant and animal groups). With no state endangered and threatened species list and little, if any organization, environmental organizations and interested citizens had little chance to prevail.

*The Atlas of Breeding Birds of Connecticut* sprang from this lack of "hard" ornithological field data with a purpose to study and organize information in a logical manner, to retrieve accurate statistics relating breeding birds to specific habitats and "blocks" anywhere in the state of Connecticut, to fine tune the information so that the burden of proof for justifying a proposed habitat destruction would fall to the developer.

The project began when a group of twenty interested Connecticut citizens, birdwatchers, and ornithologists met at Wesleyan University in October 1981 to consider launching a scientific breeding bird study. The National Audubon Society and its statewide affiliate of organized local chapters, the Audubon Council of Connecticut, made the decision to follow up on initiation of such a project. Planning took place during November 1981; from January through March 1982, regional coordinators were chosen, and the first surveys were launched that year with over two hundred participants in the field. Elsa Bumstead (National Audubon Society staff in Connecticut) helped organize the planning year; Dave Rosgen was later hired as field coordinator for the second through fifth study years, and Louis Bevier concluded the major assignment as editor of this publication.

We know that the data will be beneficial because the results of this study have already worked for protection of birds in several locations in Connecticut. Even before publication, computerization of our data in the Natural Diversity Data Base of the Connecticut Department of Environmental Protection Natural Resources Center provided data on the value of habitats at proposed projects. In one situation, a highway was redirected to preserve marsh birds, and in another a landfill site in the town of Southbury was defeated at the town public voting polls. This latter case was significant because it involved a potential negative effect upon our growing winter Bald Eagle population at Shepaug Dam, as well as upon a number of scarce breeding birds at the pro-posed site. This close but major victory was obtained because we provided data in an organized format through a scientifically legitimate study made credible by having the data as part of the Natural Diversity Data Base.

## BIOGRAPHICAL SKETCH OF ARETAS A. SAUNDERS

Aretas Saunders believed in good field science, and that has been the basis for this study and resulting publication. He published widely on the results of his meticulous bird field studies.

Born in Avon, Connecticut, on November 15, 1884, he was encouraged at an early age to pursue his interest in the study of natural history, particularly birds. Encouraged by his Aunt Beth, who gave and loaned him books on natural history subjects, he spent much of his time exploring by foot and bicycle. He later attended Yale University and, in 1907, graduated from Yale School of Forestry.

Aretas Saunders spent several years in Montana working for the United States Forest Service and then returned to New Haven, Connecticut, in 1912 to begin teaching on the subjects of geometry, physics, trigonometry, and general science. From 1914 to 1949 he taught biology at Central High School in Bridgeport, Connecticut. By all accounts, he was a wonderful and enthusiastic teacher. His passion for natural history spilled over to many of his students who later pursued interests in the same field. Saunders also served as instructor in ornithology from 1927–1940 at the Allegheny School of Natural History in New York.

Aretas Saunders was also an accomplished self-taught musician, a skill which helped a great deal in the pursuit of one of his ornithological interests, bird songs, that later led to publication of *A Guide to Bird Songs*. He carried a tuning fork in his pocket in the field and, on hearing a bird song, would hold the instrument to his ear to attempt to locate the song's first note on the musical scale; he also carried a stop-watch for accurate timing of the song. In addition to his musical skills, he was an accomplished artist.

In 1949, having retired from teaching, Saunders moved to Canaan, Connecticut, where he continued to pursue his natural history and bird interests. He was a Fellow of the American Ornithologists' Union and a top notch scientist. One of his great interests was with youth, and his philosophy included enjoyment of education. Dominick D'Ostilio, who illustrated Saunders' book *The Lives of Wild Birds*, said about Saunders that one should have pleasure and happiness in the study of living things.

Aretas A. Saunders died on April 7, 1970, at the age of eighty-five and still a Canaan resident. In 1972, the Audubon Council of Connecticut created the Aretas A. Saunders Memorial Fund for continuation of his interests in education and ornithology. This fund was created through the organizational skills of Audubon employee J. Stanley Quickmire, Jr., and donations of several public film viewing events by Roger Tory Peterson. Thus, it is most appropriate that this special publication be dedicated to this Connecticut ornithologist who had a passion for birds, natural history, and people.

*Marshal T. Case*

# A Place Where the Birds Are

It is highly probable, so favorably is [Connecticut] situated, that no equal area in the country can boast a greater number of birds than may be found within its limits.

So wrote C. Hart Merriam in *A Review of the Birds of Connecticut* from the 1877 transactions of the Connecticut Academy of Science. Thirty-six years later, John Sage, Louis Bishop, and Walter Bliss made a similar remark in the 1913 Connecticut Geological and Natural History Survey publication, *Birds of Connecticut*, noting, "over 135 species nest more or less regularly within [Connecticut's] borders, and it is probable there are few localities in our country where so many can be found within so circumscribed an area." Although this claim is not accurate in the light of current knowledge, it nevertheless indicates that the variety of species of birds breeding in Connecticut is rich relative to many parts of the United States.

For more than 75 years, the *Birds of Connecticut* provided the most comprehensive source of information on Connecticut's breeding bird populations. But with the completion and tabulation of this 1982–1986 breeding bird atlas, there is a new, more accurate status report confirming that the state continues to attract and support a great diversity of bird life. Within Connecticut's 5,009 square miles, 173 species were confirmed as nesters. New York state with 49,576 square miles of dramatically varying habitat confirmed fifty-seven more species in its atlas project, while Vermont confirmed 178 nesting species within its slightly greater 9,609 square miles.

Ecological, geological, and geographical conditions provide obvious explanations for Connecticut's bird diversity; however, further analysis of this atlas and other data will be necessary before conclusions can be drawn about the current health of the state's bird populations. The results of the atlas research reveal a better understanding of the diversity of birds in Connecticut's landscape since the earlier publications of Merriam and later of Sage, Bishop, and Bliss.

Those authors explained their observations of diversity with the ecological concept of life zones, still sometimes applied today. The southern influences of the Carolinian zone penetrate the state up the major river valleys; the Alleghenian zone rolls across our uplands and the Canadian zone reaches into the western highlands. A more recent analysis of Connecticut's ecology by Joseph Dowhan and Robert Craig (1976) considered five zones in the state, subdivided into fourteen eco-regions based on landscape, climate, vegetation, and indicator species.

Like all highly developed regions, Connecticut has faced significant environmental stresses, some of which are evident without studies of bird populations. Still, birds are widely recognized as good potential barometers for detecting subtle environmental changes, and intuitively we tend to think that the more types of birds, the better. Suitable habitat remains in Connecticut for most species of birds that colonized the region in the wake of receding glaciers thousands of years ago. New habitats created by human activity have enabled new species to invade Connecticut, while a few others have been eliminated.

Basic ecology and modern environmental analyses do not always provide simple explanations for our observations. Detailed analyses of the atlas data may reveal correlation between land use, environmental degradation, and bird species diversity. Certainly, the major effort of surveying birds across the state has provided valuable information on particular habitats and particular species. If we heed the information gained in this effort, then in twenty-five, fifty, or even seventy-five years, another breeding bird atlas can be undertaken to indicate the competence of our stewardship.

If the first pilgrims had landed on the west coast of North America, and the country had grown eastward, much of New England today might be national parks and wildlife refuges. The Connecticut River might still flow undammed through the region's virgin forests, flooding and feeding riparian wetlands and extensive salt marshes. Western tourists and bird-watchers would flock to observe the fabulous diversity of wildlife supported by such rich wilderness.

Economists and sociologists point out that Connecticut's most valuable indigenous resource is her people, most of whom are drawn to or enticed to stay in the state by the high quality of life we enjoy. Sage, Bishop, and Bliss recognized the nexus between birds and life quality in Bishop's chapter on economic ornithology, identifying "sport and means of mental enjoyment as important values attributed to birds." With some prescience Bishop observed that "to provide mental enjoyment may not seem at first sight a part of the function of the State, but there is a large and steadily increasing body of people, valuable citizens, who derive great enjoyment from listening to the songs and studying the habits of birds, who will go where birds are and stay away from where they are not." *The Atlas of Breeding Birds of Connecticut* shows us that Connecticut is still where the birds are.

*Christopher S. Wood*

# Introduction

This survey of Connecticut's breeding birds was initiated to determine what species of birds nest in Connecticut and what parts of the state are used by each of these species. Although Connecticut birds have been studied for about 160 years, there has been no previous systematic survey of the breeding species and their locations. The information gathered in this atlas provides a baseline for future evaluation of changes, both natural and human-induced, and provides a more rigorous basis for making decisions affecting the conservation of birds in the state. Changes in the Connecticut environment will undoubtedly continue to occur, but past experience indicates that forecasts of future environmental conditions are likely to be highly uncertain. It therefore behooves us to monitor present conditions of birds as closely as possible, so that when changes occur, the effects on birds will be more obvious. As an example from the past, knowledge of Osprey populations in Connecticut before the Second World War provided a baseline against which could be evaluated the sharp declines through the 1950s and 1960s; awareness of the decline provided an impetus for correcting the situation. Following the banning in 1972 of the major chlorinated hydrocarbon pesticides responsible for the Osprey declines, the population has rebounded to a considerable extent, though not back to the original level. This example shows that, once people become aware of a conservation problem, it is often possible to reverse even highly unfavorable trends. Such successful conservation efforts may require many ingredients, including skillful scientific investigation, strong conservation leadership, and public education. The continuation of breeding by the Osprey and numerous other bird species in Connecticut is due to a great extent to the time, effort, and money expended by caring people in the past. This atlas represents one such effort intended to facilitate the perpetuation of our natural heritage for the enjoyment of future generations.

The world's first atlas of breeding birds appeared in 1976 in Great Britain (Sharrock 1976). Since then, major progress has been made in the production of atlases of avian distribution in many parts of the world. Not until 1990, however, was there available a handbook of recommended standard procedures for atlases of North American breeding birds (C. R. Smith 1990); this handbook was prepared by the North American Ornithological Atlas Committee (NORAC). By that time, the Connecticut breeding bird atlas data had been collected and extensively analyzed, and consequently it has not been possible to incorporate a number of the recommendations in that handbook for this volume. Nevertheless, for those who are involved in planning for future atlas studies, the NORAC handbook will be extremely valuable.

Major planning for the Connecticut breeding bird atlas was completed during the winter of 1981–1982, and the field surveys were conducted from 1982 to 1986. Unavoidable changes in participating staff have led to some delay in the production of this volume, but we believe that the time lag compares reasonably favorably with those for all other North American regions with comparable atlases. Because this atlas was initiated before the development of widespread standard methods for such projects, certain aspects of this atlas, such as the computer programs used in assembling the data, have been unique. For the most part, however, the procedures described below are similar to those applied in other atlases.

In this volume we have attempted, in so far as possible, to keep our presentation understandable for interested people not having formal training in biological science, and at the same time we have attempted to maintain a standard in presentation like that prevailing in current scientific ornithological publications. It is thus necessary to indicate as clearly as possible the sources of our information, and we therefore provide extensive citation of both published and unpublished sources as is the regular practice in science.

## DESIGN AND METHODS

The atlas survey employed a grid system based on the U.S. Geological Survey (USGS) quadrangle system. One hundred and twenty-one 7.5 minute quadrangle maps cover the 5,009 square mile area of the state. Each quadrangle was divided into six equal-sized parts, each termed a block (see Figure 1). These blocks are approximately 10 square miles in area (25 sq km); the size of the blocks, approximately 5 km on a side, was determined following participation in the Northeastern Breeding Bird Atlas Conference where this was proposed as a standard (Laughlin 1982). The USGS

quadrangles are designated by map name and page number as published in the *Atlas of Connecticut Topographic Maps* (DEP 1992; but DEP 1982 used during the atlas), and the blocks by letters from A–F starting at the northwest corner of each quadrangle and proceeding left to right and top to bottom. The total number of blocks, including partial blocks, covering the state is 596, and 117 quadrangles contained censused blocks. Partial blocks occur at the margins of Connecticut's political boundary, and some islands surveyed in Long Island Sound were subsumed into neighboring blocks, e.g., Goose Island and Falkner Island were included in the southern tier of blocks for the Guilford quadrangle (map number 97; see Figure 1). Likewise, reports from the Thimble Islands were counted in the Branford quadrangle.

The state was divided into eight regions, each of which was assigned a coordinator to oversee coverage of blocks in that region. Regions and their coordinators were: 1) northwest, David Rosgen and Marshal Case; 2) north central, Betty Kleiner; 3) northeast, Robert J. Craig and, later, David Rosgen; 4) west central, Harold Crandall; 5) lower Connecticut River area, Clay Taylor; 6) southeast, Robert Dewire; 7) southwest, Tom Rochovansky; and 8) New Haven area, Ray Schwartz and Jim Zipp. Regional coordinators worked with the statewide coordinator—Elsa Bumstead in the first year and, subsequently, David Rosgen—in making arrangements for coverage of the blocks in their regions. The regional coordinators generally knew personally the observers within their regions and were able to plan to obtain as full a coverage of blocks as possible.

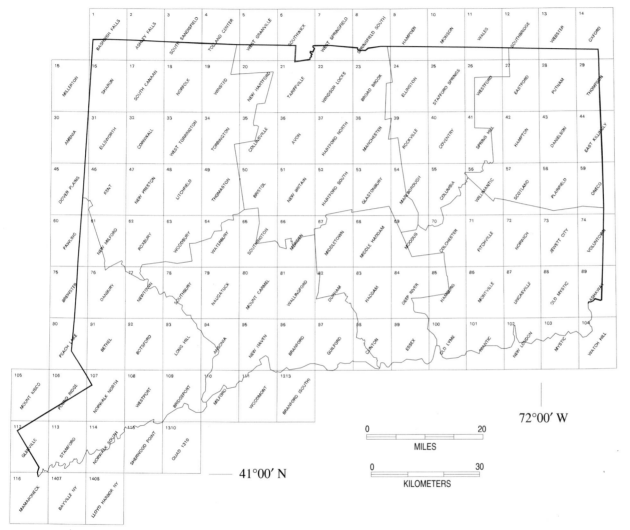

72°00′ W

41°00′ N

| 0 | | | 20 |
|---|---|---|---|

MILES

| 0 | | | 30 |
|---|---|---|---|

KILOMETERS

## HOW TO READ THE ATLAS MAPS

**USGS Quadrangles** (7.5 minute series) shown to the left were divided into six parts.

**Blocks** are identified by the quadrangle number plus the letter assigned to each part of the map.

| A | B |
|---|---|
| C | D |
| E | F |

### Breeding evidence symbols

● Confirmed
● Probable
○ Possible

The 5km × 5km square blocks are not shown within the quadrangle grid for each species map, but dots are always in the center of the blocks in which breeding evidence was reported.

**Figure 1. Index of atlas maps.** The USGS quadrangles (7.5 minute series) were divided into six equal parts, termed blocks. These blocks were assigned a letter from A–F starting at the northwest corner of each quadrangle. Quadrangles are numbered as in the *Atlas of Connecticut Topographic Maps* (DEP 1992).

9

In breeding bird atlases for Vermont and New York, it was impossible to cover all the blocks in a state, but because Connecticut is much smaller, it was possible to obtain some coverage for every block in the state. In certain areas there were too few observers located nearby to obtain detailed coverage of blocks. In such cases it was necessary to resort to "block busting," in which one or more observers spent a few hours searching in blocks which had received little or no previous coverage. Much of the block busting was done in northeastern and east-central Connecticut, and many of these areas received less coverage than blocks in other parts of the state. David Rosgen was a major participant and organizer for block busting; he was aided by observers from around the state.

Data were collected by over 500 individuals, principally volunteers, some of whom individually contributed hundreds of hours towards the success of the project. As might be expected, observers differed substantially in their skills, ranging from beginning to highly experienced birdwatchers. In view of the differences in backgrounds of observers, it has been necessary throughout the atlas project to review the submitted reports for their accuracy. Special reporting forms were made available for recording details on highly unusual breeding species, and these forms have proven to be of great value in assessing certain of the exceptional reports. Unfortunately, many of these report forms were not received or were never completed for a great number of significant reports. Through conversations with many of the observers involved, however, some of the lost data were recovered.

**Breeding Criteria Codes**

Observers were provided with printed field cards containing a list of species anticipated to occur as breeders within the state. Each card was limited to one block and one calendar year. On the card, spaces were provided by the name of each species for recording the breeding criteria codes, which were, as follows, arranged roughly in an order of increasing certainty about the occurrence of breeding.

**Observed**

X     Species (male or female) observed during the breeding season.

**Possible**

O     Species (male or female) *observed* in suitable nesting habitat during its breeding season.

S     *Singing* male(s) detected in suitable nesting habitat during its breeding season.

**Probable**

P     *Pair* observed in suitable nesting habitat during their breeding season.

T     Song or other behavioral evidence of *territory* establishment on at least two different days a week or more apart.

C     *Courtship* behavior or *copulation*.

N     Visiting probable *nest* site.

A     *Agitated* behavior or *"anxiety"* calls from adult(s).

B     Nest *building* by wrens or excavation of holes by woodpeckers.

**Confirmed**

NB     *Nest building* by all except woodpeckers and wrens.

PE  *Physiological evidence* of breeding [i. e., highly vascularized incubation (brood) patch or egg in oviduct] based on bird in hand. Used by bird banders.

DD  *Distraction display* or injury feigning.

UN  *Used nest* found. Caution is necessary because a nest must be carefully identified if it is to be used; a written verification report is required. Only permit holders may collect nests.

FL  Recently *fledged* young or downy young of Galliformes, shorebirds or waterfowl. Fledged young should be incapable of sustained flight.[1]

ON  *Occupied nest;* adults entering or leaving nest site in circumstances indicating occupied nest (includes high nests or nest holes, the contents of which cannot be seen); or adult incubating.

AY  *Attending young;* adult carrying fecal sac or food for young, or feeding recently fledged young.[1]

NE  *Nest* with *eggs.*[1]

NY  *Nest* with *young* seen or heard.[1]

[1] *Presence of cowbird egg or young is confirmation for both cowbird and host species.*

Although space was provided on the cards for recording the duration of observation, it was found that many observers did not report that information, and consequently no effort was made to assess the overall results in terms of time afield. Had this measure been recorded more consistently, it would have provided a better means for assessing the very substantial effort devoted to the project. This measure of effort would also have allowed more reliable comparisons with future atlas attempts. Although the recording of hours would have been desirable, this is not necessarily a good measure of effort since detection of breeding birds was, in many cases, made by individuals who lived in a particular block and thus noted breeding evidence incidental to their daily routines. Robbins (1990) showed that comparison of the percentage of all detections for a given species was a better method for comparison of population trends.

A small paperback handbook of atlas procedures was made available for all observers. Observers were instructed whenever possible to attempt to find evidence for placement of a species in a category with greater certainty of breeding. Instructions were given to keep disturbance to the birds to a minimum. It was pointed out that in most cases breeding can be confirmed without ever approaching a nest.

**Data entry**

Data on the field cards were transferred at the end of each field season to data forms by the regional coordinators, and then the data forms were checked by regional coordinators and David Rosgen. Under the guidance of George Zepko, Manager of User Services of the Computing Center at Wesleyan University in Middletown, volunteers entered the data on those forms into a 1022 database system running on a mainframe Digital Equipment Corporation System-20 computer at Wesleyan University. A data entry program was written to facilitate error checking and preparation for storage in the database system. It should be noted that this computer software was written before personal computers were available.

Data from each year were entered in a separate file. As data collection for each additional year was completed, the new data were merged with the cumulative data from previous years so that each species in each block was designated with the highest code recorded in any of the years up to that time. (The greater the certainty of breeding, the higher the code.) George Zepko, with the assistance of volunteers, then proofread and edited the printouts from the computer. The corrected output was made available for the regional coordinators in various summary formats after each year. This annually produced up-to-date record of species and their coded status in each block was helpful in planning in advance for the field seasons.

## Maps

The data stored at Wesleyan University were transferred to a personal computer, thus facilitating the preparation of the maps by providing a database for later use with a geographical information system (GIS), ArcInfo. Jonathan Scull assigned each block an x,y coordinate thus allowing the GIS to plot the position of confirmed, probable, and possible codes directly on the respective blocks against a digitized outline of the state without the necessity of a time-consuming placement of symbols by hand. The plots were stored as separate files later edited and printed by Louis Bevier. After final proofs of the mapped data were made, Jonathan Scull and Stacey Kingsbury produced Encapsulated PostScript files for each species for use with a desktop publishing system.

## RESULTS

Altogether, 189 species were recorded exhibiting breeding behavior during the atlas survey; 173 species and two hybrid forms were confirmed breeding in Connecticut. In addition, the Monk Parakeet and the hybrid American Black Duck × Mallard bred during the atlas period, but localities for these forms were not entered into the database. Several species that formerly bred in the state were not reported exhibiting breeding behavior during the atlas survey; they include the Peregrine Falcon, Gray Partridge (introduced and later extirpated from the state), Short-eared Owl, Sedge Wren, Dickcissel, and Henslow's Sparrow. Unlike these species, which may nest again someday (the Sedge Wren already has), the extinct Passenger Pigeon will never again build its nest in Connecticut. The Heath Hen, an extinct subspecies of the Greater Prairie Chicken, might have occurred in Connecticut at one time, and, if it did, would likely have been a breeder. Species that once bred somewhat regularly in the state and that were recorded during the atlas but only as possible or probable breeders include the Bald Eagle, Northern Harrier, and Northern Parula—the eagle now returning as a breeder, the harrier and Northern Parula nearly extirpated. Other reported but unconfirmed breeding species that have bred in Connecticut sporadically in the past were the Tricolored Heron, Black Rail, Common Snipe, and Prothonotary Warbler. Atlas participants confirmed several species that have bred in the state irregularly in the past—Pied-billed Grebe, Cattle Egret, Blue-winged Teal, Common Moorhen,

Golden-crowned Kinglet, Long-eared Owl, Red-headed Woodpecker, Vesper Sparrow, and Pine Siskin.

One result of the increased birdwatching activity in the state during the period of the atlas survey was the establishment of first documented state breeding records for Black Skimmer and Olive-sided Flycatcher. The atlas survey confirmed that breeding populations of certain species are limited in extent and should continue to be monitored—for example, American and Least Bitterns, Great and Snowy Egrets, Glossy Ibis, Sharp-shinned and Cooper's Hawks, American Black Duck, Osprey, American Kestrel, King Rail, American Oyster-catcher, Piping Plover, Willet, Upland Sandpiper, Roseate Tern, Common Tern, Least Tern, Barn Owl, Common Night-hawk, Whip-poor-will, Horned Lark, Common Raven, Golden-winged Warbler, Yellow-breasted Chat, Grasshopper Sparrow, and Orchard Oriole. Those species confirmed breeding and reported in the fewest blocks overall are listed in Table 1. Some of these are irregular breeders or species at the edge of their range, and others have populations that are declining and have been designated Endangered or Threatened in the state. Species whose success in breeding in Connecticut brings them into a realized or prospective nuisance category are the Mute Swan, Canada Goose, Monk Parakeet, and European Starling; in all four of these cases the populations of concern have come into the state as a consequence of human introductions. Those species reported in the greatest number of blocks and listed in Table 2 are species that have a widespread distribution in the state, are easy to detect, and breed in abundance and successfully in association with humans.

### TABLE 1
#### Confirmed breeding species reported in the fewest total blocks

| | | | |
|---|---|---|---|
| Cattle Egret | 2 | Olive-sided Flycatcher | 5 |
| Long-eared Owl | 2 | Glossy Ibis | 7 |
| Evening Grosbeak | 2 | Vesper Sparrow | 7 |
| King Rail | 4 | Grasshopper Sparrow | 8 |
| Black Skimmer | 4 | Yellow-cr. Night-Heron | 9 |
| Little Blue Heron | 5 | American Oystercatcher | 9 |
| Upland Sandpiper | 5 | Willet | 9 |
| Roseate Tern | 5 | Common Moorhen | 10 |

### TABLE 2
#### Breeding species reported in the most blocks
#### (ranked by total blocks and total confirmed blocks)

| | | | |
|---|---|---|---|
| Song Sparrow | 595 | Northern Flicker | 590 |
| American Robin | 593 | Common Grackle | 589 |
| Gray Catbird | 593 | House Finch | 589 |
| Black-capped Chickadee | 591 | European Starling | 587 |
| American Crow | 591 | Common Yellowthroat | 587 |
| Mourning Dove | 591 | House Sparrow | 586 |
| Northern Cardinal | 590 | Chipping Sparrow | 585 |
| Blue Jay | 590 | | |

## Coverage

The list of species reported during the atlas, and the number of blocks in which they were recorded, are listed in Appendix 1. For the most part, the goal of recording at least 50 species in each of the 596 blocks was achieved, only 28 blocks (5%) having fewer than this number. This figure is comparable to coverage achieved in the New York Atlas (Andrle and Carroll 1988), in which survey about 6% of 5,323 blocks had fewer than 50 species reported.

Adequate coverage for a block in the Vermont atlas was based on the number of species expected in a block; that number was 75 species, of which a minimum of 35 should have been confirmed (Laughlin and Kibbe 1985). That survey employed a system of priority blocks rather than attempting to survey the entire state. Of their priority blocks, 92% had adequate coverage, whereas only 32% of all blocks in Connecticut met this level of coverage, and only 39% (235 blocks ) recorded 75 or more species. This illustrates the difficulty in achieving adequate complete coverage during atlas surveys, even in a comparatively small region. It should be noted, however, that species diversity in Vermont is likely somewhat higher in each block as Breeding Bird Survey routes there average 7–10 more species than in Connecticut; therefore, the num-

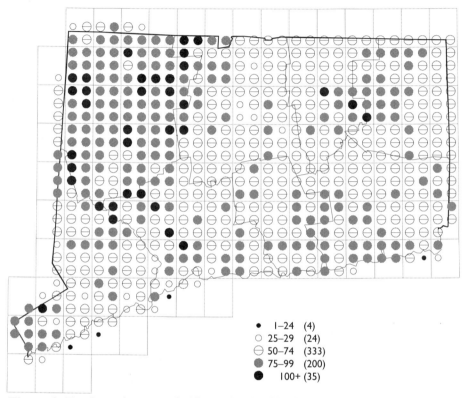

**Figure 2.** Total species recorded in each atlas block

ber of expected species per block would be lower in our state. The average number of species reported in each block during the Connecticut atlas was 71, and 35 blocks had 100 or more species (see Figure 2). The atlas database contains 42,629 records, of which 79% were confirmed or probable breeding reports. (*Please see notice on the last page regarding limitations of the atlas data.*)

14

## THE SPECIES ACCOUNTS

For each species suggested as a breeder in Connecticut during the period of the atlas survey, we have provided a species account. These accounts have been written by numerous authors who have generously given of their time on a volunteer basis. In some cases these authors have conducted extensive studies in Connecticut on the particular species about which they have written, but for most species such detailed studies have not been conducted in the state. The names of the species and their sequence follows the AOU *Check-list* and its supplements (AOU 1983).

The species accounts have four sections: an introduction to the species, its habitat requirements, the atlas results, and a discussion. The introduction includes general comments on the status and any movements of the species. Under the habitat section, an attempt was made to describe the habitat requirements as best known in Connecticut, including studies from outside the state only where relevant. The atlas results section briefly summarizes the patterns of distribution revealed by the atlas data. The discussion section in most cases reviews the historic status of the species in Connecticut and any recent trends or conservation issues. These sections are discussed in further detail in the following paragraphs.

*Introduction.* This section presents information on the species' migratory or nonmigratory status, provides an indication of the abundance of the species as a breeder in the state, and also outlines the wintering area for populations breeding in the state, information that can be important for conservation

purposes but is often lacking in field guides. In most cases where appropriate, an effort is made to identify the subspecies or groups of subspecies reported breeding in Connecticut. These names identify populations that share some feature or features over a geographic range within the species as a whole and serve as a link to studies on geographic variation, movements, and population changes of these groups. Identification of subspecies is not usually possible in the field, and observers should use caution. Although the use of subspecies is discouraged by some taxonomists today, the names are still useful in drawing attention to populations that might otherwise be ignored, especially from the standpoint of conservation issues (e.g., see the accounts for Marsh Wren and Swamp Sparrow). No subspecific determinations were made for preparation of this atlas; only references in the literature were used. Much work on the geographic variation of populations occurring in Connecticut remains to be completed.

*Habitat.* This section represents an effort to characterize for each species the breeding habitats as known for Connecticut. In a number of cases we have included brief comparisons of habitat among closely related or ecologically similar species. Although many general statements about habitat appear in the literature on birds, even in field guides, these characterizations of habitat are often either very broad (e.g., "forest") or not representative of the situation in Connecticut. As pointed out in a number of the species accounts, the habitats of particular species commonly vary geographically, so that habitat descriptions appropriate for one part of the range may not apply in another. Consequently, management and conservation efforts should be based on consideration of the local situation. Our characterizations of habitats for Connecticut birds are qualitative, and it is not clear that it is possible to devise a method for numerical comparison of habitats for such a great variety of species as breed in the state. Furthermore, the authors of the species accounts have generally not had an opportunity to investigate the particular species throughout the state. Thus the habitat descriptions presented in this volume might not apply statewide. Detailed descriptions of the nest and eggs, when reported here, are limited to observations gathered in Connecticut for the most part. Readers are directed to the annotated bibliography at the end of this chapter for books that contain general information on the nest and eggs of each species. In addition, the series of volumes on the life histories of North American birds by Bent (see Literature Cited) are an important source of such descriptions.

*Atlas results.* A most important component of the species accounts is the result of the atlas survey itself. Much of the information is expressed in the atlas maps. One problem in evaluating results of the field work in the atlas survey has been the lack of a satisfactory measure of the effort expended. Even a block with over 50 hours of coverage might not have been thoroughly covered unless time was spent at night to search for owls and goatsuckers and unless broadcasting of vocalizations was used to attract species such as rails. Furthermore, two blocks with the same number of hours of coverage might actually differ in the thoroughness of coverage if one block was always visited early in the morning and another at midday. There are also differences in the abilities of observers to detect species. Because of such unavoidable variations in coverage, emphasis has generally not been placed on individual blocks in reaching interpretations.

*Discussion.* This section presents a summary of historic status, a discussion of the results, recent population trends, and conservation issues. For the historic status, there is little information available prior to the 1830s in most cases. In reviewing the historic status of the species, we have used extensively the major summaries of Linsley (1843), Merriam (1877), and Sage et al. (1913) and supplemented these with numerous other cited sources. It has not been feasible to examine all the hundreds of references that constitute the primary literature on the breeding birds of the state. Because most authors have not assigned exact numerical values to terms of abundance, it is not possible to track minor changes in the abundance of species over the period of historic records, but a number of the major trends are clear and discussed in the appropriate species accounts. Availability of the atlas data provides a new way to consider the breeding birds of Connecticut. In numerous cases we have looked for possible new interpretations of the distributions. The resulting interpretations range from fairly solid to rather speculative, and we have tried to indicate the relative strength of the supporting evidence for those interpretations.

The number of observers contributing published and unpublished information on the birds of Connecticut has risen enormously over the past two centuries. One should remember that many of the findings and conclusions of the nineteenth century were based on far more limited numbers of observations than are available in recent decades. Therefore, statements on distribution over the state by the earlier authors could be flawed because there was at that time no statewide network of observers. Even today almost no reports come from certain parts of the state. There are surely birds present in those areas, but no one living there reports on the local birdlife. We hope that one outcome of the atlas will be to encourage those who live in parts of the state that are not extensively studied to place their observations of birds on record, such as in the seasonal reports of the *Connecticut Warbler*.

## ABBREVIATIONS USED

| | | |
|---:|:---:|:---|
| AOU | = | American Ornithologists' Union |
| BBC | = | Breeding Bird Census |
| BBS | = | Breeding Bird Survey |
| CBC | = | Christmas Bird Count |
| CTMNH | = | Connecticut Museum of Natural History |
| DEP | = | Department of Environmental Protection |
| ft | = | feet |
| ha | = | hectare |
| km | = | kilometer |
| m | = | meter |
| pers. comm. | = | personal communication |
| pers. obs. | = | personal observation |
| USFWS | = | United States Fish & Wildlife Service |

## BIASES AND LIMITATIONS

A general problem for ornithological studies in general, and for this volume in particular, is the vast quantity of published information on birds. This literature includes books and periodicals made up of thousands of titles worldwide. Much of the material is not relevant for the present volume, but nevertheless with so great a quantity of potentially pertinent material available, there is a strong likelihood that some important pieces of information will be missed. In searching the published literature, we have made extensive use of the citations in those references that we have cited, and for recent literature we have extensively used the Aves section of the *Zoological Record*. In addition to including a section of Literature Cited for sources mentioned in the species accounts, we have also provided, later in this chapter, a list of a number of general reference publications including field guides and handbooks that treat bird species breeding in Connecticut.

There are also numerous unpublished sources of data on Connecticut breeding birds. These include: 1) specimens, generally old, in museums; 2) theses completed by students at colleges and universities; 3) original field notes, a relatively small portion of which are now held in museums and other archives; 4) certain computerized databases to be mentioned later. In preparing this volume, we have generally not attempted a broad search for unpublished data; we have used and cited such materials in some cases where their existence was known to us.

Preparation of a volume of this kind requires categorizing large quantities of information. The creation of relatively neat categories tends to mask the variation so typical in biology. For example, when we categorize a species as migratory or nonmigratory, we commonly ignore a relatively small number of exceptional individuals. Thus, for example, the Northern Oriole is a migratory species, but in some years at least, one or more individuals may attempt to winter in Connecticut. In a similar fashion, most House Sparrows appear to be nonmigratory. However, apparently migrating birds have been reported from New Jersey (Broun 1972), and certain populations of this species in the Old World regularly migrate (Summers-Smith 1963).

Furthermore, our estimates of abundance of birds in the state as common, uncommon, rare, etc., are necessarily inexact because no exact counts are available. Many authors have attempted to provide quantifiable terms for abundance based on the number of individuals of a particular species that a "standard observer" might find in a single day or season, while other authors have gauged abundance on the percentage of field trips that a species is encountered by an observer. In these attempts at objective abundance estimates several subjective terms are introduced (e.g., the standard observer) and the abundance terms are rarely based on comparable field data. The number of birds found by an observer may vary depending on weather conditions, time of day, and amount of effort, and counts vary based on the experience of different observers. Species also differ in their relative detectability. These factors are difficult to standardize over a large geographic area such as a state. Therefore, we have opted to express the abundance as a comparative term based on known or estimated population sizes in the state. Every effort was made to apply these estimates consistently throughout the species accounts, particularly within the same taxonomic group (e.g., the accipiters). Comparison of abundance among species, therefore, is best within the same group.

Additional sources of data that we have not been able to utilize fully include: 1) the Breeding Bird Censuses as published formerly in *Audubon Field Notes*, then *American Birds*, and now in the *Journal of Field Ornithology*; 2) the U.S. Fish and Wildlife Service roadside breeding bird survey (see Appendix 2 for a summary of population trends based on data from these surveys); 3) summer bird counts that have been conducted in several towns during recent years and are now published in the *Connecticut Warbler*; 4) nest cards and colonial breeding bird records that are kept at Cornell University Laboratory of Ornithology; and 5) U.S. Fish and Wildlife Service Bird Banding Laboratory (Laurel, Maryland) records of birds banded in Connecticut. To make full use of these extensive resources was beyond the scope of our objective which has been to make the results of the atlas survey available.

There remain many uncertainties about the causes underlying the distributions of the breeding birds in Connecticut, but answers seem most likely to come from considering alternative interpretations and then looking for evidence with which to confirm or refute the various interpretations. If we have in some cases in the discussions speculated rather freely, it is because we believe the statement of such ideas has potentially great importance as a basis for future studies. Ideas on the factors influencing bird distribution have indeed been changing over recent decades. Conceptual changes arise through the presentation of new ideas and then the deliberate finding of evidence to support or refute those new ideas. Changes in viewpoint have occurred in the past and may be expected to continue in the future. Speculation, if used in moderation and presented explicitly, has its place as a stage in seeking scientific explanations, and such explanations should constitute a vital cornerstone of efforts for conservation.

One of the less tangible, but nevertheless important, consequences of the atlas project has been a continued heightened level of interaction and cooperation among individual birdwatchers throughout the state, and this is a promising development both for continued monitoring of the birds of the state and for promoting the conservation of those birds and their habitats for the appreciation and enjoyment of generations to come. The pleasures of conducting this atlas survey have been ours, but while recalling the fine times afield, we would be remiss not to recognize that, despite the many past successes of conservation efforts, numerous challenges remain. Those of us who watch birds have a responsibility to promote the conservation of the natural heritage that we now enjoy. One part of our efforts must be to improve our basic understanding of the natural world of birds, the subject of the chapter "Interpreting Distributions of Breeding Birds."

## ANNOTATED BIBLIOGRAPHY

The following is an annotated bibliography of some general references that include information concerning birds that breed in Connecticut:

### Field guides and identification manuals

Billings, G. 1990. *Birds of prey in Connecticut*. Rainbow Press, Torrington, Connecticut.—Provides much detail on hawks and owls in Connecticut including extensive coverage of places to look for these raptors and other birds throughout the state.

Clark, W. S., and B. K. Wheeler. 1987. *A field guide to hawks: North America*. Houghton Mifflin Co., Boston.—One of two specialty field guides covering North American hawks; see also Dunne et al. 1988.

de la Torre, J. 1990. *Owls: their life and behavior*. Crown Publishers, New York.—Review of the general biology of owls with excellent photographs by Larry Wolf.

Dunne, P., D. Sibley, and C. Sutton. 1988. *Hawks in flight: the flight identification of North American migrant raptors*. Houghton Mifflin Co., Boston.—One of two specialty guides for North American hawks; see also Clark and Wheeler 1987.

Farrand, J., Jr., ed. 1983. *Audubon Society master guide to birding*. 3 volumes. Alfred A. Knopf, New York.—A set that covers identification of birds of North America; mainly illustrated with photographs.

Fjeldså, J. 1977. *Guide to the young of European precocial birds*. Skarv Nature Publications, Tisvildeleje, Denmark.—Very young birds are often difficult to identify to species. Among the species covered by this guide are Common Loon, Mute Swan, Canada Goose, Wood Duck, Mallard, Gadwall, Green-winged Teal, Northern Pintail, Common Merganser, Ring-necked Pheasant, Bobwhite, Wild Turkey, Common Moorhen, Spotted Sandpiper, Great Black-backed Gull, Herring Gull, Roseate Tern, and Common Tern.

Grant, P. J. 1986. *Gulls: a guide to identification*. 2d ed. T & A D Poyser, Calton, England.—This book provides details for identifying the species and age categories for gulls found in North America and Europe.

Harrison, C. 1978. *A field guide to the nests, eggs, and nestlings of North American birds*. Collins, Cleveland, Ohio.—An important field guide for use in identifying nests and eggs.

Harrison, H. 1975. *A field guide to birds' nests*. Houghton Mifflin Co., Boston.—This compact photographic guide to nests and eggs by Hal Harrison includes nest measurements that are not included in the book by Colin Harrison (1978).

Harrison, P. 1983. *Seabirds: an identification guide*. Houghton Mifflin Co., Boston.—This most detailed guide for seabirds of the world by Peter Harrison includes loons, grebes, cormorants, gulls, terns, skimmers, and those ducks likely to be seen in coastal areas.

Harrison, P. 1987. *Seabirds of the world: a photographic guide*. Christopher Helm, London.—This field guide includes loons, grebes, cormorants, gulls, terns, skimmers, and other waterbirds. Smaller than the author's 1983 book, this volume is easier to carry in the field.

Hayman, P., J. Marchant, and T. Prater. 1986. *Shorebirds: an identification guide*. Houghton Mifflin Co., Boston.—Primarily an identification guide covering the world's waders; the species accounts also include information on breeding habits, movements, and geographical variation.

Kaufman, K. 1990. *A field guide to advanced birding*. Houghton Mifflin Co., Boston.—Among the problem groups included are certain herons, the accipiters, Roseate and Common Terns, *Empidonax* flycatchers, waterthrushes, and *Carpodacus* finches.

Madge, S., and H. Burn. 1988. *Waterfowl: an identification guide to the ducks, geese and swans of the world*. Houghton Mifflin Co., Boston.—The most detailed waterfowl identification manual, covering identification of all species.

National Geographic Society. 1987. *Field guide to the birds of North America*. 2d ed. National Geographic Society, Washington, D. C.—The most detailed single volume field guide covering birds of all of North America.

People starting out in bird identification might do better using the somewhat simpler guide by Peterson (1980).

Peterson, R. T. 1980. *A field guide to the birds*. 4th ed. Houghton Mifflin Co., Boston.—The latest edition of a compact and classic field guide covering birds of eastern North America; includes the best distribution maps among the field guides covering our region (fairly accurate up to the date of publication).

Pyle, P., S. N. G. Howell, R. P. Yunick, and D. F. DeSante. 1987. *Identification guide to North American passerines*. Slate Creek Press, Bolinas, California.—Although the primary goal of this book has been to assist bird banders who need to identify passerines when held in the hand, the volume will also be useful for advanced level observers watching birds at a distance in the field. Peter Pyle has published corrections for this book in *North American Bird Bander* Volume 13 (1988), pages 112–113 and Volume 15 (1990), page 147.

Robbins, C. S., B. Bruun, and H. S. Zim. 1983. *Birds of North America*. Rev. ed. Golden Press, New York.—A compact field guide covering all of North America.

Turner, A., and C. Rose 1989. S*wallows & martins: an identification guide and handbook*. Houghton Mifflin Co., Boston.—The most authoritative treatment of identification of the swallow family throughout the world.

*Handbooks including information
on breeding birds in Connecticut*

Campbell, B., and E. Lack, eds. 1985. *A dictionary of birds*. Buteo Books, Vermillion, South Dakota.—Actually a well prepared one volume encyclopedia covering birds of the world and their ecology and behavior. Generally does not cover individual species in detail.

Ehrlich, P. R., D. S. Dobkin, and D. Wheye. 1988. *The birder's handbook: a field guide to the natural history of North American birds*. Simon and Schuster, New York.—Provides a single volume summary of much information on the general biology of North American birds.

Forshaw, J. M. 1973. *Parrots of the world*. Doubleday, New York.—Includes the Monk Parakeet. (Now in several editions and reprints, some of poor quality.)

Goodwin, D. 1986. *Crows of the world*. 2d ed. University of Washington Press, Seattle, Washington.—Includes jays, crows, and ravens.

Hancock, J., and J. Kushlan. 1984. *The herons handbook*. Harper and Roe, New York.

Long, J. L. 1981. *Introduced birds of the world*. Universe Books, New York.—Includes detailed accounts on the history of introductions and establishment of Mute Swan, Ring-necked Pheasant, Rock Dove, Monk Parakeet, European Starling, House Sparrow, and a surprising number of our native birds.

Palmer, R. S. 1962–1988. *Handbook of North American birds*. 5 volumes.—Production of this major series has now ended, but the completed volumes cover loons, grebes, cormorants, herons, ibises, swans, geese, ducks, vultures, hawks, and falcons.

Short, L. L. 1982. *Woodpeckers of the world*. Delaware Mus. Nat. Hist., Greenville, Delaware.

Terres, J, K. 1980. *The Audubon encyclopedia of North American birds*. Knopf, New York.—Similar to the Campbell and Lack dictionary but written in a less scientific style; includes entries for individual species.

Voous, K. H. 1989. *Owls of the Northern Hemisphere*. MIT Press, Cambridge, Massachusetts.

*Special bibliographic aids*

Breit, V., and K. B. Clarke. 1983. *Ornithology books in the Library of Trinity College. Hartford*. Trinity College, Hartford, Connecticut.

Ripley, S. D., and L. L. Scribner. 1961. *Ornithology books in the Yale University Library*. Yale University Press, New Haven, Connecticut.

*Zoological Record*—This annually published reference work contains a section on birds (Aves) providing extensive coverage of the scientific literature on birds throughout the world.

Additional references will become available in the future. Periodicals such as *American Birds* (published by the National Audubon Society), *Birding*, and *Connecticut Warbler* as well as more technical ones such as *The Auk, The Condor, Wilson Bulletin*, and *Journal of Field Ornithology* contain listings and reviews of new books and other publications concerned with birds.

# Interpreting Distributions of Breeding Birds

Completion of this volume is a major landmark in Connecticut's ornithological history. Thanks to the cooperative effort of many people, the representation of the ranges of breeding birds in Connecticut is now far more thorough than at any time in the past. This atlas provides a body of information to be applied in making decisions affecting the conservation of Connecticut's birds. Although the publication of this atlas represents the end of a major and fruitful project, it also provides a new beginning for the present and future study of unresolved issues. The aim of this chapter is to consider the relationship of the atlas data to certain general ideas and problems concerning bird species and populations.

## Prehistoric and Historic Perspectives

As recently in geological time as 21,000 years ago the last great glacial advance of the Pleistocene Ice Ages entirely covered Connecticut with a depth of perhaps a mile or more of ice. Connecticut in that age might have resembled parts of modern day central Greenland or Antarctica, and birdwatching here would presumably have been extremely unrewarding. By 13,000 years ago, the North American glaciers were in retreat (Pielou 1991), and, with a general warming, plants and animals again invaded Connecticut from the south. An open tundra and taiga vegetation probably appearing much like that in the Canadian arctic today was gradually replaced by coniferous woodland. Large elephant-like mastodonts once roamed the Connecticut landscape (Schuchert 1914),

and dead ones might have been eaten by California Condors, which have been found together with mastodont remains in New York state (Steadman 1988). For the past 10,000 years a mixed deciduous-coniferous woodland of varying composition has prevailed (Steadman 1988).

Unfortunately, knowledge of events in Connecticut during most of the past 10,000 years is very sketchy. Study of the remains of microscopic plant pollen preserved in lake sediments combined with radiocarbon dating has indicated the prevailing plant life at different times. Such studies indicate that modern tree species have been present for 10,000 years at least. Although apparently no fossil birds of any age have been reported from Connecticut, the limited material from New York state (Steadman 1988) suggests that the bird life of Connecticut has probably been somewhat like that of the present over the past 10,000 years.

Archaeological evidence from sites occupied by native Americans reveals the past presence in Connecticut of Wild Turkeys and Ruffed Grouse (Frank Dirrigl, pers. comm.), nonmigratory species which must have bred in the state. Historic records by the European colonists before 1780 are generally too vague to provide much direct insight on most of the bird species breeding during the colonial period. One difficulty in using the written reports of the early Europeans is that they had no standard names for birds so that, even when birds were mentioned, it is often impossible to be certain of the species. Development of standard names began in the latter half of the 1700s, but even Linsley's (1843) first list for Connecticut birds reflects the inadequacy of the names used at that time.

When Europeans first arrived, Connecticut was covered with virgin forest of large trees. Native Americans had made some clearings, but the extent of these is unclear. During the colonial period and on into the 1860s the land was cleared for timber, fuel, and agriculture. By 1865, virtually all land suited for farming had been cleared. Thereafter, with the new opportunities for agriculture in the midwestern states, land use for agriculture progressively declined in Connecticut. By 1985, 59% of the area of the state was rated as forested (Dickson and McAfee 1988), but the stone walls passing through the woodlands stand as a testament to a formerly agricultural landscape.

Knowledge of the kinds of birds breeding in Connecticut grew rapidly after 1870, but statewide coverage remained poor because of the spotty distribution of those few who recorded bird observations and a lack of easy transportation to more distant points in the state. The present volume is the first effort to map the breeding ranges for birds in all parts of the state on the basis of actual evidence from the field.

## Some Limitations of Atlas Data

This atlas is based on a sampling of sites that provide an indication of the breeding ranges of the different species. A more exact mapping might have been possible through the use of smaller blocks, but in practice it would have been very difficult to find volunteer observers to cover many more blocks. One problem with blocks of any size is obtaining access. Much of Connecticut is privately owned. For example, attempting confirmation of Common Nighthawk breeding by requesting permission to visit appropriate urban rooftops would very likely be unsuccessful. In some areas such as airports and prisons, thorough coverage was not feasible due to obvious restrictions. In other areas the terrain prevented a thorough sampling. For example, deep streams in some wooded swamps could not be followed by canoe or raft due to fallen limbs across the water, while the tangle of fallen trees and dense brush in shallower water made any progress on foot discouragingly slow.

Ideally, it would be good to have data not only on the block by block distribution of the breeding birds but also on their relative numbers (Craig 1987b, Bart and Klosiewski 1989). In practice, there are substantial difficulties in estimating accurately the numbers in most avian populations (Ralph and Scott 1981). The enormously greater time required to sample population numbers has made such a sampling impractical for this atlas, and in making interpretations from the data of this atlas we should remember that numerical estimates have not been made.

## External Factors Limiting Breeding Ranges

Once the breeding ranges are mapped, as in this atlas, one can ask what factors set the range limits. Where a species has a sharply defined breeding range with large number of birds breeding at the limits of the range, we may suspect that the birds are limited by a critical substrate (Caughley et al.

1988). An example is the obvious case of landbird species whose breeding ranges abruptly end at shorelines. If, however, the density of breeding birds becomes gradually less towards the edge of the range we can suspect more subtle restrictions on the range, often with two or more factors interacting (Caughley et al. 1988). This appears to be the case for certain landbird species whose breeding ranges reach their limits within interior Connecticut, e.g., the Yellow-rumped Warbler. External factors that might interact in limiting breeding range include physical factors such as temperature, humidity, and wind, and biological factors such as food, competitors, predators, parasites, and disease-producing microbes. These factors can interact in complex ways. In general, biologists do not know exactly what combinations of factors determine such range limits. Consequently, it is difficult to predict the effects of minor or sometimes even major changes in these factors. For example, a slight increase in mean annual temperature in Connecticut over the next few decades, as during a regime of global warming, would undoubtedly have many effects on plants and animals, but it is not presently possible to predict with much assurance the outcome for particular bird species. Environmental variables do affect the breeding distributions of the birds, but because many ranges are probably affected by interaction of two or more variables, one should not expect to find a simple correspondence of, for example, altitude and the range of any particular species. Hence, a combination of overlays may be more informative than any one alone. Moreover, by expressing the environmental variables in numerical terms and considering them in statistical models, it may eventually be possible to test more rigorously ideas on the roles of different factors (e.g., in Turner et al. 1988). There are several sources of information on the factors mentioned above and they may be consulted for comparison with the maps in this atlas—for the climate of Connecticut, see Brumbach (1965); for land forms, see Bell (1985); and for a synthesis of these factors as they relate to other organisms, see Dowhan and Craig (1976).

**Expansions and Contractions of Breeding Ranges**

This atlas illustrates that the boundary of a breeding range is often not accurately described simply by a neat line crossing a map, as is often shown as a necessary simplification in field guides. Instead, the periphery of the range consists of isolated pockets or "islands" of suitable environment. Examples from this atlas include the Hooded Merganser and Alder Flycatcher. The presence of birds in such peripheral isolated sites may vary from year to year. For example, in one area of Mansfield, Hermit Thrushes were present during the summer of 1981 but not in years immediately before or after (R. Löf and G. Clark, unpublished data). Thus, range limits are not necessarily constant from one year to the next. We do not know whether birds occupying peripheral sites reproduce as successfully as birds within the main portion of the breeding range, but it is conceivable that the peripheral birds are less successful (Pulliam 1988). It appears that many, if not all, species undergo year to year fluctuations in the boundaries of their ranges.

Extensions of breeding ranges over hundreds of miles northeastward have occurred in this century for such species as Red-bellied Woodpecker, Tufted Titmouse, Northern Mockingbird, Blue-gray Gnatcatcher, and Northern Cardinal, all of which were generally absent from Connecticut as breeders as recently as 1940 (Beddall 1963 and this volume). Other breeders showing clear increases since 1920 are the herons and Killdeer, which have recovered from the slaughters of earlier decades (Zeranski and Baptist 1990). In contrast are breeding populations that have declined in recent decades, such as most grassland species, including the Upland Sandpiper, Sedge Wren, Grasshopper Sparrow, and most notably the Henslow's Sparrow, which is now gone as a breeder in Connecticut. Still other species such as the Carolina and Winter Wrens have dramatically varied in their ranges and numbers within the state.

If the breeding ranges of birds are associated with controlling external factors, then a change in one or more of these factors might correspond with each range expansion or contraction. In most cases in which relatively well supported suggestions can be proposed to account for range changes, human influences have been at work. In the cases of the Red-bellied Woodpecker, Tufted Titmouse, Northern Cardinal, and House Finch, winter bird feeding has likely been a major contributor to the breeding range expansions. These are generally nonmigratory species commonly found near feeding stations in winter and much less frequently encountered away from stations during the coldest winter days. Thus it appears possible that the provision of extra food enables these species to survive Connecticut winters and hence to maintain a breeding range covering much of the state. The Northern Mockingbird appears to present a similar case of a largely nonmigratory species which can breed in an area due to the human planting of multiflora rose, the fruits of which constitute a major component of the winter diet (Stiles 1982). These suggestions of winter food as a major limiting factor affecting the breeding ranges of nonmigratory species have not been proven, but are plausible explanations.

The decline of grassland breeding species during this century is undoubtedly related to the loss of habitat with the decrease of land used for agriculture. Some of these grassland species bred in Connecticut probably only after the opening up of the forests by the Europeans (Hurley and Franks 1976). Thus the present decrease of these birds represents in some respects a return to probable precolonial conditions.

The Winter Wren and Carolina Wren appear to illustrate the effects of climate on the breeding range. The latter is much constricted by severe winters. On the basis of experience in the Storrs area, the Carolina Wren appears to be able to withstand very cold winters when sufficient food can be reached, but the population markedly drops when deep snow blocks access to food.

Although a major climatic change occurred with the retreat of the last glaciers, it is unlikely that birds are still invading Connecticut in response to that change in view of the intervening thousands of years of relatively warm climate. Change in range in response to temperature would more likely be due to recent events such as the warming since 1850 or that since the 1940s (K. Williamson 1975). Because changes in land use have been extensive in recent decades, it is difficult to separate possible effects of temperature from those of land use. Insectivorous species such as the Blue-gray Gnatcatcher have posed a problem because causes for range expansion in New England have not been obvious (Ellison 1993), with either warming or reforestation among leading possible causes. Temperature change affects growth and composition of vegetation and insect production, and separating causes of avian range changes can be difficult.

Expansion of the range would seem usually to require either the production or survival of extra young within the original range in order to provide colonists for the new area. Thus, these changes in both the original range and the area to be colonized seem necessary. One unsettled question is whether any recent range expansions were initiated by hereditary change within the original population. No example of such an event is known, but such a change might be very difficult to detect. Consequently, changes only in the environment, and not in the birds themselves, have ordinarily been considered in the search for causes of range expansions. However, in view of evidence for inherited differences between individuals affecting the direction and distance of migration in some bird populations (Gwinner 1988), it would not be surprising if hereditary changes are found also to be involved in range expansions.

**Habitat Selection**

Whether a bird breeds in a particular atlas block depends on the presence of a suitable kind of environment or habitat, e.g., grassy fields for Savannah Sparrows and conifers for Solitary Vireos. Breeding birds of one species often use only a restricted part of all available habitats in the vicinity, and their preference is designated with the term habitat selection (Cody 1985). In the long run, over evolutionary time, habitat selection should in theory enable breeding birds to choose areas favorable for finding food and nest sites free from severe predation or parasitism.

On a more immediate basis, habitat selection is probably based on an assessment of multiple factors. The relative importance of such factors is poorly known. The ability of experienced birders to predict roughly the kinds of birds likely to breed in a particular habitat is based on the regularity with which breeding birds of particular species occur in certain kinds of associations. For example, the Chipping Sparrow is often found in Connecticut where short grass on relatively dry soil occurs in association with conifers, especially pines. In contrast, the closely related Field Sparrow occupies areas of higher grass on well drained soils, not necessarily with conifers nearby. It is conceivable that species of birds choose habitats using some of the same clues as do birders in searching for breeders of those species. For many species the size of suitable habitat appears to be important, and this aspect has in recent years attracted increased interest in view of the many human imposed changes in the Connecticut landscape.

Laboratory studies indicate that habitat selection involves both inherited and learned aspects (e.g., Raach and Leisler 1989, Grünberger and Leisler 1990). Many species of birds that breed in Connecticut vary in the habitats used over their entire geographic range (Collins 1983a, Collins 1983b, James et al. 1984). For example, the Black-throated Green Warbler in Connecticut regularly breeds in coniferous areas that look very different from the cypress swamps used in the Atlantic coastal plain. Brooks (1942) gave other examples of geographic variation in habitat selection within breeding ranges of species in the eastern United States. Little is known of the relative importance of inheritance and learning in producing such geographic differences in habitat selection.

Some species have changed their breeding sites, apparently since precolonial times. For example, Chimney Swifts now seldom use hollow trees, and Purple Martins in the Northeast now breed only in artificial nesting houses. Known nest sites of Barn and Cliff Swallows in Connecticut are entirely on human built structures. In recent decades all known nestings of the Common Nighthawk in the state have been on flat roofs. We do not know whether these new developments represent changes in habitat selection or simply reveal preexisting tolerances enabling a shift in response to changes in available habitat. However, in view of the case of the Eastern Phoebe, which places its nests both under natural overhangs and human constructed buildings and bridges, we might suspect that the changes in breeding sites represent use of human constructed equivalents of naturally available sites.

## Diversity of Breeding Species

Some blocks have more breeding species than do others. Some habitats are richer in species than are others. What determines why a certain number of species occur in a given area, rather than more or fewer species? Species diversity is measured by the number of species present in an area, sometimes weighted by their relative abundance (MacArthur 1972). In general, the variety of breeding species tends to be higher in more complex habitats than in simpler ones. Thus forest plots almost invariably have a higher number of breeding species than do similarly sized grassland areas. A variety of explanations has been offered to account for differences in species diversity of birds between areas and habitats, but no general agreement has thus far been reached.

The number of avian species breeding in one area has often been thought to result from the complexity of habitat determining the variety of ways available for bird species to obtain food (Lack 1971). Similar species of birds breeding in the same area ordinarily differ in the ways in which they forage. There has been much discussion as to whether such differences arise as a consequence of past or present competition among species (Cody 1985), or as the result of each species independently acquiring in its own evolution specialized ways of feeding that differ somewhat from the feeding habits of other species in the same area (Wiens 1989).

Still another kind of explanation for diversity of bird species in an area is that an upper limit to the number of species might be set by the variety of different kinds of nest sites available (Martin 1988). Different species feeding in similar habitats often differ in the sites used for nesting. Some examples are the daytime aerial feeders including the swifts and swallows. Other groups such as flycatchers, vireos, warblers, and sparrows also show notable differences between species in the sites used for nesting. Experiments indicate that artificial nests of the same kind placed in the same way throughout an environment are readily found by predators, whereas if such nests are hidden in different ways, predators find fewer of the nests (Martin 1988). Thus placement by each species of its nest in a site different from that used by other species should help it to avoid predation at the nest. However, it seems unlikely that any single factor alone will determine the variety of species breeding in an area (Ricklefs 1989).

Another explanation of the variety of species breeding in an area, individuals in each species are presumed to use a distinctive habitat in order to attract and keep mates (Colwell 1984). Shared features of the habitat are believed to help unite individuals within a species with other species-specific features in plumages, vocalizations, and specialized movements such as in courtship displays. Birds that do not select breeding habitat within the usual range are unlikely to attract mates. In this view, species can invade a new area and add to the total number of breeding species living in that area as long as the invading species have distinctly different habitats. However, two species having the same habitat selection for breeding, if both numerous in an area, might be expected to compete so intensely that only one survives in the area.

Possible North American examples of species pairs so similar in habitat selection that only one of the species can survive as a breeder in an area include the Black-capped and Carolina Chickadees, Red-bellied and Golden-fronted Woodpeckers, Rose-breasted and Black-headed Grosbeaks, and Eastern and Western Screech-Owls.

## Gradients of Species Diversity

Numerous birds breeding in Connecticut migrate to the tropics or subtropics and remain for six or more months through the northern winter. These species are in some respects visitors from the tropics that nest in Connecticut when the climate is most like that of the tropics. During spring and summer in the north temperate zone, including in Connecticut, a burst of production of insect life occurs over a relatively short number of weeks, and birds migrating to Connecticut from the south can take advantage of the temporary availability of food.

The variety of species of breeding birds is greatest in the tropical rain forests and is generally progressively less as one moves away from the equator into the temperate regions and then the arctic. About 80% of the world's bird species reside in the tropics where the continuous warmth frequently enables a year-round supply of such foods as nectar, fruit, and invertebrate animals. In view of such favorable features in parts of the tropics and subtropics, it has been difficult for biologists to understand what factors have led to the origin and maintenance of long range latitudinal migration in so many bird species.

The tendency for a change in number of breeding species, usually a decrease, as one moves from the equator towards the poles, is often called a latitudinal species diversity gradient. Such a gradient would be difficult to demonstrate within the confines of Connecticut because the state encompasses only a narrow band of latitude. Nevertheless, the data from this atlas and those from other published and forthcoming atlases will be useful in evaluating ideas proposed to explain latitudinal diversity gradients. One obvious factor is the greater complexity of tropical forests relative to those of the temperate zone. The more complex environment offers a greater array of possibilities for habitat selection and hence more species.

One contributing factor might be the yearly input of energy from sunlight at different latitudes. Using data from the British breeding bird atlas, Turner et al. (1988) found within Britain a strong correlation between the input of natural solar energy and a latitudinal gradient in diversity of breeding bird species. Such analyses have not yet been done for North America.

## Origin and Elimination of Species

Bird species are believed to proliferate when one species becomes separated into two geographically isolated populations. Given sufficient time in isolation without interbreeding, the two populations may diverge in their hereditary features so that they can no longer interbreed should an opportunity arise. Non-interbreeding populations of such similar birds as Willow and Alder Flycatchers are considered separate species, whereas freely interbreeding birds are members of the same species even though members of a pair may look very different such as in the case of the red and gray phases of the Eastern Screech-Owl. No examples are known in which new species of birds have evolved during the last 300 years, the time during which birds have been most carefully observed. Although little is known about the time required for the evolution of new species, it appears that evolutionary rates are generally slow, with at least centuries or perhaps millennia required for the formation of a new species.

In striking contrast is the rapidity with which species can be eliminated. Extirpated birds are those eliminated from a particular region, whereas extinct birds are those that no longer exist. The only extinct species known to have bred in Connecticut (Sage et al. 1913) was the Passenger Pigeon. Naturally occurring species that formerly bred apparently regularly but are now extirpated as breeders in Connecticut include the Peregrine Falcon, Sedge Wren, Northern Parula, Dickcissel, and Henslow's Sparrow (Sage et al. 1913). Wild Turkeys were extirpated from the state probably before 1825, but have been successfully reintroduced in recent decades. Among presently breeding species, the Bald Eagle, Piping Plover, and Roseate Tern are considered endangered or threatened under federal regulations. These and other species with small populations and a historically declining number of breeding sites in the state are particularly at risk of extirpation as breeders. Species to be watched in this regard include the Sharp-shinned Hawk, Cooper's Hawk, Northern Goshawk, Northern Bobwhite, Upland Sandpiper,

Barn Owl, Common Nighthawk, Whip-poor-will, Horned Lark, Purple Martin, Cliff Swallow, Golden-winged Warbler, Yellow-breasted Chat, and Grasshopper Sparrow. The situation in Connecticut, however, seems less threatening than the general picture globally, in which more than 10% of all bird species are believed to be in circumstances that could potentially quickly lead to extinction (Collar and Andrew 1988). Many bird species nesting in Connecticut appear to have large ranges relative to birds in many other parts of the world, especially those restricted to small islands; a large range reduces the chance of extinction arising from environmental changes in a small geographic area.

## Conservation

The data of this atlas show the breeding ranges in Connecticut for all known breeding species at one period in time. For those species especially at risk of extinction or extirpation, the maps indicate general regions of the state where changes in land use or application of toxic chemicals might have adverse effects on particular bird species. For any specific case in which land use changes or major applications of toxins are proposed, a more detailed examination of the particular sites would be necessary to predict the impacts in detail.

Human effects on the landscape and on the quality of water and air are preeminent among known factors potentially affecting breeding bird populations at the present time. Nature free of human influence no longer exists in Connecticut or elsewhere on the globe. Human activity, such as in land use, affects populations of all breeding species, albeit usually without a deliberate goal of either increasing or decreasing the number of breeders of a particular species. Advocating letting "nature take its course" with respect to conservation of birds, an attitude widely adopted in the past, can lead to neglect of birds in making decisions about use of the environment. Whether we like it or not, humanity today is, in effect, altering populations of plants and animals throughout the globe and commonly doing so without explicit long-term objectives. Wildlife management related to conservation has thus become a critical need worldwide, but it remains an open question whether human societies will recognize this need in time to avoid the huge numbers of extinctions that seem likely if present trends continue.

This atlas helps to illustrate the effects of past human activity in Connecticut. As one example, in those parts of the state that have become urbanized in recent decades, the variety of breeding birds has been sharply reduced; when suitable habitat is removed, breeding populations do not persist. In another example, from the 1940s to 1972 populations of certain raptor species sharply declined due to the wide use of DDT as an insecticide in Connecticut and elsewhere in North America. Following the national ban on the use of DDT, a number of raptor populations rebounded, but the Osprey in Connecticut has still not regained the number of breeding sites in use before 1940, and the Bald Eagle and Peregrine Falcon still have far to go in recovery.

Human activities remote from Connecticut potentially affect the status of breeders here. Deforestation is widespread in much of Latin America where many birds that breed in Connecticut migrate and spend the winter. Furthermore, continued pesticide use in some of those areas poses additional hazards for the same species. Declines have been reported for northeastern North American breeding species and particularly those that migrate to the tropics. However, it has been difficult to demonstrate unequivocally that particular causes, such as tropical deforestation, are responsible (Holmes and Sherry 1988, Hutto 1988, Askins et al. 1990). In Connecticut, regional declines of particular breeding bird species have come with major changes in land use and with the ends of outbreaks of insects such as the introduced gypsy moths. Developments unfavorable to migratory birds have been occurring on both their breeding and wintering grounds, and it is difficult to determine the long term trends of many populations and whether events on the breeding or wintering grounds are of primary importance in driving these trends. These problems clearly need continuing attention.

A predictably continuing concern within Connecticut will be the preservation of habitats. Much progress has already been made in preserving remnant fragments of shoreline and marsh environments. Preservation efforts have necessarily emphasized the rarer habitats and rarer species, but it would be desirable to have more preservation initiated before the numbers of a species or abundance of a habitat become perilously low. For some species, conservation will require a continued deliberate manipulation of the environment. For example, natural change in plant communities over a period of years will eliminate the grassland breeding bird species unless countered by mowing. Such cutting ideally should be done after the ground nesters have fledged their young.

Most of the ongoing change in the landscape of Connecticut has been directed to meet immediate economic or social goals without considering possible long-term implications for conservation of plants and animals. One tendency has been to carve up the landscape with roads and other developments that reduce the remaining natural areas into smaller and more isolated fragments (DeGraaf and Healy 1990). When such habitat fragments become too small, certain birds will no longer breed. The loss of breeding bird species through reduction and isolation of suitable forests has been well illustrated in studies in southeastern Connecticut (Askins et al. 1987). From the viewpoint of conservation, land use planning might be more effective if undertaken on a broader, regional scale rather than by a series of separate decisions on the use of relatively small parcels of land.

An optimistic approach to bird conservation seems most likely to be productive. A negative view that extirpation of certain breeding species is inevitable invites inaction and thus can be a self-fulfilling prophecy. In contrast, thinking realistically about future possibilities and acting to promote the best of these would seem far more productive. Part of this conservation effort must be the continued development of a solid foundation of scientific studies, such as this atlas, which provides a basis for making decisions concerning particular species and habitats (Robbins 1990). The historical perspective indicates that human activities in the state over the last 400 years have led to a greater diversity of habitats in Connecticut now than in precolonial times; consequently, it seems likely that the diversity of breeding bird species today exceeds that of the precolonial period. Although some breeding species have been lost, there have also been notable gains. Connecticut's breeding birdlife at present is possibly as diverse as at any time in the past 10,000 years. Birds constitute a highly valued part of our natural heritage. Public interest and enthusiasm, such as that shown by the atlas participants, play a vital role in sustaining that heritage for both present and future generations.

*George A. Clark, Jr*

# Species Accounts

*Confirmed and Probable Breeders*

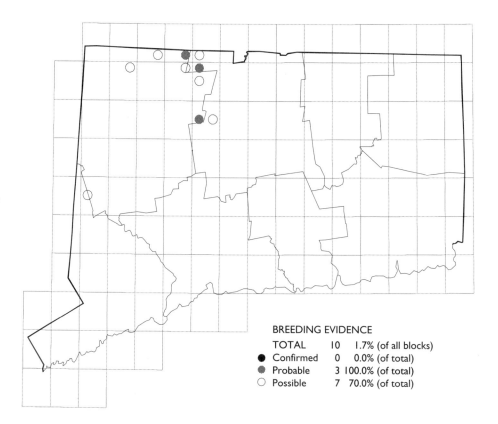

## Common Loon
### *Gavia immer*

BREEDING EVIDENCE

| | TOTAL | 10 | 1.7% (of all blocks) |
|---|---|---|---|
| ● | Confirmed | 0 | 0.0% (of total) |
| ◐ | Probable | 3 | 100.0% (of total) |
| ○ | Possible | 7 | 70.0% (of total) |

Mainly a winter visitor and transient in Connecticut, summering nonbreeders are found occasionally along the coast and at a few public water supply reservoirs in the northwestern part of the state. The Common Loon is designated as a Species of Special Concern in the state.

**Habitat**—Potential breeding sites where summering individuals are found include the larger and deeper reservoirs in Litchfield County, such as Barkhamsted and Nepaug reservoirs. The necessary requisites for nesting include large lakes or reservoirs with no shoreline development and highly restricted or closed public access (no boating). Fluctuating water levels and predation by raccoons or American Crows have caused nesting failures in Massachusetts.

**Atlas results**—The atlas did not confirm breeding from 1982 to 1986, although probable evidence was obtained in Litchfield County at Colebrook, Barkhamsted, and Nepaug reservoirs. Summering birds were reported on these reservoirs and on Candlewood Lake, Doolittle Pond, and Wangum Lake.

**Discussion**—The history of the Common Loon breeding in Connecticut is not well documented, and to date no substantive evidence for nesting exists. Historical accounts indicate that the species once bred sparingly south to Connecticut, northern Pennsylvania, northern Indiana, northern Iowa, and west to northeastern California. The

southern limit of breeding is currently well to the north in the West and Midwest while much the same in New England. Linsley (1843) did not mention breeding in Connecticut, and the first report for the state is found in Merriam (1877), who cites a report of breeding on a pond in "Easthampton." Sage et al. (1913) cite an observation by W. R. Nichols of a pair and two young at Lake Saltonstall, East Haven, in 1890 where the observer previously recorded nesting in 1878. Neither of these reports is supported by descriptive evidence nor are several reports this century, all of which should be considered suspect—Winchester in the early 1880s (Job 1908), Colchester in 1948 (Bergstrom 1960), Ansonia in 1952 (Craig 1980), Nepaug Reservoir in 1972 and 1975 (Craig 1980), and Barkhamsted in 1977 (Vickery 1977b, Craig 1980).

Adult Common Loons continue to summer on several larger lakes in northwestern Connecticut; yet despite these reports and the historical accounts, evidence of nesting in Connecticut is sadly lacking. The report of a single bird presumed sitting on a nest at Nepaug Reservoir, the site of earlier summering birds, on 31 July 1989 (Kaplan 1990) is now considered inadequate following discussions with the observer, who only saw one bird during that summer and never found a nest. In other cases, the breeding reports likely involve misidentifications of Common Mergansers (Norfolk in 1978 and 1985). On a positive note, the presence of summering loons and suitable breeding habitat in Connecticut indicates a strong potential for nesting, a possibility that should be promoted in management of the larger reservoirs. Zeranski and Baptist (1990) have suggested that recreational use of lakes might inhibit nesting in Connecticut; yet studies in Ontario show no clear relationship between nesting success and human disturbance (Ashenden 1988). It is clear, however, that loons prefer to nest in remote sections of these recreational lakes. Since 1975, Common Loons have nested in Massachusetts at Quabbin and Wachusett reservoirs, Worcester County; floating rafts, which provide stable nest sites when water levels fluctuate, have been used successfully at these localities once it was clear nesting pairs *already* were established (Blodgett and Lyons 1988).

*Louis R. Bevier*

# Pied-billed Grebe
*Podilymbus podiceps*

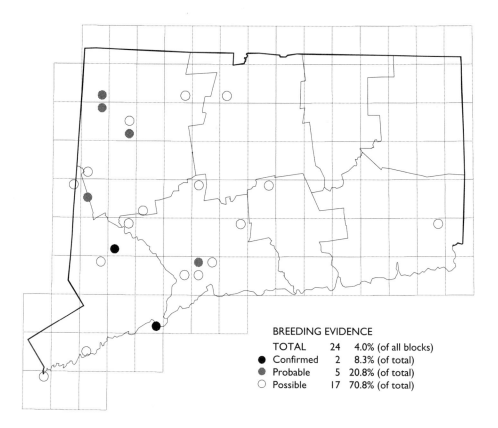

BREEDING EVIDENCE

| | TOTAL | 24 | 4.0% (of all blocks) |
|---|---|---|---|
| ● Confirmed | | 2 | 8.3% (of total) |
| ● Probable | | 5 | 20.8% (of total) |
| ○ Possible | | 17 | 70.8% (of total) |

This is the only species of grebe that breeds in the state. The Pied-billed Grebe is a rare migratory breeder designated as an Endangered species in Connecticut. Breeding individuals usually arrive in Connecticut from late March through April depending on the severity of the winter and ice conditions on lakes, ponds, and marshes. Fall migrants are more numerous and widespread. The species is irregular and rare in the state during winter, most birds moving south of New England.

**Habitat**—The Pied-billed Grebe requires quiet ponds, lakes, and sluggish streams with extensive emergent vegetation for nesting. Cattail marshes and reed laden ponds are favored for nest sites. The nest is constructed with large bulky piles of plant materials overlain with a smaller, neater, more compact layer extending two to four inches above water. The entire structure is attached and anchored to emergent vegetation, usually in shallow water less than three feet deep. Floating nests are occasionally constructed over deep water.

**Atlas results**—Confirmed breeding was reported from only two blocks: at Great Meadows, Stratford, and at Newtown. Breeding was limited to western Connecticut, the entire eastern section of the state yielding only one possible breeding record. Since the years of the atlas survey, localities in northwestern Connecticut (e.g., Miles Sanctuary, Sharon) have supported suspected breeders, and the Stratford site still holds a single pair.

**Discussion**—This grebe has apparently always been a sparse breeder in Connecticut. Merriam (1877) and Samuels (1867) stated that it bred in Connecticut but gave no details. Bent (1919) described a nest observed in Canaan in 1913. Sage et al. (1913) noted that it was a common fall migrant and cited a probable breeding record near Wilton. They also reported summer observations of this grebe in Litchfield County. Bagg and Eliot (1937) indicated without details that it nested regularly in South Windsor.

Mackenzie (1961) reported two nesting records from the Guilford area and wrote that L. B. Bishop had reported Pied-billed Grebes generally nested each summer at Lake Quonnipaug in Guilford.

Although the draining and filling of inland wetland habitat this century has obviously reduced potential nesting sites for the Pied-billed Grebe, we suspect that the breeding population is greater than the atlas data suggest. The Pied-billed Grebe is difficult to detect on its nesting grounds due to its secre-

tive nature. In addition, growth of extensive emergent vegetation limits habitat visibility and accessibility to atlas researchers. However, the species responds readily to tape playback of its song, especially in the hours immediately preceding dawn. A comprehensive survey of potential nesting habitats coupled with playback censusing of these areas would clarify the extent of breeding in Connecticut.

*Arnold Devine and Dwight G. Smith*

## Double-crested Cormorant
*Phalacrocorax auritus*

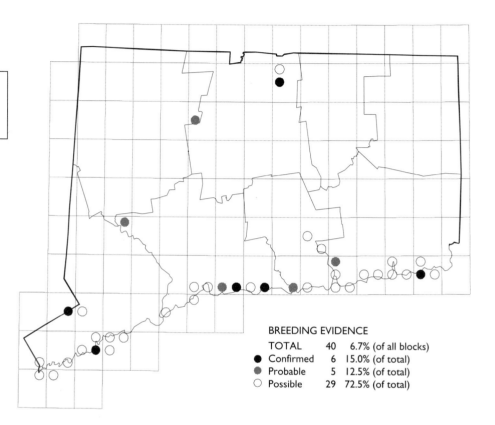

BREEDING EVIDENCE

| | | | |
|---|---|---|---|
| TOTAL | | 40 | 6.7% (of all blocks) |
| ● Confirmed | | 6 | 15.0% (of total) |
| ◍ Probable | | 5 | 12.5% (of total) |
| ○ Possible | | 29 | 72.5% (of total) |

The Double-crested Cormorant is presently a common summer breeder that is increasing in numbers. The vast majority of New England breeders (about 82%) winter from the eastern Gulf of Mexico to the south Atlantic coast (Dolbeer 1991). The nominate subspecies, *auritus*, breeds in our state and has black ornamental crest feathers on most birds unlike populations in western North America where white crest feathers are typical.

**Habitat**—In Connecticut, Double-crested Cormorants primarily nest along the coast, although they are increasingly common in summer inland along large rivers and on reservoirs, where limited nesting attempts have been noted. Cormorants require sites with little disturbance and form dense colonies on the rocky parts of coastal islands or, less commonly, in trees of these islands, e.g., on Ram Island, Stonington, and Calf Pasture Island, Norwalk. The birds can cause extensive damage to trees through guano buildup.

**Atlas results**—The cormorant population was expanding during the atlas surveys and has increased dramatically since. Nesting by cormorants is diffi-cult to confirm. Cormorants sit in large numbers on offshore rocks during the nesting season and sometimes play with nesting material. Careful observation is required to determine whether birds are nesting.

The report of birds nesting on Kings Island well inland on the Connecticut River near Enfield was checked in

1991, and no evidence of former nesting was found. If nesting occurred during the atlas period, it was not continued. Confirmation of breeding at the other inland sites is desired.

**Discussion**—No historical nesting records exist for this species in the state and it was a rare migrant through the 1800s and into the early 1900s (Linsley 1843, Sage et al. 1913). Breeding colonies began pushing south along the Atlantic coast from the Maritimes and Maine and expanding east from other populations in the northern Great Plains from 1925 to 1935 (Palmer 1962). The disappearance of cormorants prior to this time was probably the result of persecution of this alleged fishing competitor. The extent to which it has reoccupied or exceeded its previous range in New England is unknown, but the species did breed south at least to islands in Boston Harbor prior to colonial times (Veit and Peterson 1993).

The species first nested in Long Island Sound at Fisher's Island in 1977 (Bull 1981). In 1979 a single pair nested on East White Rock, Westport, and in 1982 a small colony started on Goose Island three miles offshore from Guilford. This second colony increased to 13 pairs in 1983 and 125 in 1986, whereas East White Rock was empty some years and never had more than two pairs until 1988 and 1989 when 42 and 84 pairs (respectively) nested. In 1986 almost 200 pairs were found on Gates Island off Mystic, although none had been there the year before. Nesting on nearby Ram Island began in 1989, when 500 pairs were present, and in that same year, the state's nesting population was estimated at over 1,000 pairs (Sibley and Bull 1990).

Associated with this population increase is a change in status at other seasons. In the past decade, this species has become regular in winter along the coast and inland during migration.

*Fred C. Sibley*

## American Bittern
*Botaurus lentiginosus*

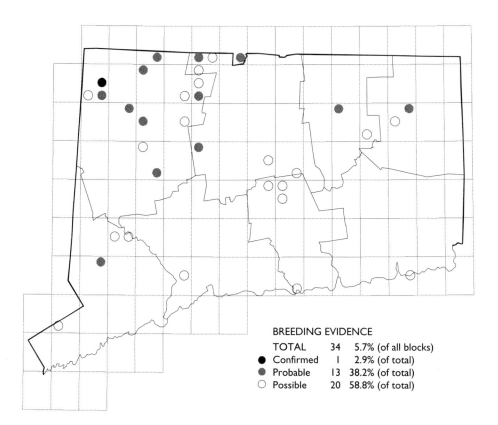

BREEDING EVIDENCE

| | TOTAL | 34 | 5.7% (of all blocks) |
|---|---|---|---|
| ● | Confirmed | 1 | 2.9% (of total) |
| ◓ | Probable | 13 | 38.2% (of total) |
| ○ | Possible | 20 | 58.8% (of total) |

This secretive bird of marshes and bogs is now a rare and local migratory breeder at interior marshes in Connecticut and has recently been designated as Endangered in the state. This species is more frequently encountered as a fall migrant in Connecticut, especially at coastal marshes; a few may linger late in fall or, more rarely, spend the winter. Spring migrants arrive in early April and are occasionally seen away from breeding localities through late May. The American Bittern breeds well north into Canada, mainly south of central British Columbia across to Newfoundland, and southward, locally, to Texas and northern Mexico; the species winters over much of the United States, parts of the West Indies, and Mexico (AOU 1983).

**Habitat**—Breeding in Connecticut is restricted to freshwater interior marshes with tall emergent vegetation, especially cattails and bulrushes. This species has nested in brackish marshes, such as at the Connecticut River mouth, but has not done so recently (Craig 1990). Broad, dense marshes are favored, although wet swales may occasionally be used for nesting provided there is dense cover. Nests may be constructed over water on a platform of bent cattail stems and leaves or, infrequently, built on dry ground at the margin of the marsh (Hancock and Elliott 1978). No more than one pair has been found occupying a single marsh in Connecticut recently. Nests with eggs have been found in late June in Connecticut (Sage et al. 1913).

**Atlas results**—The only confirmed breeding was in Sharon, but as detection of nests or young is difficult for this secretive species, the several probable localities in Litchfield County should be considered as likely nesting sites. Although several large marshes exist in northeastern Connecticut, only two blocks were reported there with probable breeding. A cluster of possible blocks in the vicinity of Cromwell indicate the strong likelihood of nesting in that area at Dead Man's Swamp, Cromwell Meadows, Wangunk Meadows, and Wethersfield Meadows.

**Discussion**—This species was formerly an uncommon to locally common breeder in extensive marshes of Connecticut. Although Merriam (1877) called the American Bittern a common summer resident, Sage et al. (1913) later described the species as rare in summer without stating whether the species had declined over the intervening years. More recently, the American Bittern has noticeably declined (Tate and Tate 1982), and Mackenzie (1961) attributed its scarcity in Guilford since the mid-1950s to draining of marshes.

The American Bittern still occupies marshes in northwestern Connecticut and marshes along the Connecticut River. From 1971 to 1987, the only locality along the Connecticut River found to have American Bitterns consistently was Dead Man's Swamp, Cromwell (Craig 1990); its territorial pumping call has been heard there over the past several years (Kaplan and Mantlik 1990). Dowhan and Craig (1976) suggested that pesticides and other chemical pollutants accumulated through fish eaten by this species were a factor in the decline of the American Bittern. Loss of breeding habitat undoubtedly has contributed to its decline, especially considering the tremendous rate of draining and filling of swamps and marshes in the state during this century.

*Louis R. Bevier*

## Least Bittern
*Ixobrychus exilis*

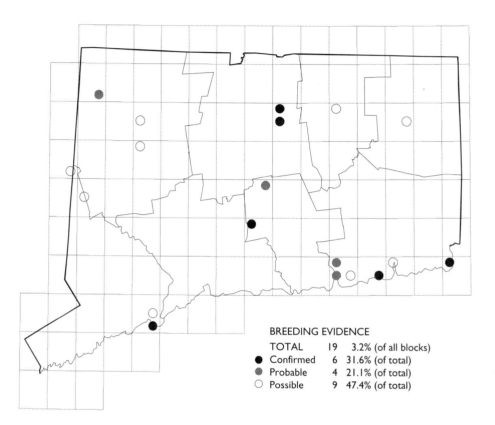

BREEDING EVIDENCE

| | TOTAL | 19 | 3.2% (of all blocks) |
|---|---|---|---|
| ● | Confirmed | 6 | 31.6% (of total) |
| ◐ | Probable | 4 | 21.1% (of total) |
| ○ | Possible | 9 | 47.4% (of total) |

This is perhaps the most secretive of our nesting herons, and it is frequently overlooked. Least Bitterns are migratory breeders in Connecticut, the population withdrawing to the southern United States in winter. Migrant Least Bitterns are rarely encountered, and most individuals seen or heard in Connecticut are at likely breeding localities. The subspecies breeding throughout the eastern United States is the nominate form, *exilis* (AOU 1957).

The familiar territorial call is a soft trebled sound, 'kwo-o-o,' but a frequently overlooked growling alarm call, 'gwaah,' can also be heard. The Least Bittern is listed as Threatened in Connecticut.

**Habitat**—Unlike the American Bittern, this species breeds both at coastal and at interior localities. Least Bitterns occur in estuarine salt and brackish marshes as well as freshwater marshes in Connecticut. Craig (1990) found the species most commonly in brackish cattail and cattail-reed dominated marshes on the Connecticut River.

**Atlas results**—Breeding was confirmed at South Windsor (Station 43), Durham Meadows, Barn Island in Stonington, Harkness State Park in Waterford, and at the margins of the Great Meadows marsh in Lordship, Stratford. In addition, two blocks near the mouth of the Connecticut River had probable breeding.

**Discussion**—Considering the tremendous loss of wetlands in the state and the fact that this was noted as a regularly occurring breeder by Merriam (1877), the species has almost certainly declined. Although comparison of the opinions of various authors is tenuous for such a secretive species, it is likely that a serious decline occurred in the late 1800s based on the comments of Sage et al. (1913), who described the species as rare. Although recent records indicate that the Least Bittern is not as scarce as it seems, the species is not abundant and is not found in many marshes that would otherwise appear suitable for nesting.

The Least Bittern was probably underreported due to its secretive behavior. Many small wetlands along the Connecticut River likely harbor several breeding pairs of Least Bittern, whereas along the coast, where observers tend to concentrate their efforts, the few localities found during this survey likely better represent the extent of breeding there. As with the American Bittern, the loss and degradation of wetlands in the state caused a reduction in the number of breeding individuals; unlike the American Bittern, however, the Least Bittern has remained a breeder coastally.

*Louis R. Bevier*

## Great Blue Heron
*Ardea herodias*

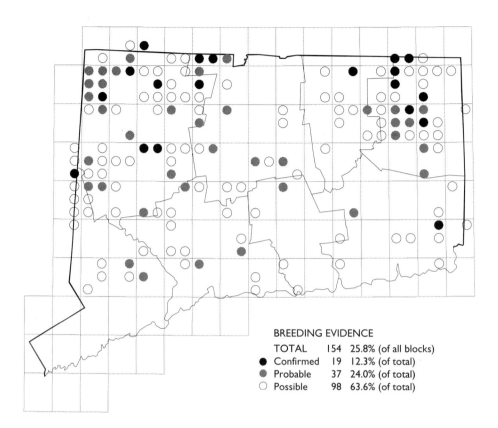

BREEDING EVIDENCE

| | TOTAL | 154 | 25.8% (of all blocks) |
|---|---|---|---|
| ● | Confirmed | 19 | 12.3% (of total) |
| ● | Probable | 37 | 24.0% (of total) |
| ○ | Possible | 98 | 63.6% (of total) |

The Great Blue Heron is an uncommon migratory breeder in Connecticut. A small number of birds winter in Connecticut along the coast and at interior sites with open water, but it is unknown whether these wintering birds also breed in the state or come from breeding sites to the north. In winter, the species becomes more prevalent as one goes further south in eastern North America (Root 1988). With a limited number of colony sites and with shrinking acreage of suitable nesting habitat, the Great Blue Heron has been designated as a Species of Special Concern in Connecticut. According to the AOU (1957) the nominate subspecies *herodias* breeds here and in most of North America except the Southeast and the West.

**Habitat**—Great Blue Herons typically nest in wet wooded areas, often by the margins of lakes, ponds, or marshes, but sometimes in wet areas in the interior of forests. The large nests are placed well off the ground in rather open trees that are often dead. Although the species is ordinarily colonial in its nesting, isolated nests have also been observed in Connecticut. The birds require relatively shallow waters for their foraging.

**Atlas results**—The major areas for confirmed breeding were in the northwestern and northeastern hills where relatively undisturbed wooded wetlands together with numerous bodies of water provide suitable conditions for breeding. The general absence of confirmed breeding records in coastal regions is striking in the case of this species.

**Discussion**—Merriam (1877) did not specifically mention breeding but noted that the Great Blue Heron was a summer resident and common during migration. Sage et al. (1913) termed the species a very rare summer resident and reported only one specific nesting record from Winchester. Craig (1978) reported confirmed breeding records in seven towns and suspected breeding in two others since 1950. During the mid-1970s, breeding populations of Great Blue Heron in Connecticut began to increase greatly (Zeranski and Baptist 1990). Craig (1978) suggested that activity of beavers had created more favorable situations for breeding. Although there is apparently no evidence that chlorinated hydrocarbon pesticides adversely affected Great Blue Herons in southern New England, the coincidence in timing of a reduction in use of chlorinated hydrocarbons with an increase in heron numbers warrants further consideration of the possibility of a connection.

For many blocks for which birds were recorded but not confirmed as breeders it is difficult to ascertain whether or not the records apply to breeding birds or simply to birds that bred in nearby blocks and traveled out to feed. The relative lack of confirmed breeding in Connecticut shoreline areas might be explained by the extensive human development there. The Great Blue Heron has the reputation of being the wariest of herons (Stone 1937). However, there is also apparently some tendency for Great Blue Herons, in contrast to most other Connecticut species of herons and egrets, to nest away from salt water as indicated by the sites of rookeries—see Bent (1926), Stone (1937), Peterson *in* Andrle and Carroll (1988), Griscom and Snyder (1955). Although Great Blue Herons once nested on Long Island (Peterson *in* Andrle and Carroll 1988) and still do on coastal islands of Maine (Gibbs et al. 1987), there might be factors in addition to human disturbance tending to limit coastal nesting by this species. Although apparently no studies have been conducted on salt excretion by Great Blue Herons, the limited tolerance for salt load in the closely related Gray Heron (*A. cinerea*) of Europe (summary in Shoemaker 1972) suggests the possibility that Great Blue Herons might be similarly limited, though many of these birds do feed in saline environments through part of the year.

*George A. Clark, Jr.*

## Great Egret
*Casmerodius albus*

The Great Egret is highly local as a breeding species in Connecticut. In the latter part of the summer and early fall, postbreeding birds wander and may occur on occasion in virtually any part of the state. The presence of such post-breeding wanderers at inland locations during the summer months has some-times been wrongly interpreted as indi-cating local breeding. The breeding population in the state is currently des-ignated as Threatened. Birds from pop-ulations in the northeastern United States apparently winter principally from North Carolina south along the east coast with the major portion in Florida and perhaps into the West Indies (Allen *in* Palmer 1962).

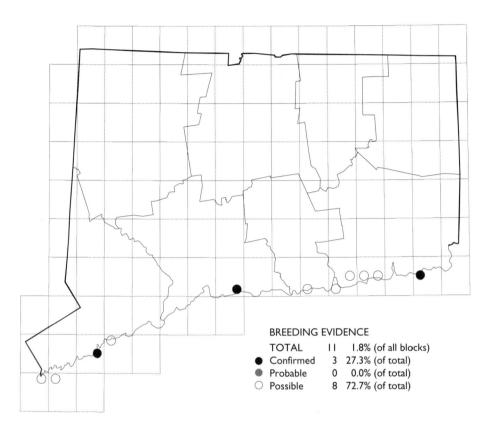

BREEDING EVIDENCE

| TOTAL | | 11 | 1.8% (of all blocks) |
|---|---|---|---|
| ● | Confirmed | 3 | 27.3% (of total) |
| ◍ | Probable | 0 | 0.0% (of total) |
| ○ | Possible | 8 | 72.7% (of total) |

**Habitat**—For successful nesting, Great Egrets require a grove of trees in a site relatively isolated from potential preda-tors such as raccoons. Such sites are typ-ically on islands. On Chimon Island off Norwalk, nests have usually been placed in the tree canopy in contrast to the nests of Snowy Egrets and Little Blue Herons that have been at lower heights in shrubs (Connecticut Audubon Society, unpub-lished data). The Great Egret also needs fairly open situations for foraging in shallow water or along the edge of the water. Foraging areas are often at a sub-stantial distance from the breeding areas, and birds must fly back and forth—for example, between Chimon Island and the mainland (Marra and Bull 1986b).

**Atlas results**—Confirmation of breeding was obtained in three blocks along the coast. Birds were found in eight other coastal blocks, but a conservative interpretation would be that no breeding occurred in those eight.

**Discussion**—Sage et al. (1913) knew of no records of breeding by Great Egrets. The species underwent a severe decline in numbers in the late nineteenth century and beginning of the next century when birds were killed to obtain feathers for the millinery trade (Bent 1926). Since full legal protection was provided in the early twentieth century, the numbers of this species have greatly increased. The first recorded breeding for Connecticut came in 1961 in the Norwalk Islands (Bull 1964; Marra and Bull 1986a).

Connecticut has relatively few uninhabited coastal islands with suitable vegetation, and therefore a great expansion of the breeding numbers of this species in the coastal area seems unlikely. This species remains rare as a breeder away from the coast in the northeastern U.S. (Peterson *in* Andrle and Carroll 1988).

*George A. Clark, Jr.*

## Snowy Egret
### *Egretta thula*

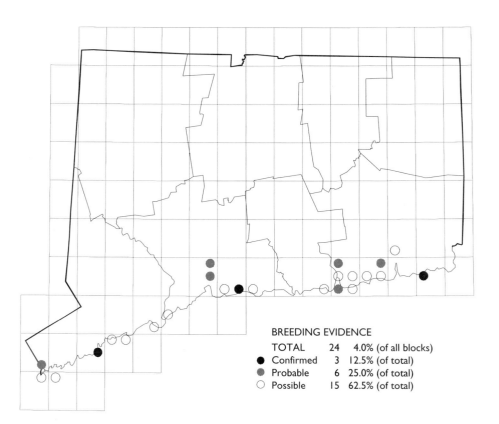

BREEDING EVIDENCE

| | TOTAL | 24 | 4.0% (of all blocks) |
|---|---|---|---|
| ● | Confirmed | 3 | 12.5% (of total) |
| ● | Probable | 6 | 25.0% (of total) |
| ○ | Possible | 15 | 62.5% (of total) |

The Snowy Egret is a migratory breeder in our state. This species is much less frequently encountered as a postbreeding wanderer in interior Connecticut than is the Great Egret. The breeding population in the state is currently designated as Threatened. In winter, birds of this species can be found over a vast area, including the southern coastal areas of the United States south through the West Indies, Central America, and South America (AOU 1983). The wintering area for those Snowy Egrets breeding in Connecticut is unknown but may extend as far south as northern South America (Hancock and Kushlan 1984).

**Habitat**—On Chimon Island of the Norwalk Islands, Snowy Egrets generally nest in shrubs. These sites contain quantities of bittersweet, blackberry, honeysuckle, and sumac (Connecticut Audubon Society, unpublished data). The birds also require feeding sites that may in some cases be located at a considerable distance from the breeding colony (Marra and Bull 1986b). Hancock and Kushlan (1984) have pointed out that habitats used by this species vary greatly over its entire range. In mixed species colonies in Connecticut, Snowy Egrets apparently typically nest lower in the trees than do Great Egrets (see above and also Palmer 1962), but nest sites for Snowy Egrets are known to vary widely from place to place and from year to year (Hancock and Kushlan 1984).

**Atlas results**—Breeding was confirmed in the same three coastal blocks as for the Great Egret. The finding of birds in summer in 21 other blocks should not be assumed to indicate breeding by this species in those blocks; summer birds may travel widely for foraging. Some of these blocks may contain important feeding sites crucial to the support of nesting in other areas.

**Discussion**—This species underwent a severe decline in numbers in the late nineteenth century and during the beginning of the twentieth century as a consequence of the commercial millinery trade. The numbers of these birds began to increase following the establishment of full legal protection in 1913 (Bull 1964). Breeding was first definitely recorded in Connecticut in 1961 (Bull 1964, Marra and Bull 1986a). The twentieth century comeback of Snowy Egret populations, like that of other similarly afflicted species, indicates the great potential for solution of many conservation problems if the problems are identified in time, the solutions recognized, and a sufficiently vigorous education program is promptly undertaken.

*George A. Clark, Jr.*

## Little Blue Heron
*Egretta caerulea*

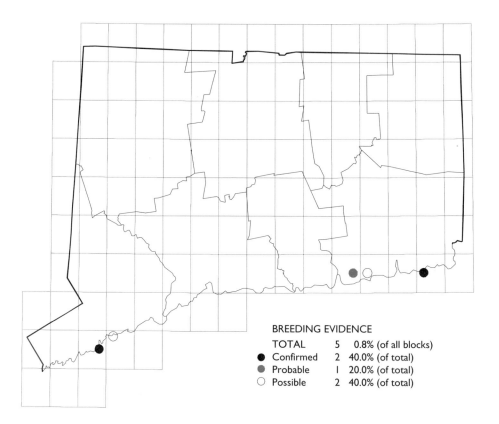

BREEDING EVIDENCE
| | | |
|---|---|---|
| TOTAL | 5 | 0.8% (of all blocks) |
| ● Confirmed | 2 | 40.0% (of total) |
| ● Probable | 1 | 20.0% (of total) |
| ○ Possible | 2 | 40.0% (of total) |

A migratory breeder, the species is very local in its breeding in Connecticut and has been designated as a Species of Special Concern. In winter, birds of this species from populations breeding in the eastern United States occur from coastal Virginia and the Gulf Coast south through much of the West Indies, Central America, and northern South America (AOU 1983, Hancock and Kushlan 1984, Palmer 1962). The Little Blue Heron is unique among herons of the world in having immatures white in plumage while mature birds are dark (Hancock and Kushlan 1984). Thus far, no one has advanced a convincing explanation as to why such a change of plumage color with age might be advantageous for this species but not for other kinds of herons.

**Habitat**—Like many other colonial nesting herons, the Little Blue Heron uses wooded sites isolated from potential terrestrial predators. On Chimon Island in the Norwalk Islands, the relatively few pairs of Little Blue Herons, like the more numerous Snowy Egrets, have nested in shrubs rather than the tallest trees (Connecticut Audubon Society, unpublished data). Little Blue Herons also require feeding areas that may be located at a substantial distance from the nesting area, and the birds then commute between these areas (Marra and Bull 1986b).

**Atlas results**—The Little Blue Heron was confirmed as a breeder in only two blocks. Sightings of the species in an additional three blocks probably do not indicate breeding in those blocks.

**Discussion**—This species did not suffer as much as did some of the other heron species from the slaughter of birds for the millinery trade (Hancock and Kushlan 1984). Nevertheless, breeding was not recorded in Connecticut until 1968, and even in more recent years the number of nesting pairs of Little Blue Herons in the Norwalk Islands has been much lower than that for Snowy Egrets (Marra and Bull 1986a).

The expansion of the Little Blue Heron into the northeastern states has been less successful than those of the Great and Snowy Egrets, two species that suffered greater losses during the period of the millinery trade in the late 1800s and beginning of the 1900s (Bull 1964, Hancock and Kushlan 1984). There has been some indication from the southeastern states that the Little Blue Heron has been adversely affected in competition for nesting sites by the invading Cattle Egret (Hancock and Kushlan 1984), but there is so far no clear indication why the northeastward expansion of the breeding range of the Little Blue Heron has been less successful than those in the Great or Snowy Egrets (Peterson *in* Andrle and Carroll 1988).

*George A. Clark, Jr.*

## Tricolored Heron
### *Egretta tricolor*

The Tricolored Heron has bred on occasion in Connecticut and is designated as a Species of Special Concern in the state. Although the species breeds primarily to our south, a few probably have attempted to nest here each year, at least in recent times. The wintering area for those relatively few birds breeding in Connecticut is unknown, but banding indicates that birds from South Carolina winter at least as far south as Panama (Hancock and Kushlan 1984). Breeding populations in North America are the subspecies *ruficollis*, which winters, in the eastern parts of its range, from Florida and the Gulf Coast south apparently into northern South America.

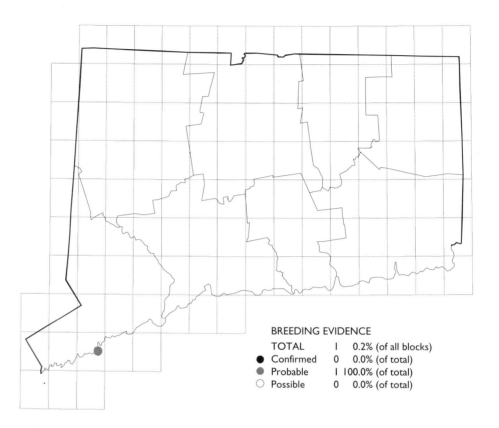

BREEDING EVIDENCE

| | | |
|---|---|---|
| TOTAL | I | 0.2% (of all blocks) |
| ● Confirmed | 0 | 0.0% (of total) |
| ◉ Probable | I | 100.0% (of total) |
| ○ Possible | 0 | 0.0% (of total) |

**Habitat**—No specific description of the breeding habitat is available for this species in Connecticut. However, from the localities in which breeding has been recorded, it may be presumed that the breeding habitat is somewhat like that of related species that nest in wooded sites relatively isolated from terrestrial predators.

**Atlas results**—During the atlas survey, the species was observed in the Norwalk Islands, where breeding was judged to be probable but not definitely confirmed. However, reports from studies conducted separately from those for the atlas indicate that breeding actually did occur in 1983.

**Discussion**—Although many sightings of this species by experienced observers exist, especially since the 1970s and 1980s, documentation of its occurrence in Connecticut has been very limited; the only known available specimen and photographic evidence for its occurrence in the state has been one skeleton in the Peabody Museum of Natural History at Yale University and one photograph by Mark Szantyr in the Connecticut Museum of Natural History collection at Storrs.

Breeding was first recorded in Connecticut in the Norwalk Islands in 1976 (Finch 1976). Subsequent breeding records are from 1977, 1979, and 1983 (Marra and Bull 1986a). This species was relatively little affected by the slaughter of herons during the period of the millinery trade of the late 1800s and early 1900s (Bent 1926). The Tricolored Heron has, along with other herons, shown in recent decades some tendency to expand its breeding range northward along the eastern seaboard, but in the case of the Tricolored Heron only a very limited number of birds have been involved. It is unknown why this species has been less successful in this regard than species such as the Great and Snowy Egrets (Peterson *in* Andrle and Carroll 1988).

*George A. Clark, Jr.*

## Cattle Egret
### *Bubulcus ibis*

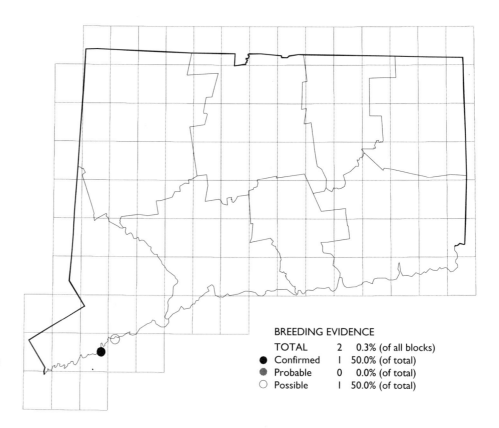

BREEDING EVIDENCE

| | | |
|---|---|---|
| TOTAL | 2 | 0.3% (of all blocks) |
| ● Confirmed | 1 | 50.0% (of total) |
| ◉ Probable | 0 | 0.0% (of total) |
| ○ Possible | 1 | 50.0% (of total) |

The Cattle Egret is a migratory breeder in Connecticut. Populations breeding in eastern North America winter from Florida south through the Greater Antilles and Central America to South America (Hancock and Kushlan 1984), but it is unknown specifically where the small number of birds that have bred in Connecticut have gone in the winter. The Cattle Egret is designated as a Species of Special Concern in Connecticut.

**Habitat**—Relatively little has been published about Cattle Egret nesting areas in Connecticut (Craig 1978). In the northeastern states the birds have nested with other herons, and studies in New Jersey indicated that Cattle Egrets can out-compete other heron or egret species of similar body size in obtaining favorable nest sites in a heronry (Burger 1978). Nests are typically placed off the ground. Cattle Egrets also require foraging areas, often in fields or other grassy areas that often have drier ground than the feeding sites commonly used by other herons. Cattle Egrets, as their name implies, often forage in pastures in association with large grazing mammals, particularly cattle in the Americas. In Connecticut, Cattle Egrets often will forage on large lawns in residential areas.

**Atlas results**—During the period of the atlas survey breeding was confirmed only in the Norwalk Islands block.

**Discussion**—This species, originally confined to the Old World, was first recorded in South America in 1880 and has subsequently spread widely throughout much of the New World (Hancock and Kushlan 1984). These birds exhibit a strong tendency to wander and this has contributed to their widespread establishment over many parts of the globe. The first nesting of the Cattle Egret in Connecticut was recorded in 1971 when 10 pairs were found breeding on Chimon Island in the Norwalk Islands (Marra and Bull 1986a). A lack of specific reports of Cattle Egrets breeding in Connecticut in many of the years since 1971 would seem to indicate that breeding has not been of annual occurrence in the state. Cattle Egrets show a strong association with large mammals that serve as "beaters" for flushing out arthropods that are eaten by the egrets. In one study, Cattle Egrets feeding with cattle obtained more food with less walking than did Cattle Egrets feeding alone (Heatwole 1965). These birds are also attracted to vehicles such as tractors, which if moving slowly in fields can apparently serve the same function of flushing arthropods for the birds (G. Clark, pers. obs.). Situations in which cattle or suitable vehicular substitutes can be found in fields located near suitable nesting sites would appear to be very limited in number in Connecticut.

The relative infrequency of this combination of habitat features would seem to limit the potential for establishment of a substantial breeding population in the state.

*George A. Clark, Jr.*

# Green Heron
*Butorides virescens*

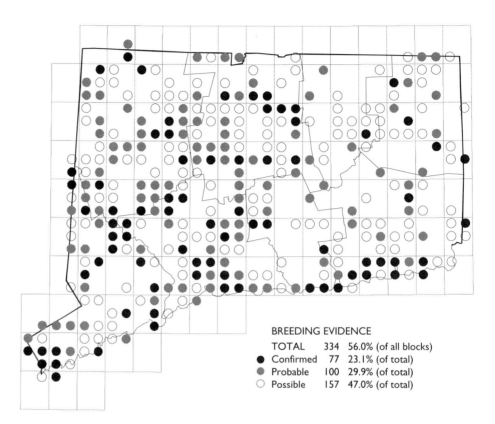

BREEDING EVIDENCE

| TOTAL | 334 | 56.0% (of all blocks) |
|---|---|---|
| ● Confirmed | 77 | 23.1% (of total) |
| ● Probable | 100 | 29.9% (of total) |
| ○ Possible | 157 | 47.0% (of total) |

This species is a widely distributed breeder in Connecticut but is not numerous. Our breeding populations are migratory, generally wintering from South Carolina, the Gulf Coast, and southern Texas south through the West Indies and Central America to northern South America (Hancock and Kushlan 1984, Root 1988). This heron is exceedingly scarce in southern New England during winter, with only nine winter records listed for Connecticut and Massachusetts (Zeranski and Baptist 1990, Veit and Petersen 1993).

Populations breeding in the eastern United States are referred to the nominate subspecies *virescens*. The Green Heron includes this and other subspecies breeding in western North America south to central and eastern Panama. (Green-backed Heron is another name used until recently.)

**Habitat**—This species nests in densely wooded vegetation along ponds, rivers, and lakes and in such sites in coastal localities including offshore islands (Hancock and Kushlan 1984, Marra and Bull 1986a). Nests are typically well concealed and located in a bush or tree from 8 to 30 feet off the ground (Sage et al. 1913), often with water beneath (Hancock and Kushlan 1984). This species tends to be less colonial than many other herons, but sometimes does nest in colonies (Sage et al. 1913). The species forages in both fresh and salt water sites (Hancock and Kushlan 1984).

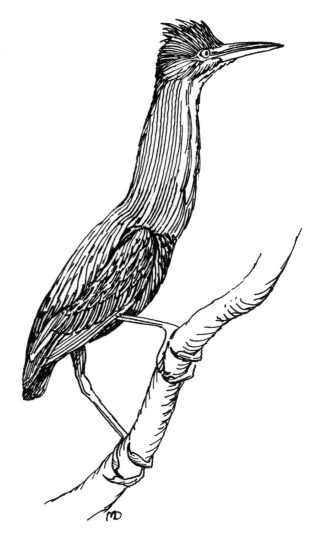

**Atlas results**—The species was found statewide, being confirmed as breeding in more than 10% of the blocks.

**Discussion**—This species was relatively unaffected by the millinery trade, and Sage et al. (1913) termed it a common summer resident. There has presumably been a decline in the abundance of this species statewide through the loss of wetlands during the twentieth century (Zeranski and Baptist 1990).

There are some surprisingly large areas in which this species was not recorded during the atlas survey. In the eastern part of the state where coverage was less extensive, some gaps might be due to insufficient coverage, but the statewide pattern indicates that this species is less widespread as a breeder than its regular occurrence in many areas might suggest. A reasonable, though untested, explanation is that the decline of agriculture in the twentieth century in the state has greatly reduced the amount of open shallow water wetland suitable for foraging by Green Herons. The species presumably cannot forage effectively in wet areas that become part of a continuous forest.

*George A. Clark, Jr.*

## Black-crowned Night-Heron
*Nycticorax nycticorax*

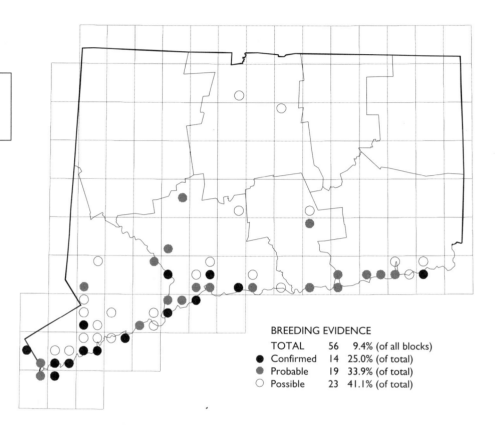

BREEDING EVIDENCE

| | TOTAL | 56 | 9.4% (of all blocks) |
|---|---|---|---|
| ● | Confirmed | 14 | 25.0% (of total) |
| ◉ | Probable | 19 | 33.9% (of total) |
| ○ | Possible | 23 | 41.1% (of total) |

The Black-crowned Night-Heron is widespread globally; however, the species is now highly local as a breeder in Connecticut. It is common at suitable sites (Marra and Bull 1986a) but is designated as a Species of Special Concern in our state, in part because so few breeding localities are known. Although regularly found along the Connecticut River valley as a migrant and nonbreeder, it is comparatively scarce elsewhere inland in Connecticut. Populations breeding in the eastern United States winter from the southeastern and Gulf Coast states south into the Caribbean islands (Hancock and Kushlan 1984); it is casual in winter north to Massachusetts (AOU 1957). A few linger until late December along the coast of Connecticut (Zeranski and Baptist 1990).

**Habitat**—On Chimon Island of the Norwalk Islands, Black-crowned Night-Herons have placed their nests in the branches below the tree canopy, in contrast to the slightly larger and more loosely constructed nests placed in the canopy by Great Egrets (Connecticut Audubon Society, unpublished notes). Black-crowned Night-Herons also require feeding areas such as marshes and shorelines that can be a considerable distance from the breeding colony (Marra and Bull 1986b).

**Atlas results**—Confirmations of breeding were obtained in 14 blocks along the coast, and it is conceivable that the birds nested in some of the 19 other coastal blocks for which the species was recorded as probable for breeding.

**Discussion**—In the nineteenth century large colonies were recorded in the interior of the state (Sage et al. 1913). There are apparently no records of nesting away from the coast in recent decades, and the species has become much less common in the interior. A similar trend in loss of breeding birds is indicated for inland parts of New York state (Levine *in* Andrle and Carroll 1988). There are indications for recent decades that even in coastal habitats this species has not overall fared so well as have other herons (Craig 1990).

Disappearance of this species as a breeder from the interior in Connecticut and New York has been attributed to loss of wetland habitat (Levine *in* Andrle and Carroll 1988, Zeranski and Baptist 1990). Although this loss can in part be attributed to human drainage and development of wetlands, the transformation of agricultural lands along waterways into woodlands during the twentieth century has presumably also contributed to a major extent to the elimination of open wetlands suitable for the foraging of this species. In contrast, in the coastal regions the estuaries and remaining salt marshes have continued to provide sufficient foraging habitat to sustain a breeding population.

*George A. Clark, Jr.*

# Yellow-crowned Night-Heron
## *Nyctanassa violacea*

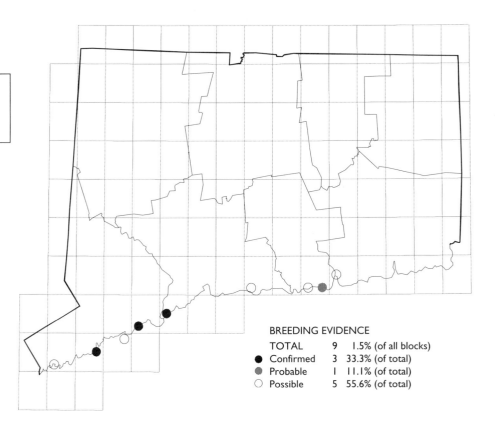

BREEDING EVIDENCE

| | | |
|---|---|---|
| TOTAL | 9 | 1.5% (of all blocks) |
| ● Confirmed | 3 | 33.3% (of total) |
| ◓ Probable | 1 | 11.1% (of total) |
| ○ Possible | 5 | 55.6% (of total) |

The Yellow-crowned Night-Heron is an uncommon and local migratory breeder in Connecticut, where it is at the northeastern limit of its range in North America. It is designated as a Species of Special Concern in our state based on its limited breeding distribution here. The species is found from western Mexico, the central United States, and Massachusetts south to eastern Brazil and northern Peru. Eastern North American populations (subspecies *violacea*) winter along the Atlantic seaboard and Gulf Coast states, with some wintering or permanently resident as far south as Panama (Hancock and Kushlan 1984).

**Habitat**—Apparently no detailed report has been made on the breeding habitat of the Yellow-crowned Night-Heron in Connecticut, but it is known that the birds nest in colonies with other kinds of herons as on the Norwalk Islands (Marra and Bull 1986a) as well as in more solitary settings (Peterson *in* Andrle and Carroll 1988). In localities where the breeding habitats have been more closely studied, the nests are often placed in trees (Hancock and Kushlan 1984). In coastal Norwalk and Darien, small groups of a few pairs in loose associations have been found nesting primarily in sycamores, with the nests frequently placed directly over roadways (Bevier pers. obs.). The herons also need habitat suitable for feeding and sometimes

commute substantial distances between the nesting and feeding areas (Marra and Bull 1986b). Crabs such as fiddler crabs constitute the major component of the diet of the Yellow-crowned Night-Heron in the northeastern United States (Riegner 1982), and salt marshes would be a primary source for such food in Connecticut.

**Atlas results**—The species was confirmed as breeding in three coastal blocks in southwestern Connecticut, and nesting was considered probable in one block along the eastern Connecticut shoreline.

**Discussion**—Bull (1964) reported six breeding pairs at Westport in 1947. In 1953, J. Malkin found two pairs nesting near South Norwalk (Nichols 1953). Subsequently there were a number of additional reports of nesting (Bull 1964, Marra and Bull 1986a). Nesting in coastal, mainland residential areas of Darien and Norwalk continues at present.

The limitation of this species to the coastal area would appear to be explained at least in part by a general lack of suitable food in the interior of the state. In contrast, the Black-crowned Night-Heron is a very versatile feeder, an attribute that might account for its former success as a breeder in the interior. The relative versatility of diet in the Black-crowned Night-Heron might also account for its remaining much more abundant than the Yellow-crowned Night-Heron.

*George A. Clark, Jr.*

## Glossy Ibis
*Plegadis falcinellus*

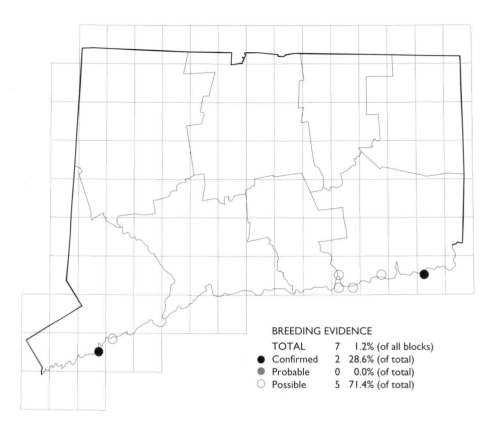

BREEDING EVIDENCE

| | TOTAL | 7 | 1.2% (of all blocks) |
|---|---|---|---|
| ● | Confirmed | 2 | 28.6% (of total) |
| ● | Probable | 0 | 0.0% (of total) |
| ○ | Possible | 5 | 71.4% (of total) |

The Glossy Ibis is an uncommon and local migratory breeder in Connecticut. It currently is designated as a Species of Special Concern here. Likely wintering areas for birds breeding in the northeastern United States are Florida and the Greater Antilles (Root 1988).

The Glossy Ibis is a widespread species, occurring in most warm temperate and tropical areas of the world. It breeds locally in the coastal eastern United States, the Greater Antilles, and, more recently, northern South America and northwestern Costa Rica; also locally in Africa, Asia, and Australia (AOU 1983). Root (1988) has commented on the relative lack of studies of this species.

**Habitat**—This species nests in colonies, often with herons, in wooded sites that are often on islands and relatively free of terrestrial predators. On Chimon Island in the Norwalk Islands, nests have been placed in shrubs and thus at a height below that of the nests of Great Egrets or Black-crowned Night-Herons (Connecticut Audubon Society, unpublished data; Craig 1978). The ibises also need foraging areas, and these can be a substantial distance from the breeding colony (Marra and Bull 1986b).

**Atlas results**—Breeding was confirmed in only two coastal blocks.

**Discussion**—As a part of a general northeastward expansion of range, Glossy Ibises were first recorded nesting in the Norwalk Islands in 1971 (Bull 1974, Peterson *in* Andrle and Carroll 1988). The species has bred in Connecticut in many, if not all, subsequent years (Marra and Bull 1986a). The first nesting on Ram Island, near Mystic, was recorded in 1984 (Sibley and Schwartz 1985).

Causes of the historic range expansion do not seem to be clear, and it is unknown what factors might be limiting the further expansion of range in this species. In the northeastern states the species appears to favor salt water habitats, though wandering birds do appear inland. Conceivably, only the coastal habitats might have sufficient suitable food and this might account for the limited range in Connecticut, a situation that would then be analogous to that suggested for the Yellow-crowned Night-Heron. The Glossy Ibis apparently can do well in competition with herons for nesting places in rookeries as indicated by the situation in the heronry at Stone Harbor, New Jersey, where in recent decades the numbers of ibises have increased sharply relative to those of many of the herons (Leck 1984).

*George A. Clark, Jr.*

## Mute Swan
*Cygnus olor*

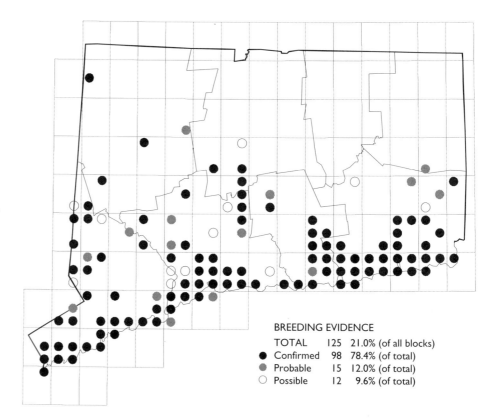

BREEDING EVIDENCE

| | TOTAL | 125 | 21.0% (of all blocks) |
|---|---|---|---|
| ● | Confirmed | 98 | 78.4% (of total) |
| ● | Probable | 15 | 12.0% (of total) |
| ○ | Possible | 12 | 9.6% (of total) |

The Mute Swan is a resident breeder that has greatly increased in numbers since its introduction to North America around 1900. While considered essentially a native bird of the central Asian steppes, the original natural range of this swan has been obscured following semidomestication and reintroduction in many parts of western Europe over the centuries. Introduced populations now are found in New Zealand, Australia, South Africa, and several areas of North America, especially the western Great Lakes region and the mid-Atlantic coast from Chesapeake Bay to Massachusetts (Long 1981).

**Habitat**—Breeding pairs usually nest in small freshwater or brackish ponds, whereas immature birds and unsuccessful breeders tend to congregate in large flocks in protected coves and river estuaries (Allin et al. 1987, Willey and

Halla 1972). As a result of their high degree of intraspecific competition, small ponds typically support only one breeding pair. The Mute Swan is almost exclusively herbivorous, and can require daily as much as 3.8 kg net weight of aquatic vegetation such as pondweed, green algae (especially sea lettuce), and eelgrass (Hatch 1988,

Willey and Halla 1972). The coastal regions have an abundant food supply and are thus especially favorable. In addition, because Mute Swans do not ordinarily migrate long distances, their inland expansion might eventually be limited by occurrence of winter ice preventing year round occupancy.

**Atlas results**—The distribution is primarily coastal, but extends inland from New Haven to Berlin inside the central lowlands and along lower stretches of the Connecticut, Thames, and Housatonic Rivers. Except for an isolated nesting near Lakeville, Salisbury, the species is almost entirely absent from the northern regions of the state, where wandering individuals are seen occasionally.

**Discussion**—A few Mute Swans were released in New York prior to 1900, but several hundred were imported in 1910 and 1912 (Long 1981). By the 1920s they were established on the lower Hudson River and Long Island, while feral populations then at Newport, Rhode Island, rapidly spread in the 1950s (Cooke and Knappen 1941). Feral birds were reported in Connecticut by the 1930s, especially Fairfield County, but establishment of breeding birds did not begin until the late 1950s to 1960s (Zeranski and Baptist 1990). No swans were reported on a midwinter waterfowl survey conducted by the DEP in 1965; however, by 1972, over 200 were counted (Merola and Chasko 1989). Data from the Christmas Bird Counts show a steady increase in numbers to a present average total of about 1500 individuals statewide (Phillip Rusch pers. comm.).

The growing numbers have been a source of concern and controversy (Hatch 1988) because under certain circumstances Mute Swans might adversely affect other waterfowl species either through aggressive interaction (such as described by Kania and Smith 1986) or exploitation of food (Chasko 1985). However, Canada geese and Mallards have been observed nesting undisturbed close to nesting Mute Swans (Eltringham 1963, Willey 1968), and a study of feeding techniques and distribution of waterfowl on the lower Thames River found that competition for food between swans and ducks was extremely limited (O'Brien and Askins 1985). During the extended observations of both territorial and nonterritorial swans in that study, no instances of aggressive behavior toward ducks were recorded.

*Elizabeth Bushnell*

## Canada Goose
*Branta canadensis*

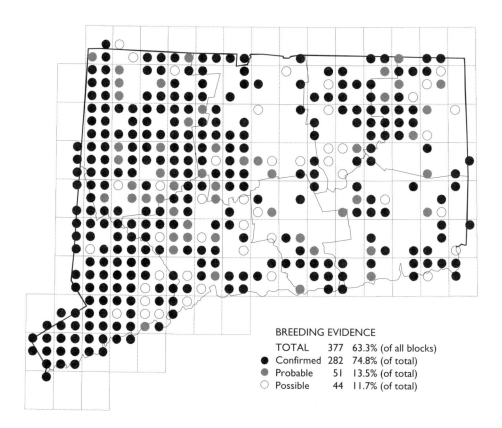

BREEDING EVIDENCE

| | TOTAL | 377 | 63.3% (of all blocks) |
|---|---|---|---|
| ● Confirmed | | 282 | 74.8% (of total) |
| ● Probable | | 51 | 13.5% (of total) |
| ○ Possible | | 44 | 11.7% (of total) |

This resident breeder has expanded its numbers and range since the early 1960s. In addition to a resident, non-migratory Canada Goose population, Connecticut is also host to migratory populations of several races including *canadensis*, *interior*, and the distinctive but scarcer *hutchinsii*, or Richardson's Goose. The winter range of these geese is determined largely by the severity of the season, which in turn determines the availability of food and open water (Hanson 1965). Thus, the Canada Goose may be widespread and abundant inland during mild winters and restricted to coastal areas during severe winters.

**Habitat**—Canada Geese frequent suburban and rural sites, in close proximity to ponds, rivers, and wetlands. The species is particularly common in parks or golf courses where lawns bordering water bodies provide forage and safety.

Canada Geese usually nest near water and prefer islands as nest sites. Nests are a scrape or shallow depression, lined with almost any available vegetation. This highly adaptable species has benefited from its association with people. Landscaping techniques that intersperse expanses of lawn with ponds, rivers,

and wetlands create excellent grazing and breeding areas, while frequent mechanical mowing of lawns maintains the grass in a preflowering, high protein state that provides good forage for geese (Converse 1985).

**Atlas results**—Breeding success in Connecticut is very high: Chasko and Conover (1988) found each pair laid an average of 5.6 eggs, and fledged 4.5 young per year. Chasko and Conover estimated an increase in this resident population from 100 to 9,000 birds between 1960 and 1988. The Atlas results reflect the now widespread breeding in the state.

**Discussion**—Until the mid-1950s, when a resident breeding population was established, the Canada Goose occurred in Connecticut only as a migrant and occasional winter visitor (Pink and Waterman 1980). Resident birds are believed to be of three origins: 1) pinioned geese released by game breeders and private aviaries after legislation abolished use of live decoy

flocks in 1935 (Heusmann 1979, Dill and Lee 1970); 2) pinioned geese stocked during restoration efforts in the Northeast; and 3) wintering migrants that do not leave in spring (Converse 1985). Restoration efforts included habitat management and establishing resident flocks of the nonmigratory giant Canada goose, subspecies *moffitti*.

*Donald E. McIvor and*
*Michael R. Conover*

# Wood Duck
*Aix sponsa*

This species is currently a common to abundant migratory breeder in Connecticut (Merola 1991). Although some are seen in the state at any time of the year, most of the breeding population winters along the Atlantic coastal plain from North Carolina to Florida (Merola and Chasko 1989).

**Habitat**—Wood Ducks prefer areas of low human disturbance, nesting near freshwater forested or shrub wetland, wooded riparian, or adjacent deciduous forest. Beaver ponds with heavy wooded cover are especially favored. This species may also use suburban and rural areas. Breeding in brackish water areas is limited. Since the Wood Duck is an obligate cavity nester, the location of a suitable tree-cavity is a prerequisite for breeding (Haramis 1990). The species readily accepts artificial nest boxes.

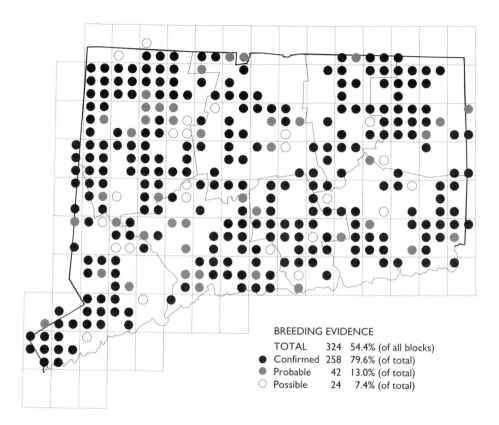

BREEDING EVIDENCE

| | | | |
|---|---|---|---|
| TOTAL | 324 | 54.4% | (of all blocks) |
| ● Confirmed | 258 | 79.6% | (of total) |
| ● Probable | 42 | 13.0% | (of total) |
| ○ Possible | 24 | 7.4% | (of total) |

**Atlas results**—The atlas was conducted when the population of Wood Ducks was high. Consequently, the results show nesting throughout the state except for coastal and urban areas. Nesting evidence is lacking for numerous inland blocks with suitable habitat.

This may be attributed to the difficulty of detecting breeding in timbered swamps, where the crepuscular birds can seek dense cover. The high ratio of confirmed to probable and possible blocks is the result of state and private nest box data.

**Discussion**—Before and during the 1800s, the Wood Duck was considered common in Connecticut (Merriam 1877, Sage et al. 1913); however, by 1900 the population reached such low numbers in New England that it was considered to be on the verge of extirpation (Griscom 1948). This decline was attributed primarily to excessive market hunting, and deforestation with its subsequent loss of tree nest cavities (Bellrose 1990). Hunting in Connecticut was stopped in 1912.

Believing that the Wood Duck was near extinction, wildlife biologists raised and released about 3,000 birds at the Litchfield-Morris Sanctuary from 1924 to 1936 (Frank 1948, Ripley 1957). Within two decades following the cessation of hunting, the Wood Duck had increased to the point that it was once again considered common to abundant in Connecticut (Mulliken 1938, Griscom 1948). Following the 1938 hurricane, which was thought to have destroyed numerous nest cavity trees (Griscom 1948), a nest box program was begun in 1941 (Frank 1948). Surveys conducted since 1948 show that the population remained stable until the mid-1960s when a decline occurred during several years of drought; since then, numbers have increased (Merola and Chasko 1989).

Connecticut is endowed with a combination of numerous freshwater wetlands and extensive deciduous forest cover, a condition highly favorable for the Wood Duck. Reestablishment of the beaver in the 1940s has also resulted in more nesting areas. The return of mature forests and subsequent rise in the population of Pileated Woodpeckers has probably resulted in more tree nest cavities. Also, the Wood Duck has adapted well to using suburban areas, unlike the Hooded Merganser and American Black Duck.

*Paul R. Merola*

## Green-winged Teal
*Anas crecca*

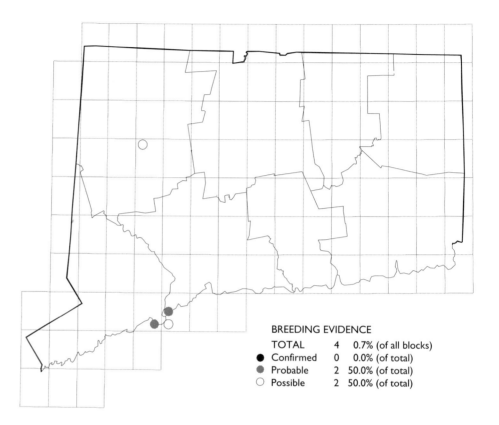

BREEDING EVIDENCE

| | TOTAL | 4 | 0.7% (of all blocks) |
|---|---|---|---|
| ● | Confirmed | 0 | 0.0% (of total) |
| ◉ | Probable | 2 | 50.0% (of total) |
| ○ | Possible | 2 | 50.0% (of total) |

This migratory species is recorded as having bred in Connecticut at least three times (Merola and Chasko 1989). North American populations of this Holarctic species are the subspecies *carolinensis*, which in the eastern part of its wintering range, extends from the Atlantic Provinces of Canada and the Great Lakes area south into northern Central America and the Caribbean islands (AOU 1983, Root 1988). Fewer than 100 birds have been found on all Christmas Bird Counts in Connecticut during a given winter (Merola and Chasko 1989).

**Habitat**—Although the Green-winged Teal is well known as a species occupying marshes, there is apparently no description of breeding habitat for birds in Connecticut. Palmer (1976) stated that the species generally prefers to nest in grass or sedge covered terrain with scattered trees or brush and usually located not far from open water.

**Atlas results**—Green-winged Teal were found in four blocks during the period of atlas field observations and were considered to be probable breeders in two of those blocks, both on the coast. However, no confirmation of breeding was obtained.

**Discussion**—Sage et al. (1913) did not mention breeding by this species in Connecticut. Apparently the first direct evidence for breeding by the species in the state came in 1962 when two broods were found during state brood surveys; an additional brood was seen during a 1974 survey (Merola and Chasko 1989). Other sightings of adults in summer have been recorded, so it is possible that additional nestings have occurred in the past (Craig 1990, Zeranski and Baptist 1990); however, summering nonbreeders are also seen.

This species has expanded its breeding range from midcontinental and northern sites into the northeastern states (Levine *in* Andrle and Carroll 1988). The range expansion has been attributed to 1) a greatly increased population following the introduction of hunting restrictions in the early part of the twentieth century, and 2) the creation of management areas that provided locally especially favorable conditions for nesting in the northeastern states (Levine *in* Andrle and Carroll 1988). The species might well be breeding more often than has been recorded for Connecticut, but difficulties in access in the areas of possible breeding have limited verification.

*George A. Clark, Jr.*

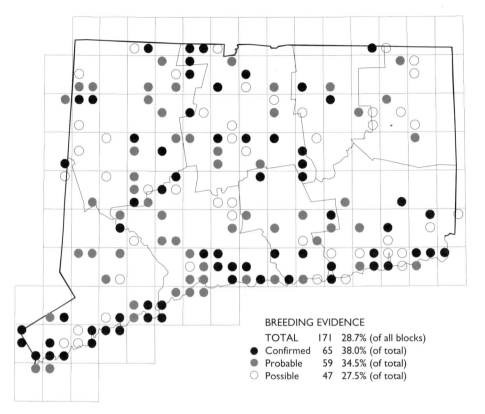

BREEDING EVIDENCE

| | | |
|---|---|---|
| TOTAL | 171 | 28.7% (of all blocks) |
| ● Confirmed | 65 | 38.0% (of total) |
| ● Probable | 59 | 34.5% (of total) |
| ○ Possible | 47 | 27.5% (of total) |

## American Black Duck
*Anas rubripes*

This native duck of eastern North America is found year-round in Connecticut, the wintering population composed largely of migrant birds originating north of Connecticut. The Connecticut breeding population winters in coastal habitats from Connecticut to Virginia. The current breeding population is uncommon and stable, although widely distributed in low densities.

**Habitat**—This species occupies rural to suburban sites with a high preference for areas with low human disturbance. It uses a great variety of wetlands during the breeding period including fresh, brackish, or saline marshes and swamps. Freshwater nesting sites are typically densely wooded shrub or forested swamps with recent beaver ponds of flooded timber being favored. In coastal habitats, both high and low salt marsh are used. Most nests are on the ground, but some nests are placed in tree cavities or crotches. At upland sites, nests may be found in woods, shrub thickets, and fields; clear cuts with woody slash are highly favored. At wetland sites, nests are constructed on raised hummocks, tussocks, or on elevated patches of dead grass. Prerequisites for nesting are nearby water, dense ground cover, and low human disturbance.

**Atlas results**—The atlas was conducted at a time when this species was probably at record low numbers; however, the atlas results show that the American Black Duck is still widely distributed, being found in both coastal and inland areas. Somewhat

surprisingly, few were confirmed nesting in northeastern Connecticut where there is excellent beaver pond habitat. Nearly all coastal blocks had some evidence of breeding, and a higher percentage of confirmations was found in coastal blocks than in inland blocks. About one third of all confirmed blocks were coastal. This may be due to higher breeding densities in salt marsh than in freshwater wetlands (Merola and Chasko 1990), but detection of nesting is easier in salt marsh than in densely wooded freshwater swamps where broods are elusive.

**Discussion**—The American Black Duck was considered rare during summer in the early 1900s (Sage et al. 1913), having been considered more common previously (Forbush 1916). The population probably suffered due to spring hunting (Forbush 1916). After conservative hunting seasons were implemented it appears that the population rebounded, and Mulliken (1938) reported it to be an abundant breeder throughout the state. The species continued to be locally common to abundant and widely distributed during the early 1950s, but a major decline began in the 1960s and continued through the 1970s (Merola and Chasko 1989). Recent surveys indicate that the population is still comparatively low but stable (Merola 1991).

The major question confronting researchers is why the American Black Duck has declined in the northeastern United States and southern Canada (Rusch et al. 1989), while the Mallard has increased so dramatically (Heusmann 1991). In Connecticut this situation has been especially pronounced during the last 30 years (Merola and Chasko 1989); whether this is cause and effect is unknown. The major reasons for the decline of the American Black Duck likely involve a combination of factors including the loss of coastal habitat prior to the tidal wetlands laws of 1969, the conversion of the Connecticut landscape to suburban habitat, and hybridization with the more aggressive and adaptable Mallard. Inland areas with low human disturbance and protected coastal areas may be the last stronghold for this species as a breeder in Connecticut.

*Paul R. Merola*

## Mallard
*Anas platyrhynchos*

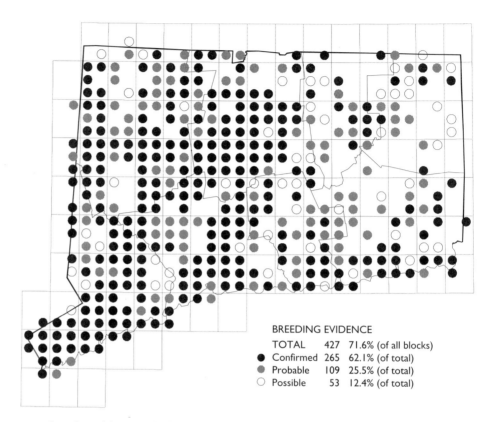

BREEDING EVIDENCE

| | TOTAL | 427 | 71.6% (of all blocks) |
|---|---|---|---|
| ● | Confirmed | 265 | 62.1% (of total) |
| ◓ | Probable | 109 | 25.5% (of total) |
| ○ | Possible | 53 | 12.4% (of total) |

The Mallard is a locally common to abundant resident breeder whose numbers have rapidly increased in the northeastern United States due to the release of captive raised birds that have now reverted to the wild and an eastward expansion of populations from central North America. While most winter in Connecticut, some move south at least as far as Georgia (Merola and Chasko 1989); numbers are augmented somewhat in fall and winter by migrants.

**Habitat**—The Mallard has shown itself to be the most adaptable of all waterfowl during its increase. It is highly tolerant of human disturbance, using all types of wetlands—urban to rural, fresh to saline, including reservoirs, rivers, urban park ponds, and marinas. The nest is constructed on the ground near water and is generally well hidden and may be placed in wooded uplands, hay fields, and on islands or dry hummocks in ponds or marshes. Occasionally a nest is found in tree crotches.

**Atlas results**—The atlas survey was conducted when the Mallard population was still increasing and expanding. The results show the Mallard to be widely distributed in the state, except for eastern Connecticut. There are fewer suburban ponds in the east resulting in lower Mallard densities. Detection of nesting is also more difficult in the dense wetland habitats used in eastern Connecticut. The Mallard readily uses densely wooded beaver ponds and saline wetlands which are considered the last strongholds for the American Black Duck in Connecticut.

**Discussion**—The Mallard was not known to nest in Connecticut during the late 1800s or at the turn of the century when it was only a fall migrant through the state (Merriam 1877, Sage et al. 1913). Escaped birds from captive flocks began nesting in Connecticut early in the century, and by 1925 the Mallard was reported nesting in most of New England (Forbush 1912, 1925). By the 1930s, the Mallard was listed as a locally common nester as a result of released birds (Mulliken 1938). The Mallard was an uncommon nester in rural marshes by 1950, and surveys indicated that the population increased rapidly from 1950 to the late 1970s (Merola and Chasko 1989). Craig (1990) noted a slight decline along the Connecticut River between 1974 and 1983. Recent surveys show the Mallard to be the most abundant of the waterfowl nesting in Connecticut (Merola 1991).

The eastward expansion of the Mallard has been accompanied by a dramatic decline in the American Black Duck; Johnsgard and DiSilvestro (1976) showed that the percentage of American Black Duck to Mallard on winter counts had declined from 96% to 48% in Connecticut between 1900 and 1974. The large scale release of the Mallard in eastern North America, including Connecticut, is probably the principal reason for the rapid population increase (Heusmann 1991, Merola and Chasko 1989).

The major question is why the Mallard has been so successful in Connecticut since 1950 while the American Black Duck has declined so rapidly during the same period. The Mallard and American Black Duck are nearly identical genetically but are quite different behaviorally (Ankney et al. 1986). The Mallard is more adaptable to human disturbance than the American Black Duck, especially during the nesting period. The Connecticut landscape has become more suburban, with numerous open shoreline ponds created during the past several decades, especially in Fairfield County. These habitat changes have pushed the American Black Duck out while at the same time creating areas which the more adaptable Mallard quickly filled.

*Paul R. Merola*

## Blue-winged Teal
*Anas discors*

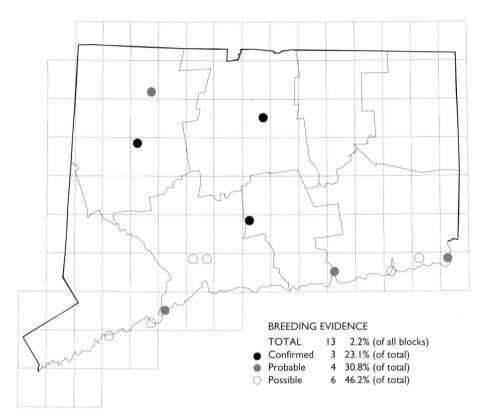

BREEDING EVIDENCE

|  | TOTAL | 13 | 2.2% (of all blocks) |
|---|---|---|---|
| ● | Confirmed | 3 | 23.1% (of total) |
| ◉ | Probable | 4 | 30.8% (of total) |
| ○ | Possible | 6 | 46.2% (of total) |

The Blue-winged Teal is a rare and local migratory breeder in Connecticut. The wintering range of birds migrating through New England extends from the mid-Atlantic states and Gulf Coast south through Central America and the Caribbean islands to its principal wintering grounds in northern South America (AOU 1983, Root 1988). Compared with other dabbling ducks of the genus *Anas*, this species has commonly been viewed as being relatively intolerant of cold conditions as reflected in its relatively southern wintering grounds and its migration dates (Ellis *in* Laughlin and Kibbe 1985, Root 1988). Long transoceanic migration flights and exposure to extensive hunting in South America are believed to have contributed to a relatively high annual mortality rate of Blue-winged Teal (Root 1988).

**Habitat**—In Connecticut the species breeds in both freshwater marshes and brackish marshes along the coast (Merola and Chasko 1989). No detailed descriptions are known for breeding habitats in Connecticut. From the Maritime provinces to the mid-Atlantic states the species nests primarily in large, open marshes, especially in tidal regions. These populations have been designated as the subspecies *orphna* (AOU 1957); however some regard the species as monotypic (Johnsgard 1979). In the midcontinental prairies of North America, the species is said to nest in fairly tall coarse grasses away from water (Palmer 1976).

**Atlas results**—Confirmations were obtained for three blocks, two along the Connecticut River and one in Litchfield County, and birds were found in an additional ten blocks.

**Discussion**—Sage et al. (1913) reported one sight record from the Quinnipiac Marshes in July as the only known report from summer. Zeranski and Baptist (1990) summarized reports of summer sightings from 1931 to 1964, including broods in South Windsor in the 1930s (Eliot 1934). Craig (1990) reported on summer occurrences in both brackish and fresh water marshes along the Connecticut River from 1974 to 1987 but did not mention any direct evidence for breeding.

The Blue-winged Teal, like other dabbling ducks that breed extensively in the midcontinental prairies, is likely limited in Connecticut by a lack of suitable habitat. Because information on the breeding of this species in Connecticut is so very limited, it is desirable that those finding evidence of breeding in the future provide details of their observations for publication. It may well be that small numbers of these birds breed annually in the state, but existing records do not provide a firm basis for evaluating the frequency of breeding.

*George A. Clark, Jr.*

## Gadwall
*Anas strepera*

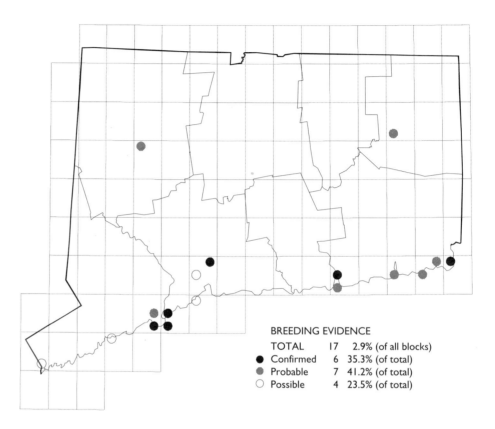

BREEDING EVIDENCE

| | TOTAL | 17 | 2.9% (of all blocks) |
|---|---|---|---|
| ● | Confirmed | 6 | 35.3% (of total) |
| ◓ | Probable | 7 | 41.2% (of total) |
| ○ | Possible | 4 | 23.5% (of total) |

The Gadwall is an uncommon migratory breeder in Connecticut (Merola and Chasko 1989). The main breeding range in North America is the central and northern Great Plains. Migrants and nesters from New England winter principally from the mid-Atlantic states and the central and Gulf Coast states south through much of Mexico; it is generally uncommon in southern New England during winter (AOU 1983, Palmer 1976, Root 1988).

**Habitat**—In Connecticut, nesting occurs in brackish marshes or impoundments along the coast (Merola and Chasko 1990). In the central portions of North America, important habitat factors are l) a vegetative cover that provides concealment for nests, 2) a dry location on land for the nest, 3) a location not readily accessible to predators, and 4) nearness to open water (Oring 1969).

**Atlas results**—Breeding by Gadwall was confirmed in six blocks along the coast. The species was thus rather uncommon as a breeder in the state, but nevertheless has apparently been doing better as a breeder than at any previous time since the start of historic records on the birds of the state.

**Discussion**—Breeding was not reported for Connecticut during the nineteenth century. Efforts during the 1960s by the state to establish a breeding population of Gadwalls by means of a captive breeding program were unsuccessful (Merola and Chasko 1989). The earliest definite reports of successful nesting came during the 1970s (Zeranski and Baptist 1990).

Although Gadwalls have been known to occur in the Connecticut River valley for many years (Craig 1990), breeding at inland locations has never been definitely confirmed for the state. Most inland marshes in Connecticut are relatively small, and these marshes generally appear to lack the high density of insects that is characteristic of the major waterfowl breeding areas of central North America; the insects are important in part as food for young waterfowl.

The species has been successful in recent decades as a breeder in management areas in western and northern New York state and on Long Island (Eaton *in* Andrle and Carroll 1988). There would thus seem to be a potential for a continuation and perhaps even some expansion of the breeding areas in Connecticut.

*George A. Clark, Jr.*

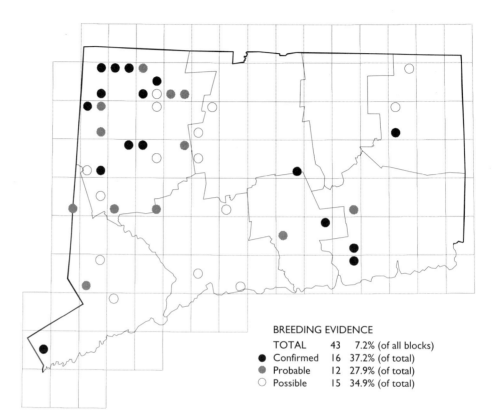

BREEDING EVIDENCE

| TOTAL | 43 | 7.2% (of all blocks) |
|---|---|---|
| ● Confirmed | 16 | 37.2% (of total) |
| ◓ Probable | 12 | 27.9% (of total) |
| ○ Possible | 15 | 34.9% (of total) |

# Hooded Merganser
## *Lophodytes cucullatus*

The Hooded Merganser is a rare to uncommon breeder. Migrant and wintering birds are seen in fresh to brackish habitats in Connecticut with wintering individuals primarily found coastally. The breeding populations of eastern North America also winter south along the Atlantic coastal plain to the Gulf of Mexico.

**Habitat**—The Hooded Merganser is secretive during the nesting period and prefers areas with low human disturbance. It inhabits rural woodland freshwater wetlands, ponds and streams and prefers clear flowing waters, such as beaver ponds, with timbered cover and shorelines. This obligate cavity nester selects trees close to water, but also readily accepts nest boxes.

**Atlas results**—The Hooded Merganser was found in few blocks, with most nesting in the northwestern hills and adjacent to the lower Connecticut River; only sporadic nesting was noted elsewhere in the state. Low human disturbance and numerous beaver ponds with clear, fast water probably make the northwestern hills more attractive than the rest of the state to the Hooded

Merganser. It is possible that the distribution is much wider than currently believed because the species occurs in low densities and is very secretive, making detection at natural cavity nest sites difficult. Checking nest boxes in the spring would help verify the actual distribution in the state. Competition for nest cavities with the more abundant and adaptable Wood Duck and a low tolerance for suburban habitats may limit the Hooded Merganser

**Discussion**—The Hooded Merganser was believed to have bred formerly throughout the eastern U.S. (Forbush 1925, Palmer 1976). However, it suffered a decline similar to the Wood Duck due to deforestation and over-hunting prior to 1900 (Palmer 1976). It was not known to nest in Connecticut in the early 1900s to 1920s, although it did nest sparingly in northern New England (Sage et al. 1913, Forbush 1925). Numbers were believed to be increasing in its eastern range during the 1930s (Palmer 1976). The first confirmed nesting since the late 1800s was in June 1937 at Farmington (Amadon 1938). Sporadic pairs or single adults were observed in the summer during the 1950s in Simsbury and Wallingford and Canaan (Zeranski and Baptist 1990). Hooded Mergansers were found nesting in boxes intended for Wood Ducks in 1961 and 1962 in New Fairfield (Beckley 1963); this behavior was widely noted beginning in the

1950s. In 1976, seven female Hooded Mergansers were banded while nesting in Wood Duck boxes in Haddam, Chaplin, N. Stonington, Goshen, and Union (DEP Wildlife Division files). By the 1980s nesting was regularly confirmed in Litchfield County and within the Connecticut River valley in nest boxes or by sightings of broods (Merola and Chasko 1989). Although the 1970–1990 population level might be slightly higher than in previous decades, the results of a recent survey indicate that the population is still very low (Merola 1991).

*Paul R. Merola*

# Common Merganser
## *Mergus merganser*

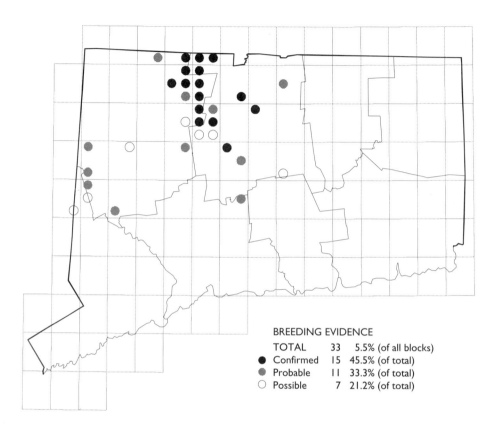

BREEDING EVIDENCE

| | TOTAL | 33 | 5.5% (of all blocks) |
|---|---|---|---|
| ● | Confirmed | 15 | 45.5% (of total) |
| ◓ | Probable | 11 | 33.3% (of total) |
| ○ | Possible | 7 | 21.2% (of total) |

Common Mergansers are uncommon and local breeders in Connecticut but are common migrants through the state. Presumably our breeders withdraw to the south, but their movements are unknown. On the Atlantic seaboard, the species is found in winter from Newfoundland to central Florida and is much less numerous than the Red-breasted Merganser. The North American populations (subspecies *americanus*) of this Holarctic species are recognized by a black bar across the base of the median wing coverts of the male.

**Habitat**—This duck nests in large cavities of trees located in woodlands along major rivers or large open reservoirs (Craig 1978, Merola and Chasko 1989). In other geographic areas, the species is known to nest in bird houses with large diameter holes (Lumsden et al. 1986).

**Atlas results**—The species was confirmed in more than a dozen blocks along waterways in the area of the Farmington River. The species thus apparently increased substantially as a breeder in the 25 years following the earliest reported nesting.

**Discussion**—The first report of breeding in the state was in 1962 (Craig 1978). In 1978 breeding was known from Barkhamsted and Colebrook (Craig 1978). The apparent expansion of the breeding range of this species to include Connecticut is presumably related to the regrowth of forests during the twentieth century. Griscom and Snyder (1955) noted nesting records in central Massachusetts in 1947 and 1954, and the increase in Connecticut might be part of a more widespread increase in populations in neighboring states, but additional information will be needed to evaluate this possibility.

It is conceivable that the species was breeding in the state at the time of European colonization and then subsequently extirpated until the recent occurrence of nesting. Kiff (1989) has summarized breeding records of Common Mergansers that represent either isolated, unrelated occurrences or traces of a former breeding range that extended far south along the Appalachians. Presence of this fish-eating species might be taken as one index of water quality, for the species is reported to occupy only clear waters for extended periods and to avoid waters in which visibility is poor (Palmer 1976).

*George A. Clark, Jr.*

# Turkey Vulture
## *Cathartes aura*

The Turkey Vulture is an uncommon to fairly common breeding species in the state, with spring migrants arriving as early as late February. This species is also a fairly common fall migrant, especially over inland areas. Winter concentrations are found occasionally, often near landfills, and the winter population has increased substantially within the past decade. Winter roosts with thirty or more individuals are documented for a number of localities statewide. Populations breeding in eastern North America (subspecies *septentrionalis*) winter principally in the southeastern United States to the Gulf of Mexico and Florida; however, breeders to the west of these populations (subspecies *meridionalis*) migrate as far as southern Brazil (AOU 1957). The species as a whole is more or less continuously distributed from southern Canada to Tierra del Fuego.

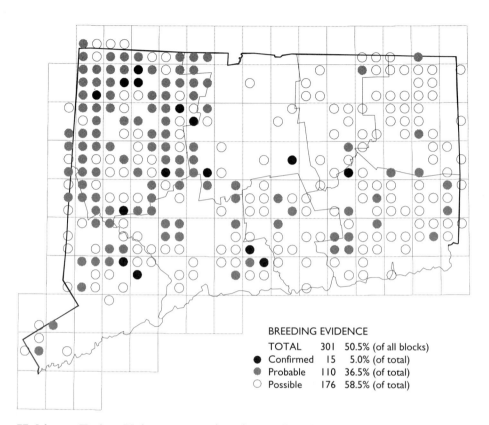

BREEDING EVIDENCE

| | | |
|---|---|---|
| TOTAL | 301 | 50.5% (of all blocks) |
| ● Confirmed | 15 | 5.0% (of total) |
| ◉ Probable | 110 | 36.5% (of total) |
| ○ Possible | 176 | 58.5% (of total) |

**Habitat**—Turkey Vultures nest primarily on cliffs and rocky ledges, and most Connecticut nests are associated with such sites. Tree cavities, hollow logs, and deserted buildings also may be used; Mackenzie (1961) reported a pair nesting in a dense hemlock forest along Lake Quonnipaug, North Guilford. Most pairs make little or no attempt to construct a nest, rather the eggs are laid directly on the rock or wood nest substrate. The Turkey Vulture requires open areas for foraging.

**Atlas results**—Turkey Vultures were recorded in all physiographic provinces of the state, but limited evidence of breeding activity was found in the north central portion and the more densely populated southwestern section.

**Discussion**—While widespread and numerous, the Turkey Vulture apparently declined in North America during the 1800s with declines in populations of bison but increased with increased availability of road-killed animals (Jackson *in* Palmer 1988). The breeding range of the Turkey Vulture has advanced northward dramatically in eastern North America since the 1920s (Bagg and Parker 1951), up to which time it was considered a casual visitor to southern New England (Merriam 1877, Forbush 1927), despite Linsley's statement that it was "not uncommon" when he was a child in the early 1800s (Sage et al. 1913).

The first record of breeding in Connecticut accepted by Bagg and Parker (1951) was a nest with two young found in a buttonwood tree (American sycamore) at Stony Creek, Branford, by William Seifert on 19 July 1947. However, those authors cited a report by Mrs. A. G. Mathers of two young found on a hillside ledge on the east side of Lake Candlewood, Sherman, on 28 July 1930 and rumors of nesting in Redding some years prior to 1947 reported by L. J. Bradley. Nesting was not found in northeastern Connecticut until 1965 (Manter 1975). Although widespread in Connecticut, the nesting range within the state is now primarily in the west, with the majority of confirmed and probable nesting records from that region.

Coleman and Fraser (1989) suggested that expansion of the Turkey Vulture in the Northeast may be correlated with the substantial increase in the White-tailed Deer population. They also noted a general consensus among researchers that important limiting factors may include: 1) the lack of large trees in mature woodland stands isolated from human activity for roosting sites and 2) the lack of suitable, undisturbed breeding sites.

*Dwight G. Smith and Arnold Devine*

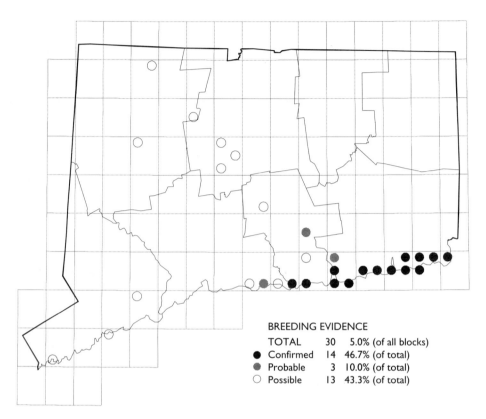

BREEDING EVIDENCE
TOTAL 30 5.0% (of all blocks)
● Confirmed 14 46.7% (of total)
◉ Probable 3 10.0% (of total)
○ Possible 13 43.3% (of total)

# Osprey
## *Pandion haliaetus*

The Osprey is a migratory breeder present from late March to September. Once endangered, its numbers have grown dramatically since the late 1970s; it is now designated as a Species of Special Concern in Connecticut. The Osprey is a common migrant from March to May and from September to early November. Most winter from Panama and northern South America south through the Amazon Basin (Poole 1989).

**Habitat**—This species occurs in coastal marshes and tidal creeks in suburban, rural, and, less often, urban areas. Although migrants rest and feed in fresh water habitats regularly, only a few nest inland along lakes and rivers. Historically, Ospreys nested atop large trees, usually isolated dead ones. Now they nest almost exclusively on artificial structures—channel markers, buoys, light towers, and, mostly, nesting poles built for this species. Current nest sites in Connecticut are typical of those found elsewhere along the coast from Cape May to southern Maine. The species is largely a coastal bird in Connecticut, and its ability to colonize fresh water habitats (e.g., large interior lakes or upstream along the Connecticut River) is still in question.

**Atlas results**—Nearly all reports were east of the Connecticut River. The Osprey nests in urban and suburban areas, although most concentrations (loose nesting colonies) are found in large salt marshes. Because both nests and individual birds are conspicuous, the atlas results are probably accurate. Clearly, a small percentage of Ospreys use fresh water habitats in Connecticut.

**Discussion**—Ospreys were abundant during the nineteenth century, especially along the coast. Although shooting, habitat destruction, and nest robbing all took a toll on these birds (Poole 1989), the species remained common (200+ nesting pairs) prior to World War II, most nesting near the mouth of the Connecticut River, especially on Great Island (Ames and Mersereau 1964). Pesticides induced a population crash from about 1950 to 1970, reducing numbers 90% to 95% (Ames 1966, Wiemeyer et al. 1975, Spitzer et al. 1978). A nationwide ban on most uses of DDT and Dieldrin (ca. 1968), plus limited import of nestlings from Chesapeake Bay (Spitzer 1978), helped stabilize numbers by the mid-1970s. New nests appeared regularly during the 1980s, especially along the coast east of Old Lyme; there were 53 active nests in the state by 1990. Recently, limited nesting has been detected west of Hammonasset Beach State Park, e.g., at the mouth of the Housatonic River.

There are several probable reasons for its current distribution: 1) Nest sites (artificial platforms) are especially abundant along the coast, where human interest in this species has been traditionally strong and management efforts concentrated. Artificial nests, scarce at inland sites, are safer from predators  (e.g., raccoons) and blowdowns than tree nests (Poole 1989). 2) The Osprey is a social species, so new colonizers are attracted by established nests and colonies, generally dispersing only short distances from natal sites (Spitzer et al. 1983). 3) Given the usual diversity and abundance of anadromous and nearshore fish along the coast, food is apparently more available to marine and estuarine nesters than to pairs dependent on fresh waters, but this hypothesis needs study. Why breeding Osprey have been slow to colonize western Connecticut remains a puzzle, especially given the speed with which they have moved west on nearby Long Island, New York. The scarcity of adequate nest sites, especially good artificial platforms, is a probable barrier.

*Alan F. Poole*

## Bald Eagle
### *Haliaeetus leucocephalus*

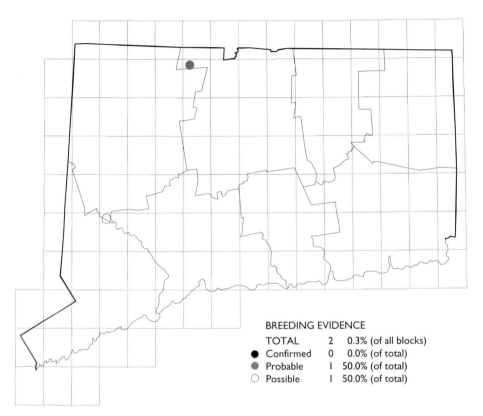

BREEDING EVIDENCE

| | | |
|---|---|---|
| TOTAL | 2 | 0.3% (of all blocks) |
| ● Confirmed | 0 | 0.0% (of total) |
| ◉ Probable | I | 50.0% (of total) |
| ○ Possible | I | 50.0% (of total) |

In Connecticut, the Bald Eagle is a rare breeder and a regular winter visitor. The fledging of two young in 1992 was the first successful breeding in the state since the late 1950s, although non-breeding birds have summered since 1975 (Grier et al. 1983, Hopkins 1992). The wintering area for Connecticut breeders is unknown. A sizable winter population composed of birds that breed to the north of the state is found along the Connecticut River and a few inland reservoirs in western Connecticut. The Bald Eagle is designated as Endangered in the state.

**Habitat**—For nesting, the Bald Eagle requires tall trees along rivers, lakes, and coastal waters remote from human disturbances. In New England, the nest tree is usually a white pine that extends above the surrounding canopy and is located, on average, within 40 meters from water (Stalmaster 1987). The pair now breeding in Connecticut are using such a nest site.

Although the major rivers of the state offer potential areas for nesting, human disturbance in those areas may be too great, as it is along the coast where the species no longer nests.

**Atlas results**—The probable report in the New Hartford quadrangle involved a pair of eagles, and the possible report in the Newtown quadrangle involved a single eagle using the site over a period of weeks. Given the bulk of an eagle's nest, it is unlikely an observer could miss finding a nest being used by such a large and conspicuous bird.

**Discussion**—It is uncertain how extensive nesting was in the past in Connecticut. A few nested, mainly near the coast, in the 1800s as indicated by Merriam (1877), Linsley (1843), and Sage et al. (1913), who together reported only five nesting sites: Fairfield-Bridgeport, Stratford-Milford, Hamden, East Haven, and Winchester. Summer sightings were widespread then as well. The species also bred near Kent until 1933 according to Kuerzi and Kuerzi (1934). Recent reports of nesting, all lacking documentation, are for Southbury in 1957 (Craig 1980), Lyme in the 1950s (Zeranski and Baptist 1990), and Barkhamsted in 1963 (two adults and two young; Craig 1980). The Bald Eagle populations in the coterminous United States sharply declined in the late 1940s when pesticides were introduced into the environment (Palmer 1988).

Since 1975, a summer population has been reported in the northwestern part of the state in the upper Farmington River watershed (Hopkins 1990). Eagles using this area remained nonbreeding until 1990 when a pair were seen billing, nest building, and copulating at Barkhamsted Reservoir. Unfortunately, the poorly constructed nest was broken apart by high winds, and the pair abandoned further nesting attempts that year. A second attempt in 1991 also resulted in failure. It was late May 1992 when the first of two young hatched following the third attempt. In 1993, the pair produced one chick. The male of this nesting pair was a bird introduced to Massachusetts in 1986, the last year of a four year program hacking captive raised eagles at Quabbin Reservoir in that state (Hopkins et al. 1993). Although nesting in Connecticut will be limited by human encroachment, a degree of habituation and continued nesting by the eagles can be anticipated, depending, in part, on the recovery of neighboring populations to the north.

*Donald A. Hopkins*

# Northern Harrier
*Circus cyaneus*

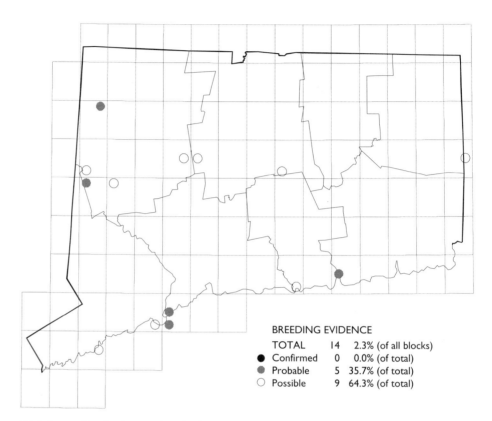

BREEDING EVIDENCE

| | | |
|---|---|---|
| TOTAL | 14 | 2.3% (of all blocks) |
| ● Confirmed | 0 | 0.0% (of total) |
| ◍ Probable | 5 | 35.7% (of total) |
| ○ Possible | 9 | 64.3% (of total) |

The Northern Harrier is an exceedingly scarce and sporadic breeder in Connecticut and has been designated as Endangered in the state. There is only one recent breeding record (see below). It is an uncommon to common migrant in fall, especially during peak migration days; spring migrants are much less common. A few individuals regularly may be observed in coastal marshes during winter.

North American breeders, subspecies *hudsonius*, of this circumpolar species winter south to Middle America, parts of the Caribbean, and northern South America. It is not known where breeding birds from southern New England migrate within this wintering range. The rich orange-buff underparts of the juvenal plumage is one of the defining characteristics of this subspecies (see Grant [1983] for a discussion on the separation of this subspecies from others).

**Habitat**—Typical nest sites in New England include extensive open freshwater or salt marshes, abandoned fields, old dune communities, extensive grasslands, and pastures. Similar areas are needed for foraging. The nest is a loosely built shallow cup lined with grasses and feathers, usually built on the ground. Harriers often forage by flying a few feet above an area and hovering when prey is seen or heard. Food consists of voles, birds, snakes, amphibians, and some insects.

**Atlas results**—Nearly half of the atlas records are from coastal marshes, such as near Lordship, Great Neck marsh, and along the mouth of the Connecticut River. Of the inland sites, six were in upland marshes in the northwestern part of the state.

**Discussion**—Comparison with early accounts suggest that the Northern Harrier has sharply declined in Connecticut in this century. Linsley (1843), Bagg and Eliot (1937), Merriam (1877), and Sage et al. (1913) all considered it a common summer resident, especially along the coast, and an abundant coastal migrant. Sage et al. (1913) noted the earliest egg date for Connecticut as 9 May (1878) and the latest as 18 June (1884). A serious decline starting early in this century was apparently first noted by Morris (1901). The continent-wide decline of the Northern Harrier in North America was caused by indiscriminate shooting (Bagg and Eliot 1937), habitat loss due to development and reforestation (Bull 1964), and pesticides (Tate 1986, Serrentino and England 1989).

The decline of the Northern Harrier in the state has been attributed to habitat loss and pesticide poisoning (Dowhan and Craig 1976); disturbances during the nesting season might be a factor as well. The presence of a pair and the sighting of a juvenile attended by an adult female at Great Meadows, Lordship, in July 1991, is the only recent record of nesting (Charles Barnard *in litt.*). Although the Northern Harrier decline is linked with development, there are coastal and upland marshes within Connecticut that could support small numbers of nesting pairs, and if further habitat loss can be avoided, these areas might serve as recolonization centers for breeding harrier populations in Connecticut. Indeed, upland nesting sites are now being used in southeastern Massachusetts (Christiansen and Reinert 1990).

*Dwight G. Smith and Arnold Devine*

## Sharp-shinned Hawk
### *Accipiter striatus*

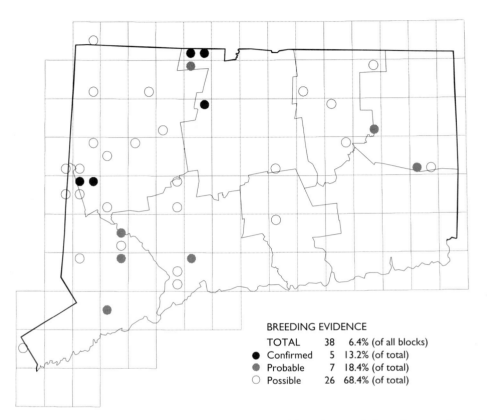

BREEDING EVIDENCE

| | TOTAL | 38 | 6.4% (of all blocks) |
|---|---|---|---|
| ● | Confirmed | 5 | 13.2% (of total) |
| ◉ | Probable | 7 | 18.4% (of total) |
| ○ | Possible | 26 | 68.4% (of total) |

The smallest of our accipiters, the Sharp-shinned Hawk is a rare to uncommon breeder in the state and is currently designated as Threatened. In contrast, this species is an exceptionally common migrant through the state and, with appropriate weather conditions during September and October, is abundant at coastal hawk watch sites such as Lighthouse Point Park, New Haven. According to data of the New England Hawk Watch, the Sharp-shinned Hawk is the second most common hawk migrating through Connecticut in late summer and fall. Most breeders in Connecticut likely withdraw to the south in winter, the Sharp-shinned Hawk being rare at that season in the state. The North American populations of this species, the *striatus* group of subspecies, winter from southern Canada to central Panama.

**Habitat**—Breeding Sharp-shinned Hawks usually arrive in Connecticut in mid to late March. Territories are established in remote and extensive woodland, often with adjacent fields or forest openings that arc uscd for foraging. In Connecticut, and elsewhere in New England, the Sharp-shinned Hawk nests in dense stands of conifers including mixed stands of hemlock, spruce, or white pine and, less frequently, mixed woodlands of white pine and oak. Nests are usually made of evergreen sticks and twigs placed 10–50 feet high in white pine, hemlock, or spruce (Sage et al. 1913, Bent 1937, Hopkins et al. 1987). Also, the platform-like nest frequently is placed in the tops of conifers. Eggs are laid in May or early June, and incubation takes about a month.

**Atlas results**—Most blocks in which the Sharp-shinned Hawk was recorded are in the higher elevations of the western and eastern portions of the state. Despite this species having a reputation for intolerance of human activity, 12% of 38 recorded blocks were in low density residential areas, and 7% were in high density residential areas.

**Discussion**—Sage et al. (1913) considered the Sharp-shinned Hawk a common summer resident from May to October. Persecution, including the infamous slaughters during migration, sharply reduced the numbers of this and the other accipiters during the first decades of this century. Since then, counts during migration indicate a substantial recovery may be underway. Like so many of our raptor species, this relatively inconspicuous and secretive nester requires a comprehensive survey to determine the size and extent of the nesting population in Connecticut.

*Dwight G. Smith and Arnold Devine*

# Cooper's Hawk
## *Accipiter cooperii*

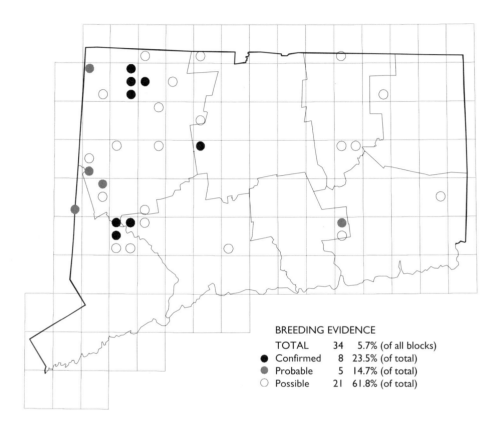

BREEDING EVIDENCE

| TOTAL | 34 | 5.7% (of all blocks) |
|---|---|---|
| ● Confirmed | 8 | 23.5% (of total) |
| ● Probable | 5 | 14.7% (of total) |
| ○ Possible | 21 | 61.8% (of total) |

This medium-sized accipiter is a rare to uncommon breeder in Connecticut. It is designated as a Threatened species within the state and has been included on the *American Birds* Blue List because of declining numbers (Tate 1986). In most years birds begin arriving in March, and courtship and nest site selection begin by early April. Banding studies have shown that Cooper's Hawks from southern New England may winter as far south as the Gulf Coast.

**Habitat**—Breeding habitat consists of deciduous or conifer stands near wetlands or open areas, such as fields, scrubby growth, or clearings. In general, the Cooper's Hawk nests in sub-mature woodlands, sometimes surprisingly close to residential areas; this contrasts with the Northern Goshawk, which selects more remote mature woodland tracts. Cooper's Hawks often use an old nesting territory, occasionally repairing a nest from previous years. The nest is typically a large and bulky affair constructed high (30 70 ft) in a hemlock, white pine, or deciduous tree. The number of eggs laid ranges from three to seven with four or five most frequent. Clutches from nine Connecticut nests held 3–5 eggs, which were laid between late April and early June. Extreme egg dates include a 28 April 1884 nest with one egg, and a 24 June 1911 nest with four eggs (Sage et al. 1913). Young begin to hatch in late June to early July. Prey brought to the young include small and medium-sized birds and small mammals, especially mice and chipmunks. Several authors have noted a relationship between chipmunk abundance and nesting success of the Cooper's Hawk.

**Atlas results**—The atlas recorded the Cooper's Hawk in 5.7% of all blocks, mostly in the western portion of the state. Over 76% of the atlas blocks in which the Cooper's Hawk was found are from the higher elevations of western Connecticut. The rest are from the northeastern portion of the state, with the single exception of a possible record from the central lowlands north of New Haven. The lack of nesting elsewhere in the state might reflect the secretiveness of nesting Cooper's Hawks rather than their distribution, as we have often found them near residential developments in northern New Jersey and elsewhere throughout their breeding range in the eastern United States.

**Discussion**—The past two centuries have seen dramatic shifts in the status of the Cooper's Hawk in the Northeast.

Samuels (1883) wrote that this hawk was once rare and more southerly in distribution and spread northward into New England in the 1800s to become one of the most abundant birds of prey in the region. To Allen (1864), Stearns and Coues (1883), and Sage et al. (1913) the Cooper's Hawk was a rather common summer resident, but by the 1920s, Forbush (1927) noted that it was less common than before. The Cooper's Hawk underwent a precipitous decline following persecution, including the slaughter of thousands along their fall migratory routes, and vastly reduced breeding productivity in more recent years caused by eggshell thinning as a result of DDT contamination. Its recovery also has been hampered by competition for nest sites with the Northern Goshawk and predation by the Great Horned Owl on adults and young at nest sites. Since the summer of 1975, Cooper's Hawks have nested in

Litchfield, New Haven, and Tolland counties and, historically, also nested in Hartford County. More recently, nesting has been detected in Windham County.

*Dwight G. Smith and Arnold Devine*

# Northern Goshawk
*Accipiter gentilis*

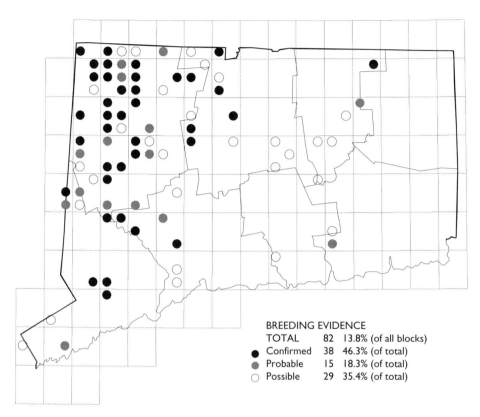

BREEDING EVIDENCE

| | TOTAL | 82 | 13.8% (of all blocks) |
|---|---|---|---|
| ● | Confirmed | 38 | 46.3% (of total) |
| ◉ | Probable | 15 | 18.3% (of total) |
| ○ | Possible | 29 | 35.4% (of total) |

The Northern Goshawk, largest of the North American accipiters, is an uncommon permanent resident and migrant in Connecticut. Nesting is concentrated in the higher elevations of western Connecticut. Pairs usually occupy a territory throughout the year and may protest vocally at intruders, especially near the nest, in any season.

**Habitat**—Although noted for preferring extensive tracts of mature old-growth woodlands, Northern Goshawks in Connecticut exhibit flexible habitat selection. Nest sites include tracts of mixed northern hardwoods and conifers (especially hemlock or white pine), pure stands of mature white or red pine often within more extensive tracts of deciduous woodlands, wetlands, and second growth deciduous stands. Most nests are located on wooded hillsides, frequently near wetlands and distant from human disturbance. Primary components of habitat selection appear to be the presence of mature, overstory trees coupled with a lack of understory cover. These features, plus a tendency to place the nest towards the base of the canopy, suggest selection of a cooler microclimate for nest sites. A nesting territory is typically occupied for a number of years. In Connecticut, courtship begins in late winter and continues through much of the spring. Nests are constructed or repaired during the courtship phase.

The following summarizes unpublished data collected by the authors and Root and DeSimone. Of 41 Connecticut nests, 19 were in conifers (red pine, white pine, and hemlock) and 22 were in deciduous trees (red oak, red maple, birches, and American beech). An

active nest is usually decorated with conifer sprigs, birch bark, and down feathers. Nests were placed in large, primary crotches of trees or at the base of horizontal limbs on average 43 feet (range 19–57 feet) above the ground. Eggs are laid in April; young hatch in a month and fledge in late June or early July. Average clutch size at 71 nests was 2.65 eggs; the average fledged was 1.68. Food brought to nests included mammals, mostly squirrels and chipmunks, and several species of birds, especially grouse, songbirds, and waterfowl. Breeding success is strongly related to the abundance of available prey, particularly chipmunks and gray squirrels, and in low prey years, Northern Goshawks either do not nest or abandon efforts early in the breeding season (Pat and Mike Redman, pers. obs.).

**Atlas results**—The Northern Goshawk shows a distinct preference for cooler climatic conditions and low human population density within the state. Almost 83% of atlas records were at higher elevations, and 71% were located in the west, with a concentration in the transition hardwood forests. Annual snowfall for 67% of nest sites averaged 50 inches or more per year, and mean monthly temperatures were 49°F or less. All confirmed and probable breeding blocks were in the least densely populated parts of the state. The few blocks in which the Northern Goshawk was recorded in the eastern portions of the state might reflect poor coverage there.

**Discussion**—The Northern Goshawk was a rare nesting species in New England at the turn of the century. Forbush (1927) listed this species as casual in summer, while Bagg and Eliot (1937) called it very rare in New England. Sage et al. (1913) reported only one Connecticut breeding record, a nest in Winchester, and considered the species a rare and irregular winter resident. The Northern Goshawk is now a firmly established breeder in Connecticut. Increased breeding is likely due to the extensive reforestation that occurred in Connecticut over the past fifty years. In addition, the maturation of largely untouched woodland tracts has greatly expanded the amount of old-growth forest, the preferred breeding habitat in the state. Protection has also been important in its recovery and spread as a breeder.

*Dwight G. Smith and Arnold Devine*

# Red-shouldered Hawk
## *Buteo lineatus*

This common hawk of Connecticut's wetlands is distributed patchily within the state. Connecticut's Red-shouldered Hawk population is largely migratory, although some individuals may winter in the state. Pairs usually return to the same territory year after year, repairing a previously used nest or constructing a new one nearby. This species has been included on the *American Birds* Blue List since 1972 because of nationwide concern over declining numbers. Although population levels in Connecticut are apparently stable, the Red-shouldered Hawk is included on Connecticut's list of Species of Special Concern.

**Habitat**—Swamps, river valleys, and bottomland forests are required for nesting; upland forests are used if adjacent to open or semi-open marshes, wet meadows, or the edges of ponds and

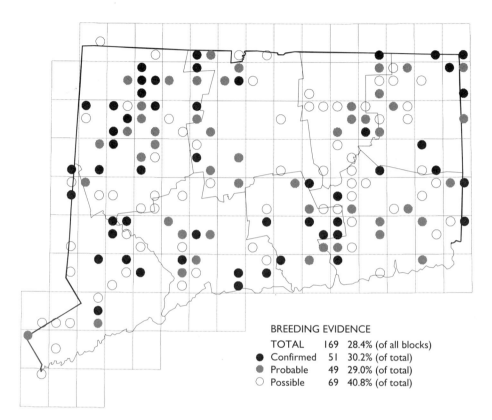

BREEDING EVIDENCE

| | TOTAL | 169 | 28.4% (of all blocks) |
|---|---|---|---|
| ● | Confirmed | 51 | 30.2% (of total) |
| ● | Probable | 49 | 29.0% (of total) |
| ○ | Possible | 69 | 40.8% (of total) |

lakes where the birds can forage. Nests are usually placed in mature canopy trees in wetland areas, hillsides adjacent to wetland areas, or, rarely, in upland woods. Of 218 nest records compiled from records in Sage et al. (1913), observations by Root and DeSimone, and by ourselves, all were in deciduous trees, mostly red oak, hickory, beech, yellow birch, and American chestnut,

which apparently was the favorite nest tree at the turn of the century when larger specimens still existed. The average height of nest placement was 40.5 ft (range 20–75 ft), and the nest typically was built in the main crotch of the tree. Most nests were decorated with sprigs of cedar, hemlock, pine, or ground-pine and lined with leaves and feathers. Feathers adhering to the nest rim plus freshly broken twigs littering the ground beneath are a sure sign that a nest is active. Eggs are laid in mid-April and hatch in mid-May. The young fledge in late June or early July. Clutch sizes of 13 nests in Connecticut averaged 3.4 eggs (range 3–6) and the number of fledged young observed at 38 successful nests averaged 2.25 and ranged from 2–5 (pers. obs. Root and DeSimone, M. and P. Redman, D. Smith).

**Atlas results**—Although the Red-shouldered Hawk was recorded in all regions of the state, they were most prevalent in the western and eastern interior sections and only slightly less widespread through the central lowlands and near the coast. Despite this statewide distribution, the choice of nest sites within each region indicates an intolerance of human activity and selection of undisturbed wetland.

**Discussion**— The rather low nesting success of this species is ascribed to intolerance of humans around nest sites, predation of adults and young by nesting Great Horned Owls and sensitivity to low numbers of prey. Several early accounts described the Red-shouldered

Hawk as the most common raptor in southern New England. Sage et al. (1913) considered them a common resident of Connecticut's lowlands, river valleys, and marshy woodlands. Bent (1937), Bagg and Eliot (1937), and Forbush (1927) suggested an inverse relationship with numbers of Red-tailed Hawks in a given area. For example, early in this century when the Red-tailed Hawk population was lower, the Red-shouldered Hawk was more common and occupied a wider variety of upland habitats, but has since declined with increasing Red-tailed Hawk numbers, a trend that has continued to the present. The factors affecting the population size mentioned above are similar for the Barred Owl, which nests in many areas with the Red-shouldered Hawk (Julio de la Torre pers. comm.).

*Dwight G. Smith and Arnold Devine*

101

---

## Broad-winged Hawk
### *Buteo platypterus*

---

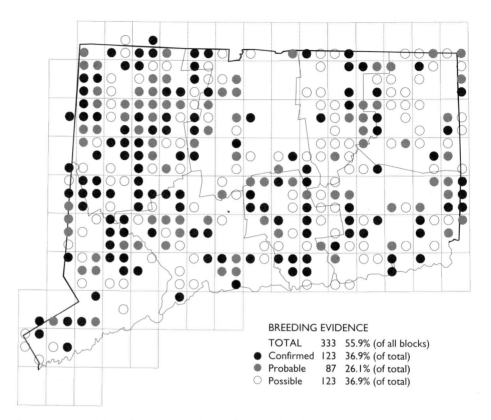

**BREEDING EVIDENCE**

| | | |
|---|---|---|
| TOTAL | 333 | 55.9% (of all blocks) |
| ● Confirmed | 123 | 36.9% (of total) |
| ◐ Probable | 87 | 26.1% (of total) |
| ○ Possible | 123 | 36.9% (of total) |

The smallest buteo breeding in Connecticut, the Broad-winged Hawk is a summer resident that ranges across the state, varying in abundance from locally common to uncommon. In Connecticut, migrating Broad-winged Hawks arrive from April through early May. Adults remain in the vicinity of their nesting territory until fall departure in September. They are rare after October. Most winter in Central America and northern South America.

**Habitat**—The Broad-winged Hawk exhibits a diversified nest site habitat selection. Although traditionally associated with deep tracts of deciduous or mixed forest, the species may also nest in isolated woodlots, often near roads and houses, and almost invariably close to a lake, pond, or wetland. About 50–70% of former nest sites are reoccupied by the same pairs. Nests are usual-ly constructed in primary crotches of deciduous trees at heights of 25–35 feet, although extremes of 10–90 feet have been reported. Sixteen Connecticut nests located in the north-western hills from 1974 to 1986 were in deciduous trees (oaks, maples, and yellow and white birches) and averaged 28 feet in height. The Broad-winged Hawk builds a nest similar to those of the Red-tailed Hawk, although some resemble the broad platform nests of the Cooper's Hawk. Broad-winged Hawk nests are usually smaller and lined with feathers, moss, bark, and dried grasses or leaves. Uniquely, Broad-winged Hawks may bring deco-rative greenery to the nest almost daily. Two to three eggs are usually laid in mid-May or early June, although Sage et al. (1913) reported a nest with three young 10 days old found on 14 May 1894 and another nest with one egg on 19 April 1884. Dates for young in the nest range from late May (more commonly June) into late July or more rarely early August. Food brought to nestlings includes small mammals, birds, amphibians, snakes, and a wide variety of insects and other invertebrates.

**Atlas results**—The Broad-winged Hawk was most prevalent in the western and eastern interior regions of the state (49% and 33% of confirmations in each region respectively ) and least common in the central lowlands and coastal regions (18.3% and 23.5% of confirmed blocks). This pattern suggests an avoidance of developed areas and indeed most ornithologists (e.g., Bent 1937, Forbush 1927, Bagg and Eliot 1937) also noted that the Broad-winged Hawk preferred woodland nesting sites far removed from human activities and landscapes.

**Discussion**—Sage et al. (1913) described the Broad-winged Hawk as a tolerably common summer resident from May to September and a common fall migrant. Their note that Broad-winged Hawks bred most abundantly in Litchfield County is reflected today in the atlas results, which revealed widespread breeding of this species in that region of the state. The North American Breeding Bird Survey results show that from 1969 to 1985 numbers of the Broad-winged Hawk increased in the less developed parts of New England but remained stable elsewhere, including most of Connecticut.

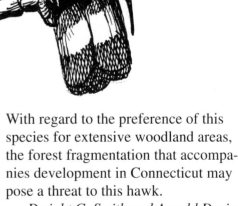

With regard to the preference of this species for extensive woodland areas, the forest fragmentation that accompanies development in Connecticut may pose a threat to this hawk.

*Dwight G. Smith and Arnold Devine*

# Red-tailed Hawk
## *Buteo jamaicensis*

This large hawk ranges widely over North America from the southern margins of the tundra to western Panama (Ridgely and Gwynne 1989). The Red-tailed Hawk may be seen throughout the year in Connecticut, but some of the population migrates southward in fall and returns in late February or early March to establish nesting territories. During winter, Red-tailed Hawks from more northern regions may migrate into Connecticut.

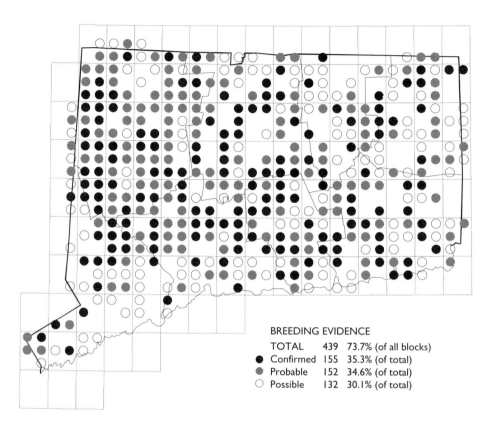

BREEDING EVIDENCE

| | TOTAL | 439 | 73.7% (of all blocks) |
|---|---|---|---|
| ● Confirmed | | 155 | 35.3% (of total) |
| ◗ Probable | | 152 | 34.6% (of total) |
| ○ Possible | | 132 | 30.1% (of total) |

**Habitat**—As elsewhere throughout their range, Red-tailed Hawks in Connecticut are generalists in choice of breeding habitat. Extensive deciduous or mixed forest, conifer stands, and woodlots all serve as nesting habitats in the state, although the species generally avoids high density residential areas. Nests usually are built in large canopy trees near ridgetops or steep hillsides, often near a meadow or other open area. Quite often, pairs use the same nest for several consecutive years; when new nests are constructed, several nests may accumulate in an old territory, the older nests in various stages of disrepair. Of 34 nests we located, 12 were in oaks, mostly red oak, four in white pine, and the rest in a variety of deciduous trees including sugar maple, pignut hickory, American elm, and black, gray or white birch. Nests averaged 46 feet in height (range 27–75 ft), were constructed of large sticks, and were often quite bulky. Most nests had deep cups lined with feathers, vines, or grasses and rims decorated with conifer sprigs of hemlock, red cedar, or pine. Red-tailed Hawks in Connecticut construct new nests or repair old ones in March or early April. Eggs are usually laid in April but egg dates range from late March to late May. Young fledge in June, or less frequently July. Prey brought to the young include squirrels, chipmunks, and a variety of birds.

**Atlas results**—The atlas results indicate that the Red-tailed Hawk is the most widely distributed bird of prey breeding in Connecticut. Although some allowance must be made for the ease of finding these conspicuous soaring and perching buteo hawks, they are undoubtedly numerous and widespread.

**Discussion**—Historically, the Red-tailed Hawk has always been reported as common in the state. Sage et al. (1913) noted them as a common resident of the interior wooded hills although much rarer along the coast. Forbush (1927) and Bagg and Eliot (1937) considered the Red-tailed Hawk reg-

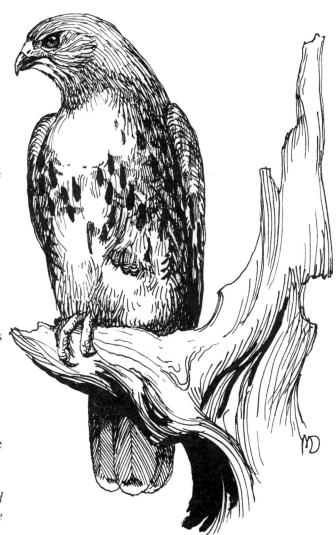

ular but less common and possibly declining, due to shooting and nest destruction. The North American Breeding Bird Survey (Robbins et al. 1986) revealed a significant positive increase in the species in the East from 1966 to 1979. These increases may have resulted from a combination of decreased persecution, increased forest fragmentation, and the natural reversion of many farmlands abandoned in the 1930s back to woodland. Breeding pairs were found in all physiographic regions and all ranges of climatic conditions that occur in Connecticut. Their abundance seems to have decreased only in heavily urbanized areas. Given their adaptability to human modified habitats, the Red-tailed Hawk population in Connecticut should remain stable.

*Dwight G. Smith and*
*Arnold Devine*

## American Kestrel
### *Falco sparverius*

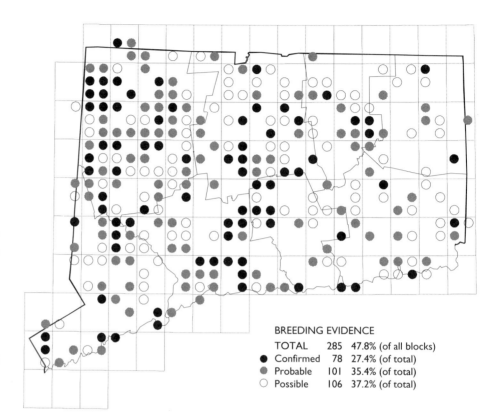

BREEDING EVIDENCE

| | | |
|---|---|---|
| TOTAL | 285 | 47.8% (of all blocks) |
| ● Confirmed | 78 | 27.4% (of total) |
| ● Probable | 101 | 35.4% (of total) |
| ○ Possible | 106 | 37.2% (of total) |

The American Kestrel is an uncommon to fairly common breeder in Connecticut. A few are seen in the state throughout the year perching on wires or foraging along the grassy shoulders of roadways; kestrels are fairly common migrants, especially in fall. The species' breeding range extends from central Alaska and much of forested Canada southward to Mexico, locally to Nicaragua, and also throughout South America to Tierra del Fuego. Most northern birds (subspecies *sparverius*), including Connecticut breeders, withdraw to the south in winter, some as far as Panama (AOU 1957).

**Habitat**—The two primary requirements of American Kestrels are open terrain for hunting and cavities, particularly tree holes, for nesting. Among its favored habitats are grassland or shrubland at the edge of forest or open coun-try with scattered trees; even urban open space is used if suitable perches and nest sites are available. In Connecticut, American Kestrels are usually seen around agricultural areas, airports, large parks, and power line rights-of-way. Kestrels most frequently capture prey on the ground or in short aerial attacks and either eat the item in its entirety or, during the breeding sea-son, may cache it in one of several pre-determined sites (Balgooyen 1976). In Connecticut, kestrels begin laying eggs in late April; natural tree cavities, flicker holes, nest boxes, or holes in buildings are most frequently used. The fledged young and adults often form family groups that remain together for several weeks before dispersing southward during the fall migration.

**Atlas results**—The species was recorded in all sections of Connecticut, although less densely in the eastern third of the state. The occurrence of suitable habitat throughout much of eastern Connecticut suggests the possibility that coverage was not as thorough there and that this falcon might be more widespread than indicated.

**Discussion**—The former status of the American Kestrel as a breeder in Connecticut is difficult to assess because its year-round presence hides a complex pattern of movements. They undoubtedly increased as farmland replaced forest and remained widespread until more recently. Sage et al. (1913) noted that they increased as a migrant at the turn of the century but characterized the breeding status as still comparatively rare, similar to what it was in the late 1800s (Merriam 1877). In contrast to Sage et al., this species was reported as a rare migrant in eastern Massachusetts between the 1880s and the 1920s but was said to be a common summer resident by the middle of the century (Griscom 1949). More recently, there is an impression of declining numbers in Connecticut. This might be due to the loss of open foraging areas following the extensive regrowth of forests and the loss of nest cavities now that dead trees are quickly cut for firewood. This trend may be at least partially mitigated by placement of nest boxes, which kestrels will readily utilize.

*Dwight G. Smith and Arnold Devine*

# Ring-necked Pheasant
*Phasianus colchicus*

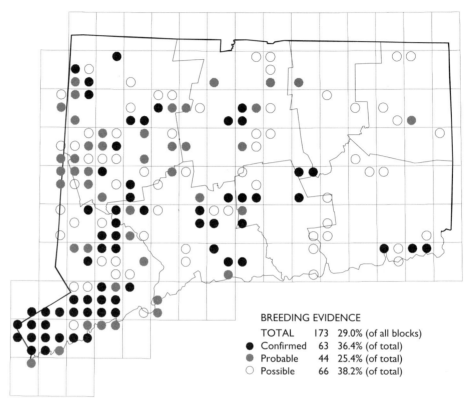

BREEDING EVIDENCE

| | TOTAL | 173 | 29.0% (of all blocks) |
|---|---|---|---|
| ● | Confirmed | 63 | 36.4% (of total) |
| ● | Probable | 44 | 25.4% (of total) |
| ○ | Possible | 66 | 38.2% (of total) |

The Ring-necked Pheasant is an introduced, nonmigratory species. Annual releases of captive-reared birds help maintain the population in Connecticut. Native to Asia, this pheasant was introduced widely in Europe prior to its being brought to North America.

**Habitat**—The Ring-necked Pheasant is a species of open country and does well in areas of grassy fields, farmland, brushy areas, and hedgerows. Although suburbs would not generally be considered prime habitat, birds may survive in such settings, particularly where grain is provided by people who feed the birds. This species does not do well in a habitat solely composed of woodland.

**Atlas results**—Ring-necked Pheasants were confirmed as breeding in a surprisingly high total of 63 blocks. Much more breeding was recorded west of the Connecticut River than in eastern Connecticut, and no breeding at all was confirmed for the northeastern corner of the state.

**Discussion**—The first recorded successful introduction into North America was of birds brought from China to Oregon in 1881 (Bent 1932). The earliest recorded successful introduction in the eastern states was of birds transported from England to New Jersey in 1887 (Bent 1932). Ring-necked

Pheasants were released in Connecticut in the late 1800s; the earliest year for which birds were reported in the wild was 1897 (Sage et al. 1913). The early releases of this species in Connecticut were made by private individuals or groups and were unsuccessful (Sage et al. 1913, Loranger 1980). Not until 1908 was stocking begun by the Connecticut State Board of Fisheries and Game (Loranger 1980). Hunting records from the mid-1920s indicate that the birds were successfully established as breeders because the numbers killed regularly exceeded the numbers stocked. Peak production of birds reared in the wild came in 1926, 1936, and 1937 (Loranger 1980). The population dropped markedly in 1943, and reproduction in the wild remained poor thereafter (Loranger 1980). Stocking has continued to the present. In recent years thousands of captive reared birds have been released annually during October and November on hunting areas that constitute less than 1% of the total land in the state (Loranger 1980). Ring-necked Pheasants do well in agricultural settings, particularly where some fields are left unplowed, spilled grain is left after harvesting, and seed-producing weeds are allowed to grow. The birds, including the chicks, frequently eat arthropods during the warmer months. In recent decades many farms have been lost to development, and since 1945, agricultural changes have been disadvantageous for maintaining a substantial breeding population of Ring-necked Pheasants. These changes include more intensive use of remaining fields, more complete harvesting of grains, and more effective control of insects and weeds.

*George A. Clark, Jr*

## Ruffed Grouse
*Bonasa umbellus*

A nonmigratory resident which is widely distributed in suitable habitat and which undergoes periodic fluctuations in numbers, being common in some years and uncommon in others. The causes of the fluctuations are still not fully understood (Atwater and Schnell 1989). The subspecies *umbellus* is found in Connecticut; the northern *togata* probably occurs in the northwest, but releases of other stock complicate the picture (Aldrich and Friedmann 1943).

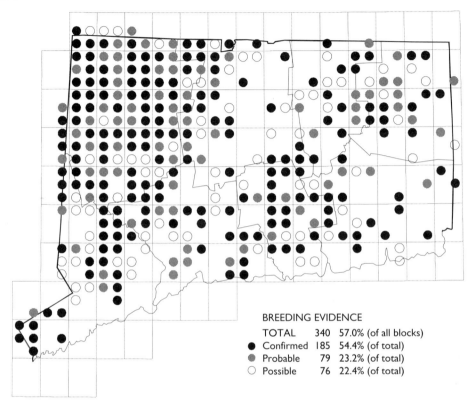

BREEDING EVIDENCE

| | TOTAL | 340 | 57.0% (of all blocks) |
|---|---|---|---|
| ● | Confirmed | 185 | 54.4% (of total) |
| ◉ | Probable | 79 | 23.2% (of total) |
| ○ | Possible | 76 | 22.4% (of total) |

**Habitat**—Ruffed Grouse are basically woodland birds but regularly enter brushy areas, and indeed benefit from the food plants that eventually grow in forest openings. Numbers of grouse tend to be higher in mixed coniferous-deciduous woodlands rather than in pure hardwoods (Johnsgard *in* Atwater and Schnell 1989). Grouse forests often have a well developed understory. Fallen logs are commonly used by males for their spring and fall drumming displays. Nests are placed on the ground. The omnivorous grouse feed on a variety of foods including seeds, berries, and insects in the warmer months, and tree buds and twigs in winter. The distribution of the Ruffed Grouse corresponds to a great extent with that of certain poplars, particularly the quaking aspen and balsam poplar (Johnsgard *in* Atwater and Schnell 1989), seeds of which are a major source of food during part of the year. Outside the breeding season, wandering grouse may appear briefly in virtually any habitat including, for example, the streets of downtown urban Hartford (James Hallett, pers. comm.).

**Atlas results**—The Ruffed Grouse was confirmed breeding in about 31% of all blocks, and birds were detected during the breeding season in an additional 26% of the blocks, thus indicating a probable use for breeding in about 57% of all blocks. Because there were relatively few observers in parts of eastern Connecticut, and Ruffed Grouse is not a species readily detected by summer block busting, it seems likely that the species breeds in more parts of eastern Connecticut than are indicated on the map.

**Discussion**—Archaeological evidence indicates that Ruffed Grouse were consumed by native Americans (Frank Dirrigl, pers. comm.). Linsley (1843), Merriam (1877), and Sage et al. (1913) considered the Ruffed Grouse to be a common species in Connecticut. Mackenzie (1961) reported the species to be regular in Guilford, and Manter (1975) noted a similar status for the Storrs area. Despite being a game species and living in an environment subject to increasing fragmentation, the Ruffed Grouse appears to have been doing relatively well in Connecticut. However, this has been achieved partly by deliberate efforts in forest management undertaken to encourage grouse, e.g., in the Coverts program jointly sponsored by the Connecticut Department of Environmental Protection and the Ruffed Grouse Society, a private organization that was founded in Connecticut.

*George A. Clark, Jr.*

## Wild Turkey
### *Meleagris gallopavo*

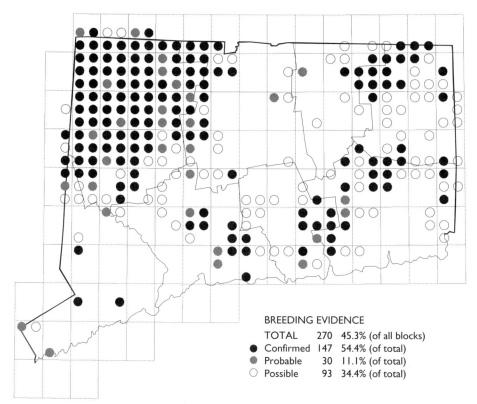

BREEDING EVIDENCE

TOTAL 270 45.3% (of all blocks)
● Confirmed 147 54.4% (of total)
● Probable 30 11.1% (of total)
○ Possible 93 34.4% (of total)

The Wild Turkey is a nonmigratory resident that was successfully reintroduced only in the mid-1970s and is now regular in many parts of Connecticut. It disappeared from much of its range as forests were cut and unrestricted harvests decimated its numbers.

The species ranges from central Mexico north, locally, throughout the eastern United States, the Rocky Mountains, and parts of the West, where introduced. Formerly it ranged to northern Maine and southern Ontario. The present range in the East is largely the result of restocking from remnant populations (AOU 1983). The domestic variety originated from the subspecies in southern Mexico; this form has pale-buffy tail-tips and uppertail coverts. It was introduced to Europe and later brought back by colonists. Eastern birds, subspecies *silvestris*, have rusty tail-tips and uppertail coverts.

**Habitat**—The Wild Turkey is a bird of mature hardwood forest, particularly with trees that produce mast, such as the oak, hickory, and beech (formerly chestnut). During winter, most congregate in flocks and roam woodlands, old fields, or harvested corn fields. These flocks break apart in early spring when males gather harems. Gobbling continues through May.

**Atlas results**—Breeding was confirmed for nearly a quarter of all blocks, indicating the rapid growth of the introduced population within a decade after its start. This illustrates that extirpated or endangered bird species can be rescued. However, strong motivation, sustained effort, patience, and adequate funding seem essential for success.

**Discussion**—The Wild Turkey is well known from Connecticut archaeological deposits (Coffin 1940 and Frank Dirrigl, pers. comm.), which indicate the use of these birds as food by native Americans. By making a number of assumptions, Schorger (1966) reached a rough estimate of a Wild Turkey population of 24,500 individuals in Connecticut before the Europeans arrived. The ensuing period of unrestricted hunting and deforestation caused the species' extirpation from the state (Sage et al. 1913). The last report in this period was of one taken by hand in deep snow at Letoket Mountain, North Branford, in the early 1800s (Linsley 1843).

In an effort to reestablish this species in Connecticut numerous releases of pen-reared Wild Turkeys were undertaken in the period from 1956 to 1970 (S. N. Jackson 1985), but these birds did not become permanently established. In 1975, through the cooperation of the New York Department of Environmental Conservation, wild trapped birds were moved from New York into Connecticut and began to breed successfully. These were birds that had survived in the Allegheny Hills of Pennsylvania and had later spread into New York. Thus the species was successfully reestablished after an absence of more than 160 years.

Further transfers of wild trapped birds were used to establish populations widely across the state, including east of the Connecticut River. The population subsequently has enlarged statewide to an estimated 3,000 to 3,500 birds by 1983 (Jackson 1985).

*George A. Clark, Jr.*

## Northern Bobwhite
*Colinus virginianus*

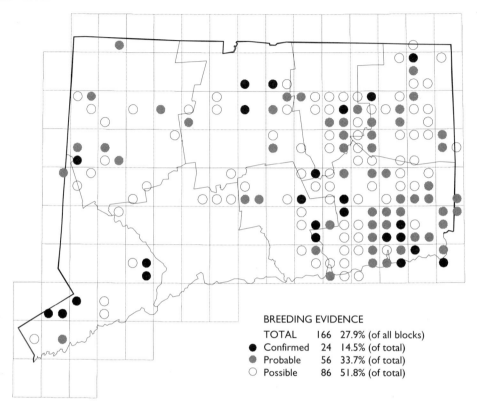

BREEDING EVIDENCE

| | | |
|---|---|---|
| TOTAL | 166 | 27.9% (of all blocks) |
| ● Confirmed | 24 | 14.5% (of total) |
| ● Probable | 56 | 33.7% (of total) |
| ○ Possible | 86 | 51.8% (of total) |

This species is a fairly common resident in eastern Connecticut in suitable habitat. It is less common west of the Connecticut River (Zeranski and Baptist 1990).

**Habitat**—Northern Bobwhites are found in old fields, farmland, and shrubby power line rights-of-way. The species is especially common in areas characterized by a mixture of woodland or brush and open fields.

**Atlas results**—Records of this species are concentrated in eastern Connecticut, but there are widely scattered records from western Connecticut. Release of Northern Bobwhite by private individuals may account for some records (Steven Hill, pers. comm.). BBS results indicate that Northern Bobwhite populations declined in Connecticut by an average of 8.6% per year between 1966 and 1989, a trend that is statistically significant. This appears to be a continuation of the long-term decline of this species since the 1800s. The situation may be more complex, however. The Northern Bobwhite was counted on two annual survey routes in Salem and East Haddam between 1946 and 1985 using methods similar to the BBS (roadside stations every 0.3 mi rather than every 0.5 mi). These surveys indicate that the population increased from 1946 to 1965, and subsequently declined (Steven Hill, pers. comm.). The average number of birds per survey point was similar from 1946 to 1951 and from 1980 to 1985, indicating that the decline since 1965 is not necessarily related to a long-term decline.

**Discussion**—The Northern Bobwhite has declined considerably since the 1800s, when they were common or even abundant (Zeranski and Baptist 1990). Although intense hunting and susceptibility to severe winters may have been contributing factors, the main cause of the population decline was probably loss of suitable habitat. The Northern Bobwhite has exceptionally specific habitat requirements. It needs low dense grass or forbs to hide the nest, dead grass stems for nest construction, patches of open ground for feeding, and some woody or brushy cover for protection in the winter (Roseberry and Klimstra 1984). All requirements are met in the varied landscapes typical of overgrazed, weedy pastures, recently abandoned fields, or farmland with fence rows or roadside verges. The conversion of much of the farmland and abandoned farmland in Connecticut into forest, and the more intensive use of much of the remaining farmland, has probably resulted in the decline of this species. For example, intensively managed hayfields do not provide good nesting habitat because open areas are not available for feeding and little dead grass remains after harvesting to provide nest material (Minser and Byford 1981).

*Robert A. Askins*

# Clapper Rail
*Rallus longirostris*

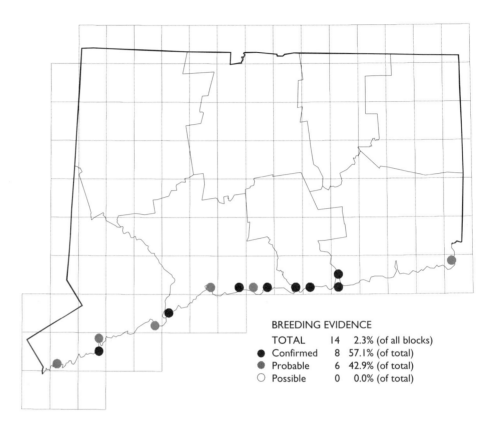

BREEDING EVIDENCE

| | TOTAL | 14 | 2.3% (of all blocks) |
|---|---|---|---|
| ● | Confirmed | 8 | 57.1% (of total) |
| ● | Probable | 6 | 42.9% (of total) |
| ○ | Possible | 0 | 0.0% (of total) |

This is a common migrant and summer resident in coastal salt marshes. A few overwinter during less severe winters. Populations in Connecticut and along most of the Atlantic seaboard (subspecies *crepitans*) are grayer and have a more muted pattern to their plumage than most of the 23 recognized subspecies of the Clapper Rail.

**Habitat**—This species lives in coastal salt marshes and tidal brackish areas even upriver along the Housatonic and Connecticut Rivers. The nest of grasses and decayed vegetation is placed on the ground and built up to a level well above the flood level of the high tide. The incubating bird often weaves grasses over the nest making a cover that once recognized facilitates the location of nests by observers.

**Atlas results**—As expected, all nesting records were coastal save for one location slightly up the Connecticut River. Indeed, even the probable reports are more than likely solid nesting locations considering how difficult the nest is to find and how infrequently observers venture into marshes.

**Discussion**—Apparently the Clapper Rail was an uncommon to rare resident in the coastal marshes during the 1800s, but the literature is not entirely consistent on this point. Both Merriam (1877) and Sage et al. (1913) listed the species as rare or uncommon, but Linsley (1843) termed it an abundant nester in the Stratford marshes. In view of the difficulty seeing the species, it is understandable that discrepancies of viewpoints might occur. One can, however, get a good idea of how abundant the species is simply by listening for its calls. In the 1920s, Howes (1928) felt it was a rare summer resident, but then things began to change rapidly. In the 1940s, the population evidently began to burgeon (Bledsoe 1988), and by the end of that decade Saunders (1950) listed it as a common species.

It remains a common coastal resident of Connecticut's marshes. Yet, with the decrease of the coastline habitat, in particular the salt marshes, the potential nesting area for this species narrows each year. The extensive marshes at the mouth of the Connecticut and Housatonic rivers still hold a large population of this species, but in Fairfield County the populations seem to have dropped. The Lordship marshes in Stratford, for example, have been greatly disturbed, and sites where nests were found in the 1960s are now gone.

The hybridization of this species with the King Rail has been covered under that species. Hybridization has occurred several times in the Connecticut marshes, and some leading authorities on rails consider the King and Clapper conspecific (Ripley 1977). Further study of the relationship between these forms in Connecticut is needed.

*Noble S. Proctor*

## King Rail
### *Rallus elegans*

This species is a rare inhabitant during the summer in both fresh and brackish water areas where they nest. Wintering birds occasionally occur in the coastal salt marshes, most consistently around the mouth of the Connecticut River. Connecticut is at or near the northeastern coastal terminus of this species' range. The King Rail is currently designated as Threatened in the state.

**Habitat**—Although the King Rail is often listed as the fresh water counterpart of the Clapper Rail, in Connecticut King Rails occur in coastal brackish marshes and interior fresh water marshes. This situation has been reported from Louisiana to Delaware and Long Island, New York (Meanley and Wetherbee 1962, Bull 1964). It nests on the ground. At coastal sites, the species is found in fresh water or brackish impoundments adjacent to salt marshes where the Clapper Rail is a common breeder.

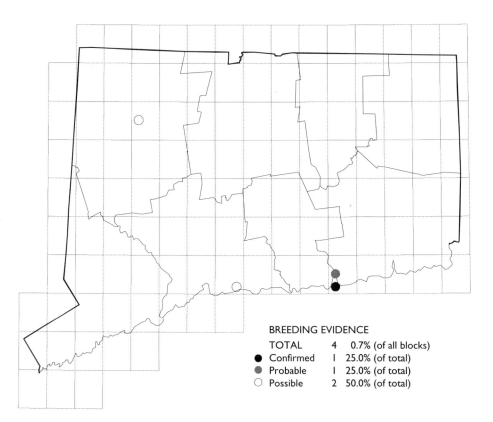

BREEDING EVIDENCE

| | TOTAL | 4 | 0.7% (of all blocks) |
|---|---|---|---|
| ● | Confirmed | 1 | 25.0% (of total) |
| ● | Probable | 1 | 25.0% (of total) |
| ○ | Possible | 2 | 50.0% (of total) |

**Atlas results**—The only confirmed nesting during the atlas period occurred in the marshes near the mouth of the Connecticut River. Probable nesting occurred farther up river (Craig 1990). One problem is the difficulty in actually finding the nest of the species. Although a ground nester, they quickly slip from the nest at the sound of anything approaching and flush some distance from the nest site. In addition, the nest is covered by grasses, often woven over the nest by the sitting bird, thus adding to the difficulty of finding the nest. The other reports came at West Torrington in a fresh water marsh and the Juniper Point marshes of Branford. A nest could not be found at either location.

**Discussion**—This species apparently has always been a rarity in the state. It was first reported by Linsley (1843). Sage et al. (1913) listed only six localities where it could be found. Mackenzie (1961) found it nesting in Guilford. Manter (1975) listed it as "casual, very rare transient" for the Storrs area. In the last ten years, favored coastal marshes for the species include: Barn Island, Stonington; Great Island, at the mouth of the Connecticut River; Guilford Great Harbor marsh; the East Haven marshes of the Trolley Museum; and Manresa, Norwalk. The only interior fresh water marshes that have consistently held King Rails are the Durham Meadow marshes, where nests were found on three occasions in the 1970s (pers. obs.). Birds have been heard here in recent springs, but nesting has not been proven. Vocalizations ascribed to the King Rail from such habitats seems reasonable; however, at coastal sites, the calling bird should be seen as the vocalizations of both King and Clapper rails can be indistinguishable. Other interior sites with reported past probable breeding include South Windsor (Station 43), Bloomfield, and Rocky Hill (Bergstrom 1960).

This species has been observed interbreeding with Clapper Rails at the mouth of the Connecticut River, Manresa (Norwalk), Milford, East Haven, and Barn Island (Stonington). In one case at Barn Island, a Clapper Rail was observed copulating with a King Rail in the brackish marsh (Bevier, pers. comm.). The inland impoundments at this locality were recently opened to salt water flushing. At the mouth of the Connecticut River, W. Burt has photographed apparent hybrid young birds, which show the features of both species. Bledsoe (1988) listed the features of an intermediate specimen, and presumed hybrid, from Connecticut—a bird found in emaciated condition at New Haven, October 1951. Observers in Connecticut are cautioned to note carefully the characters of supposed King Rails that they report, including coloration of back striping, flanks, and cheeks. Clearly, this species is very closely related to the Clapper Rail; the AOU (1983) considers the two to form a superspecies, whereas Ripley (1977) regards the King Rail as a subspecies of Clapper Rail. The two forms contact each other throughout the Clapper's range along the Atlantic and Gulf Coasts.

*Noble S. Proctor*

## Virginia Rail
### *Rallus limicola*

A migratory breeder in Connecticut, this rather secretive species is probably relatively plentiful within the limited amount of suitable habitat. It is unknown whether the small number of individuals wintering in salt marshes along the coast are year round residents of Connecticut or originate elsewhere. Major wintering areas for the species as a whole in eastern North America are from coastal North Carolina south along the Atlantic coast and west along the Gulf Coast and south into Central America (AOU 1983). Smaller subspecies of the Virginia Rail are found locally in small numbers south to Tierra del Fuego.

**Habitat**—In Connecticut, this species often breeds in fresh water marshes in which the emergent vegetation includes some cattails with an understory of grasses and sedges (Billard 1948);

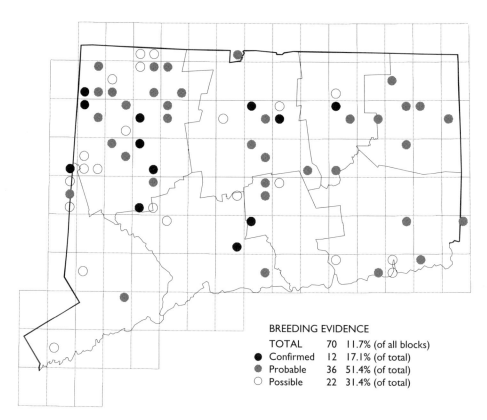

BREEDING EVIDENCE

| | TOTAL | 70 | 11.7% (of all blocks) |
|---|---|---|---|
| ● | Confirmed | 12 | 17.1% (of total) |
| ● | Probable | 36 | 51.4% (of total) |
| ○ | Possible | 22 | 31.4% (of total) |

however, a considerable range of marsh habitats from tidal brackish to palustrine is used in Connecticut (Craig 1990). Nests are constructed of materials found near the nest site and are primarily built during the second and third weeks of May (Billard 1948). Comparison of habitat use with that of the Sora is included in the account for the latter species.

**Atlas results**—During the period of intensive survey for this atlas, the species was found widely scattered across the state, with the greatest concentration of records in the northwestern hills. The fewest records came from the southern portions of the state, particularly Fairfield County. Because this species is somewhat secretive and lives in a habitat not regularly entered by

birders, there is a substantial possibility that the species could be missed. Broadcasting of tape-recorded vocalizations provides a means for detecting birds that might otherwise be missed, but such broadcasting has not been employed in many sites in which these rails might possibly occur.

**Discussion**—Apparently the first breeding evidence for the state was provided by Linsley (1843), who collected at least one egg of the species. Merriam (1877) considered the species to be an abundant breeder in both fresh and salt water marshes. However, Sage et al. (1913) termed the species a rather rare summer resident and mentioned only fresh water breeding. Although Virginia Rails do breed in the upper portions of brackish marshes (Townsend *in* Bent 1926, Craig 1990) and unditched salt marsh (Post and Enders 1970), fresh water marshes are the more usual site.

The period from 1877 to 1913 was one of extensive and often unregulated hunting which might have contributed to a decrease in the number of breeders. Because of major elimination of wetland habitats by people in Connecticut during the past 150 years, it seems quite possible that the numbers of this species have declined accordingly, but detailed documentation on the population is lacking. By broadcasting tape-recordings of vocalizations, Craig (1990) found indications of a population increase in the period from 1983 to 1987 along portions of the Connecticut River. Virginia Rails appear to tolerate a wide variety of marsh habitats (Craig 1990), and at present the species appears to be at least maintaining its numbers in the state.

*George A. Clark, Jr.*

## Sora
*Porzana carolina*

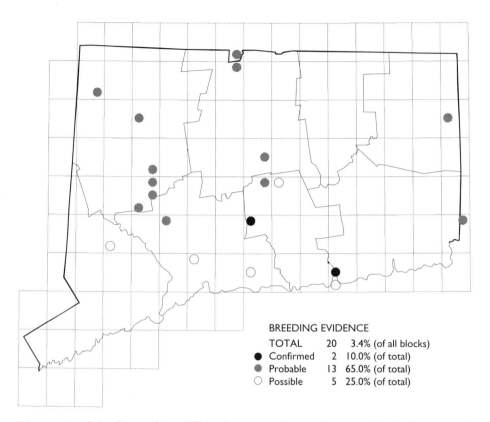

BREEDING EVIDENCE

| | TOTAL | 20 | 3.4% (of all blocks) |
|---|---|---|---|
| ● | Confirmed | 2 | 10.0% (of total) |
| ◉ | Probable | 13 | 65.0% (of total) |
| ○ | Possible | 5 | 25.0% (of total) |

The Sora is a relatively uncommon migratory breeder in Connecticut, although many birds migrate through the state. The species as a whole winters principally from the southern United States south through Central America and the Caribbean islands into much of northern South America (AOU 1983).

**Habitat**—In Connecticut, Soras nest principally in fresh water marshes, but sometimes in marshes with high salinity (Craig 1990). Billard (1948) found that Sora nests were often in a solid cattail stand, while Virginia Rails commonly used reed canary-grass or mixed coarse sedges as a nesting site. Furthermore, she found that Sora nests appeared to be in the wetter portions of the swamp, often close to muskrat houses. Water depth at Sora nests tended to be greater or the swamp bottom to be more unstable than at sites of Virginia Rail nests.

The nests of the Sora often differed from those of the Virginia Rail in having: 1) a closely knit canopy of surrounding vegetation only two or three inches above the nest and 2) a ramp from the nest to the water.

In contrast to Billard's findings, Johnson and Dinsmore (1986) found Soras in Iowa to be more prevalent than Virginia Rails in the shallow water near shore where wetland plants produced seeds eaten by Soras. They also found no strong separation in habitat between Soras and Virginia Rails, but proposed that differences in bill shape indicated different ecological roles. There appears to be considerable overlap in the habitats of these two species in Connecticut, and Billard found nests of the two species as close as 15 feet apart.

**Atlas results**—The Sora was found in only 20 blocks statewide and confirmation of breeding was obtained in only two of these blocks. Because this species is even more secretive than the Virginia Rail and broadcasting of vocalizations was not used to search for birds in all areas, the species might well have been overlooked in some localities.

**Discussion**—Although Merriam (1877) termed the species "an abundant summer resident," he did not specifically mention nesting in Connecticut and might have been referring to an influx of migrants that arrive starting as early as late July (Craig 1990). Sage et al. (1913) mentioned only five specific cases of nesting. Billard (1948) monitored fifteen Connecticut nests in one summer. Walter Bulmer (in Zeranski and Baptist 1990) estimated fifteen pairs breeding in the Great Meadows at Stratford in the late 1960s and reported that subsequent human development led to the elimination of Sora breeding in that area. Although Virginia Rails and Soras clearly overlap in habitat use, some difference, perhaps in diet, leads the Sora to be a much less common breeder in Connecticut. Although the earlier historic records are not detailed, indications are that the Sora has declined as a breeder, due at least partly to habitat loss. For many decades during the fall migration, substantial numbers of Soras were taken by hunters in Connecticut, but the large numbers indicated that most of those birds must have originated from breeding areas to the north or west. In recent decades, a drastic decrease in the number of birds has led to a sharp decline in the number of hunters and number of birds taken (Eddleman et al. 1988). The current annual take of Soras nationally is estimated to be well within sustainable levels (Eddleman et al. 1988).

*George A. Clark, Jr.*

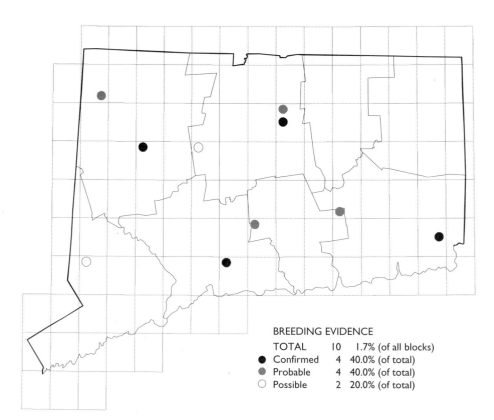

BREEDING EVIDENCE

| TOTAL | 10 | 1.7% (of all blocks) |
|---|---|---|
| ● Confirmed | 4 | 40.0% (of total) |
| ◉ Probable | 4 | 40.0% (of total) |
| ○ Possible | 2 | 20.0% (of total) |

## Common Moorhen
### *Gallinula chloropus*

The Common Moorhen is a rare and sporadic migratory breeder, mainly at large fresh water marshes. It has been designated as Threatened in the state. Migrant birds may be found in wetlands across the state in spring, from late April on, or, more frequently, in autumn from late August to mid-October, after which occasional individuals linger until December, depending on when a hard freeze occurs. Breeders from the Northeast withdraw, for the most part, to the southern coastal Atlantic states, the coast of the Gulf of Mexico, or possibly farther south to Central America.

**Habitat**—Moorhens are typically found in large, deep-water marshes with tall, dense emergent vegetation surrounding the margins of the marsh. Cattail and cattail-reed swamps appear to be the favored habitats for the species in Connecticut, although so few nest that it is difficult to specify the precise requirements within the state. Dense vegetation is frequently used to shield movements, although the species does forage in open water. The nest is a basket-like affair usually hidden in cattails or emergent shrubs of a marsh. Snakes and raccoons may be the principal predators of moorhen eggs.

**Atlas results**—Confirmed nesting was determined in four blocks. In the northwest, the Common Moorhen was found nesting in the large fresh water wetland at the White Memorial Foundation. Along the Connecticut River, the extensive wetlands preserved in South Windsor at Station 43 provided nesting for at least one pair of moorhens. Other localities with confirmed breeding included Assekonk Swamp, North Stonington, and in North Haven. Probable breeding localities included the Miles Sanctuary, Sharon; Durham Meadows, Durham; and extreme northeastern East Haddam.

**Discussion**—The Common Moorhen appears to have been a rare migrant and summer visitor in Connecticut since ornithologists first visited the region, despite G. B. Grinnell's statement that this species was a rather common summer resident during the 1870s in the Milford area (Merriam 1877); this statement was called into question by Sage et al. (1913). It should be noted, however, that there is little quantitative information in existence for comparison with past populations in the state. The first report of a nest was in 1891 at Stratford (Lucas 1891), and the first reported nesting at South Windsor was in 1930 (Bagg and Eliot 1937). The species also reportedly nested at New Haven in 1940 (Bergstrom 1960), and again at Stratford in the 1970s (Hills

1983). During the 1980s, it nested at North Haven, Litchfield, South Windsor and North Stonington. Because the species breeds sporadically, a strategy of protecting only a few known localities could fail to assure continued breeding in the state, and although considered a game bird, its rarity surely makes the species unimportant to hunting, from which it should receive full protection. The draining and filling of large fresh water marshes in the state has certainly inhibited the potential for a breeding population to take hold.

*Louis R. Bevier*

# Piping Plover
## *Charadrius melodus*

The Piping Plover is a migratory breeder, arriving in March and nesting in early April. Almost extirpated early in the century, numbers have increased steadily over the past ten years; it is currently designated as Threatened in Connecticut. Populations breeding along the Atlantic coast (subspecies *melodus*) are found in winter mainly from South Carolina to Florida and, in small numbers, in the Bahamas and Greater Antilles. The wintering area for Connecticut breeders lies somewhere in this range.

**Habitat**—Breeding is found only at coastal sandy beaches, often in association with Least Terns. Birds usually nest on the open sandy areas of beaches and as a result are frequently disturbed by people. The simple scrape of a nest is frequently near vegetation, sometimes quite dense vegetation.

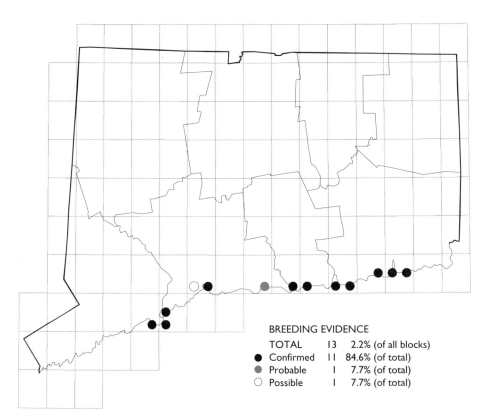

BREEDING EVIDENCE

| | | |
|---|---|---|
| TOTAL | 13 | 2.2% (of all blocks) |
| ● Confirmed | 11 | 84.6% (of total) |
| ● Probable | 1 | 7.7% (of total) |
| ○ Possible | 1 | 7.7% (of total) |

**Atlas results**—The atlas results agree well with other regular censuses conducted by the DEP. No new sites were found during the atlas surveys. The species rarely wanders from its nesting area and there are evidently very few nonbreeding birds in the state. Thus, the presence of a bird on a beach between April and August usually indicates nesting.

**Discussion**—The species was evidently never common in Connecticut as Linsley (1843) considered it rare. Although it was virtually extirpated along the east coast by 1910, its numbers recovered quickly after migratory bird regulations were passed and the species recovered its former numbers on Long Island in the 1930s. Numbers declined again after World War II with

increased development of the shoreline (Bull 1974). In Connecticut, it nested at Stratford in 1931 and at an increasing number of locations in successive years (Zeranski and Baptist 1990).

The species now occupies most sandy beaches along Connecticut's shore and has expanded to new sites in the last few years. Since 1983 there have been regular censuses, increased protection measures, and an increase of nesting pairs from 15 to 43 as of 1992. The largest numbers are found at Stratford's Long Beach, Milford Point, and Sandy Point in West Haven; all three sites are heavily used by bathers and fisherman with resultant potential for heavy disturbance. Posting of signs with information about the plovers and fencing of the nest sites has resulted in surprisingly higher success rates at the above sites than at Hammonasset Beach State Park, where there is almost no human access to the nesting sites.

*Fred C. Sibley*

# Killdeer
## *Charadrius vociferus*

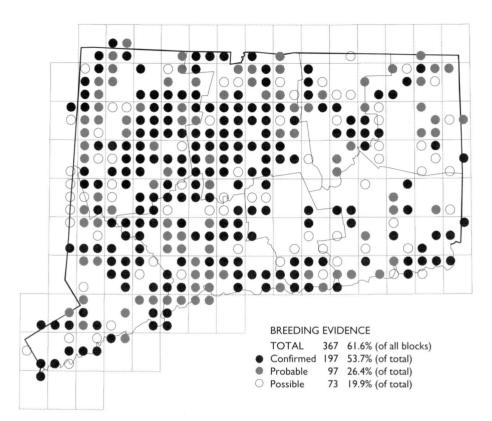

BREEDING EVIDENCE

| | TOTAL | 367 | 61.6% (of all blocks) |
|---|---|---|---|
| ● | Confirmed | 197 | 53.7% (of total) |
| ● | Probable | 97 | 26.4% (of total) |
| ○ | Possible | 73 | 19.9% (of total) |

The Killdeer is principally a migratory breeder in Connecticut. The species is presently a widespread fairly common breeder in Connecticut. In eastern North America, the species as a whole winters mainly from the south central and southeastern states south into Central America (AOU 1983, Root 1988); small numbers winter in coastal areas of Connecticut and even fewer in the interior of the state (Zeranski and Baptist 1990).

**Habitat**—A denizen of open habitats, the Killdeer often nests in upland fields with well-drained soils. Killdeer tend to favor bare ground in an open field for a nest site, but will use other areas such as mowed lawns of large cemeteries. Surrounding areas of open ground must be sufficiently large to provide food. In Connecticut, rainfall is generally sufficient that most temporarily bare ground on reasonably fertile soils shows sub-stantial growth of plants within a matter of days or a few weeks. Consequently, suitable nest sites of sufficient duration would seem to be scarce for Killdeer. In recent decades, the birds have apparently taken more and more to nesting on flat roofs (Ankney and Hopkins 1985).

**Atlas results**—Remarkably, breeding was confirmed for nearly a third of all blocks, including a great many blocks that are heavily populated by people. Killdeer breed statewide, but Hartford County can be singled out as having a relatively high density of blocks with confirmed breeding by Killdeer. Among plovers and sandpipers breeding in Connecticut, the Killdeer shows by far the greatest density of blocks with breeding.

**Discussion**—Merriam (1877) considered the Killdeer to be a "not very common" summer resident and indicated that the numbers had declined in the vicinity of Portland. Sage et al. (1913) also considered it a "rather rare summer resident" though it had apparently increased during the previous decade. Unregulated hunting in the latter part of the 1800s and early years of the 1900s apparently kept the numbers of Killdeer at a low level. Zeranski and Baptist (1990) have summarized literature reporting the increase of numbers and breeding records of Killdeer through the twentieth century following the establishment of restrictions on hunting. The increase in the breeding and numbers of Killdeer in the twentieth century illustrates the importance of the establishment of hunting regulations in the early part of the century as a result of the Audubon conservation movement (G. Clark *in* Zeranski and Baptist 1990). One of the developments apparently subsequent to that recovery has been the increased use of roofs for nesting. As in the case of the Common Nighthawk, it is generally difficult to obtain access to roofs, and we do not know whether roof-nesting Killdeer in Connecticut have sufficient breeding success to maintain their numbers.

*George A. Clark, Jr.*

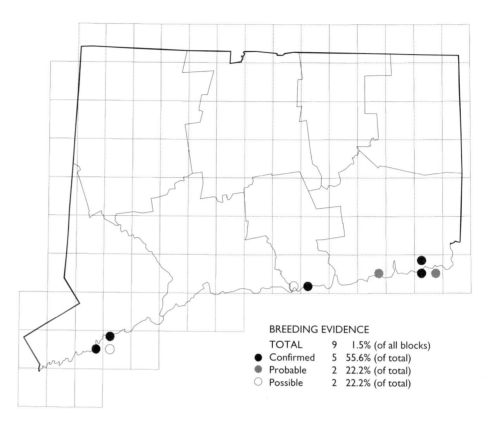

BREEDING EVIDENCE

| TOTAL | 9 | 1.5% (of all blocks) |
|---|---|---|
| ● Confirmed | 5 | 55.6% (of total) |
| ◉ Probable | 2 | 22.2% (of total) |
| ○ Possible | 2 | 22.2% (of total) |

## American Oystercatcher
### *Haematopus palliatus*

A migratory breeder in Connecticut, the species is uncommon and local in occurrence. It is designated as a Species of Special Concern in the state. Birds nesting in the northeastern United States presumably winter principally from North Carolina south along the Atlantic and Gulf Coasts to southeastern Mexico (AOU 1983).

**Habitat**—The second recorded nest in Connecticut was on a pebble beach of an isolated island (Dewire 1981), and a number of subsequent records have come from such sites of low open sandbars relatively free of vegetation (Zeranski and Baptist 1990). On Long Island, some birds have nested in salt marshes (Lent *in* Andrle and Carroll 1988). In addition to nest sites, oystercatchers also need a suitable foraging habitat for obtaining shellfish (Lent *in* Andrle and Carroll 1988).

**Atlas results**—The species was found breeding in a small number of coastal insular sites, thus documenting the increase in numbers of these birds breeding in the state. In 1983 four nestings were confirmed in the Norwalk Islands (Hand and Mockalis 1983). Confirmations of breeding in 1985 were obtained from the Norwalk Islands and two blocks in the Mystic area (Rosgen 1986). In 1986 confirmation was obtained from Westbrook (Rosgen 1987).

**Discussion**—Although oystercatchers were recorded from the state before 1840, the species was not found in Connecticut again until 1971 (Zeranski and Baptist 1990). Subsequently the number of sightings in the state began

to increase. Breeding was reported in Westbrook on Menunketesuck I. in 1980 (see *Connecticut Warbler* 2:13, 1982). Confirmation of nesting in Connecticut came in Mystic in 1981 (Dewire 1981). Lent (*in* Andrle and Carroll 1988) has traced the history of recent expansion of the breeding area on Long Island, New York, which might well have been a source for birds that came into Connecticut. Breeding records continued to come from additional sites after the period of the atlas. In 1988 a pair nested in Stonington (Taylor 1989). In 1990 breeding was attempted in Darien and Greenwich (Kaplan 1991). It remains to be seen how far this expansion of breeding areas will eventually extend. Factors involved in the spread of this species remain to be closely analyzed.

Certainly the establishment of protection after the market hunting of shorebirds as late as the early part of the twentieth century was a strong factor promoting their increase. There is some question as to the importance of other factors (Lent *in* Andrle and Carroll 1988), and this species would seem to be a good subject for a careful examination of the factors influencing its breeding distribution and abundance.

*George A. Clark, Jr.*

# Willet
## *Catoptrophorus semipalmatus*

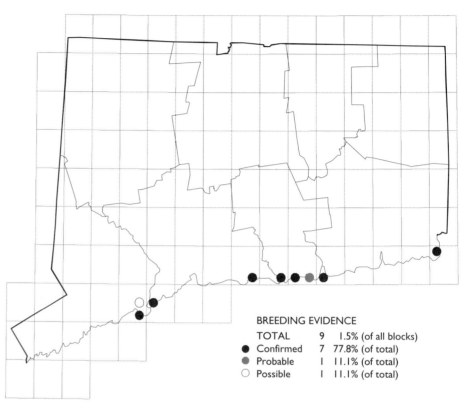

BREEDING EVIDENCE

| | | TOTAL | 9 | 1.5% (of all blocks) |
|---|---|---|---|---|
| ● | Confirmed | 7 | 77.8% (of total) | |
| ◉ | Probable | 1 | 11.1% (of total) | |
| ○ | Possible | 1 | 11.1% (of total) | |

The Willet is an uncommon and local breeder in Connecticut, arriving in late April and early May. The bulk of the breeding population departs by August and winters along the coast of the Gulf of Mexico and Florida. The Willet is designated as Threatened in the state.

Two disjunct and distinctive populations of the Willet nest in North America, Connecticut breeders belonging to the nominate subspecies *semipalmatus*, which occupies coastal salt marshes from Nova Scotia to Mexico and the Caribbean. The more western subspecies, *inornatus*, breeds in the Great Plains and intermountain regions of North America. Migrant Willets seen in Connecticut from early August through September are most likely this western subspecies, which is larger, paler, grayer (less barred below in breeding plumage), and gives a loud, shrill, tern-like alarm call.

**Habitat**—As with other populations along the Atlantic coast, Connecticut breeders occupy coastal salt marshes and nest in vegetated sites above the intertidal zone. Howe (1982) found that only unpaired males perform the conspicuous and vocal aerial displays consisting of stiff-winged glides with short, rapid wing strokes. Nests are placed on the ground in grass or at the base of small shrubs in more upland sites, such as sand dunes, bordering the marsh. Representative egg dates in Connecticut include: three eggs on 5 June 1873 and four eggs on 13 June 1980 (Sage et al. 1913, R. J. Craig field notes). Feeding territories are established usually some distance from the nest site, and both exclusive territories with fixed boundaries and shared feed-

ing areas on intertidal mudflats are used by pairs (Howe 1982). Currently, only the larger remaining salt marshes are used for nesting in Connecticut, although nesting attempts have been detected at smaller marshes.

**Atlas results**—Breeding was found near Milford Point, Great Meadows in Stratford, from the mouth of the Connecticut River west to Madison, and at Barn Island, Stonington.

**Discussion**—Until the late 1800s, the Willet presumably nested along the length of the Atlantic coast of the United States, but during this time, its eggs were collected in large numbers for food, and the adults were hunted throughout the breeding season. As a result it was extirpated between Nova Scotia and New Jersey. The species returned as a breeder on Long Island, New York, in 1966 (Davis 1968) and in New England at Biddeford, Maine, in 1971 (Finch 1971). Although no documented evidence of breeding in the form of nests and eggs existed prior to these reports for New York and Maine, it seems reasonable to guess that the species was reclaiming a part of its former range. The last reported nesting in Connecticut prior to this resurgence was in 1873 when a nest with three eggs was collected at Madison 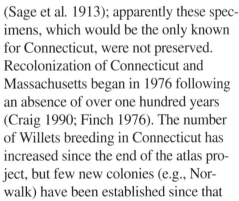 (Sage et al. 1913); apparently these specimens, which would be the only known for Connecticut, were not preserved. Recolonization of Connecticut and Massachusetts began in 1976 following an absence of over one hundred years (Craig 1990; Finch 1976). The number of Willets breeding in Connecticut has increased since the end of the atlas project, but few new colonies (e.g., Norwalk) have been established since that time. The marshes near Milford Point and Hammonasset Beach State Park have supported 6–15 pairs each over the past several years and have been the most consistently used nesting areas in the state (*Connecticut Warbler* 10:22). Craig (1990) found a maximum of two pairs on Great Island at the mouth of the Connecticut River from 1984 to 1987.

*Louis R. Bevier*

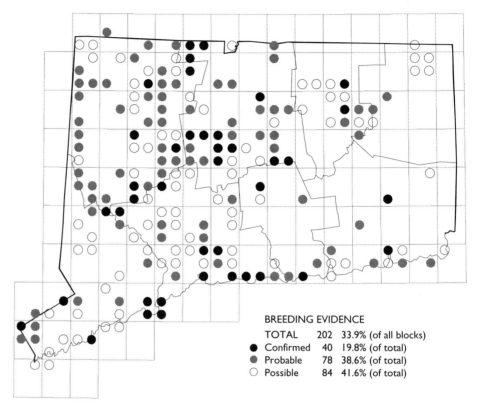

BREEDING EVIDENCE

| | TOTAL | 202 | 33.9% (of all blocks) |
|---|---|---|---|
| ● Confirmed | | 40 | 19.8% (of total) |
| ● Probable | | 78 | 38.6% (of total) |
| ○ Possible | | 84 | 41.6% (of total) |

## Spotted Sandpiper
### *Actitis macularia*

A migratory breeder which is now relatively uncommon as a nesting bird in Connecticut. The species as a whole has an enormous wintering range, extending in the east from the coastlines of the south Atlantic and Gulf Coast states south through the Caribbean islands and Central America to northern Argentina and Chile.

**Habitat**—The Spotted Sandpiper nests in open country on the ground in dry, often sandy, well drained soils with a relatively thin cover of herbaceous vegetation; in the vicinity there is a pond or lake with a shoreline suitable for foraging (Oring et al. 1983).

**Atlas results**—Altogether, Spotted Sandpipers were recorded from a third of the blocks; however, the greatest number of records were in the possible category which, in this case, could rep-

resent wandering birds that were not breeding. This is a species that might readily be missed during block busting so the absence of records in some areas might be due simply to relatively less coverage. However, the species is genuinely absent as a breeder in the relatively heavily wooded blocks.

**Discussion**—Merriam (1877) considered the Spotted Sandpiper to be a common summer resident and mentioned finding a nest within eight feet of a railroad track where trains passed hourly. Sage et al. (1913) also considered the species to be a common in summer. During the period of decline of many shorebirds due to relatively unregulated

hunting in the latter part of the nine-teenth and early twentieth centuries, the Spotted Sandpiper was less affected than many species because of its compara-tively solitary habits (Bent 1929).

The subsequent decline of this species is associated with the general reduction in the amount of open field habitat in the state. The habitat used by this species for breeding is generally ephemeral and in many localities highly dependent on agricultural activities that may either create or destroy potential breeding areas. As Oring et al. (1983) pointed out, this species quickly colonizes new sites as old sites are lost due to plant succes-sion, flooding, or predation.

Among Connecticut birds, the Spotted Sandpiper has an exceptional social system, females fre-quently having more than one mate (poly-andry) as reported from Great Gull Island in Long Island Sound (Hays 1972) and elsewhere (e.g., Oring and Knudson 1972, Oring et al. 1983). The female Spotted Sandpiper takes the lead in territorial defense and courtship, whereas the males have major duties in incubating eggs and accompa-nying young (Oring and Lank 1982). Thus both nesting site and mating sys-tem of the Spotted Sandpiper are strik-ingly different from those of the American Woodcock, the only other species of the sandpiper family that now has a wide-spread breeding distribution in the state.

*George A. Clark, Jr.*

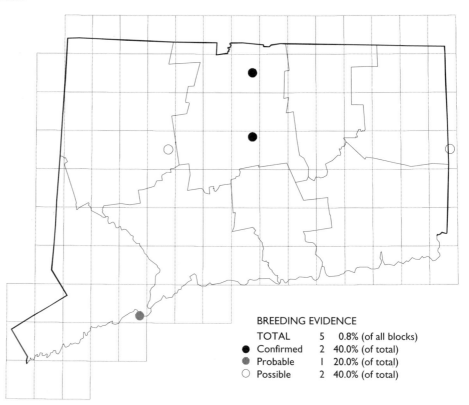

BREEDING EVIDENCE

| | | |
|---|---|---|
| TOTAL | 5 | 0.8% (of all blocks) |
| ● Confirmed | 2 | 40.0% (of total) |
| ▨ Probable | I | 20.0% (of total) |
| ○ Possible | 2 | 40.0% (of total) |

# Upland Sandpiper
## *Bartramia longicauda*

The Upland Sandpiper is now a rare breeder that is designated as Endangered in Connecticut. Occasional concentrations are seen during the fall migration from mid-July to late September; fewer spring migrants are seen from mid-April to mid-May. This species performs a long-distance migration to southern South America, wintering primarily in the drier grasslands of eastern Argentina and Uruguay; the extent of the winter range is still not well-defined (White 1988).

**Habitat**—This species is primarily a short-grass prairie nester. Dry and wet pastures, meadows, and hayfields once composed the bulk of the breeding habitat in southern New England. Extensive, open grassland of generally level topography is required; this habitat is scarce in Connecticut. Currently, the species is only found nesting in the extensive mowed grassland at airports. (Bradley International Airport, Windsor Locks, is the only locality currently.) Upland Sandpipers appear to favor areas with a few low perches, such as posts or shrubs. The grassland at airports is maintained at relatively short heights, in which the birds place their nest with over-arching grass blades that conceal the sunken nest.

**Atlas results**—Breeding was confirmed at Bradley International Airport, Windsor Locks, and Brainard Airport, Hartford. The species has since abandoned nesting at Brainard Airport. The nearby private Rentschler Airport in East Hartford was not surveyed. Although searches have been made of other airports, the results of these efforts have not been published.

**Discussion**—That this species once populated the short-grass prairie of interior North America in great numbers is well established; less certain, but of great interest, is the extent to which the Upland Sandpiper expanded its range eastward as forests were converted to farms. Although large populations may have existed in the Northeast prior to colonial times in areas of extensive natural prairie, such as at Hempstead Plains on western Long Island (Bull 1964), the increase in suitable habitat almost certainly allowed the species to become a common breeder in Connecticut during the 1800s (Merriam 1877). Whatever increases the species may have enjoyed at the hands of man were soon erased, however, through extensive shooting and, later, destruction of open habitats through building developments. In earlier times, breeding in Connecticut appears to have been concentrated nearer the coast rather than along the Connecticut River Valley (Bagg and Eliot 1937), although the species was found nesting at scattered interior sites such as Torrington, Litchfield, and Winchester (Sage et al. 1913). By early in this century, numbers were clearly dwindling, and breeding had become more sporadic, with nesting at Glastonbury in 1948, Suffield in 1959, and Fairfield 1966 (Zeranski and Baptist 1990). More recently nesting was known from Brainard Airport, Hartford and at Windsor Locks (above). The few pairs at Hartford last nested in 1989. Small concentrations of Upland Sandpipers (4–12) have been seen regularly at Sikorsky Airport in Stratford during late summer and fall; this site is important to migrant Upland Sandpipers and could support breeding.

*Louis R. Bevier*

137

## Common Snipe
### *Gallinago gallinago*

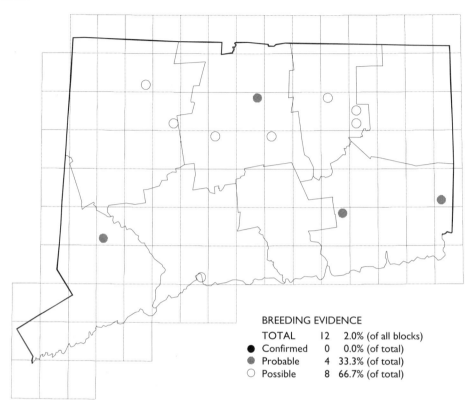

BREEDING EVIDENCE

| | TOTAL | 12 | 2.0% (of all blocks) |
|---|---|---|---|
| ● | Confirmed | 0 | 0.0% (of total) |
| ● | Probable | 4 | 33.3% (of total) |
| ○ | Possible | 8 | 66.7% (of total) |

Only one historical breeding record in the state exists for this species, and there are no recent confirmed records. Common Snipe nesting in northeastern North America winter principally from the latitude of the mid-Atlantic states south through Central America and the West Indies into northern South America (Tuck 1972). Small numbers winter in Connecticut.

**Habitat**—Craig (1978) reported the occurrence of summer birds in Connecticut in a slightly brackish grassy marsh and in a tussock marsh through which flowed a small stream heavily overgrown with smartweeds. More generally, the species breeds in open areas of marshes, bogs, and meadows (Craig 1978, Eaton *in* Andrle and Carroll 1988). Nests are usually situated in or near tall cover such as alder or grass (Eaton *in* Andrle and Carroll 1988).

**Atlas results**—During the atlas there were a number of reports of displaying snipe in the month of May, but none of these can be taken as definitely indicating breeding in the state. The most common territorial display, often termed "winnowing," occurs sporadically at any time of year, although it is most intense and continuous on the breeding grounds (Tuck 1972). A pair was found at Tolland Marsh in Tolland twice in early June of 1983, but it is unknown whether breeding occurred.

**Discussion**—The only confirmed nesting of the species in Connecticut was recorded by Sage and Coe on 13 May 1874 at Portland, where they found an adult on a nest with three eggs (Sage et al. 1913). Craig (1978) listed six areas of the state in which breeding was suspected to have occurred since 1950, and he indicated the presence of summering birds at unspecified locations in the state. Confirming this species is potentially difficult. Most observers do not enter the wet areas where nests are most likely to be discovered. Once the eggs hatch, the 'winnowing' display is rarely given (Eaton *in* Andrle and Carroll 1988), and the snipe become difficult to locate. Partially grown young, if they can be found and identified, would provide a confirmation of breeding, but fully grown juveniles are very difficult to distinguish from adults (Hayman et al. 1986). By August juveniles generally associate with other young rather than with adults (Tuck 1972) so that a direct comparison of young and adults may not then be possible in the field. As discussed above, the evidence for breeding of this species in Connecticut in recent years is equivocal. Regardless of whether breeding is occurring, Connecticut lies towards the southern limit of the breeding range for the species. As pointed out by Tuck (1972), throughout much of the regular breeding range of this species, the underlying soil is highly organic and the wet areas tend to dry out in late July. The birds then move into other habitats and become more gregarious. Speculatively, it may be suggested that more southern marshes might be unfavorable for breeding because they lack the kind of organic soils favored by these birds; the southern soils perhaps lack sufficient quantities of those animal foods obtained by probing with the long bill.

*George A. Clark, Jr.*

# American Woodcock
*Scolopax minor*

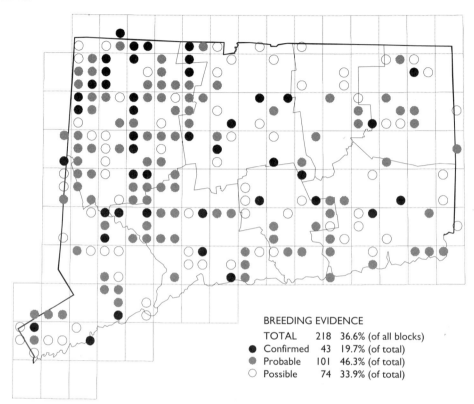

BREEDING EVIDENCE

| | TOTAL | 218 | 36.6% (of all blocks) |
|---|---|---|---|
| ● | Confirmed | 43 | 19.7% (of total) |
| ● | Probable | 101 | 46.3% (of total) |
| ○ | Possible | 74 | 33.9% (of total) |

This species is a fairly numerous migratory breeder in Connecticut, apparently wintering principally in the southeastern Atlantic seaboard states (Owen 1977). The display flight of the American Woodcock is arguably the most spectacular courtship among Connecticut's birds.

**Habitat**—This species commonly nests in low immature patches of hardwoods with a moist soil and near a field edge. However, occasionally nests are situated in a field of herbaceous vegetation not far from the edge of such a woods. Also important for this species is a display ground, commonly a patch or field of ragged grasses growing in a well drained soil. A stream or wet area is typically nearby. Earthworms, which are the major food, are sought, often by probing, in moist soil under the immature woodlands

(Hudgins et al. 1985). The American Woodcock is one of two Connecticut breeding species with a high dependency on earthworms; the other species, the American Robin, seeks worms through a more limited part of the year and generally in a habitat very different from that used by woodcock. Suitable sites with the necessary features for breeding by woodcock may

occur along the edges of fields or streams or in gaps in relatively continuous forest. During spring migration, displaying woodcock are widespread in Connecticut, even in suburban areas, but many of these birds eventually move away from areas near human residences from which dogs or cats traverse habitat seemingly otherwise suitable for woodcock breeding.

**Atlas results**—Woodcock were found in more than a third of all blocks, but confirmed as breeders in far fewer. The nests and young are often difficult to find so the number of confirmations is actually impressive. Because the birds breed substantially earlier than most species in the state and before the time of the most survey activity for the atlas, it seems likely that the birds could have been missed in many of the areas from which they were not reported including a number of blocks in eastern Connecticut where block busting was necessarily widely used. However, the absence of records from many of the more highly settled areas of the state is probably accurate.

**Discussion**—Merriam (1877) ranked the species as common through the summer, but Sage et al. (1913) noted a decrease in the number of breeding birds. Mendall and Aldous (1943) reported the woodcock to be a fairly common summer resident in scattered localities in Connecticut. Between the mid-1960s and the mid-1970s there was a substantial increase in the number of birds reported as harvested over the entire range within which the species is hunted (Owen 1977). In recent decades there has been a decrease in suitable habitat for breeding throughout much of the range, including Connecticut (Owen 1977). The change from a largely agricultural landscape to the extensive human settlement and more mature forests of the present has been to the detriment of breeding woodcock. It is remarkable that a bird so specialized as the American Woodcock has such a widespread distribution. One challenge for future conservation efforts will be to try to maintain a substantial breeding population of this species in the state.

*George A. Clark, Jr.*

## Laughing Gull
### *Larus atricilla*

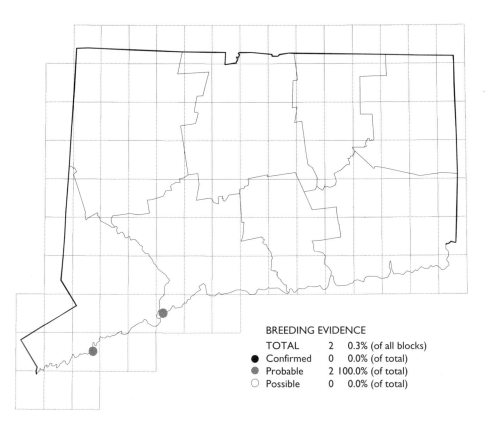

BREEDING EVIDENCE

| | TOTAL | 2 | 0.3% (of all blocks) |
|---|---|---|---|
| ● | Confirmed | 0 | 0.0% (of total) |
| ◓ | Probable | 2 | 100.0% (of total) |
| ○ | Possible | 0 | 0.0% (of total) |

The Laughing Gull is a migratory species that breeds principally to the south of Connecticut, to northern South America, and in scattered colonies to the north in Massachusetts and Maine. There is no evidence of breeding in this state, but it is regular here in summer. It has bred in that part of its range along the Atlantic Ocean as far north as Nova Scotia (last in 1962) and on Machias Seal Island in southern New Brunswick (last in 1981) (AOU 1983, Erskine 1992). In the survey for the New York state breeding bird atlas, the only active colony was at Jamaica Bay on Long Island (Lent *in* Andrle and Carroll 1988). Some birds from the Northeast could conceivably winter as far south as Central America (Nisbet 1971).

**Habitat**—Laughing Gulls nest both in salt marshes and in drier habitats such as sandy beaches (Lent *in* Andrle and Carroll 1988).

**Atlas results**—The species was present in summer for at least a week in two coastal blocks.

**Discussion**—Breeding of Laughing Gulls has never been reported from Connecticut, but because the state lies within the breeding range of the species and birds have frequently been seen along the coast in summer, there remains a possibility that the species might nest in Connecticut. Linsley

(1843) reported the occurrence of the species at Stonington. Merriam (1877) suggested the possibility that some might breed on islands in Long Island Sound, but no evidence has been found to support his speculation. Sage et al. (1913) indicated that the bird was never common in Connecticut and knew of apparently only two individuals present since the time of Merriam's report. Subsequently in the twentieth century, numbers of sightings along the coast increased (Zeranski and Baptist 1990). In recent decades the rapid southward expansion of the range of breeding of the Herring Gull has, through direct and indirect kinds of competition, often adversely affected the nesting of Laughing Gulls in New Jersey and elsewhere along the Atlantic coast (e.g., Burger and Shister 1978, Burger 1979). It thus seems unlikely that Laughing Gulls could establish themselves within a breeding colony of Herring Gulls in Connecticut. Furthermore, establishment of a new breeding area may be difficult because of the colonial nesting; birds are likely to prefer to nest in traditional areas where breeding has been successful in the past rather than attempt to nest in a new area.

*George A. Clark, Jr.*

## Herring Gull
### *Larus argentatus*

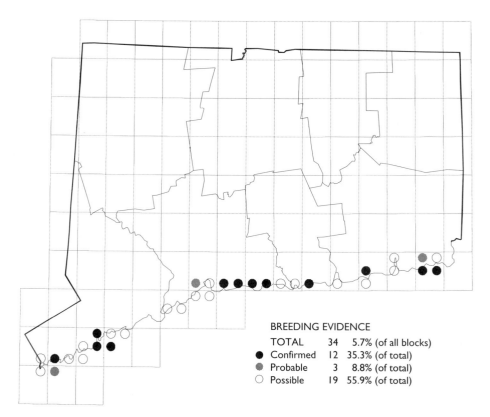

BREEDING EVIDENCE

| | TOTAL | 34 | 5.7% (of all blocks) |
|---|---|---|---|
| ● | Confirmed | 12 | 35.3% (of total) |
| ◉ | Probable | 3 | 8.8% (of total) |
| ○ | Possible | 19 | 55.9% (of total) |

The Herring Gull is a common to abundant breeder that only began nesting in southern New England early in this century and now nests south to North Carolina. The breeding population in Connecticut has remained fairly constant over the last twenty years.

The species as a whole occurs around the Northern Hemisphere. Populations in western Europe and eastern North America have burgeoned this century. The subspecies breeding in North America is *L. a. smithsonianus.*

**Habitat**—As a nesting species, the Herring Gull is confined mainly to offshore islands with occasional nesting in salt marshes. Both rocky and heavily vegetated islands are used with nests built on bare rock, sand, or even well back in the vegetation with a direct and well beaten path to the edge.

**Atlas results**—This species has been regularly censused since 1977, so there is a second yardstick for judging the atlas results. As with other species nesting and roosting on rocky islands, it is difficult to differentiate nesting from resting without a close check. Thus, all of the possible nestings on the map, with one exception, were likely not used during the atlas period. However, isolated occurrences of individual nests in salt marshes or other unlikely situations are found in some years. The possible nesting reported at the mouth of the Thames River is a colony on White Rock in New London harbor. As the map clearly shows, nesting is confined to areas where there are offshore islands. The bulk of the population is in the Norwalk Islands, although the largest number of sites are in the Thimble Islands, Branford. At the eastern end of the state, the Connecticut colonies are vastly out-numbered by the nearby colonies on Fisher's Island, New York, and Sandy Point, Rhode Island.

**Discussion**—Evidently the Herring Gull was never a breeder in Long Island Sound until the 1930s (Bull 1974). The first reported nesting in Connecticut was in 1942 with a rapid and dramatic increase since then. The species now nests on almost every unoccupied offshore rock and island with a total state population of about 3,000 pairs. This increase has been attributed to the greater availability of food at landfills. With changing landfill practices now, it will be interesting to see if numbers remain high.

Herring Gulls are present in Connecticut year-round, with numbers greatly augmented by northern popula-tions in winter. The degree to which Connecticut breeders move south is unknown. Herring Gulls winter south in North America to Panama.

Very few of the islands provide a con-stant environment, and the population regularly shifts from one island to another under human pres-sure, encroaching vegetation, or, more recently, competition with cormorants. Even a moderate egg removal program results in considerable population reduction, and a more vigorous effort results in complete abandonment of the island. A comparison with censuses of cor-morants from 1977 to present shows a decline in gull populations at given islands several years before the cor-

morants actually built nests. In some cases the Herring Gulls are quickly pushed off the island by the cor-morants, and in others the process is rather prolonged.

*Fred C. Sibley*

# Great Black-backed Gull
## *Larus marinus*

The Great Black-backed Gull is a fairly common resident breeder. This species began nesting in the state only in the 1950s and is apparently still expanding its range southward. The species breeds on both sides of the North Atlantic.

**Habitat**—Nesting is restricted to offshore islands and, rarely, salt marshes and protected coastal mainland sites. During the summer, Great Black-backed Gulls rarely venture far inland; only occasional immature birds are found at inland reservoirs and along rivers. Birds frequently feed at landfills outside of the breeding season.

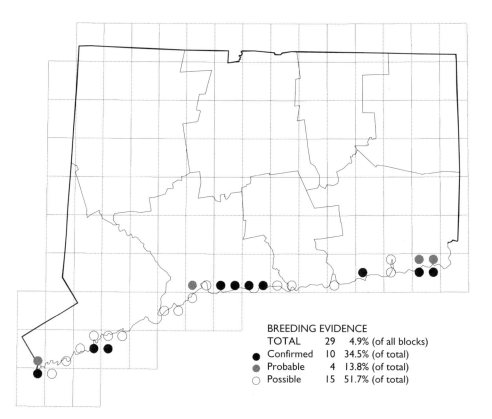

BREEDING EVIDENCE
| | | |
|---|---|---|
| TOTAL | 29 | 4.9% (of all blocks) |
| ● Confirmed | 10 | 34.5% (of total) |
| ◉ Probable | 4 | 13.8% (of total) |
| ○ Possible | 15 | 51.7% (of total) |

**Atlas results**—This species has been censused very completely every three years since 1977 (Sibley and Bull 1990), and these figures are a good check on the accuracy of the atlas results. The species only occasionally nests on the mainland (as at Millstone Neck); a boat is usually needed to verify nesting. Some possible and probable sites in New Haven and Greenwich were found later not to have breeding birds; other sites were difficult to access. Nesting obviously concentrates where there are offshore islands, e.g., the Mystic area, the Thimble Islands, and the Norwalk Islands.

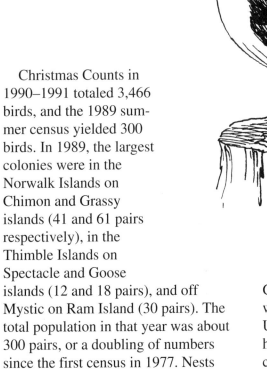

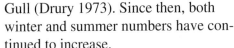

**Discussion**—This species was a regular but rare winter visitor to Long Island Sound until the early part of this century, when the southernmost breeding colonies were in Nova Scotia. An increase in winter numbers as well as summer occurrences started in the 1920s, and by the 1930s, nesting birds had colonized Massachusetts (Drury 1973). Breeding reached Long Island in the 1940s, and the first nesting in Connecticut was during the 1950s (Meade *in* Andrle and Carroll 1988, Zeranski and Baptist 1990). The 1930s through the 1960s was a period of tremendous population growth in New England for the Great Black-backed Gull (Drury 1973). Since then, both winter and summer numbers have continued to increase.

Christmas Counts in 1990–1991 totaled 3,466 birds, and the 1989 summer census yielded 300 birds. In 1989, the largest colonies were in the Norwalk Islands on Chimon and Grassy islands (41 and 61 pairs respectively), in the Thimble Islands on Spectacle and Goose islands (12 and 18 pairs), and off Mystic on Ram Island (30 pairs). The total population in that year was about 300 pairs, or a doubling of numbers since the first census in 1977. Nests were found on 36 islands, 10 of these having only a single pair of birds. The species is usually found with Herring Gulls although many of the single pairs were the only gulls on the island. Unlike the Herring Gull, this species has continued to nest in the presence of cormorant colonies and a few pairs seem to select tern colonies as nesting sites.

*Fred C. Sibley*

147

## Roseate Tern
### *Sterna dougallii*

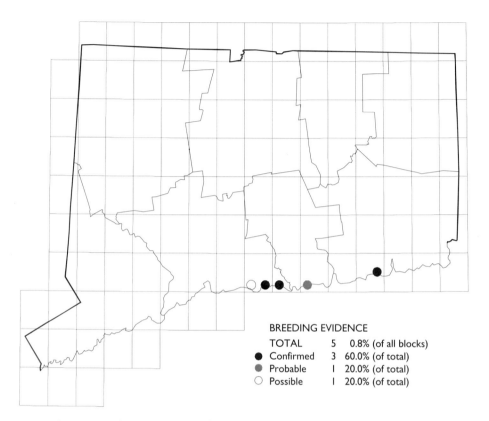

BREEDING EVIDENCE

| | TOTAL | 5 | 0.8% (of all blocks) |
|---|---|---|---|
| ● | Confirmed | 3 | 60.0% (of total) |
| ● | Probable | I | 20.0% (of total) |
| ○ | Possible | I | 20.0% (of total) |

This state and federally endangered species is a migratory breeder with between 3,000 and 3,200 pairs nesting in coastal northeastern North America from Long Island, New York, to southern Nova Scotia (Nisbet 1980). About 6% of this population nests at Falkner Island, 5 km south of Guilford (USFWS 1989). In late summer, juveniles and pre-migratory adults are seen frequently in small numbers at Milford Point, but most move quickly to other staging areas off eastern Long Island, Cape Cod, and southern Maine (Nisbet 1984; Spendelow et al., unpubl. data). Roseate Terns migrate mainly offshore.

The main wintering grounds for populations breeding in the Northeast are in northern coastal South America from Colombia to eastern Brazil, with most winter recoveries from Guyana (Nisbet 1984). Comparatively few healthy birds are actually seen on the wintering grounds, suggesting most birds feed well offshore during the day and return to land only to roost at night. Adults begin returning to the northeastern breeding colonies as early as late April.

**Habitat**—Roseate Terns in northeastern North America almost invariably nest with Common Terns, usually on islands less than 5 ha in area. Nesting habitat varies considerably from site to site (Nisbet 1981); throughout most of its range, however, the Roseate Tern nests in sheltered sites under vegetation, debris, or rocks (Gochfeld and Burger 1987, Burger and Gochfeld 1988, Nisbet 1989). At Falkner Island such sites are scarce and most pairs nest in man-modified sites inside boxes or half-buried tires; the pairs that use these modified sites are more successful than those using naturally-occurring sites on this island (Spendelow 1982, 1991a). Compared to the Common Tern, the Roseate Tern has a narrower range of preferred foraging habitat more dependent on physical features than on the presence of predatory fish (Safina 1990a, 1990b).

**Atlas results**—In Connecticut, most Roseate Terns breed on Falkner Island, a part of the Stewart B. McKinney NWR, where they are protected and managed by the research staff of the Falkner Island Tern Project. A few pairs nest irregularly at the following localities: Shore Rock, New London; Waterford Island, Waterford; Duck Island, Westbrook; Tuxis Island, Madison; and the Thimble Islands, Branford.

**Discussion**—Once described as numerous, the breeding population of Roseate Terns in the Northeast declined severely due to plume hunting in the 1870s and 1880s, increased rapidly, following protection, to a peak of about 8,500 pairs in the 1930s, and declined again to a minimum of about 2,500 pairs in

the late 1970s (Nisbet 1980). In 1987, the USFWS declared this population endangered. Historical data on birds nesting in the Guilford area were given in Mackenzie (1961), and population estimates for Connecticut from 1900 to 1982 were given by Spendelow in Kress et al. (1983). The breeding population at Falkner Island, the third largest colony in this region, remained fairly stable at about 175 pairs from 1986 to 1991 (Spendelow, unpubl. data); research suggests, however, that nesting at Falkner Island is maintained by immigration from Massachusetts and New York (Spendelow 1991b). The relatively low reproductive success and irregular use of other colony sites in Connecticut probably is due to a com-

bination of several factors including: lack of suitable nesting habitat; predation by gulls, night-herons, rats, ants, etc.; human disturbance; and possibly a lack of suitable nearby foraging areas. Safina et al. (1988) discussed evidence for prey limitation of both Common and Roseate tern reproduction at a colony in New York, and Safina (1990b) also showed that the foraging activity of predatory bluefish lowers the foraging success for Roseate Terns more than for Common Terns.

*Jeffrey A. Spendelow*

## Common Tern
*Sterna hirundo*

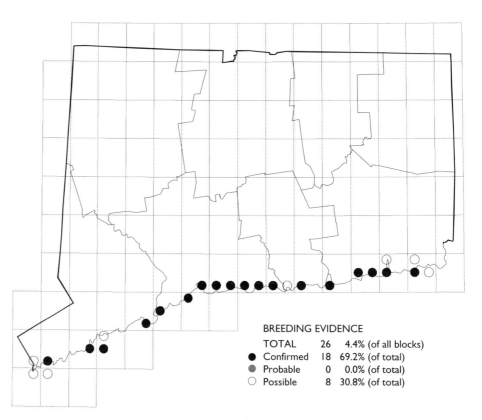

BREEDING EVIDENCE

| | TOTAL | 26 | 4.4% (of all blocks) |
|---|---|---|---|
| ● | Confirmed | 18 | 69.2% (of total) |
| ◉ | Probable | 0 | 0.0% (of total) |
| ○ | Possible | 8 | 30.8% (of total) |

This widespread migratory breeder has undergone a dramatic regional population increase during the 1980s and now nests, in at least small numbers, in virtually every coastal atlas block in Connecticut; it is, however, designated as a Species of Special Concern here. The largest breeding colony in the state is at Falkner Island, 5 km south of Guilford. Large numbers of young and adults can be seen during postbreeding dispersal from August to September at premigratory staging areas at West Haven and Milford Point. The wintering range of birds breeding in the Long Island Sound region stretches from the southern U.S. to coastal South America as far south as Peru on the Pacific coast and southern Brazil on the Atlantic coast (Austin 1953; Spendelow et al., unpubl. data); a few birds may follow large rivers into interior South America (DiCostanzo 1978).

**Habitat**—Common Terns in northeastern North America nest in various habitats on offshore islands or mainland beaches (Spendelow and Patton 1988). In Connecticut and New York, they use the same types of sandy, gravelly, rocky, and sparsely vegetated habitats as Roseate Terns but prefer open and exposed sites where both species nest together (Cooper et al. 1970, Hays 1975, Spendelow 1982, Gochfeld and Burger 1987). They also are relatively more successful when nesting at salt marsh sites (Buckley and Buckley 1982). Compared to Roseate Terns, Common Terns forage over a greater variety of habitats, forage more successfully over predatory bluefish, and are more likely to feed over deeper water and to form large flocks (Safina

1990a, 1990b). Common Terns also are more likely to feed near the mainland, and some pairs defend shoreline territories that may be more than 10 km from their breeding colony (Nisbet 1983).

**Atlas results**—Common Terns were confirmed nesting at 18 colony sites and may have nested at another 8 sites along the Connecticut coast. As in the late 1970s and the early 1980s, the greatest concentration of both colony sites and breeding birds is in the central coastal sections of the state in New Haven County, although an increasing number of sites are used in the western part of Long Island Sound. A combination of factors might account for the population increase throughout the 1980s including: (a) protection of terns from competition, predation, and disturbance by gulls and humans at several colony sites, especially Falkner Island; and (b) a greater capability, compared to the Roseate Tern, to colonize new sites and increase productivity in response to increases in abundance and/or availability of small fish.

**Discussion**—Once described as abundant, the northeastern breeding population of Common Terns was severely reduced by plume hunting in the late 1800s, but increased in the early 1900s following the passage of protective legislation. By the early 1970s the population had again decreased due, in part, to competition for colony sites and predation by expanding gull populations, and to disturbance from increased human activity in or near the colony sites (see "Summary and Overview" by Nisbet in Kress et al. 1983). Data on the historical status of Common Terns before the 1970s in Connecticut were summarized by Zeranski and Baptist (1990), and population estimates from 1900 to 1982 were summarized by Spendelow in Kress et al. (1983). Sibley and Schwartz (1985) estimated a 1983 statewide population of 1,836 breeding pairs at 17 colony sites; the 1989 census estimated 3,923 pairs at 16 colony sites (Bull, unpubl. data). Since 1978, the largest colony in the state, at Falkner Island, increased from about 1,500 to more than 4,000 breeding pairs in 1991 (Spendelow, unpubl. data).

*Jeffrey A. Spendelow*

## Least Tern
### *Sterna antillarum*

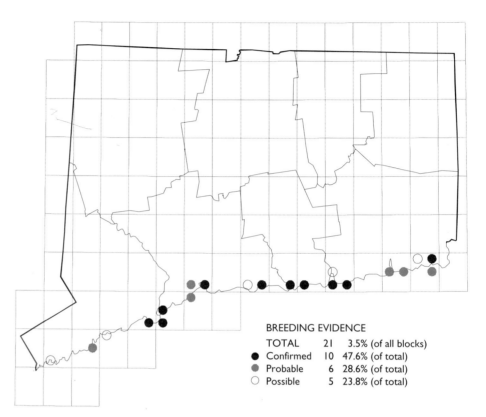

BREEDING EVIDENCE

| | TOTAL | 21 | 3.5% (of all blocks) |
|---|---|---|---|
| ● | Confirmed | 10 | 47.6% (of total) |
| ● | Probable | 6 | 28.6% (of total) |
| ○ | Possible | 5 | 23.8% (of total) |

The Least Tern is an uncommon migratory breeder in Connecticut. Although it is fairly numerous, breeding sites are quite limited here and often heavily used by people. Birds return to the state beginning in early May and nest by late May. Following a staging period in late summer when immatures and adults associate in moderate-sized flocks at the larger coastal estuaries, especially Milford Point, they migrate south, usually by early September. A late report for 10–11 October 1894 inland at Eastford (C. M. Jones 1931; date and locale in error in Manter 1975), is in fact a Black Tern (specimen, Univ. of Iowa).

Atlantic coast populations (nominate *antillarum*) are listed as Threatened by USFWS and have that status here. Breeders in the Northeast winter in the Caribbean and coastal northern and eastern South America (AOU 1983).

**Habitat**—This is strictly a coastal bird never found far from the salt water. Nesting colonies are on open sandy beaches. Unlike other terns nesting in Connecticut, this species tends to select mainland sites rather than isolated nearshore islands and tends to form small colonies. Least Terns typically use beaches that are washed over by winter storms, which maintain open sandy conditions. This is at odds with attempts to manage breeding colonies at a few permanent sites, when historically birds would shift from one beach to another depending on the conditions. Adults mainly forage nearshore over Long Island Sound, whereas fledglings require protected water near the colony.

**Atlas results**—This species receives annual monitoring by state DEP personnel; the confirmed reports from Guilford and Stonington were not noted in annual reports to DEP during the years of the atlas, and some of the probable and possible blocks were in areas not known to be used for nesting. During the atlas, most birds nested in only a few colonies, with over 1,000 at Sandy Point, West Haven, being the largest. Other important colonies were at Long Beach, Stratford, and Milford Point, Milford. All these areas receive heavy use from bathers and fishermen.

**Discussion**—The Least Tern was nearly extirpated by market hunting during the late 1800s, and our knowledge of its status prior to that time is fragmentary. It was probably a regular migrant and summer visitor here since the species was abundant as a breeder in southeastern Massachusetts during the early 1800s (Nisbet 1973). Birds from colonies outside the state were seen in late summer, but for a number of years in the early 1900s very few were reported. Protection began in 1913, and numbers gradually increased thereafter,

with the first nest on Long Island since 1882 found in 1926 (Bull 1964). The first *known* nesting in Connecticut was in 1960 at Sherwood Island, Westport (Bull 1964) and at Guilford in 1961 (Mackenzie 1961). By 1977, a few hundred pairs were in the state, and between 1983 and 1986, the population rose to 1,500 pairs. These birds were evidently from the north shore of Long Island since 90% of banded birds captured came from there (Sibley and Schwartz, unpubl. data). After 1986, the population declined somewhat and has stabilized at 750–850 pairs.

Major reproductive failures have been caused by severe weather and predation by Black-crowned Night-Heron. A late June high storm tide coupled with a few cold days killed half the young at Sandy Point in 1986 and washed away most nests at Long Beach. Night-Heron predation at Menunketesuck Island, Westbrook, has reduced fledging success to under 10%, while similar predation at Sandy Point has stopped all renesting attempts.

In 1989, Least Terns nested on Cockenoe Island in the Norwalk group. This was the first known nesting away from the mainland. In other states, the terns may use dredge spoil islands, and creation of habitat for the terns would probably be beneficial.

*Fred C. Sibley*

## Black Skimmer
*Rynchops niger*

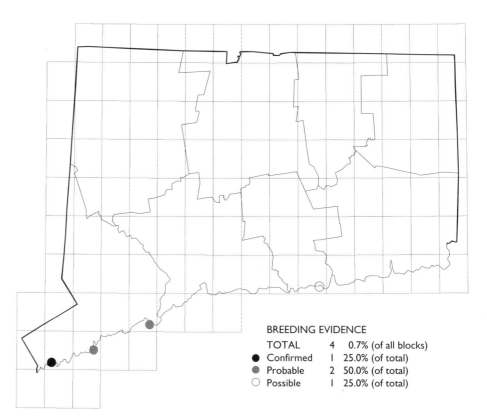

BREEDING EVIDENCE

| | | |
|---|---|---|
| TOTAL | 4 | 0.7% (of all blocks) |
| ● Confirmed | 1 | 25.0% (of total) |
| ◉ Probable | 2 | 50.0% (of total) |
| ○ Possible | 1 | 25.0% (of total) |

A migratory species that first nested in Connecticut during the atlas survey. This is the only nesting attempt by this species here. Individuals of the subspecies *R. n. niger* breeding in eastern North America presumably winter principally from Florida and the northern shores of the Gulf of Mexico south to the northern Caribbean islands and Nicaragua (AOU 1957). Burger and Gochfeld (1990) have published a major study of the ecology and behavior of this species.

**Habitat**—The one locality in which a single nesting was attempted in Connecticut was on a sandy shoal (Baptist 1982). More generally, the very simple nests of this species are typically placed on open, fairly level, stretches of sand with relatively little vegetation growing nearby (Peterson *in* Andrle and Carroll 1988; pers. obs.).

**Atlas results**—This section is largely based on Baptist's (1982) article, which may be consulted for additional details. On 20 June 1983 Charles Pettengill watched two skimmers sitting on a sandy shoal between two granite outcrops on Bluff Island in Cos Cob Harbor, Greenwich. Continuing presence of the birds led to a suspicion that nesting might be occurring, and this was confirmed on 14 July, when John Bova and George Simpson found and photographed three eggs in the nest. Unfortunately, the nest and eggs were washed away by a high tide on 18 July. Baptist (1982) published a photograph of that nest. There was no evidence for breeding in other blocks in which skimmers were observed during the atlas survey.

**Discussion**—The species was first recorded from the state in 1883 (Sage et al. 1913). One additional occurrence in Connecticut during the nineteenth century came in 1894. The species has become much more common in the northeastern states during the twentieth century (Stone 1937, Peterson *in* Andrle and Carroll 1988). Although nesting has been suspected in Connecticut on several occasions (Zeranski and Baptist 1990), only once has breeding been confirmed. For successful breeding Black Skimmers require sandy coastal areas that are free of predators, tidal flooding, and human disturbance. Such conditions are met on nearby Long Island in New York state (Peterson *in* Andrle and Carroll 1988), but Connecticut has very little area that meets all these criteria, and it is therefore not anticipated that skimmers will become established as regular breeders in the state. It is conceivable that appropriate habitat might be artificially created and maintained, but this would involve considerable expense and effort. In addition to the requirements for the nesting area, it is also necessary that there be a sufficient supply of small fishes that can be taken from the surface of saline waters.

*George A. Clark, Jr.*

## Rock Dove
*Columba livia*

The Rock Dove, commonly called the pigeon, is a widespread resident breeder in Connecticut, found regularly in urban and some suburban areas, and those farming areas having livestock. Many areas of suitable habitat have local flocks numbering from dozens to hundreds.

**Habitat**—This species generally requires nest sites with a ledge or overhang of some kind providing an overhead shield for the nest. Urban and industrial architecture having nooks, crannies, and ductwork is often suitable. Around farms where livestock are kept, barns and silos provide suitable ledges for nesting. Road and railway bridges are also commonly used. Rock Doves prefer nest sites well off the ground where risk of predation is less (Savard and Falls 1981). Woodland areas ordinarily lack suitable nest sites, and Rock Doves tend to avoid wooded habitats. In addition to sites for nesting, habitat for Rock Doves must include sufficient grain or seeds, generally provided either directly or indirectly by people. Food discarded by people is regularly used, and Rock Doves can be readily attracted by handouts of bread or grain. Rock Doves in farming areas consume grain spread during feeding of livestock and seeds in the manure.

**Atlas results**—The map indicates a strong association of the Rock Dove with urban areas and with sites where livestock are kept. The Rock Dove is a rather conspicuous species and thus relatively easy to find, and yet it was not found in some predominantly wooded blocks that were intensively surveyed.

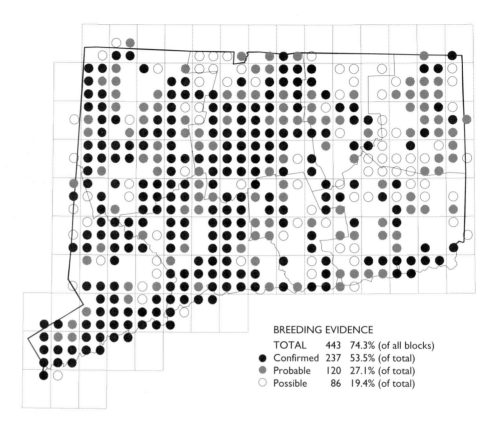

BREEDING EVIDENCE

| | TOTAL | 443 | 74.3% (of all blocks) |
|---|---|---|---|
| ● | Confirmed | 237 | 53.5% (of total) |
| ● | Probable | 120 | 27.1% (of total) |
| ○ | Possible | 86 | 19.4% (of total) |

**Discussion**—Rock Doves were apparently first introduced into eastern North America in the 1600s (Schorger 1952), and feral domestic birds have long been established in Connecticut. Linsley (1843) noted the presence of this species in Connecticut but did not report on either its distribution or abundance. Merriam (1877), in commenting on Linsley's work, listed the Rock Dove as one of six species "which scarcely deserve to be mentioned among our native birds." The widespread failure of observers to include the Rock Dove in lists of wild birds was continued by Sage et al. (1913), who failed to place the Rock Dove even in their list of introduced species. This tradition of not reporting Rock Doves has contributed to a very incomplete historic picture of this species in the state. In its current distribution, the Rock Dove, like the European Starling and House Sparrow, shows a strong association with people.

Rock Doves have both human admirers, who often deliberately feed the birds, and detractors, who view pigeons as creating excessive messiness, especially by their droppings. Long term and humane solution of problems caused by Rock Doves in urban or industrial settings can often be achieved in part through architectural design and by placing physical barriers such as screenings that prevent Rock Doves from entering places where their presence is unwanted. It appears that Rock Doves cannot be eliminated over

the long term from particular localities by trapping or killing because wandering birds will eventually replace ones that are removed. Rock Doves that fail to perform properly as racing pigeons are one source for addition of birds to the feral populations. Among the flocks of feral Rock Doves in Connecticut such drop-outs from racing can be recognized by their special leg bands. It is apparently unknown whether such drop-out racing pigeons successfully breed in the wild.

*George A. Clark, Jr.*

## Mourning Dove
*Zenaida macroura*

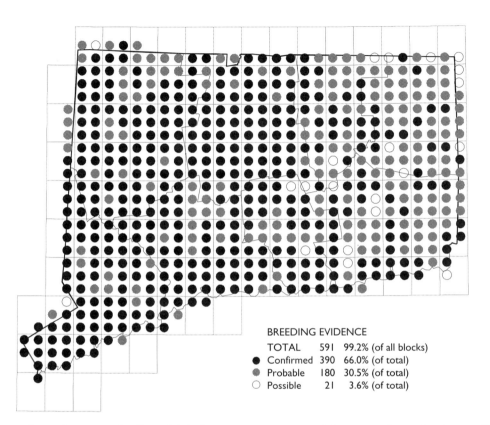

BREEDING EVIDENCE

| | TOTAL | 591 | 99.2% (of all blocks) |
|---|---|---|---|
| ● | Confirmed | 390 | 66.0% (of total) |
| ● | Probable | 180 | 30.5% (of total) |
| ○ | Possible | 21 | 3.6% (of total) |

The Mourning Dove breeds commonly in Connecticut, where most of the breeding population arrives in March and departs in October. The greatest numbers are observed during the peak migration periods of these same months in fall and spring. The familiar soft cooing from early morning through the evening signals the establishment of a Mourning Dove territory in the neighborhood. The Mourning Dove is a widespread breeder across North America from southern Canada to southern Mexico and, sparingly, to western Panama; northern populations are migratory, moving well south in winter. Breeding populations in Connecticut are referable to the subspecies *carolinensis*, which breeds in eastern North America west to the natural limits of the prairie grassland. This subspecies is significantly darker and slightly shorter-billed than the western subspecies, *marginella*, which does stray to the Atlantic seaboard in migration (Aldrich and Duvall 1958).

**Habitat**—This species nests in open woodland, agricultural areas, parks, open space, and tree-lined streets of cities and suburbs. The male brings twigs to the female who builds a loose saucer-shaped platform of a nest in a tree crotch or on a branch, stump, fence post, rock outcrop, or in a vacated songbird nest. There are two or more broods per season, each typically with two eggs. The sexes share incubation, which lasts about two weeks; the young spend about two weeks in the nest before fledging. Nestlings are first fed pigeon milk produced in the crop by both parents and then later fed seeds.

The Mourning Dove feeds on the ground in fields, agricultural areas, along roadsides, and other open areas. Mourning Doves feed chiefly on the seeds of grasses and weeds but also consume some insects.

**Atlas results**—The atlas revealed that Mourning Doves are widely distributed throughout the state. The success of this species in Connecticut and elsewhere in its range may be at least partly attributed to its adaptability to human modified habitats, which provide a suitable mix of woodland (in the form of shade and other ornamental trees and shrubs for nesting and roosting), lawns, and fields for foraging.

**Discussion**—The Mourning Dove probably was common and widespread during the colonial era and was noted as abundant throughout southern New England before 1850 by Forbush (1927). Persistent hunting of this game species for food and for sport eventually caused widespread population declines, so that by the latter part of the 1800s, it was rare and accidental in Connecticut with only a few records

from the decades at the turn of this century (Merriam 1877, Sage et al. 1913). Following protection and control of hunting, the Mourning Dove population recovered and continued to increase from the 1930s onwards (Griscom and Snyder 1955). Numbers recorded on Christmas bird counts in the state show an almost continuous increase of the winter population in Connecticut during the past several decades; this increase corresponds with population increases in New England revealed by the North American Breeding Bird Surveys (Robbins et al. 1986). The Mourning Dove also has benefited from the increased availability of bird feeders, and at least part of the increase in wintering populations in the Northeast is due to the supplemental

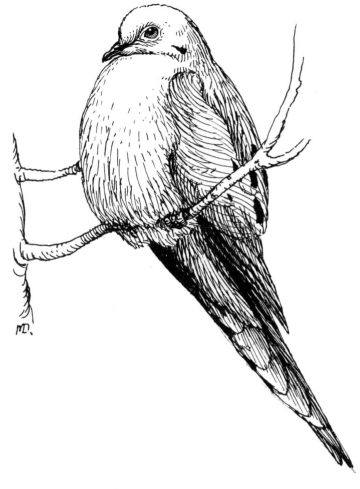

food provided at local bird feeding stations, where some birds remain all year rather than migrating.

*Dwight G. Smith and Arnold Devine*

## Black-billed Cuckoo
### *Coccyzus erythropthalmus*

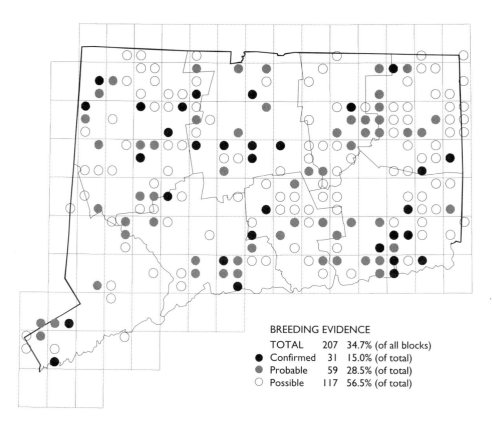

BREEDING EVIDENCE

| | TOTAL | 207 | 34.7% (of all blocks) |
|---|---|---|---|
| ● | Confirmed | 31 | 15.0% (of total) |
| ◉ | Probable | 59 | 28.5% (of total) |
| ○ | Possible | 117 | 56.5% (of total) |

This species is a migratory breeder with a widespread distribution in Connecticut. Its numbers in the state fluctuate greatly, being at a maximum during outbreaks of caterpillars. The species winters in tropical portions of South America. In recent decades the highest numbers of Black-billed Cuckoos have been recorded during outbreaks of the introduced gypsy moth. There are indications that the numbers of cuckoos increase during successive years in areas where gypsy moth outbreaks persist for several years.

**Habitat**—This species commonly nests in brushy or "edge" sites, often located on a boundary between woodlands and more open countryside. Bent (1940) summarized earlier information on nest sites including ones from Connecticut. Nests generally are placed not far off the ground, common-ly being under 6 feet in a shrub or tree, but have been found in Connecticut as high as 18 feet and above (H. W. Flint cited in Bendire 1895).

**Atlas results**—The Black-billed Cuckoo was reported from only slightly more than a third of the blocks, but those localities and those with confirmation of breeding are widely scattered over the state. Because the species is rather secretive, it might be overlooked on a short visit, as during block busting, and this might account for the absence of reports from some blocks. Another complicating factor is the presence of caterpillar outbreaks, such as occurred for the gypsy moth in parts of the state during the atlas survey; Black-billed Cuckoos would be much more likely to be found in the vicinity of such outbreaks. The map suggests that, in general, Black-billed Cuckoos are not found breeding in the more highly urbanized areas of the state.

**Discussion**—Black-billed Cuckoos have been present in the state since the earliest detailed reports on birds (Linsley 1843). Merriam (1877) considered this species to be common. Sage et al. (1913) noted a decline since the 1890s. Robbins et al. (1989b) reported a major decline for this species on Breeding Bird Surveys in North America from 1978 to 1987, following on an earlier decline in southern New England. Because this species remains relatively little studied, it is difficult to generalize about its characteristics. These cuckoos appear to have a strongly nomadic tendency (Sealey 1985), moving from site to site and favoring regions with numerous caterpillars. On the one hand, it seems possible that the regrowth of the forests in Connecticut might have adversely affected this species, in view of the tendency for it to nest in brushy or edge sites. On the

other hand, the regrowth of forests in this century has presumably increased the possibilities for caterpillar outbreaks that would favor the cuckoos. Although further detailed study focused on this species would be highly desirable, it is among the potentially more difficult species to study in the state in view of the frequently sparse populations. Interpretations of trends in the breeding numbers is difficult without comparing corresponding data on caterpillar trends during the same period.

*George A. Clark, Jr.*

## Yellow-billed Cuckoo
*Coccyzus americanus*

The Yellow-billed Cuckoo is a migratory breeder that winters in the warmer (northern) portions of South America. It is widespread in Connecticut but numerous apparently only in years of caterpillar outbreaks. It appears that Yellow-billed Cuckoos increase their clutch size in years of food abundance (Fleischer et al. 1985).

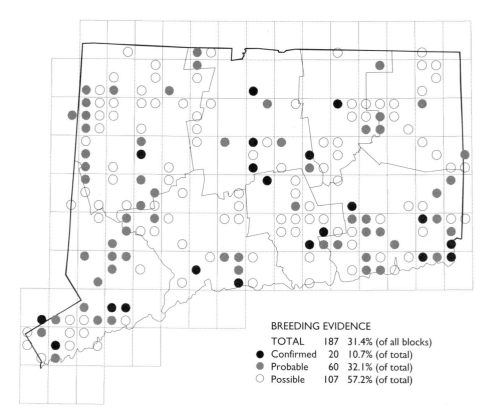

BREEDING EVIDENCE

| | TOTAL | 187 | 31.4% (of all blocks) |
|---|---|---|---|
| ● | Confirmed | 20 | 10.7% (of total) |
| ● | Probable | 60 | 32.1% (of total) |
| ○ | Possible | 107 | 57.2% (of total) |

**Habitat**—Yellow-billed Cuckoos most commonly occur in brushy or edge situations rather than in dense thick woods (Sage et al. 1913, Bent 1940). Nests are usually 5–10 feet off the ground, with 40 feet as a recorded maximum from Connecticut (Sage et al. 1913).

**Atlas results**—Yellow-billed Cuckoos were found throughout the state. Relative to the Black-billed Cuckoos, more Yellow-billed Cuckoos were found in the southwestern and western portions of the state. Although the frequencies of possible breeding, probable breeding, and confirmations of breeding were similar for the two species, the Black-billed was reported and confirmed slightly more often over the state as a whole.

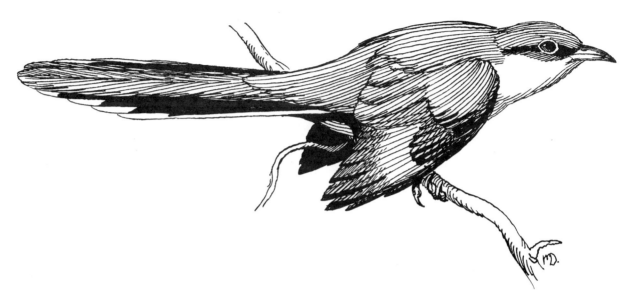

**Discussion**—Merriam (1877) and Sage et al. (1913) indicated that the species was common in Connecticut in the period of their surveys. Results of the roadside Breeding Bird Survey indicate that the species as a whole significantly increased in numbers from 1966 to 1978 and then significantly decreased between 1978 and 1987 (Robbins et al. 1989b). The Yellow-billed Cuckoo and the slightly smaller Black-billed Cuckoo appear to be remarkably similar in behavior and ecology both in Connecticut and elsewhere (see, for example, Hall 1983). Their vocalizations are sufficiently alike that considerable caution should be used in mapping their distributions by the use of calls only. The atlas results fit the general picture of the Yellow-billed Cuckoo as more southern in its breeding range (AOU 1983). Unlike most pairs of similar species of birds in Connecticut, it is not presently possible to suggest with confidence any clear difference in habitat or nest site between these species. It would be valuable to have a detailed comparative study of these species where they breed in the same area, but such a study might be difficult in view of the secretiveness of these species and the sharp fluctuations in their abundance.

*George A. Clark, Jr.*

163

# Barn Owl
*Tyto alba*

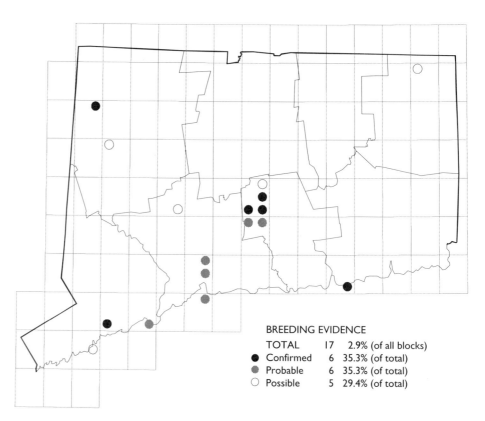

BREEDING EVIDENCE

| | TOTAL | 17 | 2.9% (of all blocks) |
|---|---|---|---|
| ● | Confirmed | 6 | 35.3% (of total) |
| ◉ | Probable | 6 | 35.3% (of total) |
| ○ | Possible | 5 | 29.4% (of total) |

The Barn Owl occurs throughout the tropical and temperate regions of the world. This distinctive tawny and white, "ghostlike" owl breeds widely across the United States. Susceptible to colder weather, this species shows a more localized distribution in the northern part of its range. Although widely distributed, the Barn Owl has declined in much of its range in the United States and was on the Blue List from 1972 to 1981; it was downgraded to Special Concern on this list in 1982 when the species had shown a positive response to nest box programs (Tate 1986). The Barn Owl is listed as Threatened in Connecticut.

**Habitat**—A remarkably adaptable species, the Barn Owl may utilize a variety of structures for nesting, often in close proximity to people. Known nest sites in Connecticut include church steeples, water tanks, barns, bridges, and buildings (both occupied and abandoned). Natural nest sites, such as tree hollows and caves, are found, but infrequently. Nest boxes may be used if placed near suitable foraging habitat, which includes extensive fields, marshes, or farm land that supports a rodent prey. Small mammals such as shrews, meadow mice, deer mice, house mice, and rats are favorite prey, but a variety of birds also are taken, especially in spring and summer. Nesting depends on prey availability and may occur from February through August. Normally, 5 to 7 eggs are laid in April or May, and young hatch in about a month. Several recent nests produced an average of 4.3 young (range 2–7 young; George Zepko pers. comm.).

**Atlas results**—The Barn Owl occurs in much of Connecticut, except the northeast; breeding evidence, however, was recorded in only 17 blocks, just 6 confirmed. Additional nest sites have been found in Fairfield in 1978, Milford in 1980 and 1987–1989, Norwalk in 1992, and Greenwich in 1992. Most of these records are from the densely populated central lowlands and near the coast. Most nesting has been near Milford or Middletown; these might represent groups of related individuals as it is known that fledged young will colonize adjacent areas. The absence of Barn Owls from the highlands illustrates their intolerance of extended periods of cold and snow cover. Why the Barn Owl is not found elsewhere in the central lowlands or along the coast is less obvious, as suitable habitat exists.

**Discussion**—The Barn Owl has apparently increased in Connecticut during this century, being one of the several southern species to enter the Northeast during this period. Sage et al. (1913) called it a very rare visitor from the south. They compiled records from previous authors, listing 13 records from 1841 to 1911, plus an additional number from New London County. Most of these reports were from 1891 onward and included the first nest found in Connecticut—at the same locality in Winchester in 1892 and 1893. Bagg and Eliot (1937) cited nesting at Cromwell and South Windsor in the 1920s. Craig (1980) lists several towns with nesting: Fairfield, 1932–1933; Westport, 1944; Windsor, 1950; North Haven, 1952; and New Haven, 1960s. Although gradually increasing during this period, Barn Owls apparently remained scarce. Mackenzie (1961) listed only three recent sightings for Guilford between 1948 and 1958.

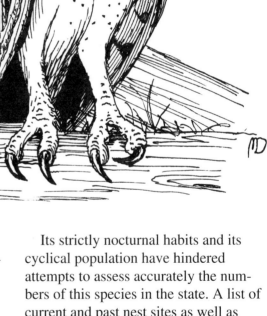

Its strictly nocturnal habits and its cyclical population have hindered attempts to assess accurately the numbers of this species in the state. A list of current and past nest sites as well as thorough survey of the state is needed.

*Arnold Devine and Dwight G. Smith*

# Eastern Screech-Owl
*Otus asio*

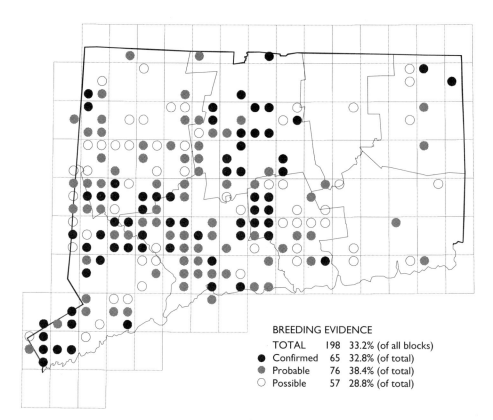

BREEDING EVIDENCE

| | TOTAL | 198 | 33.2% (of all blocks) |
|---|---|---|---|
| ● | Confirmed | 65 | 32.8% (of total) |
| ◉ | Probable | 76 | 38.4% (of total) |
| ○ | Possible | 57 | 28.8% (of total) |

The breeding range of the Eastern Screech-Owl extends from the foothills of the Rockies east to the Atlantic Coast, northward into southern Canada and south to the Gulf Coast and into Mexico. It was on the Blue List in 1981 and was listed as Special Concern in 1982 and 1986 because of declining populations (Tate 1986). In Connecticut, the Eastern Screech-Owl occurs as an uncommon to locally common permanent resident throughout much of the settled portions of the state. All three color forms—rufous, gray, and an intermediate chocolate brown—of this pigeon-sized owl with ear tufts may be seen in the state.

**Habitat**—Connecticut surveys confirm the abundance of Eastern Screech-Owls in suburban habitats and also in urban open space such as city parks and cemeteries (D. G. Smith et al. 1987, Lynch and Smith 1984). Their numbers decline in the more rural, remote areas of Connecticut and in heavily industrialized areas. Eastern Screech-Owl breeding habitat in Connecticut is diverse and includes tracts of hardwood or mixed forests, woodlots, old apple orchards, wooded suburban neighborhoods or, less frequently, forested wetlands, brushy growth, or tree-lined city streets. Their primary nesting requirement is a tree cavity although nest boxes placed in trees or on tall poles for wood ducks, kestrels, or owls are often appropriated. Nest site selection in Connecticut occurs in late February or early March, and 2–7 eggs (based on 26 Connecticut nests) are laid in late March or April. Young typically fledge in late May or early June and remain in company with the adults for another two months, perfecting hunting skills, learning to avoid enemies, and finding shelter, which usually consists of a diurnal roosting site in a tree cavity or dense vegetation (D. G. Smith et al. 1987). Prey during the breeding season consists of small mammals, birds, and insects. Nestlings are also fed small fish, amphibians, reptiles, earthworms, crayfish, grubs, and caterpillars.

**Atlas results**—The atlas data reveal that the Eastern Screech-Owl occurs in all physiographic regions of the state. They are, however, much more prevalent in the settled regions of the central lowlands, coastal shore, and southern the western hills. Eastern Screech-Owl occurrences sharply decline in the northern hardwoods and transition hardwoods of hemlock and white pine that occur in the northwest part of the state. This distribution may reflect the its low tolerance of cold and extended periods of snow cover (Mosher and Henny 1976). Also, these remote and rugged locations are home to the larger owls, such as the Great Horned Owl and Barred Owl, which prey on the Eastern Screech-Owl. Surprisingly, the

atlas results suggest that the Eastern Screech-Owl is absent or at least uncommon in the hills of northeastern Connecticut. While our own surveys revealed Eastern Screech-Owls in many areas there, it is apparently absent, or at least scarce, in many areas of that region based on the experience of other observers there. The western part of the state was more thoroughly censused, however.

**Discussion**—The Eastern Screech-Owl was considered common in Connecticut by Sage et al. (1913). Accounts in Bagg and Eliot (1937), Bent (1938), and Forbush (1927) suggest that it was more common in southern New England earlier in this century when the region was a broken mosaic of farm land and scattered woodlots. The natural reforestation that followed loss of farms reduced the area of suitable habitat for the Eastern Screech-Owl within the state

and may have contributed to their decline. A summary of the North American Breeding Bird Surveys conducted from 1965 to 1979 revealed significant continent-wide population declines (Robbins et al. 1986), suggesting a need for management measures to enhance Eastern Screech-Owl populations in the Northeast and other areas.

*Dwight G. Smith and Arnold Devine*

## Great Horned Owl
### *Bubo virginianus*

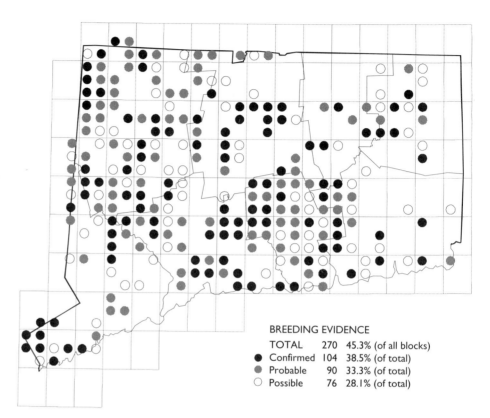

BREEDING EVIDENCE

| | | | |
|---|---|---|---|
| TOTAL | | 270 | 45.3% (of all blocks) |
| ● Confirmed | | 104 | 38.5% (of total) |
| ● Probable | | 90 | 33.3% (of total) |
| ○ Possible | | 76 | 28.1% (of total) |

The range of this large, powerful owl includes most of the western hemisphere, from the subarctic forests in Alaska and Canada southward to the tip of Tierra del Fuego. In Connecticut and the rest of New England, Great Horned Owls are largely nonmigratory and usually occupy a territory throughout the year for several years. Fledged young may appropriate adjacent territories in late fall or winter but sometimes wander widely in search of an unoccupied territory. In some years there is a major southward movement of Great Horned Owls from the north into Connecticut.

**Habitat**—Throughout its range, the Great Horned Owl occurs in a wide variety of habitats and climates, from deserts to tundra edge to dense forests. In Connecticut, Great Horned Owls are almost invariably found in mature upland forests. They show a decided preference for the edges of the forest, however. They may also nest in open farmland or even residential areas where small woodlots are available for roosting and nesting. The only habitat requirements for this adaptable owl include suitable trees, often conifers, for concealed roosting sites during daylight hours, and nearby open habitats such as power line clear-cuts, pastures, croplands, meadows, or marshes for hunting.

Our earliest breeding raptor, the Great Horned Owl advertises territorial occupancy in late fall and selects a nest site in December or January, often using an abandoned nest of a Red-tailed Hawk, Osprey, American Crow, heron, or even squirrel. Less frequently used nest sites include tree hollows, ledges or niches on cliffs, or on structures such as a tower, bridge support, or outbuilding. Most Great Horned Owl nests in Connecticut were located on dry, heavily wooded hillsides, forests along traprock ridges, forested wetland, or suburban woodlots. Ten of 21 nests were in oaks, mostly red oak, two each were in white pine and hemlock, and the rest were in a variety of deciduous trees. Great Horned Owls renovated the appropriated nests only to the extent of occasionally lining the cup with feathers and decorating the rim with sprigs of greenery. Egg dates for 12 nests in Connecticut ranged from 11 February to 20 April. Young were in the nest from 12 March to the end of May, sometimes June. Eleven Connecticut nests produced an average of 1.37 young per nest (range 1–4 young). Among food items brought to the nest were rabbits, squirrels, mice, and a variety of small and medium-sized birds. Nesting Great Horned Owls also preyed on both adults and young of several other nesting raptors, including Northern Goshawk, Barred Owl, Eastern Screech-Owl, Red-shouldered, Red-tailed, Cooper's, and Broad-winged Hawks.

**Atlas results**—The Great Horned Owl was recorded in all physiographic provinces of Connecticut but appears to be most widespread in the south-central and western regions and least prevalent in the eastern hills. Adequate habitat, including large tracts of mature woodland, occur in much of the eastern Connecticut, so the apparent rarity of Great Horned Owls in this region might indicate incomplete coverage during the atlas.

**Discussion**—Great Horned Owl populations in Connecticut may have increased during this century. Sage et al. (1913) described this owl as a common resident, especially in the wilder parts of Connecticut, but Forbush (1927) and Bagg and Eliot (1937) regarded the Great Horned Owl as an uncommon resident throughout much of New England. Reforestation, including plantings of conifer stands by water

companies, plus legislated protection of these and other raptors undoubtedly contributed to the apparent population increase. The distribution of Great Horned Owls in the state illustrates their adaptability to varied climate conditions and comparative tolerance of human activity.

*Dwight G. Smith and Arnold Devine*

169

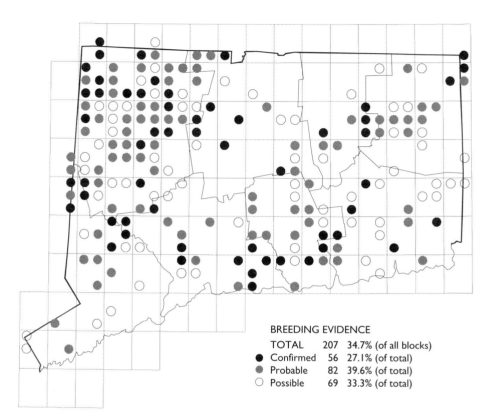

BREEDING EVIDENCE

| | TOTAL | 207 | 34.7% (of all blocks) |
|---|---|---|---|
| ● | Confirmed | 56 | 27.1% (of total) |
| ● | Probable | 82 | 39.6% (of total) |
| ○ | Possible | 69 | 33.3% (of total) |

## Barred Owl
### *Strix varia*

This species and the Eastern Screech-Owl are the state's most numerous owls, but the Barred Owl is certainly our most spectacular nocturnal vocalist. The Barred Owl is less widespread and has a more patchy distribution in the state than either the Great Horned Owl or Eastern Screech-Owl (C. F. Smith 1978). Formerly said to occur only east of the Rocky Mountains (Bent 1938), in the past thirty years the Barred Owl has dramatically expanded its range into the Pacific Northwest from southeastern Alaska to northern California. This species is essentially sedentary, with some fall and winter movements, throughout its range from southern Canada to southern Mexico. The nominate subspecies *varia*, with feathered toes and brown as opposed to blackish striping below, is the subspecies breeding in northern North America, including our state (Ridgway 1914).

**Habitat**—The Barred Owl requires mature hardwoods, preferring areas near wetlands. Wooded swamps, bottomlands, hollows, river valleys, or forested slopes near wet areas—marshes, bogs, semi-open swamps—are typical of the locales used by this nocturnal counterpart of the Red-shouldered Hawk in Connecticut. Nest site selection begins in early spring. Nests are typically in large natural cavities of trees or hollows in the top of broken snags; some pairs use the remains of Red-shouldered Hawk or Northern Goshawk nests. Barred Owls also may nest in vacated crow, heron, or squirrel nests (Bent 1938) or in appropriate nest boxes placed in trees in forested wetlands (L. Fischer pers. comm.). Trees used for nesting include sugar and red

maple, beech, yellow birch, white pine, and hemlock. In Connecticut, eggs are usually laid between mid-March and mid-April. Clutches in 53 nests in the state ranged from 2 to 4 eggs (average of 2.2 eggs). Incubation lasts about a month, and young fledge from mid-June into early July. The young remain with the adults for several weeks. During the post-fledging period, the owls of a family may roost together in the upper canopy of deciduous and coniferous trees during daylight hours.

**Atlas results**—Although the atlas shows Barred Owls in all physiographic provinces of the state, the species was most prevalent in the northwest and parts of the northeast. That fewer than ten blocks had confirmations in the central lowlands and coastal lowlands probably reflects the Barred Owl's key habitat requirements of old growth tracts of woodland removed from areas of human activity.

**Discussion**—The overall abundance of the Barred Owl appears to have changed little in the past century, but the geographic distribution of abundance within the state has shifted. The Barred Owl was considered a rather common resident of thick woods and perhaps the most common owl in southern New England (Stearns and Coues 1883, Bent 1938). In Connecticut, it was a common resident along the coast and somewhat scarcer in the interior (Sage et al. 1913). This distribution pattern is now reversed, with the Barred Owl being more common in the interior than near the coast in Connecticut (C. F. Smith 1978). Barred owl management efforts in Connecticut should be directed towards preservation of mature woodland, especially more extensive tracts with snags and partly dead trees.

*Dwight G. Smith and Arnold Devine*

## Long-eared Owl
*Asio otus*

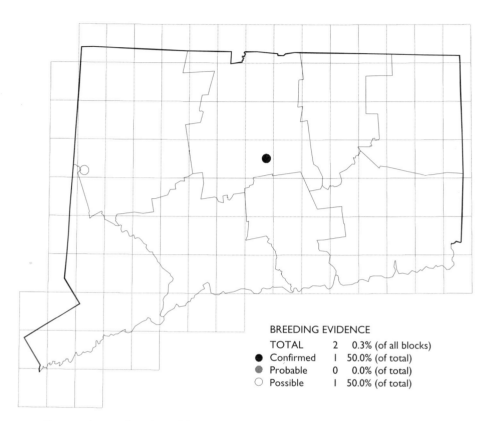

BREEDING EVIDENCE

| | | |
|---|---|---|
| TOTAL | 2 | 0.3% (of all blocks) |
| ● Confirmed | 1 | 50.0% (of total) |
| ◉ Probable | 0 | 0.0% (of total) |
| ○ Possible | 1 | 50.0% (of total) |

This crow-sized owl is included on Connecticut's list of Endangered species. Rare and difficult to locate, Long-eared Owls are generally found in the state during late fall and winter at roost sites at several localities, typically near the coast and in groves of junipers or other small conifer plantings near wetlands (Smith and Devine 1993). Several individuals may roost in the same conifer stand and even in the same tree. This species no longer nests regularly in the state.

**Habitat**—This species requires dense, cool conifer stands for roosting and nesting and adjacent open areas such as clear-cuts, fields, pastures, crop lands, or marshes for hunting. Their winter food, determined from pellet accumulations at roost sites, is mostly small mammals (voles, mice, and shrews), although an increase in the number of birds eaten is seen during spring. Long-eared Owls usually nest in an abandoned hawk, crow, heron, or squirrel nest, almost always in thick conifers or the riparian vegetation along streams and lakes. They are quiet and secretive while nesting; consequently, very little is known of their breeding biology in Connecticut. Almost all known breeding records date from the last century. Generally, the Long-eared Owl nests from mid-March to mid-May.

Egg dates for Connecticut nests are from late April and early May, while young have been seen in nests during April, May, and June. For example, on 2 April 1898 five eggs were found in a crow's nest high in a hemlock in Eastford (Sage et al. 1913). Other reported nesting locales in the state include Berlin, Ellington, Bristol, Woodbridge, and North Branford (Sage et al. 1913).

**Atlas results**—This owl was found in only two atlas blocks: one confirmed occurrence south of Glastonbury and another possible site near Kent in western Connecticut. The single recent breeding locality in Connecticut, found during the atlas, was at a known roost site close to extensive marshlands along the Connecticut River. This nest was found with young in April 1982. The observer reported that the nest was destroyed by crows (R. Cech; see Hand and Mockalis 1982). Also within the last ten years, D. G. Smith has observed pairs in riparian vegetation near Durham Meadows in late March and individuals in conifers adjacent to farmland near Lakeville in early April and in Orange in mid-April; these might have been late migrants but probably represented nesting pairs.

**Discussion**—The Long-eared Owl has always been considered a rare breeding species in New England. It was considered rare in Connecticut during the 1800s (Stearns and Coues 1883, Forbush 1927), and early in this century it was considered a common winter visitor and a rare summer resident (Sage et al. 1913).

Factors that limit the Long-eared Owl breeding population in Connecticut are poorly known but may include habitat loss and possibly predation by the Great Horned Owl or Barred Owl. Reforestation in Connecticut reduced the amount of open habitat used by Long-eared Owls for hunting, although their occurrence in some areas almost every winter suggests that adequate habitat is available. Additionally, Sage et al. (1913) described the owl as rare in the late nineteenth century when most of the state was farmland. Reforestation probably contributed to population increases of both the Barred Owl and the Great Horned Owl, which prey on Long-eared Owls and compete with them for nest sites. Unfortunately, the

factors that limit the numbers of Long-eared Owls in Connecticut are unknown, and effective management of this species within the state awaits a more extensive survey of their population status and habitat needs.

*Arnold Devine and Dwight G. Smith*

# Northern Saw-whet Owl
*Aegolius acadicus*

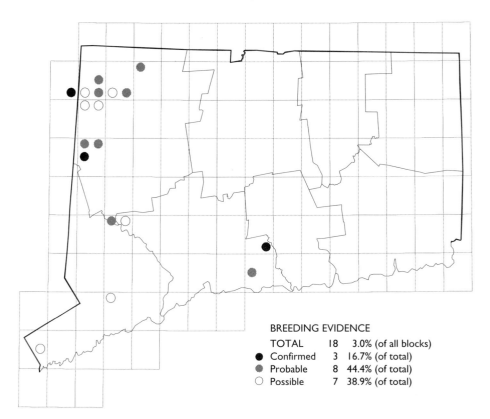

BREEDING EVIDENCE

| | | |
|---|---|---|
| TOTAL | 18 | 3.0% (of all blocks) |
| ● Confirmed | 3 | 16.7% (of total) |
| ◉ Probable | 8 | 44.4% (of total) |
| ○ Possible | 7 | 38.9% (of total) |

The breeding range of the Northern Saw-whet Owl extends from southern Canada and the northern United States southward in the mountains and higher elevations to Mexico in the West and along the Appalachians into Virginia and North Carolina in the East. This small owl is an uncommon to rare breeder in Connecticut and is currently designated as a Species of Special Concern in the state because so few localities for nesting are known.

Predominantly a winter resident here, Saw-whet Owls regularly migrate into Connecticut in late October and November and may take up residence in the same tract of conifers or mixed woods each year. Individuals remain on winter territories until late March. The size of this winter population varies and may be substantial in some years, probably due to changes in prey abundance and snow cover.

**Habitat**—Throughout most of its range, and in Connecticut, the breeding habitat of the Northern Saw-whet Owl is poorly defined. Conifer woodlands or mixed deciduous and conifer woodlands, often near wetlands, are the most commonly used habitat, provided trees with natural cavities are available for nesting. This species will use nest boxes (Cannings 1987). Nest sites in Connecticut have included low cavities in snags of sugar maple, elm, and red maple in wetlands and upland woods, often with shrub cover. Nesting phenology of known nests is somewhat varied: a nest in a red maple in Marlborough fledged five young in early May 1977 (Devine pers. obs.); one in an old crow nest in Winsted had three young in May while another had five eggs on 1 April 1887 (Sage et al. 1913).

**Atlas results**—Confirmed breeding was reported from scattered locales, with at least three nesting pairs found. The species was recorded in 18 blocks within two of the state's four physiographic regions. The species is conspicuously absent in the central lowlands and eastern portions of the state, and only four records (one confirmed) are from the coastal areas. Most breeding records are from western Connecticut with a notable concentration of 12 records within six contiguous topographic quadrangles in the northwest corner of the state. The lack of atlas records for the east is unexpected because suitable habitat is available there; incomplete coverage here partly accounts this pattern. The lack of breeding records in the lowlands may be due to habitat loss and human disturbance. It is also possible that because the Northern Saw-whet Owl is so easily overlooked, it is more common and more generally distributed within the state than the atlas records indicate.

**Discussion**—Traditionally, the Northern Saw-whet Owl has been regarded as a rare to uncommon winter visitor that rarely nests in the state (Sage et al. 1913, Mackenzie 1961, and Manter 1975). The first summer report in many years was that of two to three at Pleasant Valley, Barkhamsted, in July, but no nesting was noted (Carleton 1965). A nest found in Marlborough in 1977 was reported as the first modern breeding record for the state (photograph of juvenile; Vickery 1977a). This was followed in 1978 by three nesting pairs in Sharon and suspected nesting near Storrs (Vickery 1978).

*Arnold Devine and Dwight G. Smith*

175

# Common Nighthawk
## *Chordeiles minor*

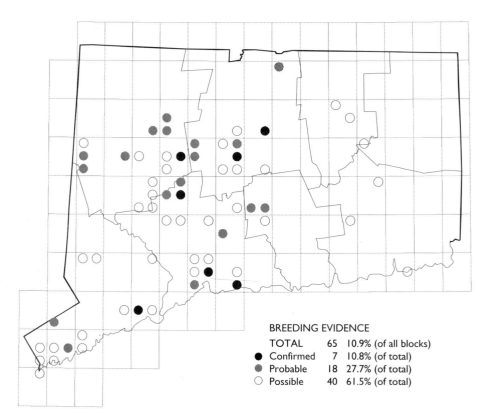

BREEDING EVIDENCE

| | TOTAL | 65 | 10.9% (of all blocks) |
|---|---|---|---|
| ● | Confirmed | 7 | 10.8% (of total) |
| ● | Probable | 18 | 27.7% (of total) |
| ○ | Possible | 40 | 61.5% (of total) |

This migrant breeder winters throughout South America south to northern Argentina (AOU 1983). Although many Common Nighthawks migrate across Connecticut, especially in fall, the number of birds breeding in the state in recent decades is probably not great. It is designated as a Species of Special Concern in the state.

The breeding subspecies in most of the eastern United States is nominate *minor*, which is generally larger and darker than other populations of this highly variable species. Most people recognize the deep booming sound made by the wings as a bird pulls out of a steep display dive; a nasal *peent* is also quite distinctive, especially when heard in cities where woodcock, which give a similar call from the ground, are less likely to be heard.

**Habitat**—At present as far as known, breeding is confined to the larger cities in which nesting occurs on flat roofs covered with gravel or similar materials. Formerly, the species in Connecticut nested on bare ground or rock in open areas, as this species still does in other parts of its range, such as in desert areas of western North America. Insofar as we can judge a nighthawk's perspective, a gravel roof appears to substitute for a patch of gravel in open countryside.

**Atlas results**—The species was mainly found in the larger cities, and probable or confirmed breeding was limited to only 25 blocks in the entire state.

**Discussion**—Linsley (1843) and Merriam (1877) ranked the Common Nighthawk as indeed common; however, by 1913 Sage et al. considered the bird to have become rare in the breeding season over most of the state. Sage et al. refer to persecution of the birds in pastures, and this is apparently a reference to shooting of the birds by mis-informed men who considered these birds to be valueless pests (Bent 1940). Sage et al. (1913) listed rocks and bare spots in pastures as primary breeding sites but did mention that the species also rarely nested on flat roofs of buildings in cities, localities which have now become the preponderant, if not the only, sites. Thus during the twentieth century there has been a dramatic shift in the predominant kind of site used for nesting. Although the species continues to breed in Connecticut, it is difficult to determine how successful this species is. Property owners or managers are often understandably reluctant, because of insurance and other concerns, to allow access to roofs, and thus it is difficult to obtain data on breeding success. We do not know whether the Connecticut birds are self perpetuating or to what extent birds breeding in Connecticut might originate elsewhere. Availability of suitable nest sites or a supply of insects for food might be potentially limiting factors in the urban setting (Armstrong 1965).

*George A. Clark, Jr.*

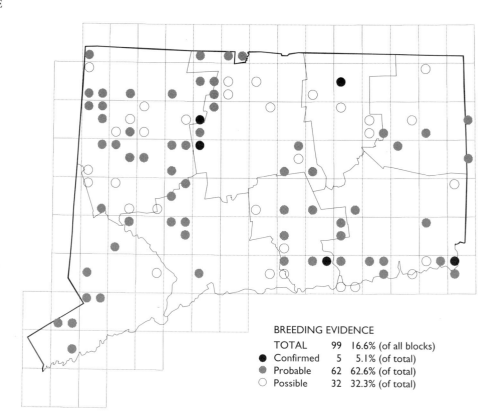

BREEDING EVIDENCE

| | TOTAL | 99 | 16.6% (of all blocks) |
|---|---|---|---|
| ● | Confirmed | 5 | 5.1% (of total) |
| ◕ | Probable | 62 | 62.6% (of total) |
| ○ | Possible | 32 | 32.3% (of total) |

# Whip-poor-will
## *Caprimulgus vociferus*

The Whip-poor-will is a migratory breeder in Connecticut. The species has been widespread as a breeder though apparently less common than in coastal states to the south. The Whip-poor-will is designated as a Species of Special Concern in Connecticut based on a perceived decline in breeding numbers.

Birds breeding from southern Canada and throughout the eastern United States are the nominate subspecies *vociferus*, which winters from the southeastern United States and northern Mexico to Costa Rica, where rare, and western Panama (two records; Ridgely and Gwynne 1989). The calls and egg color of birds breeding in the southwestern United States south to Honduras differ markedly from the "Eastern" Whip-poor-wills, suggesting possibly different species (Stiles and Skutch 1989).

**Habitat**—Whip-poor-wills are found in scrubby immature woods or areas of regrowth following disturbance in more mature forests. Sites are often on relatively dry, sandy soils; plant growth on such soils may be retarded, thus retaining a more open canopy that is favored by the birds. Because Whip-poor-wills apparently find their insect food by sight (Mills 1986), dense forest is an unsuitable habitat. In contrast to the wooded areas used by the Whip-poor-will, the Common Nighthawk, originally an occupant of open country, now occurs in urban sites.

**Atlas results**—The Whip-poor-will was found to be widespread in the state, but difficulties observing the species led to a low rate of confirmations of breeding.

Because block busting efforts were conducted principally during daylight and less effort was expended to find nocturnal species, there is a strong possibility that the species was missed in less intensively surveyed blocks. Whip-poor-wills call to the greatest extent on moonlit nights (R. J. Cooper 1981, Mills 1986) and hence are most easily found then. On darker nights, Whip-poor-wills may call only during the period of twilight at dusk and dawn and hence may be difficult to detect without special effort.

**Discussion**—Linsley (1843) rated the Whip-poor-will as common for the state though he noted that they had become somewhat rare in Fairfield County. Both Merriam (1877) and Sage et al. (1913) considered the species to be common in the state.

The spread of extensively developed suburbs near cities has eliminated much breeding habitat for Whip-poor-wills in the state. Seemingly suitable habitat for Whip-poor-wills appears to exist more widely across the state than indicated by the number of localities found during the atlas survey. This apparent discrepancy might be due to problems in obtaining adequate coverage for a species difficult to detect or might reflect a genuine shortage of birds. Because Whip-poor-wills have not been closely monitored by any long term survey, there is no firm basis for determining whether their numbers in the state have changed. Nevertheless, there is at least a suspicion that the species is now less common than formerly, and Breeding Bird Survey data for southern New England support this impression. Observers in Vermont and New York have perceived a decline in the Northeast, and both Kibbe (*in* Laughlin and Kibbe 1985) and Sibley (*in* Andrle and Carroll 1988) suggested that this might be linked to losses of silk moths (Saturniidae), a major source of food for Whip-poor-wills. From a conservation viewpoint, this a species for which we need to know more.

*George A. Clark, Jr.*

## Chimney Swift
*Chaetura pelagica*

A migratory breeder, the earliest Chimney Swifts often appear at the end of April or early May and then, if the weather turns cold, disappear for some days until warmer weather returns. It is believed that during the spring cold periods the birds are in their roosting or breeding sites and remain inactive at a reduced body temperature that helps them to save substantial energy during those cold periods when virtually no arthropods are available for capture in the air. Most winter in the western Amazon Basin and migrate through Central America and the West Indies (AOU 1983).

**Habitat**—As the name of the species implies, this swift nests primarily in chimneys; they also use ventilation ducts, walls of buildings, and other human structures as nest sites (Tyler *in* Bent 1940). The Chimney Swift origi-

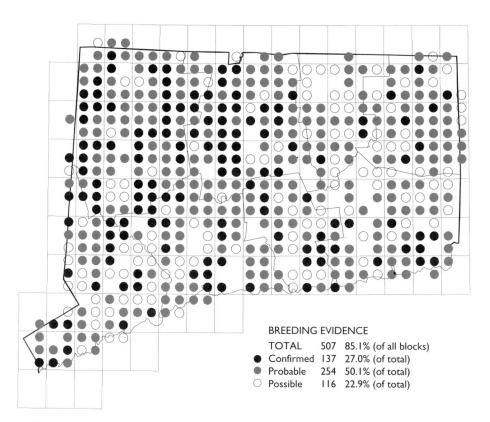

BREEDING EVIDENCE

| | TOTAL | 507 | 85.1% (of all blocks) |
|---|---|---|---|
| ● | Confirmed | 137 | 27.0% (of total) |
| ● | Probable | 254 | 50.1% (of total) |
| ○ | Possible | 116 | 22.9% (of total) |

nally nested in trees but no such sites have been reported from Connecticut in this century. In addition to a site for a nest, the birds need access to twigs used in nest construction and a source of arthropod food obtained while in flight. The birds forage over a wide variety of habitats, often flying over open water and presumably capturing emergent aquatic insects.

**Atlas results**—Chimney Swifts were observed in about 85% of the blocks and confirmed as breeding in more than 27%. Because obtaining access to potential nest sites was generally not practical, confirmations usually came from observations of swifts entering and leaving chimneys (Sibley *in* Andrle and Carroll 1988). Lack of detection of birds in particular blocks might be due to either insufficient coverage, as presumably in some eastern Connecticut blocks, or to absence of the birds because of a lack of nest sites.

**Discussion**—For the precolonial period there is no evidence on how abundant the birds might have been. Through the nineteenth century and into the twentieth century the Chimney Swift has been a common breeder in Connecticut. Apparently there has been a decline in numbers in recent decades (Zeranski and Baptist 1990) as with modern construction there are fewer chimneys with broad openings and other characteristics suitable for the nesting of swifts.

This is an appealing species that conceivably could be lost as a breeder in a relatively short time. It has become a common practice in Connecticut to put screening over the tops of chimneys to exclude raccoons, bats, and other unwanted animals. Furthermore, many people do not want swifts in their home chimney because the birds make some noise and because of a potential mess and even a fire hazard if the chimney is later used without cleaning. If the num-

bers of swifts are dwindling, and if current ideas about chimneys are maintained, it seems conceivable that this species could become much less frequent as a breeder, even to the point where construction of special nest chimneys or towers might become desirable as a means of maintaining the species as a breeder in the state.

*George A. Clark, Jr.*

## Ruby-throated Hummingbird
### *Archilochus colubris*

*'Tis an exceeding little Bird, and only seen in Summer, and mostly in Gardens, flying from flower to flower, sucking Honey out of the flowers as a Bee doth; as it flieth not lighting on the flower, but hovering over it, sucking with its long Bill a sweet substance.*

> —The Honorable John Winthrop,
> Governor of Connecticut, 1670

The first written account known of a hummingbird in the United States (Tyrrell and Tyrrell 1985) refers to the formerly common Ruby-throated Hummingbird, now an uncommon migrant breeder in Connecticut. The species winters primarily in Middle America from sea level to 3,000 m from northwestern Mexico to Costa Rica, occasionally north to southern Florida and south to western Panama (Blake 1953, Ridgely and Gwynne 1989, Stiles and Skutch 1989). For eastern North America, this species is the single representative of the Trochilidae, a New World family of

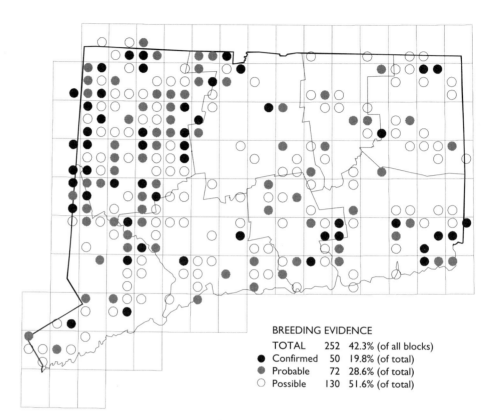

BREEDING EVIDENCE

| | TOTAL | 252 | 42.3% (of all blocks) |
|---|---|---|---|
| ● | Confirmed | 50 | 19.8% (of total) |
| ◓ | Probable | 72 | 28.6% (of total) |
| ○ | Possible | 130 | 51.6% (of total) |

some 340 species with the greatest species density in tropical lowland habitats—more than a dozen species coexist in some areas (Feinsinger and Colwell 1978). The gradient of species impoverishment is repeated in temperate South America, with only a single species reaching the highest latitudes (the Green Firecrown, *Sephanoides sephaniodes*) (Johnson and Goodall 1965).

**Habitat**—Forest openings and woodlands, edges, and gardens in rural areas are used for nesting while a greater variety of open habitats are used in migration. Nests are commonly placed on minor branches of deciduous trees (sometimes in hemlock), well protected by upper branches, and often over running water (Bent 1940).

**Atlas results**—The block counts for this species suggest that the Ruby-throated Hummingbird now prefers the wooded hills of northwestern Connecticut, while it is scarce or absent from urbanized areas. The local abundance and distribution of hummingbirds elsewhere, both during non-breeding periods and during the breeding season, is highly correlated with the flowering phenology of favored host plants (Feinsinger and Colwell 1978). One may surmise that the same is true for the Ruby-throated Hummingbird in Connecticut, driving not only present status but historical changes in distribution and abundance. The popularity of hummingbird feeders and the cultivation of nectar plants in gardens may also play a role.

**Discussion**—Ruby-throated Hummingbirds were once considerably more common in the state. Linsley (1843) and Merriam (1877) both listed them, unequivocally, as common; Stearns and Coues (1883) rhapsodized that it is "so common, that it is no remarkable thing to see a perfect galaxy 'starring' on some flowery stage…" A sequence of observers listed the bird as common in neighboring states through the 1930s (Zeranski and Baptist 1990). In Connecticut, however, Sage et al. (1913) had already declared the hummingbird not as common as formerly, although still found nesting "in the shade trees of the city streets." Today, the Ruby-throated Hummingbird is absent from urbanized areas in Connecticut (Zeranski and Baptist 1990), areas which, of course, steadily increased in prevalence over the decades since 1900. In fact, the species is now sufficiently uncommon in Connecticut that no contemporary student of avian behavior or population biology has found it an attractive subject for scientific study.

*Robert K. Colwell*

# Belted Kingfisher
## *Ceryle alcyon*

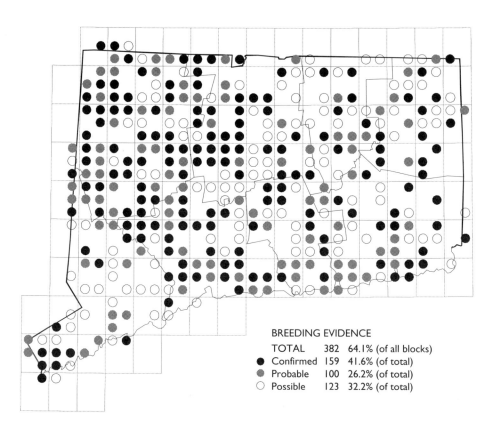

BREEDING EVIDENCE

| | TOTAL | 382 | 64.1% (of all blocks) |
|---|---|---|---|
| ● | Confirmed | 159 | 41.6% (of total) |
| ◕ | Probable | 100 | 26.2% (of total) |
| ○ | Possible | 123 | 32.2% (of total) |

This distinctive denizen of waterways is a unique and endlessly interesting component of Connecticut's avifauna. The combination of crested large head, long pointed bill, blue-gray and white coloration (females also have a reddish belly band), and stocky build make the species easy to recognize in the field. Even when not seen the loud rattling call reveals the presence of the species from the wetland habitat it haunts. In general, the Belted Kingfisher can be considered an uncommon migratory breeder, departing gradually in late fall from September to November when food becomes scarce or water-bodies icebound. They return to the state in March-April after the spring ice thaw. During warmer winters a sizable population may overwinter; in most winters a few individuals remain throughout the season along coastal Connecticut and on tidally influenced rivers and their tributaries.

**Habitat**—Being predominantly fish-eating, the Belted Kingfisher has habitat requirements dictated by the availability of aquatic and marine environment. Any water body with a suitable supply of small fish may be used for hunting. Although fish is the species' principal prey, other dietary items include frogs, crayfish, bivalves, small birds, and insects. Two methods used in foraging are 1) flying along the shoreline and hovering over potential prey, or 2) sitting on a high perch overlooking water. When a prey is detected the bird plunges headfirst into the water and seizes the prey in its powerful bill. Nests are placed in banks along rivers, streams, lakes, ponds, and occasionally far from water at railroad cuts or sand and gravel pits. Horizontal burrows 3–7 feet long are excavated in the soil by both sexes using a combination of bill and feet. Burrows terminate in nest chambers about six inches by ten inches and lined with fish bones and scales from ejected pellets (Bent 1940).

**Atlas results**—The atlas reveals that the Belted Kingfisher is a widespread breeding species recorded in 64.1% of all blocks. Breeding records are evenly distributed throughout the state with the minor exception within the southern tier of the Eastern Highland. Suitable habitat exists within that area and therefore the lack of breeding data is presumably a result of the lesser degree of coverage in the region.

**Discussion**—A review of the literature suggests that the status of the Belted Kingfisher in Connecticut has historically remained unchanged. Sage et al. (1913) stated that they were a common summer resident from April to October but rarely wintered. Forbush (1927) likewise called this species a common summer resident and suggested that a few individuals may be permanently resident throughout the year where there is adequate open water for foraging. More recently, Robbins et al. (1986) reported no significant long term trends but did note a population drop in the east attributed to the cold winter of 1976–1977.

*Arnold Devine and Dwight G. Smith*

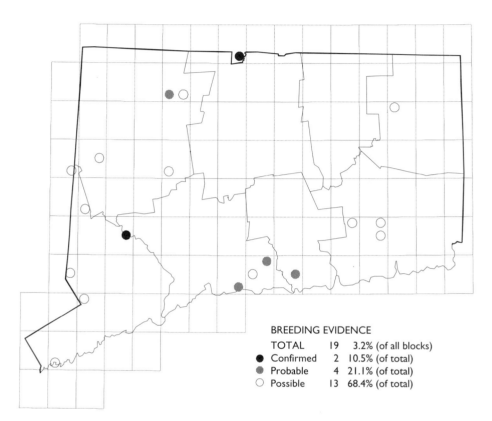

BREEDING EVIDENCE

| TOTAL | 19 | 3.2% (of all blocks) |
|---|---|---|
| ● Confirmed | 2 | 10.5% (of total) |
| ● Probable | 4 | 21.1% (of total) |
| ○ Possible | 13 | 68.4% (of total) |

## Red-headed Woodpecker
### *Melanerpes erythrocephalus*

This is one of the rarest breeding birds in the state and close to extirpation as a breeder; it is designated as Endangered in Connecticut. The species is a regular migrant, most commonly seen from late September to mid-October along the coast; it is less frequent in spring. Its movements are erratic at other times of the year, sometimes wintering when acorn or beech mast is high. The Red-headed Woodpecker molts very late, thus birds with grizzled gray-brown heads may be seen into winter. The slightly smaller nominate subspecies, *erythrocephalus*, occurs in Connecticut; however, no subspecific determination of migrants or breeders has been made.

**Habitat**—Red-headed Woodpeckers breed in open woodland, as along the margins of farm fields, or in wooded swamps; they usually nest in dead trees or trees with dead limbs. During winter, they eat some fruit and forage for dormant insects behind loose bark, more so than the Red-bellied Woodpecker.

**Atlas results**—The only confirmed reports in recent years were found during the atlas survey. These were at Congamond Lakes, Suffield, 1984–1985 (S. Kellogg), and Newtown, 1986 (H. Crandall).

**Discussion**—There are reports of an abundance of Red-headed Woodpeckers breeding in parts of Connecticut before 1840 (Linsley 1843, Merriam 1877). Unfortunately, in most nonscientific literature from the period before 1840, almost any species of woodpecker might be termed "red-headed," so it is difficult now to assess the status of any particular species at that time.

The Red-headed Woodpecker apparently has been a local and rather erratic breeder in Connecticut since the mid-1800s (Craig 1978). Over the last 150 years, this species has become scarcer throughout much of its range in the eastern United States, although peak populations to our south were found in stands of dead and dying chestnut trees at the height of the chestnut blight (Hall 1983). The disappearance along the eastern seaboard of savanna-like conditions favored by this species would seem to have been a principal cause of its decline. Other factors attributed to its decline include the loss of nest sites through competition with the introduced European Starling (J. Jones 1987, Potter 1987, Ingold 1989) and increased mortality along highways, perhaps caused by this species' habit of foraging close to the ground in pursuit of flying insects and thus frequently being struck by cars. Nevertheless, Red-headed Woodpeckers were already scarce in Connecticut before motor vehicles were prevalent and before the starling invaded Connecticut about 1900 (Kalmbach 1931). A decline of the Red-headed Woodpecker in Connecticut before 1840 might have been associated with the widespread removal of large trees for fuel, timber, and agricultural land. Also, during the 1800s, Red-headed Woodpeckers were often considered undesirable because of their feeding on fruit crops and hence were sometimes shot in large numbers (Audubon 1831, Beal 1912), though no examples of extensive shooting are known from Connecticut.

Seemingly suitable nesting sites are not now being used in the state, perhaps because of the low numbers of birds that reach Connecticut. In contrast, the closely related Red-bellied Woodpecker, which is similar in size to the Red-headed and of somewhat similar ecology and behavior (Jackson 1976), has in recent decades successfully invaded the state.

*George A. Clark, Jr.*

187

# Red-bellied Woodpecker
## *Melanerpes carolinus*

A resident breeder which has dramatically expanded its numbers and range since 1960. People often mistakenly use the name "red-headed woodpecker" for this species, probably because adult males have a bright red crown.

**Habitat**—Suburban and rural, open deciduous woodland. Commonly nests in dead snags, usually of living trees, with the nest hole on the underside of an inclined limb. During winter, birds will visit bird-feeders to eat seed as well as suet.

**Atlas results**—During the time of the atlas survey, a growing population of Red-bellied Woodpeckers was found throughout the nonurban coastal areas of Connecticut and at lower elevations into the central parts of the state. Only the higher elevations and northern border regions lacked the Red-bellied.

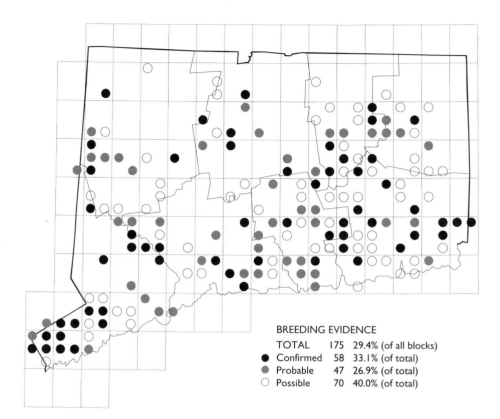

BREEDING EVIDENCE

| | TOTAL | 175 | 29.4% (of all blocks) |
|---|---|---|---|
| ● | Confirmed | 58 | 33.1% (of total) |
| ● | Probable | 47 | 26.9% (of total) |
| ○ | Possible | 70 | 40.0% (of total) |

**Discussion**—By the 1950s, Red-bellied Woodpeckers bred along the east coast of North America north only to southeastern Pennsylvania (Bull 1964), although a few records of single birds extended back over many decades in Connecticut (Sage et al. 1913). A major range expansion in the northeastern and midwestern United States was underway in the 1950s (Bull 1964, Meade *in* Andrle and Carroll 1988, Wolinski 1988). Occasional individuals appeared in Connecticut during this time with breeding reported from Farmington as early as 1963 (Carleton 1963a, Luppi 1985). The numbers of Red-bellied Woodpeckers and their known breeding localities in the state increased through the 1970s (Craig 1978, Luppi 1985). Breeding as far east as Old Lyme was known by 1974 (Finch 1975). By the early 1980s, an advancing northeastern wave of the population had reached as far as Windham and Tolland counties (G. A. Clark, Jr., pers. obs.). By the close of the 1980s, the Red-bellied Woodpecker still appeared to be expanding its numbers and range (Ripley 1988) and had become, in many parts of Connecticut, the third most often noted woodpecker, trailing only the Downy Woodpecker and Northern Flicker.

A major question is why the Red-bellied has been so successful, expanding its numbers and range, while the closely related Red-headed Woodpecker has been faring so poorly. In the twentieth century, the regrowth of woodlands and loss of extensive open habitats has created environments more favorable to the Red-bellied, which commonly breeds in a more closed woodland with edges nearby, in contrast to the almost savanna-like conditions commonly frequented by the Red-headed. The Red-bellied Woodpecker is apparently more versatile in feeding habits, in part because of a significantly longer tongue which enables capture of food items in crevices beyond the reach of a Red-headed (Kilham 1963). During winter in Connecticut, the Red-bellied Woodpecker is often found near feeding stations where sunflower seeds are taken. This species may be among those which have been helped in expanding their range northward by the increase in human provision of food for wintering birds (Meade *in* Andrle and Carroll 1988). Much of the range expansion appears to occur in winter when Red-bellied Woodpeckers are known to wander, and a trend to milder winters may have aided the dramatic expansion of the species (Todd 1940). Also, the decline of the Red-headed Woodpecker probably has assisted the expansion of the Red-bellied, for where the two species coexist, the Red-headed often excludes the Red-bellied from favored habitat (Williams and Batzli 1979).

*George A. Clark, Jr.*

189

# Yellow-bellied Sapsucker
## *Sphyrapicus varius*

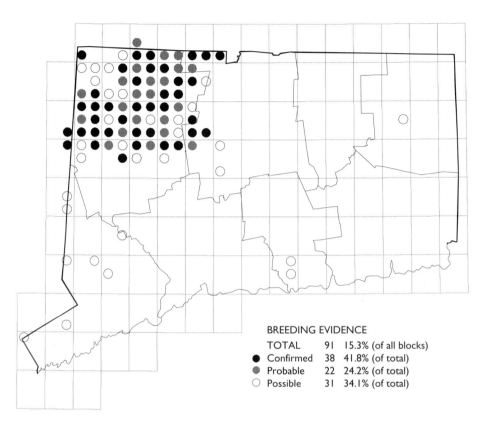

BREEDING EVIDENCE

| | TOTAL | 91 | 15.3% (of all blocks) |
|---|---|---|---|
| ● | Confirmed | 38 | 41.8% (of total) |
| ◐ | Probable | 22 | 24.2% (of total) |
| ○ | Possible | 31 | 34.1% (of total) |

The Yellow-bellied Sapsucker is a shy and retiring woodpecker that is easily overlooked except during the breeding season when its distinctive territorial drumming resonates throughout the hills and valleys of Connecticut's western highlands. Both sexes participate in the drumming ritual, which begins with a short roll and ends with five or six disconnected rhythmic taps. A distinctive slow tapping is also used for communication. In Connecticut, the Yellow-bellied Sapsucker is an uncommon migrant and a rare and locally uncommon nester. Fall migration begins in September and continues into November; peak migration is generally observed during mid-October along the coast. The species returns to breed in April (occasionally late March) and May. During winter a few stragglers linger mainly along the southern coastline and major river basins.

**Habitat**—Deciduous and mixed deciduous-coniferous woodland are the preferred habitat of the Yellow-bellied Sapsucker during the breeding season. They display a strong preference to nest in aspen, alive or dead, but also use dead birches (Kilham 1983). At other times of the year, the species occurs in most types of woodlands and orchards. Areas harboring sapsuckers can be recognized immediately by the species' woodworking technique—rows of vertical and horizontal holes drilled into the sides of trees. These holes penetrate the soft cambium layer beneath the bark, filling with sap and attracting insects. The Yellow-bellied Sapsucker makes regular rounds of these sap wells, lapping up the sugary sap and feeding on the insects with its long brush tipped tongue.

**Atlas results**—The Yellow-bellied Sapsucker clearly is associated with sparsely populated areas of cooler climate in the state. All confirmed and probable breeding records were concentrated at higher elevation in the northern tier of western Connecticut. Approximately 85% of all atlas records occurred in the transition and northern hardwood forests of the state.

**Discussion**—The first confirmed breeding record of the Yellow-bellied Sapsucker for Connecticut was at Winchester in 1893 (Sage et al. 1913). The species was considered "not very common" in Litchfield County around the turn of the century (Job 1908), and near New Haven, where it was only a migrant, it was rare (Merriam 1877). Job also indicated that it might have been fairly common in the fall in Litchfield County. Sage et al. (1913) identified the Yellow-bellied Sapsucker as a common spring and fall migrant, whereas Bagg and Eliot (1937) concluded the species was becoming more

numerous than 25 or 50 years earlier. Summarizing the historical literature, Zeranski and Baptist (1990) concluded that the species had increased as a migrant, winter visitor, and breeder in historic times. More recently, Robbins et al. (1986) noted that the Yellow-bellied Sapsucker had decreased in southern New England during the period 1965–1979, attributing the decline to the severe winters of 1976 and 1978.

The Yellow-bellied Sapsucker clearly has extended its breeding range into Litchfield County south through the Berkshire Mountains, and increased breeding activity is likely a result of the extensive reforestation which has occurred in Connecticut during this century. It is intriguing to speculate whether the Yellow-bellied Sapsucker will continue its southward breeding range expansion.

*Arnold Devine and Dwight G. Smith*

# Downy Woodpecker
*Picoides pubescens*

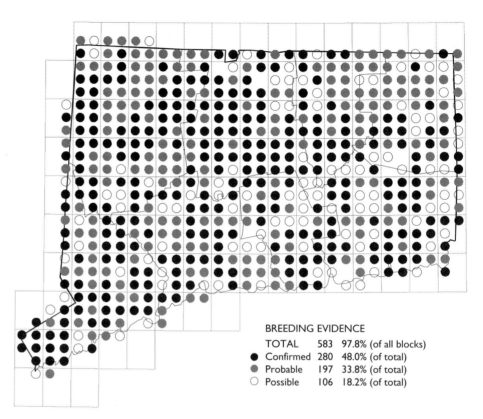

BREEDING EVIDENCE

| | TOTAL | 583 | 97.8% (of all blocks) |
|---|---|---|---|
| ● | Confirmed | 280 | 48.0% (of total) |
| ● | Probable | 197 | 33.8% (of total) |
| ○ | Possible | 106 | 18.2% (of total) |

Connecticut's smallest member of the woodpecker family and one of the most familiar because of its habit of visiting bird feeders during winter. A common to fairly common permanent resident throughout the state and an uncommon to fairly common woodland denizen in winter. This woodpecker has the interesting habitat of excavating a cavity or using a nest box for roosting during cold winter nights.

**Habitat**—This species will use almost any habitat that includes some trees for nesting and roosting, including mixed and deciduous woodlands, orchards, parks, and wooded residential neighborhoods along wooded streams and ponds. This species will use shorter, second-growth woods and scrub oaks unlike the Hairy Woodpecker, which seems to require stands of larger trees.

The female selects the cavity site which is excavated from late April to May. This cavity may be from 5–50 feet high usually in dead or decaying parts of trees, snags, or stubs. The entrance to the nest is usually camouflaged in bark, moss, or lichen. Eggs are laid in mid to late May, and incubation lasts about twelve days, with the young fledging in about three weeks, which is about a week faster than other species of woodpeckers in the state. A juvenile dependency period follows fledging. This species eats insects, fruits, seeds, and sap, the latter especially in early spring. Downy Woodpeckers may be seen foraging for insects in the stems of dried herbaceous growth, including cut corn.

**Atlas results**—The atlas recorded this species in 97.8% of the state's survey blocks, confirming its widespread distribution in Connecticut. Blocks in which it was not reported all contained suitable habitat, suggesting that it might have been overlooked, which is not surprising considering this species becomes quite secretive during the nesting cycle. The increasing availability of feeders, especially suet feeders and others specifically set out for woodpeckers, may aid the winter survival of this species, thereby contributing to the observed population increase that seems to have occurred over the last several decades.

**Discussion**—All early accounts describe this species as a common resident (Linsley 1843, Merriam 1877, Sage et al. 1913). Writing about New England generally, Forbush (1927) also described the Downy Woodpecker as common, especially in winter. More recently, Robbins et al. (1986) noted that the Downy Woodpecker was increasing over much of its range and that the highest breeding densities were found in Connecticut, Kentucky, and Maryland.

Although considered essentially a resident, significant movements of Downy Woodpeckers are noted, especially in fall. The extent to which some Connecticut breeders might move south is unknown. Likewise, the origins of winter visitors is unclear. Subspecies are poorly delimited (Bull 1974, Mengel 1965) and unlikely to illuminate movements within the East.

*Dwight G. Smith and Arnold Devine*

# Hairy Woodpecker
## *Picoides villosus*

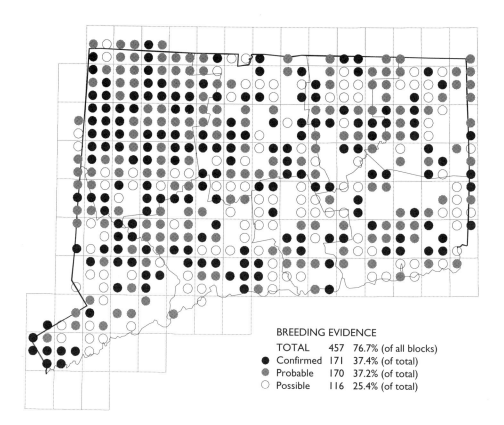

BREEDING EVIDENCE

| | TOTAL | 457 | 76.7% (of all blocks) |
|---|---|---|---|
| ● | Confirmed | 171 | 37.4% (of total) |
| ● | Probable | 170 | 37.2% (of total) |
| ○ | Possible | 116 | 25.4% (of total) |

This species is a resident breeder that occurs throughout most of the state, although it is less common than the Downy Woodpecker. It is more conspicuous in fall and winter, when some individuals may enter towns and cities and appear at feeders.

**Habitat**—The Hairy Woodpecker favors mature woodland, forested wetlands, wooded edges of streams and ponds, and, less commonly, submature woods, well wooded urban open space, and orchards. It is rarely found in developed areas. The nest cavity is excavated 5–60 feet high in a tree, snag, or, rarely, a telephone pole. Eggs are laid from late April through May, and incubation is about 13–14 days; young remain in the nest nearly four weeks. Primarily insectivorous, the Hairy Woodpecker eats caterpillars, grubs, ants, grasshoppers, and also spiders.

**Atlas results**—The atlas indicates that the Hairy Woodpecker has a widespread but patchy distribution within the state. It was most prevalent in the northwestern sector, which is the most heavily forested part of the state, and was less often found in the urbanized southern and central sectors, where its localized occurrence indicates use of wooded parks and preserves and even, in some cases, mature trees of town and city parks and streets. Its absence in heavily urbanized areas may reflect competition for nest sites with the European Starling and the House Sparrow (Ehrlich et al. 1988).

**Discussion**—The status of the Hairy Woodpecker in Connecticut apparently has changed very little since the 1800s. To Merriam (1877) the Hairy Woodpecker was not a common permanent resident, whereas according to Sage et al. (1913) it was tolerably common, more so in winter, probably indicating its greater conspicuousness at that season rather than a real increase in numbers. Forbush (1927) thought the Hairy Woodpecker was common throughout most of New England except Connecticut and Rhode Island, where he termed the species rare. This difference might have been merely a matter of interpretation rather than an a change in numbers. In the past decade the Hairy Woodpecker was widely reported as declining and was placed on the *American Birds* Blue List from 1975 to 1982; it was later listed there as a Species of Special Concern in 1986 (Tate 1986).

*Dwight G. Smith and Arnold Devine*

# Northern Flicker
## *Colaptes auratus*

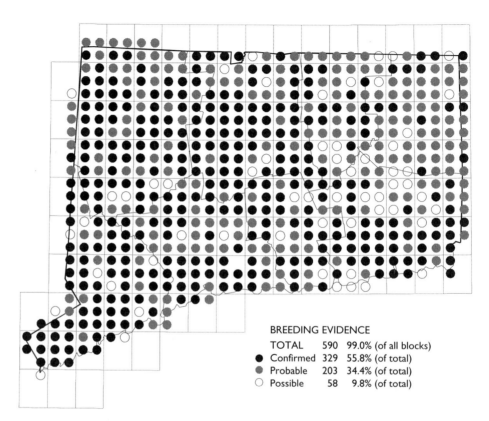

BREEDING EVIDENCE

| | TOTAL | 590 | 99.0% (of all blocks) |
|---|---|---|---|
| ● | Confirmed | 329 | 55.8% (of total) |
| ● | Probable | 203 | 34.4% (of total) |
| ○ | Possible | 58 | 9.8% (of total) |

The Northern Flicker is a common and widespread breeder within the state, especially in the more rural agricultural areas. It is a common migrant from March through most of May and from mid-September through October. It is rare inland during winter but occurs uncommonly along the southern coastal regions at this season; Connecticut breeders likely withdraw to the south but to an unknown extent.

This widespread North American member of the woodpecker family has several identifiable subspecies that fall into distinct groups, three of which have been treated as separate species. The "Yellow-shafted" Flicker (*auratus* group) breeds in Connecticut.

**Habitat**—The Northern Flicker inhabits open woodland, orchards, and shade trees of towns and cities. It is a cavity nester, using dead snags, poles, fences, and, less commonly, holes in banks or cliffs, barns, silos, or boxes. This is a conspicuous bird in spring when males produce their loud, piercing, repeated calls from the tops of trees, telephone poles, and even television aerials. The male selects the nest site and excavates the cavity, which may be usurped by European Starlings or squirrels. There is typically one brood per season in Connecticut, but renesting may occur if the first nest is destroyed. Eggs are laid in late April and early May; incubation lasts about two weeks; and young fledge in 24–28 days. Flickers forage on the ground to a greater extent than other woodpeckers but also look for insects in and behind bark and decaying limbs. Their food consists of ants, nuts, acorns, small fruits, and seeds.

**Atlas results**—The Northern Flicker was reported in most of the atlas blocks in the state, confirming its widespread distribution and apparently stable status within the state. If, as suggested, competition with the European Starling has reduced the flicker population, these effects have not caused a contraction of its range yet. It is worth noting, however, that one of the blocks in which flickers were not reported is in the heavily urbanized greater New Haven area, which has a correspondingly high population of European Starlings. It will be interesting to monitor the flicker in the coming decades to determine the influence of the starling on this woodpecker's population.

**Discussion**—Prior to the introduction and spread of the European Starling, the Northern Flicker was apparently a common nesting species in southern New England. Although occasionally hunted for sport, the Northern Flicker was listed as a common summer resident in Connecticut by Sage et al. (1913) and in southern New England in general by Forbush (1927). Results of the North American Breeding Bird Survey show this species as the most commonly detected of the woodpecker family in Connecticut (Robbins et al. 1986). The survey also revealed a significant decline in numbers between 1965 and 1979 (Robbins et al. 1986), a decline generally attributed to competition with the European Starling for nest sites. Kilham (1983) noted that the more aggressive starling is able to usurp a nest site from a pair of Northern Flickers.

*Dwight G. Smith*
*and Arnold Devine*

# Pileated Woodpecker
## *Dryocopus pileatus*

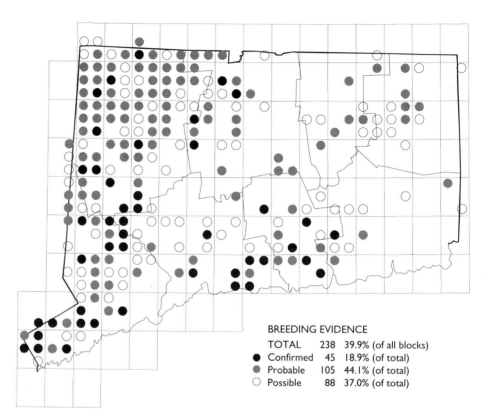

BREEDING EVIDENCE

| | TOTAL | 238 | 39.9% (of all blocks) |
|---|---|---|---|
| ● | Confirmed | 45 | 18.9% (of total) |
| ◉ | Probable | 105 | 44.1% (of total) |
| ○ | Possible | 88 | 37.0% (of total) |

This handsome bird is Connecticut's largest woodpecker. It is identified by its striking black and white plumage and long red crest. The Pileated Woodpecker is an uncommon permanent resident occurring in large tracts of mature woodland. Although normally wary and difficult to study, its distinctive loud, slow drumming resonating through woods normally reveals the presence of this species long before it is actually seen. This cavity nesting species uses old nesting chambers for roosting during the remainder of the year. The Pileated Woodpecker population, once severely depressed, is recovering and expanding its range.

**Habitat**—The Pileated Woodpecker is found in mature deciduous or mixed deciduous-conifer woodlands of uplands or forested wetlands, wooded parks, suburbs, or urban open space.

An essential habitat requirement is the presence of large, old timber. A large territory is established in extensive tracts of woodland or smaller woodlots connected by wooded corridors (Christy *in* Bent 1939). Large oval or rectangular cavities excavated in boles or limbs of dead standing timber, stumps, or fallen trees reveal the presence of Pileated Woodpeckers; this species also strips bark from dead trees and limbs to reach wood borers (Hoyt 1957). The nest cavity is excavated 12–65 feet high in a tree limb, snag, or stump. Eggs are laid in late April to mid-May and are incubated by both sexes for 15–18 days; the parents feed the young regurgitated food, consisting of insects, fruit, nuts, and acorns. The young fledge in about four weeks.

**Atlas results**—The Pileated Woodpecker was reported in 39.9% of the state's atlas blocks. The highest concentration was found in the northwestern hills, which corresponds to that portion of Connecticut with the most extensive areas of mature forest. Mostly absent or widely scattered in the central and coastal areas which are the most heavily urbanized. The northeastern section of the state shows a wide area of probable breeding; despite the strong bias in observer effort, which was less in the northeast, this pattern probably correctly depicts the distribution of the species in the state. The population of Pileated Woodpeckers appears to be smaller and more scattered in northeastern Connecticut.

**Discussion**—Historically, the Pileated Woodpecker population has been linked with the amount of available forested habitat. Deforestation that accompanied settlement sharply reduced its population, and the species was absent or rare in Connecticut during the late 1800s (Merriam 1877, Griscom and Snyder 1955). Even by the early 1900s Sage et al. (1913) still considered it a very rare breeder in the state. Population recovery followed reforestation and especially the maturation of woodlands; by the 1920s the species nested locally and by the 1970s it was fairly common, especially in western Connecticut (Zeranski and Baptist 1990). According to Robbins et al. (1986), the Pileated Woodpecker population has remained stable within the last two decades. They further noted that the population seems to be adjusting to increasing urbanization, provided that areas of mature woodland with connecting corridors remain (Christy *in* Bent 1939).

*Dwight G. Smith and Arnold Devine*

199

# Olive-sided Flycatcher
*Contopus borealis*

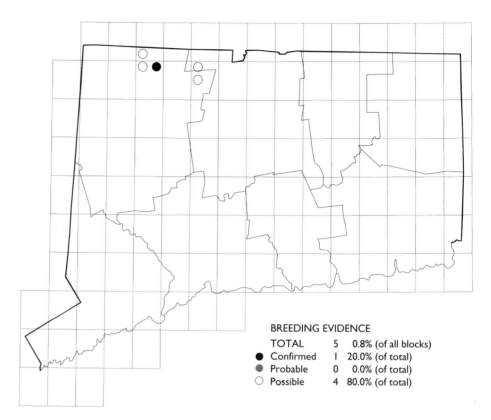

BREEDING EVIDENCE

| | TOTAL | 5 | 0.8% (of all blocks) |
|---|---|---|---|
| ● | Confirmed | I | 20.0% (of total) |
| ◉ | Probable | 0 | 0.0% (of total) |
| ○ | Possible | 4 | 80.0% (of total) |

This migratory species is an accidental breeder in Connecticut, the only documented breeding record for the state having occurred during the period of this atlas. The Olive-sided Flycatcher is presently designated as a Species of Special Concern in the state.

The Olive-sided Flycatcher is a rather late migrant through the state in spring, typically mid to late May, and an early migrant in fall, primarily from late August to mid-September. An active observer in the state may see one or two in migration, usually birds atop a dead snag of a tree. Olive-sided Flycatchers are usually silent in migration, their characteristic whistled song, 'quick-three-beers,' or incessantly repeated, short call 'pip-pip,' seldom heard in the state. This species generally migrates west of the Appalachians to wintering grounds in the mountains of northwestern South America and, to a lesser extent, Central America (AOU 1983).

**Habitat**—Nests are typically placed in conifers, characteristically in open areas where dead trees (snags) are present in a woodland setting such as occurs in valleys where beavers create a pond with standing dead trees and with live conifers nearby on the surrounding slopes (Fichtel *in* Laughlin and Kibbe 1985, Peterson *in* Andrle and Carroll 1988). The breeding record for Connecticut occurred at an extensive, high elevation black spruce bog (about 1,300 ft elev.) with many dead snags and conifers.

**Atlas results**—The single confirmation was at Beckley Bog, Norfolk, in late June and July 1983, when a *recently* fledged bird was seen attended by a pair of adult birds, one singing and the other calling agitatedly close by the fledgling (J. Souther, pers. comm.). The description of the fledgling mentions several features indicative of juvenal plumage for Olive-sided Flycatcher and indicates that the bird was very recently fledged. Another bird was heard singing west of this locality in 1986 and at Beckley Bog again in 1987 (G. Billings, pers. comm.). Also, possible breeding was noted at Barkhamsted Reservoir during the atlas.

**Discussion**—Any report of breeding for Olive-sided Flycatcher in the state should be treated with great scrutiny, and observers are cautioned to make a special effort to obtain satisfactory photographic documentation. This species was considered rare in Connecticut by Merriam (1877), who believed a few sometimes bred in the northern hills. He had no direct evidence for breeding and based this statement on known breeding in the Berkshires of Massachusetts. Early in the 1900s, the species was listed as a rare migrant (Sage et al. 1913). Among the fall records reported by those authors is a report of a pair with three young near Danbury in 1903. It is

unclear if they believed these birds had bred there; based on the dates of observation and the proximity of New York, this is best considered unsatisfactory as a breeding record. Zeranski and Baptist (1990) cite a reported nesting at Stamford in 1897, but that report should probably be questioned based on the locality; Bull (1974) rejected a breeding report from a similar low elevation locality at Newburgh, New York, citing confusion with Eastern Wood Pewee. Likewise, reports of sporadic breeding since the late 1960s in the northwest hills (Zeranski and Baptist 1990) should probably be treated as incorrect without further evidence for verification.

Although the nearby breeding population in the Adirondack Mountains of New York appears unchanged over the past century (Peterson *in* Andrle and Carroll 1988), a decline has been noted over the past several decades in the Appalachians, Nova Scotia, and central New England (Hall 1983, Tufts 1986, and Robbins et al. 1986 respectively). These authors cite no major changes in the breeding localities and no apparent reason for this decline on the breeding grounds. One must wonder if this

Neotropical migrant could be affected by loss of wintering habitat.

*Louis R. Bevier*

# Eastern Wood-Pewee
## *Contopus virens*

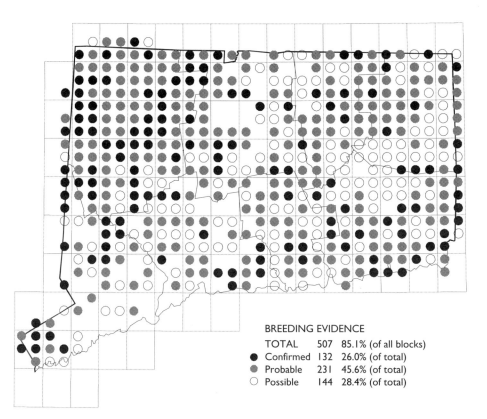

BREEDING EVIDENCE

| | TOTAL | 507 | 85.1% (of all blocks) |
|---|---|---|---|
| ● | Confirmed | 132 | 26.0% (of total) |
| ◉ | Probable | 231 | 45.6% (of total) |
| ○ | Possible | 144 | 28.4% (of total) |

The Eastern Wood-Pewee is a common migratory breeder in Connecticut. It migrates principally along the Caribbean slope of Central America, more rarely through the western Bahamas, and winters in northern and western South America from Colombia and Venezuela south to Peru and western Brazil (AOU 1983).

**Habitat**—The species breeds in mature deciduous woodland or mixed deciduous-coniferous forest, often with the presence of a forest gap, an opening through which sunlight can penetrate further into the forest than in areas with an unbroken canopy. Sage et al. (1913) mention the use of shade trees, frequently elms, and orchards as nest sites in Connecticut, but elms are now largely gone, due to introduced disease, and no records of nesting in orchards are known for the state in recent decades.

**Atlas results**—The Eastern Wood Pewee was widespread in the state and appeared to be lacking principally in the highly urbanized parts of the state as along the central valley and coast.

**Discussion**—The species has apparently been common as a breeder in the state throughout the nineteenth and twentieth centuries (Zeranski and Baptist 1990). The maturation of woodlands statewide during the twentieth century has promoted an increase in the numbers of this species, but this gain

has been offset to an unknown extent by loss of breeding habitat in cities and towns particularly through the elimination of shade trees and reduction of areas not covered by buildings or pavement. The apparent decline in the use of orchards as breeding sites might conceivably be related to 1) modern programs of pruning or mowing or 2) introduction of more effective chemical controls of arthropod pests resulting in less arthropod food for flycatchers in orchards, but these and other possible explanations need further study. Two earlier studies examining habitats of the Eastern Wood-Pewee and Least Flycatcher reached contradictory conclusions. Hespenheide (1971), in a study conducted in five states including Virginia but not Connecticut, found that wood-pewees occur in woods with a lower density of vegetation than the habitats used by Least Flycatchers. However, D. W. Johnston (1971), in a study in Virginia, supported the conclusions of two earlier studies on Least Flycatchers that the wood-pewee lives in a habitat with a greater density of vegetation. Perhaps the difference in conclusions of Hespenheide and Johnston is attributable to local differences in the habitats used by the two species.

*George A. Clark, Jr.*

# Acadian Flycatcher
## *Empidonax virescens*

The Acadian Flycatcher is an uncommon migratory breeder in Connecticut, where it is near the northeastern limit of its range. Breeding localities are quite localized within the state, and the species is rarely encountered as a migrant away from such sites. Acadian Flycatchers arrive by mid-May and generally depart by late August. This species winters from Costa Rica to western Venezuela (AOU 1983).

**Habitat**—In Connecticut, the species is found in wooded sites characteristically along streams or other waterways with a fairly dense canopy of trees overhead and a relatively open understory. Sites are often near ponds or open fields. Although breeding birds to the south of Connecticut are often in areas of deciduous trees (Bull 1964), most Connecticut sites contain many conifers.

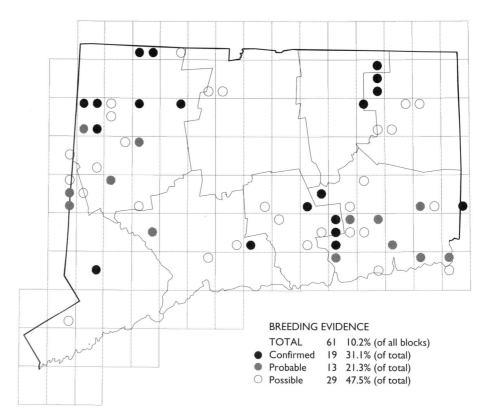

BREEDING EVIDENCE

| | TOTAL | 61 | 10.2% (of all blocks) |
|---|---|---|---|
| ● | Confirmed | 19 | 31.1% (of total) |
| ● | Probable | 13 | 21.3% (of total) |
| ○ | Possible | 29 | 47.5% (of total) |

**Atlas results**—Confirmations were obtained from 19 blocks that were widely spread across the state. A nest in Union was placed in a deciduous tree on a branch that extended horizontally so that the nest was located about five feet above a stream (pers. obs.), but most of the nests for which details were reported during the atlas survey were located over land.

**Discussion**—Sage et al. (1913) knew of breeding records in Connecticut only for Fairfield County, from Stamford west. Later in the century, Bull (1964), writing of birds in the greater New York City area, indicated that the species was no longer present as a breeder in Fairfield County. Breeding birds again appeared in the state in the 1960s (Zeranski and Baptist 1990). For

a time the best known breeding site in the state was at Devil's Hopyard State Park of East Haddam (Proctor 1978). Starting in 1970, the species began to appear as a summering bird in the northeastern part of the state where it subsequently became regular in a few localities (Manter 1975). Breeding was first recorded from Guilford in 1977 (Proctor 1978). By 1985 the species began to occur regularly in summer for several years in the New London area (Askins 1990).

The Acadian Flycatcher has undergone marked changes in status within the state, having apparently disappeared for a time as a breeder and then successfully advanced again from the south. As part of that same northward advance, recolonization also occurred in adjacent southeastern New York state (Eaton *in* Andrle and Carroll 1988). The causes of the retreat and reinvasion have apparently not been addressed. Increasing maturity of trees along waterways of the state has presumably been one factor facilitating the reestablishment of breeding in the state. For West Virginia, Hall (1983) noted that breeding Acadian Flycatchers were most common in "certain moist mixed deciduous forests," usually along streams, and that most nests were located over water. The literature thus suggests a transition from use of deciduous to more coniferous habitats from south to north in the range of this species.

*George A. Clark, Jr.*

# Alder Flycatcher
## *Empidonax alnorum*

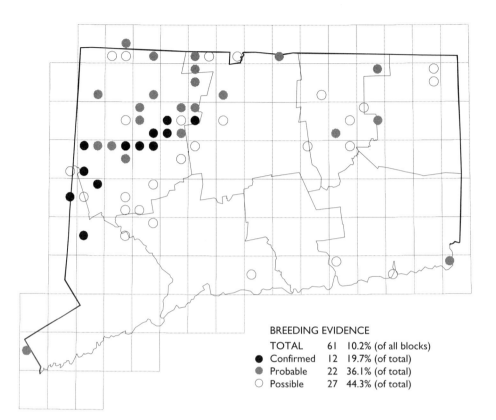

BREEDING EVIDENCE

| | | |
|---|---|---|
| TOTAL | 61 | 10.2% (of all blocks) |
| ● Confirmed | 12 | 19.7% (of total) |
| ◉ Probable | 22 | 36.1% (of total) |
| ○ Possible | 27 | 44.3% (of total) |

The Alder Flycatcher is a rare and local migratory breeder that winters in South America. Because Alder and Willow Flycatchers are virtually inseparable by measurements even when held in the hand (Seutin 1991), present ideas on the difference in their wintering ranges were initially based on Gorski's studies (1969b, 1971) of responses of wintering birds to broadcasting of tape-recorded vocalizations given by birds on the breeding grounds. He recognized that Alder Flycatcher gives a distinctive 'pit' call, which distinguishes it from the Willow Flycatcher's lower 'whit' call. He thus identified Willow Flycatchers in Panama and only Alders in South America, indicating a leapfrog migration in which the more northern breeding Alders migrate further south for the winter. The songs also differ—the Alder produces a buzzy 'fee-bee-o' and the Willow an explosive 'fitz-bew.'

**Habitat**—This species occupies areas with an interspersion of low vegetation including shrubs with trees over eight feet high in the vicinity of streams or other open water. The nest is characteristically a cup with straggling pieces of vegetation hanging beneath and placed low and not over water, less than three feet off the ground in thickets of hawthorn, spiraea, buttonbush, or alder.

**Atlas results**—Breeding was primarily in the northern part of the state, especially the northwest. Apparently, the Alder Flycatcher's range in New England extends southward through the Berkshires into northwestern Connecticut and southward sparingly through the hills of central Massachusetts into northeastern Connecticut, where it is presently an erratic summer visitor.

**Discussion**—Because this species has been officially recognized as distinct from the Willow Flycatcher only since 1973 (*Auk* 90:415–416), accurate details of its historic status are sketchy. Presumably this species has been breeding in Connecticut since colonial times, but evidence to support this assumption is limited. Sage et al. (1913) reported finding three nests 1–2 feet off the ground at Litchfield in 1905, the nest height clearly indicating Alder Flycatchers. Enders and Magee (1965) recorded both Alder and Willow Flycatchers in the summer at Litchfield, and their survey led to Gorski's detailed investigations (1969a, 1970a, 1970b) of these birds in that area. Using color banding and sound spectrographic analysis of vocalizations, Gorski found no evidence for interbreeding between the two song types, thus confirming the conclusion of Stein (1958, 1963) that the Traill's Flycatcher should be separated into two species. In the Litchfield area, habitat and nest structure of the Alder Flycatcher were like those reported by Stein from other states.

The idea that the Alder Flycatcher has been partially replaced by an expanding population of Willow Flycatchers is discussed in the account for the latter. At present, the Alder Flycatcher is a regular breeder only in northwestern Connecticut. Singing non-breeders are noted in summer south in the west to Greenwich, Fairfield County, and in the east to Chaplin, Windham County. Exceptional was an Alder Flycatcher present throughout the summer of 1974 at Deep River along the Connecticut River Craig (1975).

Because the status of this species may be changing relatively rapidly, continued monitoring is desirable. The Alder Flycatcher is recognized by vocalizations including the 'wee-bee-o' song and a sharp 'pip' call note that is slightly higher pitched (about 1,000 hertz higher) than that of the Willow Flycatcher. The Alder builds an untidy cup nest unlike the neat cup built by the Willow Flycatcher. Alder and Willow Flycatchers might be relatively easily missed by observers in view of the similarities of their vocalizations, a frequent silence even when present in numbers, and the use of habitats that are often not easily penetrated by people.

*George A. Clark, Jr.*

# Willow Flycatcher
## *Empidonax traillii*

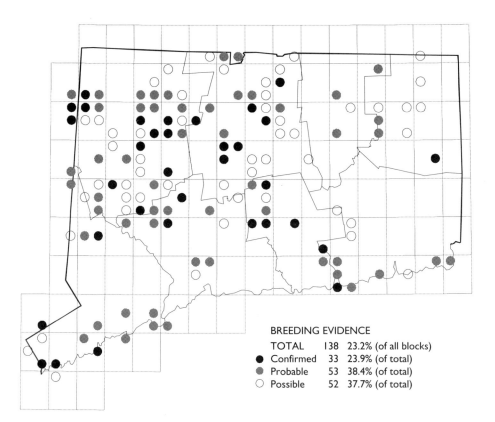

BREEDING EVIDENCE

| | TOTAL | 138 | 23.2% (of all blocks) |
|---|---|---|---|
| ● | Confirmed | 33 | 23.9% (of total) |
| ● | Probable | 53 | 38.4% (of total) |
| ○ | Possible | 52 | 37.7% (of total) |

The Willow Flycatcher is an uncommon migratory breeder. Based on the calls of wintering birds, this species is known to winter from southern Mexico to Panama (Gorski 1969b, AOU 1983). The overall wintering range is not well known, however, and where Connecticut breeders winter is unknown. The Willow Flycatcher has several subspecies, with *E. t. traillii* said to breed into New England (Browning 1993). These eastern populations might be expected to winter further south in Central America than western birds, following a pattern seen in other species.

**Habitat**—The Willow Flycatcher breeds in wet brushy areas. Nests are commonly placed in dense stands of willow shrubs over seven feet high with moist soil or water beneath. The nest is a neatly constructed cup commonly placed about four feet off the ground.

**Atlas results**—The Willow Flycatcher was found to be a widespread breeder in western Connecticut but less common in the eastern part of the state.

**Discussion**—A good historic record is lacking because Willow and Alder flycatchers have been recognized as separate species only since 1973 (*Auk* 90:415–416). The Willow Flycatcher has been expanding its range in the mid-Atlantic states and into the Northeast (Finch 1973, Hall 1983). Bull (1974) commented that the 'fitz-bew' song type only recently had spread to Long Island. These birds possibly originated from southeastern populations, subspecies *traillii*, as the midwestern form, *campestris*, was already known as a breeder in western New York (Browning

1993). Of interest regarding the presence of this species in New England in the past is a comment by Bagg and Eliot (1937) on the summer presence of an apparent Willow Flycatcher in the Connecticut River valley of Massachusetts. Unfortunately, no information exists on the presence of Willow Flycatchers in Connecticut before the 1960s. Enders and Magee (1965) found this species and the Alder Flycatcher during summer at the White Memorial Foundation in Litchfield, and consequently Gorski undertook a detailed study there (1969a, 1970a).

The idea that the northeastern range expansion of the Willow Flycatcher has involved replacement of the Alder Flycatcher has been presented repeatedly (Stein 1963, Bull 1964, Barlow and McGillivray 1983, D. R. C. Prescott 1987). A thorough compilation of the evidence, however, is still needed. Conflicts between Willow and Alder Flycatchers occur relatively frequently where they occur together (Gorski 1970a), and these conflicts together with a preconception that coexistence of two similar species might be unstable might have led observers to anticipate replacement of one species by the other. Nevertheless, growth of trees and shrubs during plant succession might result in loss of habitat suitable for Alder Flycatchers while habitat suitable for Willow Flycatchers was being formed; thus a change in vegetation might give an impression of a competitive replacement of one flycatcher species by the other. Better documentation is needed on the question of competitive replacement. In midwestern and far western North America, Willow Flycatchers are exceptionally varied in their breeding sites, using not only wet sites such as occur in Connecticut but also much drier upland

sites (de Smet and Conrad 1988, Frakes and Johnson 1982, Stedman 1987, Zink and Fall 1981, and pers. obs.).

*George A. Clark, Jr.*

## Least Flycatcher
### *Empidonax minimus*

The Least Flycatcher is a fairly common but local migratory breeder in the state. The species winters in Middle America from northern Mexico to Nicaragua and casually to Panama (AOU 1983).

**Habitat**—In Connecticut the species breeds in areas where shrubs or saplings are mixed with shorter herbaceous vegetation. The sites are typically within, or adjacent to, a woodland. There is often open water or a wetland nearby. Breeding sites of the Least Flycatcher are commonly drier than those used by either Willow or Alder Flycatchers. Sage et al. (1913) mentioned orchards and shade trees as breeding habitat, but such areas are not widely used by Least Flycatchers in Connecticut at present. Detailed evaluations of Least Flycatcher habitats outside Connecticut have been provided by Hespenheide (1971) and D. W. Johnston (1971).

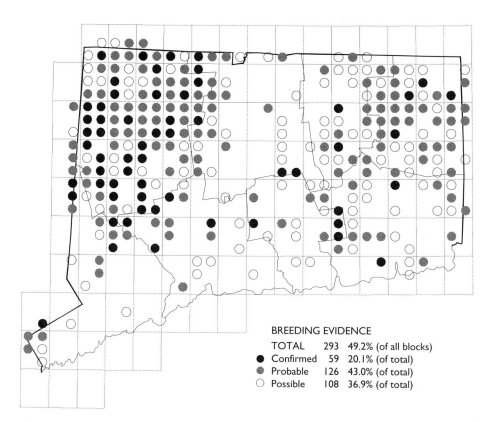

BREEDING EVIDENCE

| | | |
|---|---|---|
| TOTAL | 293 | 49.2% (of all blocks) |
| ● Confirmed | 59 | 20.1% (of total) |
| ● Probable | 126 | 43.0% (of total) |
| ○ Possible | 108 | 36.9% (of total) |

**Atlas results**—Survey during the atlas indicates that the northwestern and northeastern highlands have been the major areas for breeding of Least Flycatchers. The birds tend to be lacking as breeders at lower elevations along the coast and in the Connecticut River valley. Appropriate habitat in southwestern Connecticut is inexplicably scarcely occupied.

**Discussion**—The species has evidently occurred on a regular basis in the state throughout the nineteenth and twentieth centuries (Sage et al. 1913, Zeranski and Baptist 1990). However, during the latter century the species has become rare in Fairfield County (Zeranski and Baptist 1990), even though apparently favorable habitat remains plentiful there (L. Bevier, pers. comm.).

Adjacent to Connecticut in south-eastern New York state near New York City, observers in recent years have noted a decline in this species (Conner *in* Andrle and Carroll 1988), thus agreeing with the findings from south-western Connecticut. Because the disappearance of this species has occurred near a highly urbanized area, the search for explanations might logically include effects attributable to urbanization. If, for example, air pollution originating from urban areas affected availability of certain kinds of arthropods, effects might be detected in declines or absence of species of insectivorous birds, but evaluation of such possibilities will require further study. There are certainly many conceivable causes for the decline of the Least Flycatcher along the coast, and this remains a challenging problem. Absence of the species as a breeder in much of the Connecticut River valley might be explained as due to a lack of suitable habitat. On a statewide basis, increasing maturity of woodlands might be expected to reduce the amount of habitat available for Least Flycatchers.

*George A. Clark, Jr.*

211

# Eastern Phoebe
## *Sayornis phoebe*

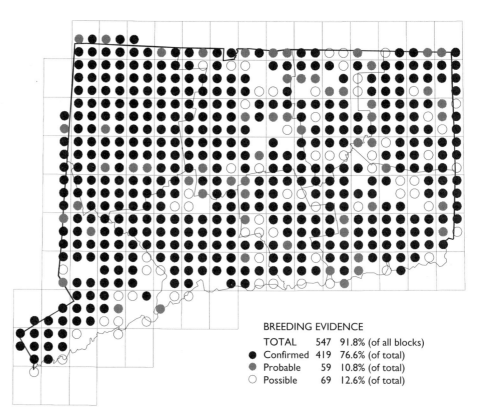

BREEDING EVIDENCE

| | TOTAL | 547 | 91.8% (of all blocks) |
|---|---|---|---|
| ● | Confirmed | 419 | 76.6% (of total) |
| ● | Probable | 59 | 10.8% (of total) |
| ○ | Possible | 69 | 12.6% (of total) |

The Eastern Phoebe is a widespread and common migratory breeder. The species winters, in the eastern part of its range, principally from Virginia and the Ohio valley south into southern Florida and Mexico (AOU 1983). Within the United States in early winter the species is most prevalent along the Gulf Coast and in Florida (Root 1988). In association with its greater tolerance of cold conditions relative to other flycatchers, the Eastern Phoebe consumes comparatively more fruit, though insects are, as in the North American flycatchers generally, a major component of the diet while the birds are in the breeding areas (Bent 1942).

**Habitat**—A major requirement for nesting by phoebes is the presence of an overhang above a surface upon which the nest is built. Structures of human construction including buildings and bridges often provide the necessary features, but the birds also use more natural sites as may be provided along earthen banks, upturned roots of fallen trees, or rock ledges. Eastern Phoebes regularly select sites with some trees nearby and usually with a fairly open understory if there is a canopy above. Sites may be anywhere from well inside a forest to suburban yards. Streams or other bodies of water are often present close to the nest sites. Nest construction requires mud and thus at least a temporary supply of wet soil at not too great a distance from the nest site.

**Atlas results**—The species was found in more than 90% of all blocks and confirmed as a breeder in a high percentage of those blocks. Because the

212

species is readily approachable and often nests in close proximity to people, obtaining confirmations of breeding is often easier than for many other species. Apparently only the highly urbanized areas of the state entirely lack this species.

**Discussion**—The species has apparently been common in Connecticut throughout the nineteenth and twentieth centuries (Sage et al. 1913). Human construction has presumably greatly increased the number of potential nest sites for this species relative to conditions in precolonial times. Nevertheless, it appears that, as in the case of many hole-nesting species, the Eastern Phoebe is still potentially limited by the availability of nest sites combined with the territoriality of the birds. If people were to increase the number of suitable nest sites in suburban and rural areas, it seems probable that an even larger breeding population could be sustained in the state. The specialization of nest structure in phoebes undoubtedly provides substantial protection from adverse weather, and conceivably is advantageous in making the nest relatively less accessible for terrestrial predators than would be a nest cup suspended in vegetation.

*George A. Clark, Jr.*

## Great Crested Flycatcher
*Myiarchus crinitus*

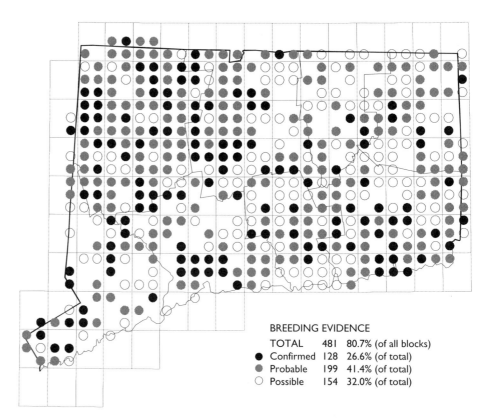

BREEDING EVIDENCE

| | | | |
|---|---|---|---|
| TOTAL | | 481 | 80.7% (of all blocks) |
| ● | Confirmed | 128 | 26.6% (of total) |
| ● | Probable | 199 | 41.4% (of total) |
| ○ | Possible | 154 | 32.0% (of total) |

The Great Crested Flycatcher is a migratory breeder. It winters from central Florida south into Cuba and from southern Mexico south into northern South America (AOU 1983). In Connecticut it is a common breeder in suitable habitat.

**Habitat**—This species typically nests in holes in trees in mature woodlands, either deciduous or mixed coniferous-deciduous, usually in the vicinity of a forest gap such as near the edge of a pond in the woods. Suburban areas are also used for breeding, and the birds have been known to accept nest boxes (Bent 1942).

**Atlas results**—Found in over 80% of all blocks, the Great Crested Flycatcher is a widespread breeder in the state. The species is lacking from highly urbanized areas. Some of the gaps in range indicated for eastern Connecticut may represent the difficulty of finding this species during block busting towards midsummer when the birds become relatively quiet (Levine *in* Andrle and Carroll 1988).

**Discussion**—Sage et al. (1913) considered it widespread as a breeder but noted that it was ranked as rare in the Litchfield area at that time. Maturation of the forests of the state through the twentieth century presumably has augmented the numbers of this species.

Of the two largest flycatcher species breeding in Connecticut, the Great Crested Flycatcher uses principally the wooded areas, whereas the Eastern Kingbird uses sites that are more open. Among species of birds nesting in holes in the state, the Great Crested Flycatcher is exceptional in being on average the latest of such species to return on migration to the breeding grounds. If the common belief is correct that availability of nest sites is generally limiting for populations of hole-nesting birds, there is a question whether Great Crested Flycatchers have any special features in their biology to enable them to obtain nest sites after other Connecticut hole-nesters including, to name only birds, Wood Ducks, mergansers, certain owls, woodpeckers, swallows, titmice, nuthatches, bluebirds, starlings, and House Sparrows have already taken holes. One evident feature is that Great Crested Flycatchers tolerate a wide range of kinds and sizes of nest hole (Bent 1942). However, there are also marked differences in the types of nesting cavities favored by the different species. Waterfowl and Barred Owls use nest cavities that are likely to be far larger than used by the flycatchers. In contrast, chickadees, titmice, nuthatches, and bluebirds commonly use cavities with entrances that would not accommodate the flycatchers. Starlings and House Sparrows tend to avoid the wooded habitats that are frequently used by Great Crested Flycatchers. Thus, the combination of cavity and entrance size and wooded sites favored by Great Crested Flycatchers would seem to be sufficiently inappropriate for other species to assure the availability of cavities for the flycatchers despite their relatively late return to the breeding area.

*George A. Clark, Jr.*

## Eastern Kingbird
### *Tyrannus tyrannus*

The Eastern Kingbird is a common migratory breeder in Connecticut. The species winters in South America to northern Argentina and is a common migrant through Mexico and Central America (AOU 1983).

**Habitat**—This species occurs around open areas including ponds, lakes, marshes, fields, and lawns. The nest is typically placed in a tree near and often overlooking such an open area. The species occurs in park, suburban, roadside, and agricultural areas, as well as more natural settings.

**Atlas results**—The species was found in 97% of the blocks and confirmed as breeding in more than three quarters of all blocks. The species is lacking apparently only in highly developed urban centers that lack parks or in extensive

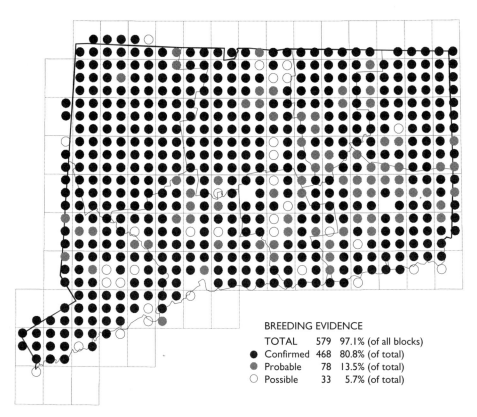

BREEDING EVIDENCE

| | TOTAL | 579 | 97.1% (of all blocks) |
|---|---|---|---|
| ● | Confirmed | 468 | 80.8% (of total) |
| ● | Probable | 78 | 13.5% (of total) |
| ○ | Possible | 33 | 5.7% (of total) |

unbroken stands of woodland. Presence of the species is usually relatively easy to detect because the birds often perch conspicuously in the open and call frequently. Eastern Kingbirds often reveal their breeding activity in an area by defending their eggs and young with aggressive mobbing of a variety of larger birds including potential preda-

tors of egg and young. One of the less common nest sites found during the survey for the atlas was in Eastford on the top of an ordinary wooden utility pole standing along the roadside (pers. obs.). Bull (1974) reported nesting of Eastern Kingbirds on telephone poles.

**Discussion**—The species has apparently been common continuously throughout the nineteenth and twentieth centuries (Zeranski and Baptist 1990). Mackenzie (1961), in studying the birds of Guilford, found that Eastern Kingbirds were more common during the 1940s than in the 1950s; conceivably this difference could be attributable to the widespread application of pesticides used in the 1950s. Unfortunately, no comparable data are available from Guilford after the reduction in use of pesticides during the early 1970s. The Eastern Kingbird exhibits strong territoriality of pairs and insectivory in Connecticut, but in the wintering areas of Amazonia the birds are associated in flocks and are fruit-eating (Fitzpatrick 1980), thus undergoing great seasonal changes in behavior, though perhaps no more dramatic than the seasonal changes of American Robins which also become much more gregarious during the times of year when they are eating fruits.

*George A. Clark, Jr.*

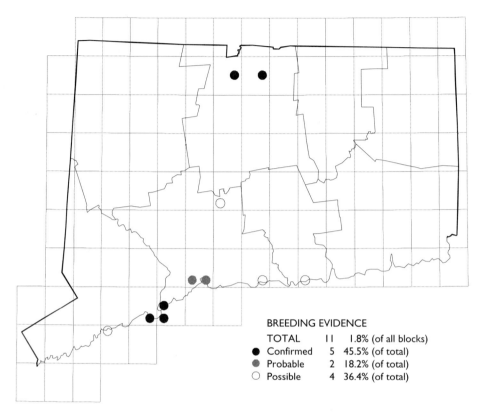

BREEDING EVIDENCE

| | | | |
|---|---|---|---|
| TOTAL | | 11 | 1.8% (of all blocks) |
| ● | Confirmed | 5 | 45.5% (of total) |
| ◍ | Probable | 2 | 18.2% (of total) |
| ○ | Possible | 4 | 36.4% (of total) |

## Horned Lark
### *Eremophila alpestris*

The Horned Lark has a circumpolar distribution extending south to the northern regions of Africa and South America. It is currently a rare breeder designated as Threatened in the state; it is commonly seen as a migrant and winter visitor in Connecticut (Zeranski and Baptist 1990).

As many as twenty-one subspecies of the Horned Lark have been recognized from North America (AOU 1957), with the "Prairie" Horned Lark (*E. a. praticola*) identified as breeding in Connecticut (Bull 1964). The various named populations of the Horned Lark are not well-defined and grade from one into the next. The "Prairie" Horned Lark falls into a group of comparatively small races with a whitish eyebrow, unlike the yellow-browed winter visitors from the north of the nominate subspecies *alpestris* (Dwight 1890). Bull (1974) did not recognize as dis-

tinct another pale-browed race (*hoyti*) that Sage et al. (1913) stated occurs in Connecticut in winter.

Horned Larks winter throughout most of their breeding range, except in the high arctic regions (AOU 1983). Connecticut breeders probably withdraw to the south in part as far as South Carolina and west possibly to Texas (AOU 1957).

**Habitat**—In Connecticut, the Horned Lark breeds on beaches and open areas mostly along the coast (Mackenzie 1961), as suggested by its early common name of Shore Lark (Bent 1942). They also breed regularly in grassland surrounding Bradley Airport, Windsor Locks (Crossman 1989), which is also typical habitat for this species. Horned Larks generally prefer open areas, par-

ticularly fallow agricultural fields, and are not likely to be found in areas with substantial cover.

**Atlas results**—The confirmed breeding areas were as expected along relatively undisturbed coastal areas and large expanses of open grasslands.

**Discussion**—The Horned Lark was only known as a migrant and winter visitor in Connecticut until the late 1800s (Merriam 1877), and the "Prairie" Horned Lark, now breeding in the state, was probably most common in the eastern Great Plains before east-

ern forests were cleared (Hurley and Franks 1976). The eastward expansion of that subspecies' breeding range is well chronicled by Forbush (1927), who stated that the first breeding record for New England was in 1889, only shortly before the first breeding in Connecticut in 1891 (Sage et al. 1913).

Horned Larks are relatively skittish while on the nest and probably do not tolerate direct human presence well (Bent 1942; Wachenhut et al. 1983). This may account for the lack of breeding records on other coastal sites. The absence of records in Fairfield and Litchfield counties, where breeding

was known early in this century, is probably due to the abandonment of agriculture followed by development or ecological succession. In agricultural areas in the western United States, destruction of nests and injury to adults often occurs during tillage for spring weed control. Although methods have been developed to mitigate these losses, tillage may account for declines where mechanized farming continues (Rodgers 1983). A decline was detected for the Northeast from 1965 to 1979 (Robbins et al. 1986).

*George Gale*

## Purple Martin
*Progne subis*

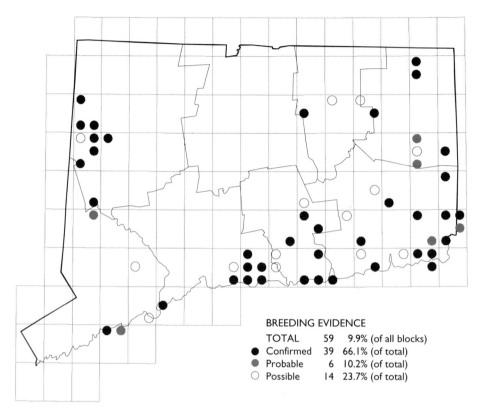

BREEDING EVIDENCE

| | | |
|---|---|---|
| TOTAL | 59 | 9.9% (of all blocks) |
| ● Confirmed | 39 | 66.1% (of total) |
| ● Probable | 6 | 10.2% (of total) |
| ○ Possible | 14 | 23.7% (of total) |

The Purple Martin is an uncommon and local migratory breeder in Connecticut, where it is now designated as a Species of Special Concern. As a migrant, it frequents open areas. Martins may be seen with other migrant swallows, but in general the species tends to move in small groups of its own. Never common, it is usually found in close proximity to a nesting site. During fall, aggregations of adults and young numbering in the hundreds have been recorded. The species migrates through Middle America, mainly coastally, and winters in the Amazon Basin south to southeastern Brazil (AOU 1983).

**Habitat**—Purple Martins are found in both suburban and rural situations in the state. There is a marked preference for the shoreline and the nearby interior. They feed over extensive open areas and favor sites with large bodies of water nearby. Although formerly nesting in hollow trees and cliff face crevices, such as are still used in the West, within Connecticut martins are entirely dependent on nest boxes. Much time has been spent studying the nest site preference of the Purple Martin as many people wish to entice them to their yard. A few things seem to be necessary to attract martins: 1) extensive open areas over which they can feed; 2) a cleared area for some distance around the nesting box, known as a swoop zone; 3) nearby open water. Other factors as yet unclear seem to influence acceptance of a site. Some nest boxes placed in seemingly ideal locations have gone unused for years. In contrast, sites seemingly lacking all the key features are sometimes used.

Since many houses are erected with the intent of establishing an avian pest control system, it should be noted that stomach content analysis (R. F. Johnston 1967) shows them not to eat as many mosquitoes as had been thought. Beetles and flies are much more important in their overall diet.

**Atlas results**—Thirty-nine blocks had confirmed breeding, including a coastal concentration and a cluster along the upper Housatonic River valley. Scattered sites to the interior, especially in the eastern portion, are in direct relation to larger bodies of water.

**Discussion**—As with other swallows that have benefited from human clearing of the state, the Purple Martin also has shown ups and downs with the changes in vegetation. Originally they might have used tree nesting cavities, but as the land was cleared and as people erected nesting boxes, the fortunes of martins increased. Merriam (1877)

listed the Purple Martin as locally abundant, undoubtedly in reference to colonies. By the late 1800s and early 1900s, the Purple Martin had sharply declined and was certainly feeling the impact of the rapid increase of both the House Sparrow and the European Starling, both of which use many of the available nest sites (Bagg and Eliot 1937). By the 1920s, the populations were reduced to only limited spots (Forbush 1927). Throughout this history, the most used nesting locations have been coastal, and this remains so to the present.

Always known for fluctuations in their populations, based on factors including bad weather and parasites (Moss and Camin 1970), the Purple Martin still has an uncertain fate in the state. With numerous houses being erected, a year of high return populations from the south may see new colonies established in many areas. But, as shown in the past, these new colonies can disappear just as quickly as they appear, and for seemingly unknown reasons. Build-up of external parasite populations in nesting sites would be expected to promote frequent shifts of nesting areas.

*Noble S. Proctor*

221

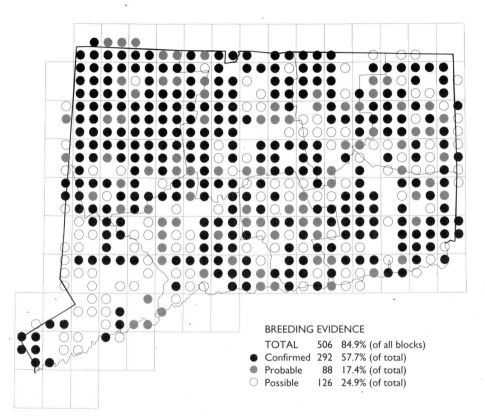

## Tree Swallow
### *Tachycineta bicolor*

This migratory breeder has increased in numbers over the last twenty years throughout the Northeast (Robbins et al. 1986). The species winters chiefly in the southeast United States, also the Bahamas, the Greater Antilles, and south through Central America to Costa Rica and casually to northern Colombia (AOU 1983, Ridgely and Gwynne 1989). Tree Swallows are casual into early winter north to Massachusetts and are usually the first swallows to return to New England in spring.

**Habitat**—A wide variety of habitats are used in both rural and suburban areas. They prefer open fields, marshlands, coastal salt marshes, and woodland edges often near water. Nest boxes and natural tree cavities are widely used as well as abandoned woodpecker holes. Principally aerial insect feeders, they also eat bayberries during stress

BREEDING EVIDENCE

| | | | |
|---|---|---|---|
| | TOTAL | 506 | 84.9% (of all blocks) |
| ● | Confirmed | 292 | 57.7% (of total) |
| ◓ | Probable | 88 | 17.4% (of total) |
| ○ | Possible | 126 | 24.9% (of total) |

periods and in fall migration. In fall it is common to see flocks numbering in the hundreds swoop low over fields and cover the coastal bayberry bushes in a feeding frenzy. This ability to feed on fruits, instead of full dependency on insects, allows this species to arrive very early in the spring and often stay late into fall and at times even into early winter!

**Atlas results**—The map shows that breeding was confirmed in nearly half of all the atlas blocks. The pattern also shows that areas with "nesting trails" for Eastern Bluebirds were often used by Tree Swallows. In many areas where nesting was not confirmed, recent surveys have shown current occupancy by these birds.

**Discussion**—The population of Tree Swallows has risen and fallen associated with human alteration of the environment. Merriam (1877) listed them as common, but the clearing of the forests during the latter part of the 1800s into the early 1900s left nest site availability at a low point. Sage et al. (1913) reported them as a rare summer resident. Since reforestation of the state and abandonment of farmlands, the population has increased to perhaps its highest numbers to date. During the 1960s and continuing to the present, nest box programs for Eastern Bluebirds and Wood Ducks enhanced many areas as Tree Swallow nesting sites, and the swallows were quick to use such boxes. More recently, nest boxes placed especially for Tree Swallows have been deployed in a variety of locations. This has greatly increased the breeding population throughout the state and New England (Robbins et al. 1986). Increased beaver activity throughout the state has led to flooding and the killing of trees. Nest holes excavated in these dead trees by woodpeckers attract early migrant Tree Swallows. Having a defense range with a radius of nearly 50 feet from the nest box means that colonial nesting, which is occasionally seen, occurs only in an area with a high density of food (Robertson and Gibbs 1982). During the second nesting of the season, young birds from the first clutch can often be seen assisting in raising the young of the second brood. This helping by birds other than the breeding pair sometimes involves even adult birds (Skutch 1987). Presumably these birds often have some attachment with the family from previous seasons. However, adult helpers sometimes are birds that have lost their own clutch and appear to adopt another family to help raise its young (Kuerzi 1941).

*Noble S. Proctor*

# Northern Rough-winged Swallow
## *Stelgidopteryx serripennis*

This summer resident is found through-out the state and can be a common migrant in both spring and fall. The species as a whole breeds across most of North America from southeastern Alaska, across southern Canada, and south to the highlands of Costa Rica; northern populations winter south to Panama (AOU 1983).

**Habitat**—The species occurs in coastal, suburban, and rural areas where there is water. It commonly nests in holes in walls, drainage pipe open-ings of abutments, crevices in old stone foundations, especially along rivers where bridges once crossed, and in retaining walls along the coast. On occasion, they use dirt banks for nest-ing, sometimes using abandoned holes of the Belted Kingfisher or former Bank Swallow colonies.

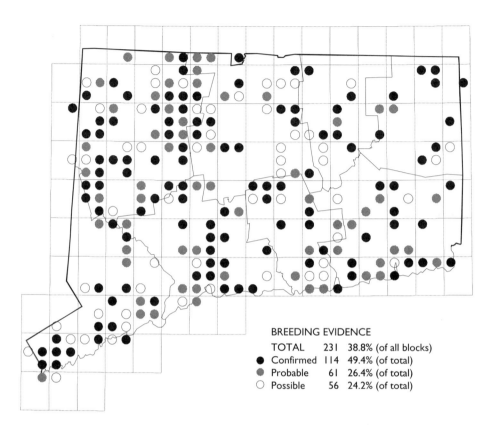

BREEDING EVIDENCE

| | TOTAL | 231 | 38.8% (of all blocks) |
|---|---|---|---|
| ● | Confirmed | 114 | 49.4% (of total) |
| ◉ | Probable | 61 | 26.4% (of total) |
| ○ | Possible | 56 | 24.2% (of total) |

**Atlas results**—An overview of the map shows the relationship between this species and large bodies of water, rivers, and the coastline. When com-pared to the Bank Swallow, this species appears to have adapted much better to living near people and along the coast. The Bank Swallow needs open sand and dirt banks in which to nest.

**Discussion**—This species has slowly increased in numbers over the last l00 years. The first record occurred in the late 1800s (Bagg and Eliot 1937). By early this century, Sage et al. (1913) listed it as tolerably common on the coast. The spread of this species inland appears to have been rapid. Turner and Rose (1989) state that "in New England, Rough-winged Swallows

were rare visitors in the last century but now breed there regularly." In the last 20 years, the population has remained rather constant. They are aerial feeders, mainly over water rather than open fields, except in migration. Those requirements, coupled with limited availability of potential nest sites in banks, stone edifices, and other man-made structures limit the birds' options.

This species tends to return to its nest sites each year (Lunk 1962), and therefore nest availability is at a premium for returning young of the previous year. They do not use nest boxes and very rarely nest in holes in trees (Turner and Rose 1989). When found on the periphery of Bank Swallow colonies, they appear to be using the abandoned holes of the Bank Swallows rather than excavating their own. This has also been alluded to in studies by others (Bent 1942). The family remains as a unit while the young are fed by the parents, but then the group dissolves.

*Noble S. Proctor*

# Bank Swallow
## *Riparia riparia*

The Bank Swallow is an uncommon to fairly common localized breeder in Connecticut; it can be fairly common as a migrant in fall but is less numerous in spring. North American breeders winter principally in northern and central South America. This species has an exceptionally large breeding range that extends around the northern portion of the globe. The English name in the Old World is the Sand Martin.

**Habitat**—This is not a city bird but one of rural open areas, especially near water, over which it will feed. It is totally dependent on sand banks and sloughed off embankments on woodland edges. Because of the transitory nature of such sites, colonies rarely are found over the long term at one locality. Nests may be excavated up to 40 inches deep, and new sites are usually dug each year (Turner and Rose 1989).

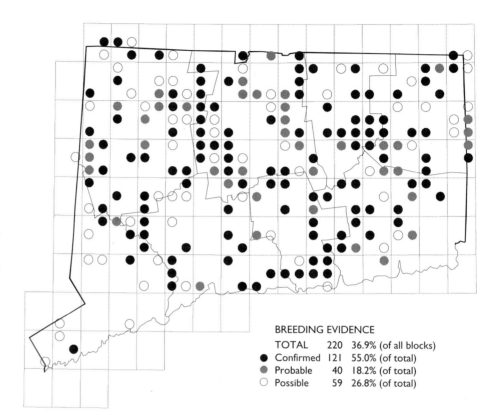

BREEDING EVIDENCE
TOTAL 220 36.9% (of all blocks)
● Confirmed 121 55.0% (of total)
◉ Probable 40 18.2% (of total)
○ Possible 59 26.8% (of total)

**Atlas results**—Major sand deposits along river systems remain prime excavation sites for construction companies, and on the map populations can be seen lining the major river and stream valleys. Some of the sand pits used during the atlas years are now gone; very few long term sites are known from the state. This variability of nesting sites is seen throughout its vast breeding range (Turner and Rose 1989). It is also interesting to note how few coastal sites were located. At several coastal locations adequate sand banks can be found, yet the species seems not to nest in such places. Several of these sites are in protected state parks, and if colonies were established, they might lead to long term success.

**Discussion**—The literature indicates that this species was locally common from the time of the earliest ornithological records for the state (Sage et al. 1913). Banks suitable for nesting can be produced by stream or river erosion, but probably human construction, sand pits, and digging at landfills have been the principal sites for nest colonies in Connecticut in recent decades. Completion of local construction projects and abandonment of sand pits can be detrimental for future nesting in specific localities. As seen on the map, numerous colonies were located throughout the state, but one should remember that nesting sites change with time. Prime banks for nest excavation can disappear in one day! In general, it appears that the species is dropping in numbers in the eastern and central part of its North American range but increasing in the west (Robbins et al. 1986). Weather can inflict mass mortality due to erosion after severe rains in early summer.

*Noble S. Proctor*

227

## Cliff Swallow
### *Hirundo pyrrhonota*

This uncommon migrant and summer resident nests at scattered localities, mainly in western Connecticut. Cliff Swallows usually are seen with flocks of other migrating swallows, and seldom form large flocks of their own species in eastern North America. This is usually the latest swallow to return to the state, being rare before late April. (In the western part of its range, Cliff Swallows may return by late February, but date of arrival is highly variable.)

The species breeds from Alaska and central Canada south to central Mexico. Cliff Swallows migrate chiefly through Middle America and winter in southern South America, although a few are said to winter as far north as Costa Rica (AOU 1983, Stiles and Skutch 1989). The subspecies across northern North America, including Connecticut, is nominate *H. p. pyrrhonota* (Browning 1992).

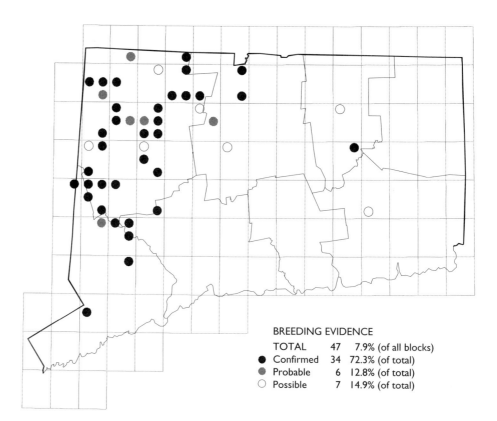

BREEDING EVIDENCE

| | TOTAL | 47 | 7.9% (of all blocks) |
|---|---|---|---|
| ● | Confirmed | 34 | 72.3% (of total) |
| ◉ | Probable | 6 | 12.8% (of total) |
| ○ | Possible | 7 | 14.9% (of total) |

**Habitat**—This species prefers open areas near water. The availability of suitable structures for nesting and for obtaining mud are the limiting factors. In Connecticut, as in much of the species' range, nesting colonies are on concrete structures, such as bridges and dams. Nests may also be placed on old wooden structures and natural cliff faces, but such sites are not used here.

**Atlas results**—Most breeding sites are in the western part of the state, especially along the Housatonic River and its watershed. The lone eastern site is in Columbia. One hopes that the species will spread into areas along other water courses with newly established concrete bridges. This has happened throughout the west north to southern Alaska.

**Discussion**—The Cliff Swallow was more widespread and found in greater numbers in the past, although Bagg and Eliot (1937) suggest that the species invaded southern New England in the early 1800s. Merriam (1877) called it a common resident during the 1870s, but this was apparently the peak of its numbers here as a dramatic decline was noticed by the early 1900s (Bull 1964). This decline was seen throughout much of the East, with a resurgence of breeding in the southeast beginning in the 1940s (Mengel 1965, Hall 1983). The species has not returned to its former status, however, and is increasing only very slightly or not at all in Connecticut at present.

Several proposed reasons for this change have been suggested. Clearing of land and erection of barns during the 1800s created a fine setting for Cliff Swallows and possibly promoted their increase. Their decline parallels two factors: 1) the slow reforestation of the state this century, and 2) the rapid increase of the highly competitive House Sparrow, which has been observed usurping nests of the Cliff Swallow (Samuel 1969). The idea that painted surfaces of buildings are less suitable for anchoring the mud nests has been repeated many times (Forbush 1927, Bull 1964). However, Cliff Swallows use such sites in the Midwest and the West (Emlen 1954), suggesting that this is not a cause of the decline. Oddly, eastern populations still do not tend to nest on painted surfaces. Cliff Swallows rely to some degree on suitable alternate nesting sites being available, colonies typically shifting after several years at one location. There would seem to be fewer such sites available now with the regrowth of forests.

In the 1960s and 1970s, the Cliff Swallow was listed as Endangered (Craig 1978). Since then, however, concrete bridges and dams have brought a slight upsurge to the colonies in the western part of the state. The rough surface and overhangs may provide a highly favorable substrate for attachment of nests. The species is not given any special status at present.

*Noble S. Proctor*

## Barn Swallow
*Hirundo rustica*

The Barn Swallow is a common summer breeder and migrant that has adapted very well to coexistence with people. Barn Swallows typically return to Connecticut in mid-April. Departure to the south begins in late summer, with peak numbers reached during late August. Connecticut breeders likely winter in South America; the species as a whole winters chiefly from Costa Rica to southern South America (AOU 1983). Migrants from eastern North America cross the Gulf of Mexico, unlike the Cliff Swallow, which follows a mainland route south through Middle America. The subspecies breeding in North America is *H. r. erythrogaster* (AOU 1957), which is distinguished from other subspecies by the presence of a thin or interrupted dusky breast band (rather than a broad band) and orange tinted underparts of adults in spring (Phillips 1986).

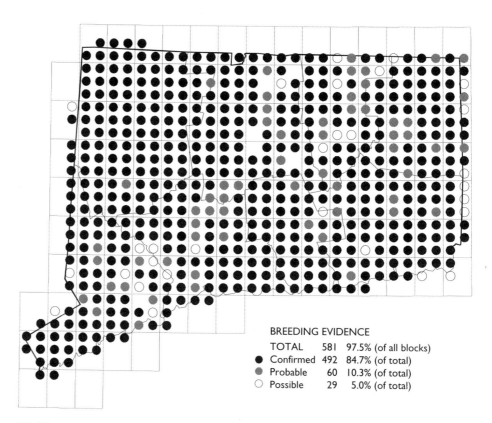

BREEDING EVIDENCE
TOTAL   581   97.5% (of all blocks)
● Confirmed   492   84.7% (of total)
● Probable   60   10.3% (of total)
○ Possible   29   5.0% (of total)

**Habitat**—Both a suburban and rural species, it can also be found at the periphery of large cities, at times nesting in the center of these cities. The Barn Swallow is a bird of open country and farmland and seems to favor areas near lakes and ponds. It is not found nesting in heavily forested areas. Originally a nester in caves and on cliff faces, the populations have expanded everywhere as people have constructed structures that substitute for rocky nesting ledges. The nest is a cup of grass and mud and is lined with feathers. In general, the birds nest in small colonies or isolated pairs, returning to their nest areas each year, with the males being more faithful to such areas than the females (Turner and Rose 1989).

**Atlas results**—As might be expected, the species was found nesting in nearly 98% of the blocks with only the most densely urbanized city centers lacking the birds.

**Discussion**—Although the status of the Barn Swallow as a common breeder has not changed much since Linsley (1843) and Merriam (1877) wrote about the species in Connecticut, it likely benefitted from land clearing and farming practices in early colonial times. The species was seen expanding its numbers in the southwestern United States along with the spread of agriculture there (Phillips 1986). However, not being a species of woodlands, its range almost certainly has changed over the last century, during which time the state has gone from nearly 70% cleared for farming to nearly 60% wooded. The Barn Swallow continues to breed around the remaining open fields and human habitations in Connecticut and is still abundant.

Among the swallows, this species is probably better known by people than any other. The most often used name in English-speaking countries is simply "Swallow," but it also has in some cases the names of "Chimney Swallow" or "House Swallow," reflecting its affinity for nesting close to human structures.

*Noble S. Proctor*

231

## Blue Jay
### *Cyanocitta cristata*

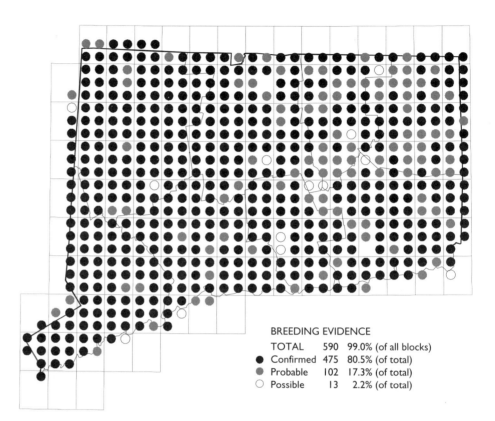

**BREEDING EVIDENCE**

| | | | |
|---|---|---|---|
| TOTAL | | 590 | 99.0% (of all blocks) |
| ● | Confirmed | 475 | 80.5% (of total) |
| ● | Probable | 102 | 17.3% (of total) |
| ○ | Possible | 13 | 2.2% (of total) |

The Blue Jay is a widespread and numerous breeders in the state. There is a regular southward migration through the state in fall, when jays may be abundant, and a return in spring. The winter status is highly variable, evidently dependent on supplies of natural food with more birds present in winter when food supplies such as acorns are abundant (K. G. Smith 1986). Although occasional sharp fluctuations in the wintering populations are seen, summer populations are more uniform from year to year and apparently are unaffected by the winter numbers.

Blue Jays in the Northeast are said to belong to the race *bromia*, which is characterized by relatively extensive white markings in the wings and tail and a darker blue above (Phillips 1986). The races of the Blue Jay are not well-defined and probably not useful in determining movements of these populations, but some may winter south to Louisiana and Georgia (AOU 1957).

**Habitat**—Blue Jays breed in a wide range of habitats including rural, suburban, and urban parks. Although nests are usually placed in a tree, jays are versatile in selecting nest sites and have been known to nest in Connecticut on a rafter inside a shed (G. A. Clark 1968).

**Atlas results**—The Blue Jay was one of the most widespread breeding species in the state. Although nests are often difficult to find and adults are generally more secretive and less vocal while nesting, jays tend to be conspicuous when feeding their young out of the nest, thus contributing to the very high percentage of confirmations of breeding.

**Discussion**—As far back as there are historic records, the Blue Jay has been known as a regularly occurring breeding bird in the state. Merriam (1877) termed the Blue Jay "an abundant resident; frequently seen about the city." Sage et al. (1913) considered it a "common summer resident." Although reports from New York and Massachusetts indicate that the Blue Jay was initially a rural bird and only secondarily moved into cities (Bagg and Eliot 1937, Sibley *in* Andrle and Carroll 1988), the historic records from Connecticut do not provide documentation of that shift in this state. Such trees as oaks and chestnuts produce such large nuts for propagation that their rate of spread without assistance is very slow. Johnson and Webb (1989) have suggested that the habit of Blue Jays to hoard such nuts was a major factor in the relatively rapid spread of such trees northward in northeastern North America following the retreat of the ice sheets in the last major glaciation.

The conditions in Connecticut are currently quite favorable for Blue Jays. Because these birds are a major predator on the eggs and young of smaller birds, the prevalence of Blue Jays has been viewed as potentially detrimental for the breeding of numerous species that migrate to the tropics (Yahner and Scott 1988, Terborgh 1989). It would be of interest to have more information on the factors affecting Blue Jay populations in order to determine how current human practices in modifying landscapes and in bird feeding are affecting the numbers of breeding jays. Although still numerous, jay numbers in eastern North America have declined according to Breeding Bird Survey data from 1966 to 1987 (Robbins et al. 1989b).

*George A. Clark, Jr.*

## American Crow
*Corvus brachyrhynchos*

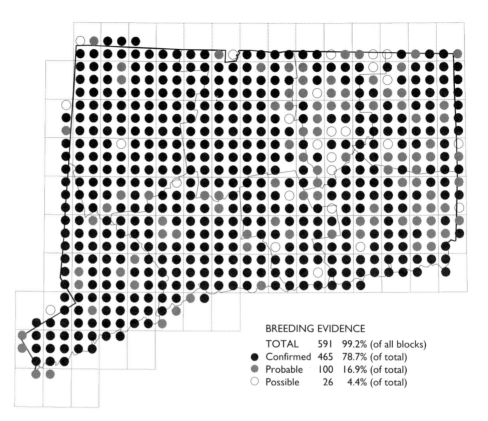

BREEDING EVIDENCE

| | TOTAL | 591 | 99.2% (of all blocks) |
|---|---|---|---|
| ● | Confirmed | 465 | 78.7% (of total) |
| ● | Probable | 100 | 16.9% (of total) |
| ○ | Possible | 26 | 4.4% (of total) |

The species occurs throughout the year in the state, but at least some migration of American Crows has been observed within Connecticut (Sage et al. 1913), although it is not known whether those migrants originated in the state. A withdrawal in winter from the northern part of the range of the species is known to occur, but little is known about where those birds go.

**Habitat**—American Crows are wide-ranging in suburban and rural parts of the state. Territories are large, averaging 42.1 hectares (104 acres) in one Massachusetts study (Chamberlain-Auger et al. 1990). In general, crows are associated in a family group which participate together in defense of a territory (Kilham 1989, Chamberlain-Auger et al. 1990). Nests are ordinarily well concealed and placed typically near the tops of trees, often in conifers but also in deciduous trees. Crows generally require open ground, such as lawns, fields, or roadsides for much of their omnivorous foraging, but such open tracts need not be large.

In Connecticut, where vultures are usually not abundant, crows are major scavengers and are often seen feeding on carcasses of mammals or birds that have been struck by vehicles on highways. In suburban areas where crows have been effectively protected against shooting they are much more approachable than in rural areas where they have often been subjected to shooting; a similar situation has been reported from Wisconsin (Knight et al. 1987). In suburban areas and landfills, American Crows regularly feed on garbage. Moreover, in some localities at least, the birds tear open plastic garbage bags put out by the roadside for collection. The frequently seen mobbing of crows by smaller birds during the breeding season suggests the importance of crows as predators on eggs and young of numerous species. American Crows have also on occasion caused substantial losses of seedling corn plants in Connecticut (Heichel and Washko 1976).

**Atlas results**—This species is widespread throughout the state, recorded in virtually every block and confirmed as nesting in more than three quarters of the blocks.

**Discussion**—The species has been considered common at least since the 1840s (Linsley 1843). The American Crow would seem to have potentially benefited greatly from the deforestation that began in the colonial period. Growth of the human population along with agricultural development and an increasing production of garbage over more recent decades would seem to have contributed to an overall increase in crow populations. As a versatile feeder and scavenger, the American Crow seems to have excellent prospects for continued success in the state.

It would be desirable to know more about the status of Connecticut crows. In the nonbreeding season within the state some roosting aggregations number in the thousands of birds, but careful counts of such flocks has apparently not been reported. We know relatively little about where the birds in these aggregations breed, or to what extent, if any, there might be major movement of birds breeding in Connecticut to out of state in the nonbreeding season. American Crows tend to be wary and difficult to study relative to many other species, and elucidation of the population biology of crows in Connecticut continues to provide challenges for future study.

*George A. Clark, Jr.*

## Fish Crow
*Corvus ossifragus*

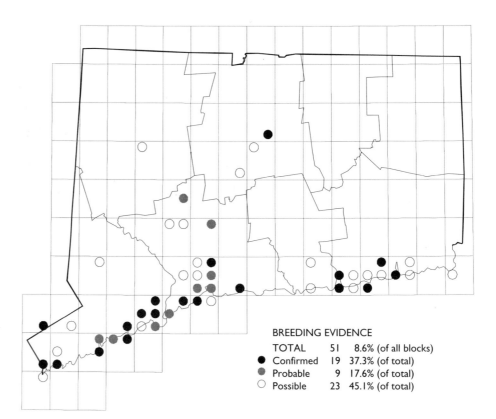

BREEDING EVIDENCE

| | TOTAL | 51 | 8.6% (of all blocks) |
|---|---|---|---|
| ● | Confirmed | 19 | 37.3% (of total) |
| ● | Probable | 9 | 17.6% (of total) |
| ○ | Possible | 23 | 45.1% (of total) |

The Fish Crow is a migratory breeder near tidal salt water. It is common along the coast but infrequent in the interior along major rivers. The number that remain during winter or move into the state then is not well known. Most are found with coastal aggregations of American Crows. Along the Connecticut River, Fish Crows are scarce and local but occur as far north as Springfield, Massachusetts (Veit and Petersen 1993). In its entire range the Fish Crow extends from southern Maine south along the Atlantic coast to Florida and along the Gulf Coast as far west as Texas (AOU 1983).

The Fish Crow and American Crow are very similar and distinguished in the field only by the more nasal sounding voice and smaller size of the Fish Crow. Suspected Fish Crows found in interior Connecticut should be identified with caution. As is well known, young American Crows often sound somewhat like Fish Crows, and the size difference is often difficult to evaluate in the field without careful comparison.

**Habitat**—The Fish Crow is expected only in coastal areas or along major rivers and thus not far from major bodies of water. Nests are placed in either coniferous or deciduous trees; Bent (1946) surveyed information on Connecticut nests. So far as is known, Fish Crow foraging is much like that of the American Crow, with both species being opportunistic omnivores. Fish Crows do much scavenging on the shoreline and have been sometimes abundantly represented at coastal landfills where garbage has been readily available. In many respects the behavior of Fish Crows resembles that of American Crows (e. g., in McNair 1985), but the Fish Crow has been much less studied.

**Atlas results**—Nearly all confirmations of breeding came from within a few miles of the shore but with one interior confirmation from the Connecticut River valley and other interior records from along major waterways. This species is clearly linked to the vicinity of water and particularly salt water. In recent decades the development of landfills has presumably facilitated the range expansion of the Fish Crow.

**Discussion**—The northeastern range of the Fish Crow has broadened to some extent in recent decades (Bonney *in* Andrle and Carroll 1988, Zeranski and Baptist 1990), but this range expansion has not been so dramatic as those of a number of other species such as the Red-bellied Woodpecker, Tufted Titmouse, Blue-gray Gnatcatcher, or House Finch.

Presumably the Fish Crow has as yet undescribed specializations that are advantageous for living in tidal areas. In contrast, most passerine species are poorly equipped for survival in highly saline environments. Although non-passerine seabirds have special glands for salt excretion in the head, such structures are unknown among passerines, which must use other mechanisms for eliminating excess salt (Poulson 1969). The smaller size of the Fish Crow relative to the American Crow might also be a specialization related to salinity of water. In other parts of North America there are also coastal crows of a body size smaller than the American Crow, e.g., the Mexican Crow (*C.

imparatus*) and the Northwestern Crow (*C. caurinus*). Because bird species of larger size are often dominant to smaller ones (G. A. Clark 1979), it might be expected that Fish Crows would be socially subordinate to American Crows, yet Fish Crows remain numerous and are not being replaced by American Crows. A study of the interaction of these species might help to explain the success of Fish Crows in the coastal environment.

*George A. Clark, Jr.*

# Common Raven
*Corvus corax*

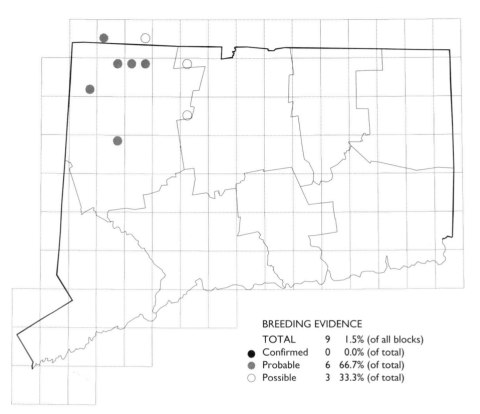

BREEDING EVIDENCE

| | TOTAL | 9 | 1.5% (of all blocks) |
|---|---|---|---|
| ● | Confirmed | 0 | 0.0% (of total) |
| ● | Probable | 6 | 66.7% (of total) |
| ○ | Possible | 3 | 33.3% (of total) |

The Common Raven is a scarce, but increasing, resident breeder that has colonized southern New England in the past twenty years. In eastern North America, the Raven is resident from the Maritime provinces of Canada (where common), the Adirondack Mountains of New York, and south sparingly throughout the higher portions of the Appalachian Mountains from Pennsylvania to northern Georgia (AOU 1983). It is designated as a Species of Special Concern in the state.

**Habitat**—Breeders are found in mountainous or hilly terrain with rocky out-croppings and cliff faces within primarily coniferous or mixed deciduous woodlands. In Connecticut, nesting has occurred in relatively undisturbed areas with restricted public access. Rock ledges with a protective overhang have been the only nest sites used, although the species also nests in coniferous trees and has done so recently in Massachusetts. The bulky stick nest is often reused over several years.

**Atlas results**—Common Ravens were observed exhibiting apparent courtship behavior at several localities in Litchfield County during spring and early summer in the last years of the atlas survey. An account of three grown and flying young on Canaan Mountain, Canaan, 22 June 1986, involved a sec-ond-hand report and, unfortunately, lacked a descriptive account required for inclusion in this atlas (Varza and Rosgen 1987). If the identification was correct, the possibility that the birds came from a nest in Massachusetts was not eliminated.

**Discussion**—The Common Raven only recently began nesting in Connecticut and was only a casual visitor in the past (Sage et al. 1913). Ravens might once have been resident in Connecticut as Bull (1974) and Forbush (1927) have inferred that the species was a widespread breeder in New York and Massachusetts at least until the time of European settlement in the 1600s. Recent excavations in New York indicate that ravens inhabited that state as long as 9,500 years ago (Peterson *in* Andrle and Carroll 1988).

The recent range expansion was first noted along coastal Maine during the 1940s (Griscom and Snyder 1955). The species spread westward in the 1960s to Vermont (Oatman *in* Laughlin and Kibbe 1985), and the first confirmed nesting in Massachusetts was in 1982 at Quabbin Reservoir (W. J. Davis 1989). Ravens have increased in that state dramatically since then. Late fall and winter reports in Connecticut began in the late 1970s, primarily in the northwest-

ern portion of the state (Baptist 1991). Breeding was first suspected in the state in 1986 at Canaan Mountain, but surprisingly, the first nest for the state was found in northeastern Connecticut. Two young were photographed in a nest at Boston Hollow, Ashford, in 1988 (photograph at CTMNH). Nesting was suspected here in 1987. Litchfield County remains the center of the raven's distribution in Connecticut, however. In 1987, nest construction was reported on Red Mountain, Sharon, and three young were fledged there in

both 1988 and 1989; four young fledged there in 1990 (*fide* John McNeely). In 1989, nesting occurred on rock ledges at Barkhamsted Reservoir where eleven young fledged from three nests; in 1990, those nests fledged 8 young (D. Rosgen, pers. comm.). Numerous sightings during May and June in recent years in Kent, Cornwall, Canaan, Thomaston, and several other towns in the northwest suggest a continued increase in Connecticut.

*Louis R. Bevier*

## Black-capped Chickadee
### *Parus atricapillus*

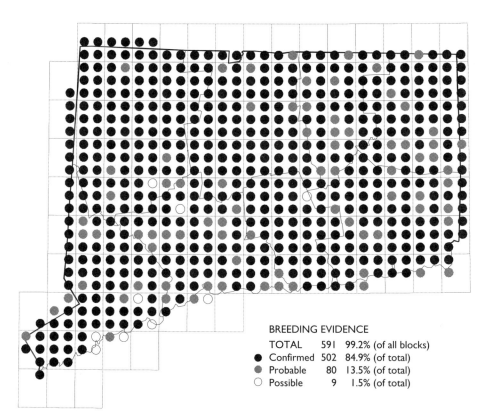

BREEDING EVIDENCE

| | TOTAL | 591 | 99.2% (of all blocks) |
|---|---|---|---|
| ● | Confirmed | 502 | 84.9% (of total) |
| ● | Probable | 80 | 13.5% (of total) |
| ○ | Possible | 9 | 1.5% (of total) |

The Black-capped Chickadee is a common resident breeder in Connecticut. Large waves of transient chickadees have been recorded, typically in the fall, but these are probably immatures. One individual banded in Litchfield in April and recovered 10 days later in New Hampshire was the only one of over 3,000 banded at that station that was ever recovered elsewhere. Other permanent residents banded in midwinter have been mist-netted within 1.6 km of the banding station during the nesting season and vice versa. These permanent residents exhibit a high degree of site fidelity as evidenced by a high return rate (Loery and Nichols 1985).

**Habitat**—Chickadees are a forest interior-edge species. They may be found during the nesting season at the edge of or in an opening of a second-growth forest habitat or along a water course.

Here they excavate their own cavities in the dead stub or branch of a Gray Birch or other tree with a soft interior and firm, decay resistant bark. Less often they may be found nesting closer to human habitation in a bird box.

**Atlas results**—The map illustrates how widespread Black-capped Chickadees are as a nesting species in Connecticut.

They were confirmed as nesters in 84.9% of the blocks in which they were found and probably could have been confirmed in most of the others if the latter had been studied more intensively.

**Discussion**—Chickadees have been reported as a common member of Connecticut's avifauna as far back as we have records (Merriam 1877, Sage et al. 1913). Recently, an attempt has been made to monitor their population dynamics by collecting banding recapture data at a White Memorial Foundation banding station in Litchfield, Connecticut (Loery and Nichols 1985). In addition to the expected minor fluctuations, the data indicate there were two at least local population crashes in the last 30 years—during 1968 and 1984–1985. The 1968 crash occurred in the same year that Tufted Titmice, moving up from the south, became established as a territorial species in the Litchfield area (Loery and Nichols 1985). Two characteristics of this crash suggest it was the result of interspecific competition: 1) it was a short-term decline; observations of possible interspecific competition between Great Tits (*Parus major*) and Blue Tits (*Parus caeruleus*) in Europe indicate that at such times niche shifts can occur almost immediately (Dhondt 1989); 2) estimates of age-specific survival rates of the Litchfield chickadee population suggested that the survival rate of first-year birds declined more than that of adults in the years of

Tufted Titmouse establishment (Loery et al. 1987). Again, work with Great and Blue Tits indicates that interspecific competition operates mainly on juvenile males (Dhondt 1989). If the above analysis is valid, it would imply that evidence for interspecific competition may often go undetected because of its temporary nature.

Black-capped Chickadees are generalists as far as habitat requirements are concerned and have probably benefited from the recent rapid expansion in the numbers of suburban bird feeders (Kricher 1981). Severe winter temperatures do not seem to be a problem for them, particularly where there is an abundant food supply available at winter feeders (Loery and Nichols 1985). Throughout the state chickadees are still far more abundant than the only other nesting parid, the Tufted Titmouse. It will be interesting to see if they remain so in the future (Kricher 1981).

*Gordon Loery*

# Tufted Titmouse
*Parus bicolor*

The Tufted Titmouse, although not as abundant as its parid relative the Black-capped Chickadee, is nevertheless a common resident breeder in Connecticut. Comparing the relative numbers of these two species is often difficult because the louder call of the titmouse may be heard at greater distances making it more likely that chickadees will be undercounted. The difference in numbers recorded on the Warren and North Woodbury U.S. Fish and Wildlife Service Breeding Bird Surveys in northwestern Connecticut is consequently always much less than the difference found at the nearby White Memorial Foundation banding station. Data collected at the banding station indicate that although the titmouse population has increased since it became established as a breeding species in the late 1960s, there are still several times as many resident chickadees in the area.

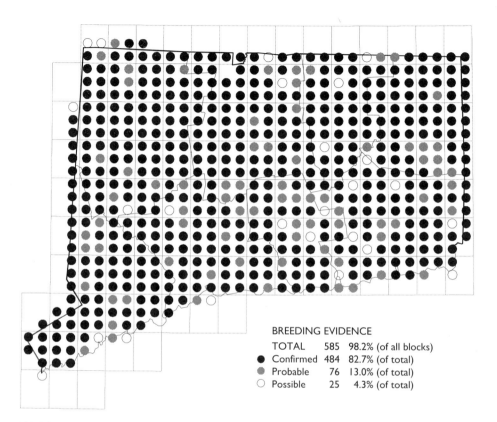

BREEDING EVIDENCE

| | TOTAL | 585 | 98.2% (of all blocks) |
|---|---|---|---|
| ● | Confirmed | 484 | 82.7% (of total) |
| ◉ | Probable | 76 | 13.0% (of total) |
| ○ | Possible | 25 | 4.3% (of total) |

**Habitat**—The Tufted Titmouse, like the Black-capped Chickadee, is a forest interior-edge species. It prefers a more mature hardwood forest, often nesting in mixed hardwood oak forests on ridges. The Tufted Titmouse may also be found nesting along watercourses where there are mature forests or in a suburban area with large trees. In such places they usually make use of a natural tree cavity or a deserted woodpecker or nuthatch hole. They are less apt to occupy a man-made bird box than some other cavity nesters.

**Atlas results**—The map indicates that titmice are now almost as widespread a nesting species as chickadees in Connecticut. They were reported as confirmed nesters in 80.7% of all blocks as compared to chickadees, which were confirmed in 83.7%.

**Discussion**—The Tufted Titmouse is a relatively recent addition to the list of breeding birds found in Connecticut, although it was a rare visitor through the 1800s (Merriam 1877). Cruickshank (1942) reported them as extremely uncommon east of the Hudson River up to the 1940s. The first reported nesting was in 1949 at Westport in the southwest corner of Connecticut (Zeranski and Baptist 1990), and the first sightings at the opposite corner of the state were in 1959 at Storrs (Manter 1975). By 1967 they were nesting as far as New London, and by 1968 they were established as a territorial species as far north as the White Memorial Foundation in Litchfield (Loery and Nichols, 1985). The Tufted Titmouse began nesting throughout the state during the 1970s. Thus, in about twenty years they succeeded in extending their nesting range across the state, perhaps with the help of an increasing number of suburban bird feeders and despite the possible handicap of having to cross the Connecticut River (Kricher, 1981). Banding recapture data collected at a banding station at the White Memorial Foundation since 1958 suggest that in the process they at least temporarily disrupted the local chickadee population (Loery and Nichols, 1985), but this interspecific competition, if it did in fact take place, was apparently very quickly reduced by niche shifts. Since they appear to occupy a somewhat narrower ecological niche with more specialized habitat requirements than chickadees it remains to be seen if they will eventually become as abundant as chickadees or even outnumber them this far north (Kricher, 1981).

*Gordon Loery*

# Red-breasted Nuthatch
## *Sitta canadensis*

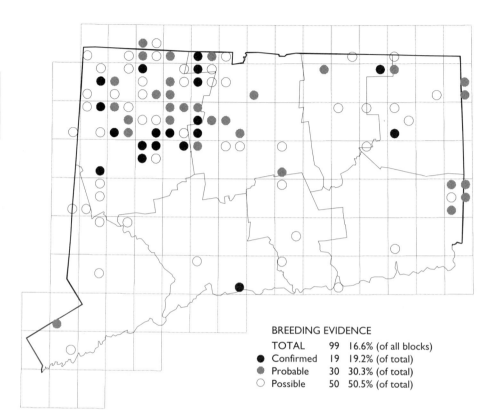

BREEDING EVIDENCE

| | | |
|---|---|---|
| TOTAL | 99 | 16.6% (of all blocks) |
| ● Confirmed | 19 | 19.2% (of total) |
| ● Probable | 30 | 30.3% (of total) |
| ○ Possible | 50 | 50.5% (of total) |

This species is an erratically migratory breeder that nests chiefly in the eastern and western highland portions of the state where it is locally regular. Major migratory movements southward occur in many winters, often, but not necessarily, in alternate years (Bock and Lepthien 1972). In the years of major southward flights, migrants are often readily detected by the distinctive vocalizations of the species. In such years, many Connecticut breeders presumably winter in the southeastern United States; it is not known to what extent Connecticut breeders might winter in the state during such flight years. These erratic migrations are believed to be a response to failure of production of cones, the seeds of which are a major source of winter food.

**Habitat**—The Red-breasted Nuthatch is closely associated with coniferous or mixed coniferous-deciduous woodland, though often this species spends much time foraging in deciduous trees. Nests are placed in cavities, commonly in dead trees or limbs, though bird houses are used on occasion (Bent 1948). Trees located over water and killed by long term flooding of small areas of woodland in a coniferous setting are a frequent site for nesting; beavers can thus help to cre-ate a favorable setting for Red-breasted Nuthatches. Food items that cannot be directly swallowed are placed in crevices for pounding, and consequently the presence of rough bark surfaces is advantageous for this species.

**Atlas results**—The strongholds of the breeding range of this species are in the more coniferous parts of the northern

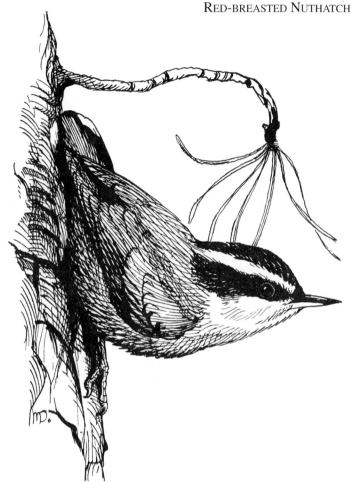

hills, but outlying records with one confirmation from coastal Connecticut indicate an apparent potential for breeding of this species in virtually any part of the state in which a suitable woodland might become established. The strong affinity of this species for coniferous woodlands is reflected in the distribution shown on the map. The general absence of extensive coniferous woodlands or plantations away from the western highlands and a small portion of the eastern highlands would seem to explain the observed distribution.

**Discussion**—Neither Linsley (1843) nor Merriam (1877) mentions the nesting of this species in the state. Sage et al. (1913) cited two breeding records from the 1800s in the northwestern hills. Unfortunately, the historic records are too few to trace the possible changes of breeding range within the state, but presumably the regrowth of forests and particularly the establishment of coniferous plantations in the twentieth century have facilitated a spread of the breeding populations in the highland portions of the state.

A detailed study of the interactions between Red-breasted and White-breasted Nuthatches in an area of overlap would be of interest. Lack (1971) pointed out that these species commonly avoid possible competition with one another due to the difference in their habitats, but he further suggested that where the two coexist their size difference would lead to a difference in diets that would reduce competition between them. However, apparently no detailed study of behavior and foraging has been conducted in an area of overlap.

*George A. Clark, Jr.*

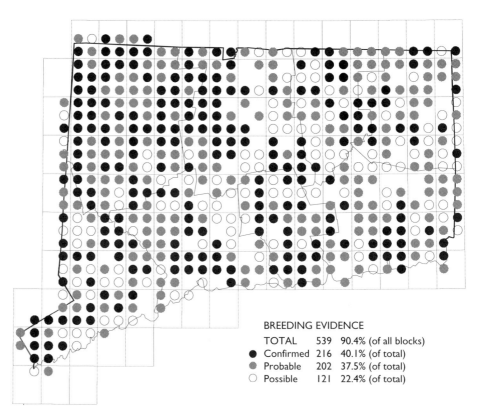

**BREEDING EVIDENCE**

| | TOTAL | 539 | 90.4% (of all blocks) |
|---|---|---|---|
| ● | Confirmed | 216 | 40.1% (of total) |
| ● | Probable | 202 | 37.5% (of total) |
| ○ | Possible | 121 | 22.4% (of total) |

## White-breasted Nuthatch
### *Sitta carolinensis*

A resident breeder of regular occurrence over most of the state. The frequency of dark-crowned females was thought to separate populations in the Northeast, where such a pattern is rarely seen, from populations in the South, where it is frequent. However, Wood (1992) has shown that this pattern and other characters are clinal; he includes all eastern North American populations in the subspecies *S. c. carolinensis*.

**Habitat**—This species is associated with mature deciduous trees. It nests in cavities of relatively large diameter limbs or trunks, most commonly well above the reach of a person standing on the ground (Stauffer and Best 1982). The use of bird houses also has been recorded (Bent 1948). This species commonly forages on main trunks and limbs. A suitably rough bark is advantageous in providing crevices from which arthropods can be extracted and for holding large prey or seeds where they can be hammered with the bill. Because this species, unlike others foraging on tree trunks, spends much time with the head facing downward, it presumably encounters prey not likely to be found by other species.

**Atlas results**—The White-breasted Nuthatch is a widespread breeder in mature hardwoods, but apparently is absent from some highly urbanized areas and some areas of extensive farmland. Because they are not densely distributed and are relatively quiet by early June, some breeding might have been missed in poorly covered blocks.

**Discussion**—Linsley (1843) termed this species common. Merriam (1877) noted that the species was not common as a breeder within the city of New Haven. Sage et al. (1913) suggested that the numbers of White-breasted Nuthatches had declined since some earlier, unspecified time, but they did not suggest a reason for such a decline. Stone (1937) reported the absence of this species as a breeder in the coastal pine areas of the mid-Atlantic states, and this was also reported for Cape Cod (Hill 1965), although a breeding population was present in the mature forest of Naushon Island to the south of Cape Cod (Griscom and Snyder 1955). More recent literature indicates some expansion of the breeding range of this species in recent decades into certain coastal areas in the northeastern United States (D. A. Sibley 1988, Bonney *in* Andrle and Carroll 1988). Connecticut has so little area of coastal pinewoods that an absence of breeding there would not be clearly detectable from the atlas data, but, in general, White-breasted Nuthatches in this state tend to avoid entering extensive stands of conifers

(pers. obs.).

Apparently no explanation has been proposed for the lack of breeding in the coastal pinewoods in the northeastern United States, but it could be that removal of hardwoods in those areas during the 1800s, or even earlier, eliminated potential nest sites, and that the recent expansions of breeding range are a consequence of growth of hardwoods to a suitably large size. It would be of interest to have information on the nest sites used by White-breasted Nuthatches where they occur in areas having a high frequency of conifers. Winter diet might also contribute to limiting the breeding range of resident White-breasted Nuthatches, because this species spends less time feeding on cones than other species of North American nuthatches (C. C. Smith and Balda 1979).

*George A. Clark, Jr.*

# Brown Creeper
## *Certhia americana*

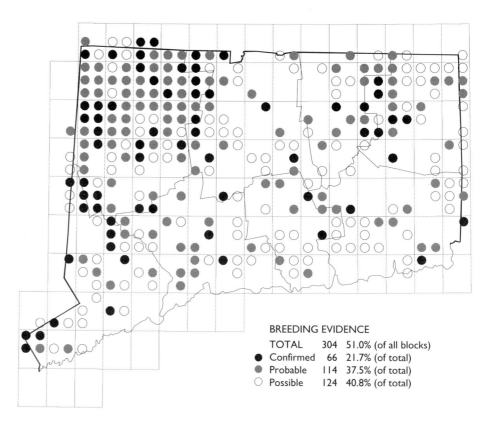

BREEDING EVIDENCE

| | TOTAL | 304 | 51.0% (of all blocks) |
|---|---|---|---|
| ● | Confirmed | 66 | 21.7% (of total) |
| ◉ | Probable | 114 | 37.5% (of total) |
| ○ | Possible | 124 | 40.8% (of total) |

The Brown Creeper is an inconspicuous, cryptically colored bird, aptly named for its drab brown plumage and habit of creeping up tree trunks. Its thin, high-pitched call and musical song are usually the first clues to its presence.

In Connecticut, it is an uncommon breeder. Although termed a year-round resident, many migrate south and others from the north arrive for the winter. Migrants return in April while some wintering birds and residents already have begun singing. The bulk of fall migrants occur in late September and October. Numbers in winter vary. Creepers often flock with titmice, nuthatches, and chickadees.

The Brown Creeper breeds across the boreal zone of Canada south in the Appalachians to Tennessee and from Alaska to California; it is also resident in mountains from Arizona to Nicaragua (AOU 1983). Variation in the species is clinal; in the Northeast, populations are intermediate between the subspecies *americana* of eastern Canada and *nigrescens* of the southern Appalachians (Webster *in* Phillips 1986).

**Habitat**—Brown Creepers use deciduous and mixed deciduous-conifer woodland, pine forests, and, especially, forested wetlands with mature standing timber. Large trees, dead or diseased, are used for nesting. Nest are cup-shaped and partly or wholly placed beneath peeling or loose bark; more rarely a rotted tree cavity or unused woodpecker nest is used (Bent 1948). Eggs are incubated by the female for two weeks; young fledge in about two weeks. Food consists mostly of invertebrates and some seeds and nuts.

**Atlas results**—The Brown Creeper is widely distributed as a breeding species throughout the state with breeding activity recorded in all physiographic provinces. Most records are from western Connecticut, and breeding records become more sporadic along the coast, the central lowlands, and upland areas of the east. Second growth forest that lacks mature trees is probably the most important factor influencing Brown Creeper distribution in the state, especially in the southern tier of the uplands in eastern Connecticut. Undoubtedly, as forests there mature, the Brown Creeper population will increase.

**Discussion**—Large scale clearing of Connecticut's pristine forests during the colonial era sharply decreased suitable habitat for the Brown Creeper, and it was much less common than at present. Reforestation in the late 1800s resulted in a very slow return of this species as a breeder in Connecticut. Merriam (1877) noted that the Brown Creeper nested in the state but provided no nesting details. Sage et al. (1913) listed only wintering records, and Forbush (1927) called it a common migrant but uncommon to rare in Connecticut. The first nest record of this century is from Norwich in June 1928 (Bagg and Eliot 1937). Since then, the Brown Creeper population has expanded dramatically within the state, and it is now a well established breeder. Breeding bird surveys indicate that it is still increasing in southern New England (Robbins et al. 1986).

*Arnold Devine and Dwight G. Smith*

## Carolina Wren
*Thryothorus ludovicianus*

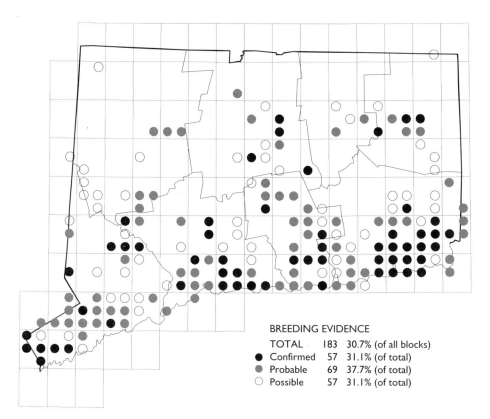

BREEDING EVIDENCE

| TOTAL | 183 | 30.7% (of all blocks) |
|---|---|---|
| ● Confirmed | 57 | 31.1% (of total) |
| ● Probable | 69 | 37.7% (of total) |
| ○ Possible | 57 | 31.1% (of total) |

The Carolina Wren is the largest of the wrens in Connecticut. Although the loud ringing song of this species is easy to recognize, the bird itself can be exceedingly difficult to locate in its favorite habitat. The Carolina Wren is currently an uncommon to locally common permanent resident in Connecticut; it is most common along the coastal slope and becomes uncommon and rare in the higher elevations along the state's northern boundary. Their status appears to fluctuate depending on the amount and duration of snow cover during winter, with marked decreases after severe winters.

**Habitat**—A creature of the undergrowth, the Carolina Wren prefers shrubby field, thicket, and edge habitats, such as shrubs and tangles near water, swampy areas, understory growth along forest edges, woodpiles, and thickets in open woodland. The species is most common in thickets and tangles along the coast. Nests are normally built in natural cavities of trees or stumps, woodpecker holes and bird houses, and sometimes the open crotch of trees or upturned roots. Occasionally nests are placed in a hole in a bank, stone wall, building, or mailbox (Bent 1948, H. H. Harrison 1975).

**Atlas results**—Breeding evidence was found in 30.7% of all blocks within all physiographic regions of the state. The species was most prevalent near the coast and inland along some rivers. Records were scarce in the higher elevations of western and eastern Connecticut, where snowfall accumulations are higher and average winter temperatures colder.

250

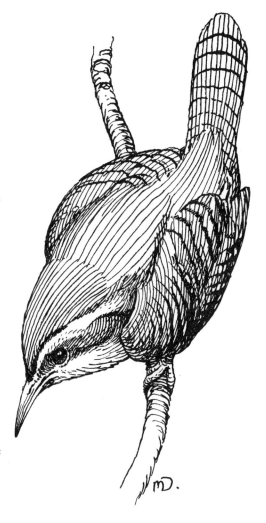

**Discussion**—The Carolina Wren has made periodic invasions into the state from the south since the 1800s. Merriam (1877) thought that it was a rare summer resident in the Connecticut River valley and along the southern border of the state. Sage et al. (1913) considered this wren a rare resident of the coastal slope, "having appeared and actually increased during the last few years." The species has periodic population fluctuations and was virtually decimated from Connecticut after two successive severe winters during 1903-1905 (Sage et al. 1913; Bagg and Eliot 1937). In addition, Bent (1948) and Forbush (1929) also summarize tremendous population crashes in New England attributed to severe winter conditions (excessive cold with deep and long periods of snow cover). Sage et al. (1913) reported the first breeding records for Connecticut: a pair with two fledged young near Bridgeport on 13 June 1895,

and a nest with five eggs in Chester found on 15 July 1901.

In the past decade, the species' population and range has expanded dramatically within Connecticut. Presumably a longer spell of relatively mild winters has contributed to this increase. A record 741 birds was recorded during the 1990–1991 Christmas bird counts. The number of birds found on these early winter counts has increased since 1978–1979 (except during 1982–1983, when just 33 birds were counted). The dramatic increase of the species in Connecticut can probably be attributed to two main factors—the recent trend toward milder winters and especially the proliferation of bird feeding stations. This wren frequents feeding stations to feed on suet and sunflower seed during the lean months of winter.

*Arnold Devine and Dwight G. Smith*

## House Wren
*Troglodytes aedon*

The House Wren is a common migratory breeder in Connecticut. During migration, it is common to fairly common, with peak spring movement in mid-May and peak fall movement in mid-September; it is quite rare during winter (Zeranski and Baptist 1990). House Wrens are territorial and very aggressive during the nesting season; a pair will destroy nests of other House Wrens that are within their territory (Belles-Isles and Picman 1986a).

The species, in the broadest sense, is found over most of North and South America. Northern populations are migratory, whereas Central and South American populations are sedentary (AOU 1983). Connecticut breeders, which are part of the eastern subspecies *T. a. aedon*, likely winter from the southeastern United States to northern Mexico (AOU 1957).

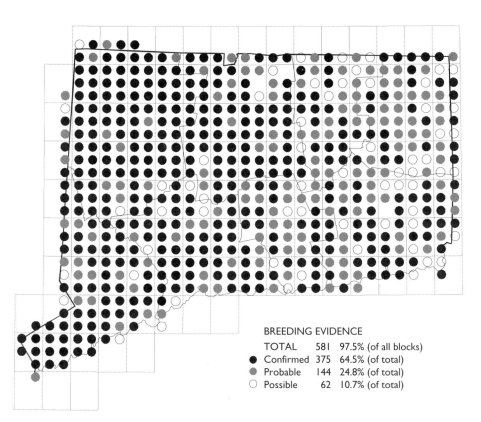

BREEDING EVIDENCE

| | TOTAL | 581 | 97.5% (of all blocks) |
|---|---|---|---|
| ● | Confirmed | 375 | 64.5% (of total) |
| ● | Probable | 144 | 24.8% (of total) |
| ○ | Possible | 62 | 10.7% (of total) |

**Habitat**—This species usually breeds in habitats near humans, such as woodland edges, agricultural areas, orchards, gardens, and urban parks. House Wrens nest in natural holes, such as woodpecker holes or cavities in trees; they occasionally use the nests of other birds (Belles-Isles and Picman 1986b). Males may build several nests, only one of which will be used; they also readily uses nest boxes. In Connecticut, the House Wren often has two broods per year, with the first brood in May. This species competes for territories and nest sites with the Carolina Wren, House Sparrow, and European Starling.

**Atlas results**—The atlas results show that the House Wren was a widespread nester, breeding evidence being report-

252

ed in nearly all blocks. Blocks not reporting House Wrens were widely scattered with no evident pattern, suggesting insufficient coverage by observers in those blocks.

**Discussion**—House Wren abundance and distribution has apparently changed several times over the last two centuries. In the early 1800s it was considered common (Linsley 1843), but by the late 1800s Merriam (1877) listed it as not abundant. By the early 1900s Sage et al. (1913) considered it a tolerably common summer resident in orchards but not abundant and apparently decreasing. Those authors cited the spread of House Sparrows as a possible cause of this decline, noting that the House Wren was seldom heard in New Haven where it was previously common. A short time later, Forbush (1927) called the House Wren a locally common summer resident in New England. Numbers increased somewhat after the 1930s (Griscom and Snyder 1955), when the species also expanded its range south into the southeastern United States (Mengel 1965). Robbins et al. (1986) noted that numbers on Breeding Bird Survey routes had increased in the East from 1965 to 1979.

*Dwight G. Smith and Arnold Devine*

253

## Winter Wren
### *Troglodytes troglodytes*

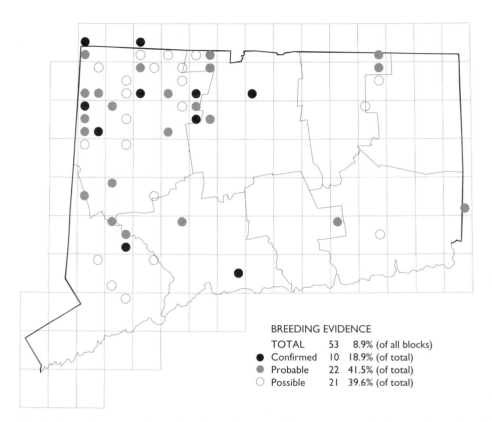

BREEDING EVIDENCE

| | | | |
|---|---|---|---|
| TOTAL | | 53 | 8.9% (of all blocks) |
| ● | Confirmed | 10 | 18.9% (of total) |
| ● | Probable | 22 | 41.5% (of total) |
| ○ | Possible | 21 | 39.6% (of total) |

The Winter Wren is usually encountered as a spectacular disembodied voice of dark, damp forests. When seen it is often briefly glimpsed scurrying rodent-like over moss covered logs and rocks.

This wren's status in Connecticut is complex. It is an uncommon and local breeder in Litchfield County, limited areas of northeastern Connecticut, and a few other areas with suitable habitat. The species also winters in Connecticut in small numbers; most are recorded on the coastal plain, for example, 2.6 per 100 party hours from 1978 to 1989 on the Greenwich-Stamford Christmas Bird Count. Most birds winter in the southeastern states south to northern Florida and east Texas.

This is the only member of the wren family found in the Old World; the species as a whole ranges throughout temperate areas of the Northern Hemisphere. Populations in eastern North America are assigned to the sub-species *T. t. hiemalis* (AOU 1957). The songs of these birds are more similar to Eurasian populations than they are to birds in western North America (Kroodsma and Momose 1991). The call notes of eastern birds also differ from western birds, eastern birds giving softer doubled notes similar to the calls of the Song Sparrow and western birds giving sharper notes similar to the calls of the Wilson's Warbler (Bevier, pers. comm.).

**Habitat**—The Winter Wren is generally associated with conifers and water. Cool, narrow ravines and swamps forested with conifers, often hemlock in Connecticut, are typical haunts. Abundance of dead timber and slash appears necessary to provide nest sites, song perches, and feeding sites. They may show a preference for conifers because these shallow-rooted trees often topple, thus providing an abundance of soil-filled root clusters for sites of primary and dummy nests. Craig (1987b) recorded a population density of 3 birds per 100 ha in mature hemlock-northern hardwoods forest in Ashford and Union.

**Atlas results**—The atlas project reports reflect the Winter Wren's restriction to swamps and ravines wooded with conifers. About 90% of blocks with reports have terrain exceeding 150 m (500 ft) elevation. The Winter Wren may be further constrained by its need for older forest with much standing and fallen deadwood because many forests in Connecticut are young and often kept free of deadwood. The increase of the Winter Wren in Connecticut appears to be due to maturation of forest on abandoned farmland both in Connecticut and in nearby states (Bonney *in* Andrle and Carroll 1988, Ellison *in* Laughlin and Kibbe 1985).
**Discussion**—The Winter Wren's nest-

ing range in Connecticut has increased during the last century. A parallel increase also occurred in New York state (Bonney *in* Andrle and Carroll 1988). The only summering Winter Wrens reported in the nineteenth and early twentieth centuries were in Sages Ravine, Salisbury (Sage et al. 1913). This area was devastated by fire in the 1920s and none were found there in 1932 (Kuerzi and Kuerzi 1934). Summering birds were later found in Canaan in 1936, and Ashford in 1939 (Zeranski and Baptist 1990). The species has summered annually in the latter town since 1960 (Manter 1975). The Winter Wren expanded into a few sites in southern Connecticut during the 1970s (G. E. Palmer 1972, Zeranski and Baptist 1990). Cold winters in the southeastern United States in 1977–1978 and 1978–1979 caused sharp declines in Winter Wren populations, reversing an increasing trend documented by BBS data (Robbins et al.

1986). The species has rebounded strongly from the decline with those survey data showing an annual increase of 7% from 1978 to 1987 (Robbins et al. 1989b).

*Walter G. Ellison*

255

# Marsh Wren
*Cistothorus palustris*

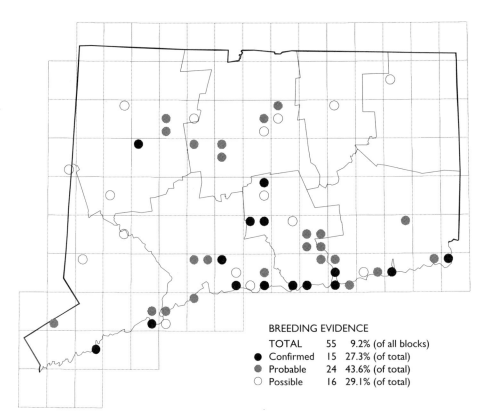

BREEDING EVIDENCE

| | TOTAL | 55 | 9.2% (of all blocks) |
|---|---|---|---|
| ● | Confirmed | 15 | 27.3% (of total) |
| ● | Probable | 24 | 43.6% (of total) |
| ○ | Possible | 16 | 29.1% (of total) |

An uncommon to locally common migratory breeder. This species is easily detected by its incessant singing, a rapid bubbling series of notes followed by a guttural trill. Two weakly differentiated subspecies are reported from Connecticut—inland freshwater populations referable to *C. p. dissaeptus*, and coastal salt marsh breeders referable to nominate *C. p. palustris*. The freshwater *dissaeptus* winter well south of the breeding range from southern Florida to southwest Mississippi, whereas the coastal populations of Connecticut withdraw southward to milder portions of the Atlantic coast, some lingering into early winter just south of the state (Phillips 1986). The status and differentiation of these races needs clarification in Connecticut.

**Habitat**—Marsh Wrens nest in taller emergent vegetation, such as cattail-reed swamps. They are found primarily in coastal and estuarine salt and brackish marshes as well as inland along the Connecticut River. Saunders (1922) noted that Marsh Wrens in Connecticut preferred swamps with narrow-leaved cattail. Bulrushes and cord-grass are sometimes used for breeding but are frequented more during the post-breeding period (Craig 1990). Marsh Wrens also are an uncommon and local breeder in freshwater cattail swamps in western Connecticut. The woven nests are usually built over water on upright stems; males may construct several dummy nests and are highly territorial, aggressively defending their nesting territories from other Marsh Wrens and larger birds, such as Red-winged Blackbirds (Verner and Engelsen 1970).

**Atlas results**—Confirmed nesting was found at the remaining few healthy salt marshes along the coast from Norwalk to Stonington. Inland, nesting was found at Durham Meadows, Cromwell Meadows, and Bantam Lake. Many sites along the Connecticut River were probably missed because the marshes there are difficult to access. Freshwater breeding populations away from the Connecticut River may have been overlooked since many isolated swamps exist. The virtual absence of this species as a breeder in northeastern Connecticut, where suitable habitat exists, is difficult to explain; the species is considered only transient in this region and there are no historic breeding records (Manter 1975).

**Discussion**—No evidence of a dramatic change in status is known for the state, although Sage et al. (1913) did not mention any inland freshwater breeding populations. Bagg and Eliot (1937) noted only one population away from coastal salt marshes—a "populous and long-established colony at South Windsor." This population apparently has declined.

Some populations have been affected adversely by draining and filling of wetlands coincident with the tremendous loss of coastal marshes in the state. Similar declines have been noted in New York for interior populations (Connor *in* Andrle and Carroll 1988). Marsh Wrens are still locally common, and the species is common in marshes along the Connecticut River to Portland, with highest population densities in transitional and cattail marshes (Craig 1990).

Neither Ridgway (1904) nor Bull (1974) recognized a coloration difference between inland and coastal breeders, and Ridgway included the race *dissaeptus* under the name Prairie Marsh Wren, *C. p. iliacus*. Zeranski and Baptist (1990) describe coloration differences that refer to this Midwestern race and not to the more eastern *dissaeptus*. More recently, Phillips (1986) has maintained recognition of *dissaeptus*, which he describes as dull brown on the uppertail

coverts, flanks, crown, and nape, in contrast to nominate *palustris*, which is duller, grayer, and largely black on the anterior upperparts; neither is washed with rusty on the belly. These races are not safely identified in the field. An evaluation of the status of these two forms in Connecticut would be worthwhile as only one or two populations of *dissaeptus* may remain in the state.

*Louis R. Bevier*

# Golden-crowned Kinglet
## *Regulus satrapa*

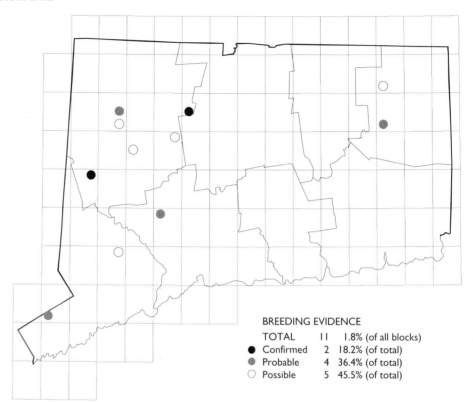

BREEDING EVIDENCE

| | TOTAL | 11 | 1.8% (of all blocks) |
|---|---|---|---|
| ● | Confirmed | 2 | 18.2% (of total) |
| ◉ | Probable | 4 | 36.4% (of total) |
| ○ | Possible | 5 | 45.5% (of total) |

This diminutive bird is a rare and local migratory breeder in Connecticut. The species breeds from southern Alaska across Canada and south in the Appalachians to North Carolina and in mountains of the West south through California and Arizona to Guatemala. Breeding birds in the Northeast belong to the eastern subspecies *R. s. satrapa*, which has a shorter bill, grayer back, and shorter white border to the crown than other races (Phillips 1991).

No information is available on the wintering areas of Connecticut breeders; eastern populations, though, winter from southern Canada to central Florida, the Gulf Coast, and northern Mexico (AOU 1957). The species regularly winters in the state and is locally common and widespread in some years. Along the Atlantic seaboard, wintering abundance is generally greatest south of the latitude of Washington, D. C. (Root 1988).

**Habitat**—The species often nests high in conifers (especially spruce), within predominantly coniferous, or mixed coniferous–deciduous forest.

**Atlas results**—Confirmation of breeding was obtained for two blocks in the western highlands, and records of occurrence were obtained from nine other blocks.

**Discussion**—Sage et al. (1913) did not mention occurrence of the Golden-crowned Kinglet in summer, much less breeding. The first report of nesting was in 1934 at Salisbury, Litchfield County (Kuerzi and Kuerzi 1934). Two additional summer records for that county are cited by Zeranski and Baptist (1990)—Sharon in 1936 and Litchfield in 1973. Other recent reports

of breeding come from Bloomfield in 1990 and in New Hartford, Granby, Morris, and West Hartford in 1991 (Kaplan 1991, 1992). Unfortunately, most of these reports lack detailed information. The first, and apparently only, breeding record for eastern Connecticut came from Union in 1974 (Suchecki 1974b); adult birds were observed carrying food to the nest which was located high off the ground in an area that was later greatly altered by lumbering (pers. obs.).

In southern New England, the Golden-crowned Kinglet is principally a bird of higher elevation coniferous forest, reaching its southern limit in the extension of the Berkshire Hills that just reach northwestern Connecticut. The deliberate establishment of stands of conifers and the natural maturation of forests containing conifers have facilitated the breeding of this species in other parts of the state and at lower elevations. Bull (1974) and Andrle (*in* Andrle and Carroll 1988) outlined a history of the expansion of the breeding range in New York state where conifer plantings appear to have been an especially significant factor in providing new areas for nesting. The species can be relatively inconspicuous on the breeding ground, so Connecticut observers in areas of mature conifers should be on the lookout for possible additional localities of nesting.

*George A. Clark, Jr.*

259

## Blue-gray Gnatcatcher
*Polioptila caerulea*

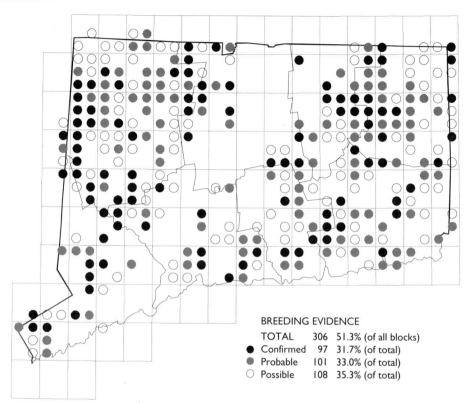

BREEDING EVIDENCE

| | TOTAL | 306 | 51.3% (of all blocks) |
|---|---|---|---|
| ● | Confirmed | 97 | 31.7% (of total) |
| ● | Probable | 101 | 33.0% (of total) |
| ○ | Possible | 108 | 35.3% (of total) |

The Blue-gray Gnatcatcher's appearance suggests a miniature mockingbird and its voice a tiny Gray Catbird. This active insectivore is a migratory breeder in Connecticut that has expanded its range into New England during the last half century (Ellison 1993). It is generally uncommon in Connecticut at present; however, it is fairly common but local in eastern Connecticut and Litchfield County. It winters in peninsular Florida, the Bahamas, Cuba, the Gulf Coast, and southward through Middle America to Honduras. The subspecies occurring is nominate *caerulea*.

**Habitat**—Gnatcatchers may live in any habitat with trees from abandoned pastures and urban parks to mature hardwood forest. They avoid largely coniferous woodland but often are found in pine-oak woodland in the southeastern United States. In New England, they are seldom seen far from a stream, river, or standing water. In Connecticut, they occur mainly in mesic streamside woodland of oak, hickory, and maple but also in silver maple and cottonwood on floodplains of major rivers. Population densities on Breeding Bird Censuses conducted in Connecticut include 11 per 100 ha in second-growth hardwoods (Magee 1968–1987), 10 per 100 ha in young hardwoods released after clearing of red pine (Magee 1979–1987), and 7 per 100 ha in mesic mixed hemlock and northern hardwoods (Craig 1987b).

**Atlas results**—The map shows that the Blue-gray Gnatcatcher is well established in Connecticut. It was particularly widespread in Litchfield, Windham, and New London counties with reports in

over 60% of the blocks in each. It is odd that few were found along the upper Connecticut and lower Housatonic River valleys, although the loss of floodplain woodland in these areas has been severe, leaving little usable habitat. The species was also seldom reported from Hartford, New Haven, and Fairfield counties apparently because of suburban and urban development of woodlands. Robbins et al. (1989a) consider this species sensitive to habitat fragmentation; the Blue-gray Gnatcatcher's frequent use of edge suggests a need for more careful study of the reason for this apparent sensitivity. The patchy distribution of gnatcatchers in the state probably reflects the establishment of core populations and subsequent spread.

**Discussion**—During the nineteenth and early twentieth centuries, the Blue-gray Gnatcatcher was a very rare bird in Connecticut. Sage et al. (1913) listed only seven reports, of which two were, in fact, misplaced reports from Wauregan, Rhode Island (Purdie 1877). Reports of vagrant gnatcatchers increased in the 1920s and 1930s (Griscom 1923, Bagg and Eliot 1937). The majority of these reports were autumnal and coastal. In the spring of 1947 huge numbers of gnatcatchers were seen north of their breeding range with several nestings in northern New Jersey (Bull 1964), and one unsuccessful nesting was in Fairfield, Connecticut (Saunders 1950). Subsequent spring invasions occurred in 1954 and 1956. Further nestings in Connecticut in the 1950s were reported from Weston, Mansfield, and Bloomfield (Bull 1964, Lougee 1957, Nichols 1959). By the end of the 1960s the Blue-gray Gnatcatcher remained rare and bred only sporadically. Several major spring flights occurred during the 1970s and led to the establishment of the species over much of New England. These spring flights rather than the appearance of autumn reverse migrants better explains the mechanism of range expansion of the species in the Northeast (Ellison 1993). Recent BBS trends show increases over the last twenty years (Robbins et al. 1989b).

*Walter G. Ellison*

## Eastern Bluebird
*Sialia sialis*

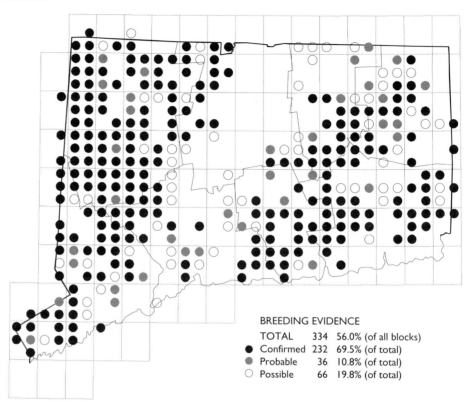

BREEDING EVIDENCE

| | TOTAL | 334 | 56.0% (of all blocks) |
|---|---|---|---|
| ● | Confirmed | 232 | 69.5% (of total) |
| ◓ | Probable | 36 | 10.8% (of total) |
| ○ | Possible | 66 | 19.8% (of total) |

A partially migratory breeder. Some birds winter in Connecticut and others pass through during migration. As a breeder the species is now uncommon but regular in the more rural parts of the state.

**Habitat**—Eastern Bluebirds commonly frequent clearings or fields containing elevated perch sites such as trees, bushes, and fences from which these birds drop down to obtain food on the ground (Pinkowski 1979a). Margins of large fields or openings in woodland are among the habitats used.

Bluebirds require suitable nesting cavities, either in trees or bird houses. Pinkowski (1979b) found in Michigan that individual bluebirds are flexible in using either natural sites or bird houses for nesting. Because bluebirds often require a minimum of at least five acres of territory per pair (Krieg 1971), it is unrealistic to expect to attract large numbers of birds to breed in a small area.

**Atlas results**—Eastern Bluebirds were located in more than half the blocks and breeding was confirmed in nearly 40% of all blocks. Relative to many other species, the total number of blocks in which birds were found but not confirmed breeding is relatively low, indicating a high frequency of confirmation of breeding for those blocks within which bluebirds were found. The high confirmation rate might be attributable to 1) special effort by observers for this species known to be of special interest and 2) the relative ease of obtaining confirmations when the birds are using bird houses that can be readily located and observed.

**Discussion**—Linsley (1843) reported that Eastern Bluebirds were common, and Merriam (1877) termed the species abundant during summer, an evaluation shared by Sage et al. (1913). Sage et al. (1913) reported a great reduction in numbers following a severe winter in the south in 1895 but that the species had recovered its former abundance by 1898. Authors of more recent decades (e.g., Mackenzie 1961, Manter 1975) have indicated that the species is less common than reported from the nineteenth century and early part of the twentieth century.

The number of Eastern Bluebirds breeding in the state appears to have declined from the early part of this century to the present. The decline cannot be readily attributed to competition for nest sites following the introduction from Europe of the aggressive House Sparrow because the latter species was already considered abundant in the 1870s (Merriam 1877). The spread of the European Starling into Connecticut provided an even stronger competitor for nest sites, but starlings can only use relatively large cavities. It seems quite possible that the decline of bluebirds is partly associated with loss of open habitats in the twentieth century along with the regrowth of forest and the spread of human developments that have not provided the habitat requirements of bluebirds. Programs, now regularly undertaken in different parts of the state, to set out nest boxes for these birds appear to have substantially increased their numbers in recent years (Rosgen and Zingo 1993).

*George A. Clark, Jr.*

# Veery
## *Catharus fuscescens*

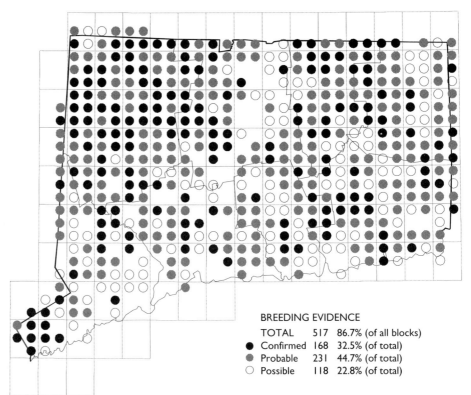

BREEDING EVIDENCE

| | | | |
|---|---|---|---|
| TOTAL | | 517 | 86.7% (of all blocks) |
| ● Confirmed | | 168 | 32.5% (of total) |
| ◍ Probable | | 231 | 44.7% (of total) |
| ○ Possible | | 118 | 22.8% (of total) |

The Veery is a common and widespread migratory breeder in the state. It migrates chiefly across the Gulf of Mexico and winters from Colombia to Brazil. Populations in the Northeast are the subspecies *C. f. fuscescens* (Phillips 1991).

**Habitat**—The Veery is found in lowland woods, thickets, and swamps, especially with dense undergrowth. Research in Kent indicates preference for areas with thickest cover 3–10 ft above the ground and the most moist substrates. Habitat overlap with the Wood Thrush was considerable in this study. The Veery was more common in thickets and early successional woodland, however, and occupied slightly cooler microclimates. Additionally, shrub cover averaged slightly higher in Veery than in Wood Thrush territories, and the former species extended into slightly wetter areas (Bertin 1977). Enders and Magee (1965) document the occasional occurrence of the Veery in tussock-sedge swamp.

**Atlas results**—The Veery was found virtually throughout the state. The areas where the species is least represented are along the coast, in the Connecticut River valley, and in the vicinity of larger cities (e.g., Bridgeport, Danbury, New Haven, and Waterbury), presumably all for the lack of appropriate habitat. The smaller fraction of blocks with confirmed breeders of the Veery than the Wood Thrush may reflect the more secretive nature and more difficult habitat (wetter, thicker vegetation) used by the Veery. Additionally, Veery nests are harder to locate. I found eight Wood Thrush nests for every Veery nest in my study of the two species in Kent (Bertin 1975).

**Discussion**—Veery abundance may have increased over the previous century with forest succession on abandoned farmland (Zeranski and Baptist 1990), but this species has been a common breeder in Connecticut since first reports. Mackenzie (1961) records increasing abundance of the Veery and its greater proximity to inhabited areas in Guilford over the period 1940–1960. Griscom (1923) reported the Veery as locally absent from the coastal plain in the New York City area, and Forbush (1929) likewise from some coastal regions of southern New England. Atlas results from coastal Connecticut also show a spotty distribution. Bagg and Eliot (1937) state that the Veery is more common than the Wood Thrush at higher elevations in Massachusetts, although Connecticut atlas results are inadequate to verify this. Since the Veery occupies much the same habitat as the Wood Thrush, the lack of the former in some blocks in urban and agricultural areas may reflect a requirement for more extensive areas of appropriate habitat. Zeranski and Baptist (1990) also cite fragmentation of deciduous woods as a potential reason for Veery decline around urban and suburban areas. Area requirements may not reflect territory size per se, since territories as small as 0.25 acres have been recorded (Harding 1925), and densities of over 1 pair per 2.5 acres have been recorded in Connecticut breeding bird censuses.

*Robert I. Bertin*

## Swainson's Thrush
### *Catharus ustulatus*

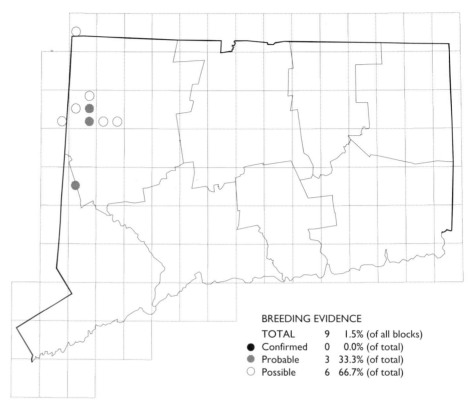

BREEDING EVIDENCE

| TOTAL | 9 | 1.5% (of all blocks) |
|---|---|---|
| ● Confirmed | 0 | 0.0% (of total) |
| ◉ Probable | 3 | 33.3% (of total) |
| ○ Possible | 6 | 66.7% (of total) |

The Swainson's Thrush has not yet been proven to breed in Connecticut, even though a small and declining population breeds in spruce-fir forests not far to the north in the Berkshires of Massachusetts (Veit and Petersen 1993). The species as a whole breeds in boreal forests from central Alaska to southern Labrador and south in the Appalachians to West Virginia, in the Rocky Mountains to New Mexico, and, in willow and alder thickets, through the Pacific lowlands to southern California (AOU 1983).

The Swainson's Thrush is a common migrant through Connecticut, especially in autumn, when most are detected as nocturnal migrants heard passing overhead. The species frequently sings on spring migration and may be heard at stop-over points in the Northeast; occasional late-lingering individuals are heard into early summer here in Connecticut.

**Habitat**—Swainson's Thrushes found during summer in Connecticut have favored white pine-hemlock woodlands in the higher elevations of the northwestern corner of the state. During migration, the species occurs in a broad range of wooded habitats.

A characteristic bird of the northern spruce-fir forests, it also breeds in beech-maple-hemlock woodlands, as in New York (Dilger 1956, Bull 1974), and occasionally in deciduous forest at the lower limit of spruce, as in West Virginia (Hall 1983). Conifers seem required. This applies only to the "Olive-backed" Swainson's Thrush which breeds from central British Colombia and the Great Basin east and includes the subspecies *swainsoni* and *appalachiensis*, the latter breeding in New England.

**Atlas results**—Apparently territorial birds were reported during the atlas in Sharon and at Lake Candlewood. Both areas have extensive hemlock stands.

**Discussion**—The Swainson's Thrush remains a regular, common migrant as listed by Merriam (1877) and Sage et al. (1913). There is no known evidence for nesting in Connecticut, although Barkhamsted, Salisbury, and Sharon were reported as areas of suspected breeding by Craig (1978). The basis for this statement is not given. If nesting occurs in the state, it is limited and should be carefully documented with due caution for late-lingering males. Localities with potential for breeding exist in the Northwest Highlands ecoregion of Dowhan and Craig (1976); the higher elevations and natural occurrence of spruce and fir exist only in this region of Connecticut.

The Swainson's Thrush has been declining in many parts of its range both in the West and the East. In New England and the Appalachians, it has disappeared as spruce forests have been cut (Griscom and Snyder 1955).

The olive-backed races mentioned above, including New England breeders, apparently winter in South America from Colombia to northern Argentina, whereas the russet-backed Pacific and interior races winter in Middle America from central Mexico to Costa Rica, thus suggesting a division of wintering areas as seen in the Gray-cheeked (South America) and Bicknell's Thrushes (Hispaniola) (Ramos *in* Phillips 1991).

*Noble S. Proctor*

# Hermit Thrush
## *Catharus guttatus*

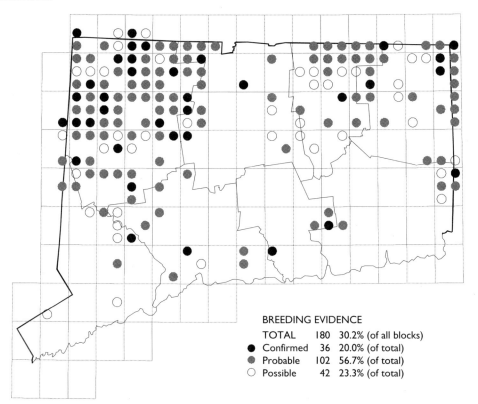

BREEDING EVIDENCE

| | TOTAL | 180 | 30.2% (of all blocks) |
|---|---|---|---|
| ● | Confirmed | 36 | 20.0% (of total) |
| ◉ | Probable | 102 | 56.7% (of total) |
| ○ | Possible | 42 | 23.3% (of total) |

The Hermit Thrush is an uncommon to locally fairly common nester in scattered localities. It is a fairly common spring and fall migrant in the state. A few birds regularly are found into early winter; these are likely not local breeders.

The breeding distribution of the Hermit Thrush is similar to that of the Swainson's Thrush, except that in the West, the Hermit Thrush is not found breeding in lowlands. The species winters over much of the United States south to northern Mexico. Populations from most of Canada east of the Rockies and throughout the East are assigned to the subspecies *C. g. faxoni* (AOU 1957, but see Phillips 1991).

**Habitat**—The Hermit Thrush breeds in a broad range of woodland, including more open forest and edge habitats. It is more tolerant of drier woodlands than the Veery and Wood Thrush, which are dominant in the wetter areas where the species overlap. Open stands of hemlock or white pine are often used.

In Connecticut, the species is generally found at moderate elevations and higher. Much foraging takes place on or near the ground. The nest is constructed on the ground, only occasionally at various heights above the ground in shrubs or trees (Forbush 1929).

**Atlas results**—The confirmed nesting sites are concentrated in the hilly areas of the northwest portion of the state. The mixed evergreen forests and varied topography of northeast Connecticut also support extensive breeding. In general, breeding is not found along the coastal lowlands of the state. The nest is difficult to find, and many probable sites might have had nesting pairs.

**Discussion**—So many have written about the song of the Hermit Thrush that little can be added here, except to say that we in Connecticut also have the great fortune to hear the sweet, ethereal notes of this species in our forests. As a migrant and winter visitor, the status of the Hermit Thrush appears to be unchanged. The breeding range in the state, however, has increased. Up to the late 1800s, the Hermit Thrush was a comparatively scarce breeder in southern New England, principally at higher elevations in western Massachusetts Forbush (1929). By the early 1900s, it was not uncommon and bred at more localities. Sage et al. (1913) reported that the species nested regularly only in the northwestern portion of the state and cited individual nest records from one in Hartford County in 1887 through several in Litchfield County in later years. If the Hermit Thrush expanded its breeding range into northeastern Connecticut, as appears to have occurred, then the timing of this is poorly known. It presumably increased there in the early 1900s.

The ability of the Hermit Thrush to breed successfully in open woodlands and edge habitats is likely a positive factor related to its increase, especially relative to the Wood Thrush and Veery, which were found to be decreasing during the 1980s according to Breeding Bird Survey data (see Appendix 2). A detailed study of population trends in the state does not exist, however, and a perceived overall decline in numbers related to habitat loss lacks evidence.

*Noble S. Proctor*

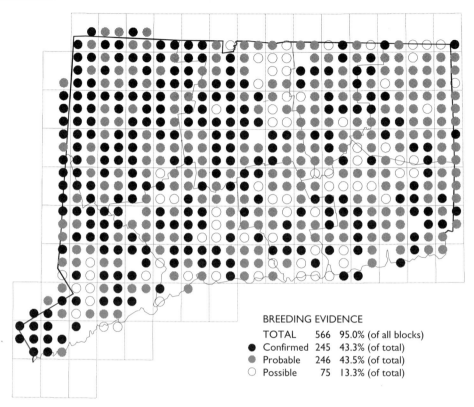

BREEDING EVIDENCE

| | TOTAL | 566 | 95.0% (of all blocks) |
|---|---|---|---|
| ● | Confirmed | 245 | 43.3% (of total) |
| ● | Probable | 246 | 43.5% (of total) |
| ○ | Possible | 75 | 13.3% (of total) |

## Wood Thrush
### *Hylocichla mustelina*

In Connecticut, the Wood Thrush is a common and widespread migratory breeder that winters from northern Mexico to Costa Rica, sparingly north to Texas and casually south to northwestern Colombia. This is a characteristic bird of the eastern broadleaf deciduous forests. The species has comparatively recently increased to the north in the Canadian Maritimes (Erskine 1992), and an increase in spring migrants noted over the past 50 years in Massachusetts (Veit and Petersen 1993) might be related to this.

**Habitat**—Moist deciduous and mixed coniferous–deciduous woodland, especially near streams or other wetlands. Uncommon or absent in early successional woodlands. Research in Kent indicates preference for forest with a maximum canopy height of at least 35–40 ft, as well as for areas with the most moist substrates, and the thickest herb and shrub cover (Bertin 1975, 1977). The species is absent from woods whose undergrowth has been removed by grazing (Saunders 1936, Dambach 1947), but occasionally occurs in park-like areas and around human dwellings (Eaton 1914, Forbush 1929, Bagg and Eliot 1937). The densest populations in Connecticut Breeding Bird Censuses reported in *American Birds* were in mixed upland habitat and swamp (up to 1 pair per two acres).

**Atlas results**—Evidence of breeding was found throughout the state.

**Discussion**—Abundance may be greater now than in recent centuries because of the greater extent of forests today (Zeranski and Baptist 1990), although the species was listed as very common and generally distributed in Connecticut during the last century by Minot (1877). A northward range extension in New England during the 1900s was observed in Massachusetts, although the species was apparently common in Connecticut throughout this period. Forbush (1929) reports the Wood Thrush as less common than formerly in southern New England early in this century. Robbins et al. (1986) report increasing abundance on New England Breeding Bird Survey routes between 1965 and 1979. Bagg and Eliot (1937) report a decreased abundance in Massachusetts at elevations over 1,000 ft, but atlas results are not sufficiently detailed to evaluate this statement for Connecticut. Field observations in areas of varied relief show that the Wood Thrush often gives way to the Hermit Thrush on the upper portions of hills, although the absence of Wood Thrush from such areas is probably due to greater dryness, thinner vegetation cover, or greater distance from streams rather than to elevation per se. The presence of the Wood Thrush in urban and agricultural blocks suggests that extensive, unbroken areas of suitable habitat are not required by this species. See under Veery for a comparison with the habitat of that species.

*Robert I. Bertin*

## American Robin
### *Turdus migratorius*

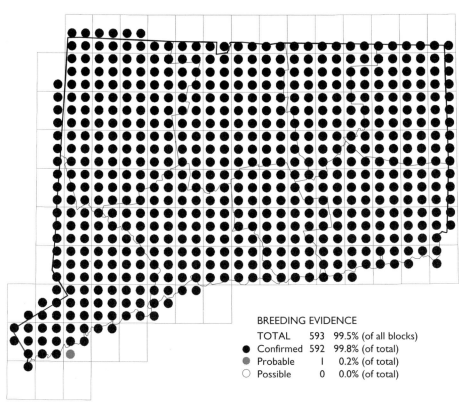

BREEDING EVIDENCE

| | TOTAL | 593 | 99.5% (of all blocks) |
|---|---|---|---|
| ● | Confirmed | 592 | 99.8% (of total) |
| ● | Probable | 1 | 0.2% (of total) |
| ○ | Possible | 0 | 0.0% (of total) |

The American Robin is a migratory breeder found commonly statewide. This species is so widespread as to be highly appropriate in its status as the official State Bird of Connecticut. Although some robins winter in the state, most are found in the southeastern and south-central states south to northern Central America at that season; the nominate subspecies breeds in Connecticut (AOU 1957, 1983). This species has been the subject of numerous behavioral and ecological studies, only a few of which can be cited in this account.

**Habitat**—Nests are placed in trees or shrubs near lawns or other areas of short grass or bare ground. Early in the season before the leaves emerge on the deciduous trees and shrubs, nests are often placed in conifers, but later nests can be placed in any tree providing suitable cover (Savard and Falls 1981). Mud is required for nest construction and is readily available virtually anywhere in Connecticut. Earthworms constitute a major portion of the diet especially from March through May (pers. obs.), but earthworms are generally not readily detected in stomach contents, so that a careful and highly detailed survey of American Robin food habits based on stomach samples from specimens collected decades ago did not show the major dependency of these birds on earthworms (Wheelwright 1986). Earthworms or, especially later in the season, arthropods taken from lawns or other short grass areas appear to be essential for breeding American Robins. Experiments by Eiserer (1980) on the mowing of lawns confirm that

American Robins have a strong preference for closely cut grass which presumably greatly facilitates their locating earthworms and arthropods. The birds begin to include fruits (e.g., honeysuckles) in their diet at least as early as the beginning of June (pers. obs.), and fruits of a great variety are a major component of their diet during summer and fall (Wheelwright 1986).

**Atlas results**—The American Robin is among the most widely distributed species in the state and was confirmed as breeding in virtually every block.

**Discussion**—Presumably American Robins greatly increased in numbers as a consequence of clearing of forests after the arrival of Europeans in Connecticut. By the time of Merriam (1877) the bird was stated to breed abundantly.

The American Robin is commonly asserted to have been originally an exclusively forest bird, but, if so, it was then presumably occupying parts of forests in which successful foraging on a relatively open ground was possible during at least the spring.

Although the American Robin is in some respects a specialized bird, for example, as a songbird that specializes in feeding on earthworms for a part of the year, it is apparent that suitable habitat exists throughout Connecticut. The widespread creation of lawns with scattered shrubs and trees has provided a highly favorable situation for robins. An increased presence of cats and raccoons in the vicinity of human dwellings undoubtedly adversely affects the breeding success of robins, but overall the species appears to benefit greatly from human manipulations of the landscape.

*George A. Clark, Jr.*

## Gray Catbird
### *Dumetella carolinensis*

The catbird is a migratory breeder, common in suitable habitat and widely distributed throughout the state. Small numbers winter in lowland areas, particularly near the coast. The species winters chiefly from the southeastern United States south to Panama, Bermuda, and the Greater Antilles.

**Habitat**—Catbirds nest low (usually 2–6 ft above ground) in dense shrubbery or tangled thickets, frequently in the vicinity of swamps, streams, or wet meadows. The species will also nest on the ground or in trees, occasionally at some height; Bent (1948) records two broods in Stamford that were successfully reared 20 feet up in a pine. Catbirds are found in a range of habitats, from hedgerows or shrubs in sub-

urban yards to woodland edges and cattail marshes. They are absent from dense woods. The nest is constructed of sticks, twigs, leaves and grasses, and lined with fine rootlets or shredded bark. In the spring, males sing from an exposed perch above dense cover.

**Atlas results**—The Gray Catbird's adaptability as a nester is amply illustrated by the atlas survey, which confirmed breeding in over 95 percent of all blocks throughout the state and which showed an impressive confirmation rate of 96.3%.

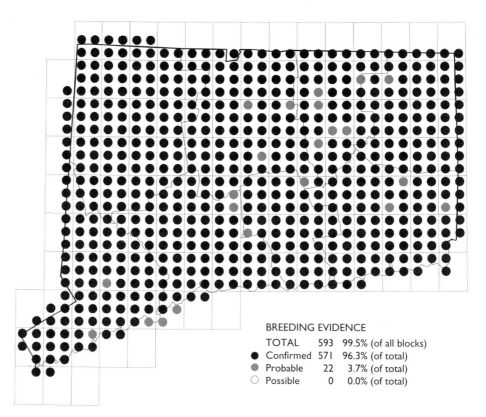

BREEDING EVIDENCE

| | TOTAL | 593 | 99.5% (of all blocks) |
|---|---|---|---|
| ● | Confirmed | 571 | 96.3% (of total) |
| ◉ | Probable | 22 | 3.7% (of total) |
| ○ | Possible | 0 | 0.0% (of total) |

**Discussion**—Considered an abundant summer resident in Connecticut by Sage et al. (1913), the Gray Catbird has fared well in spite of the extensive changes to the landscape that have occurred in this century. Regrowth of cut-over forests and development of rural areas have favored a species able to exploit dense second growth and suburban plantings. Able to subsist on a vegetable diet in the absence of insect food, the Gray Catbird has taken advantage of mild winters by feeding on the fruits of such locally abundant plants as bittersweet, poison ivy, and multiflora rose.

Its widespread distribution would suggest that the Gray Catbird finds Connecticut an excellent place to breed. There is no corner of the state that does not afford suitable habitat for this resourceful nester. Its tendency to eject eggs of the Brown-headed Cowbird from its nest (Bent 1948) affords it protection from brood parasitism, and it does not seem to have suffered from competition with its close relative the Northern Mockingbird, whose numbers have increased dramatically in Connecticut in recent years. Given its current status and apparent longtime abundance, any future change in Connecticut's Gray Catbird population would be of great significance.

*Frederick Purnell, Jr.*

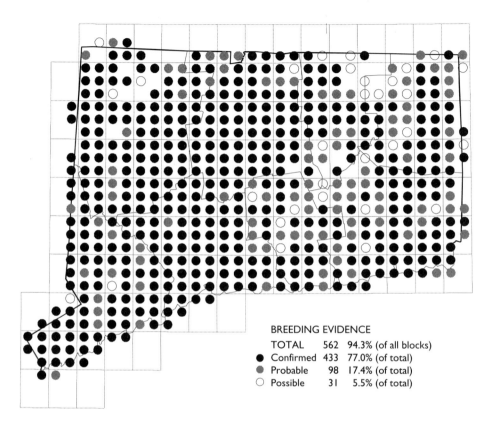

## Northern Mockingbird
### *Mimus polyglottos*

The Northern Mockingbird is essentially a resident, some withdrawing in winter from northernmost localities and higher elevations. The range and numbers of mockingbirds in Connecticut, and the East in general, have increased dramatically over the last three decades. The subspecies occurring is the eastern one, *M. p. polyglottos*.

**Habitat**—An adaptable nester, mockingbirds breed in urban, suburban, and rural areas. They build nests of dead twigs, grass, and rootlets low in bushes or small trees, frequently near human habitations in towns and suburbs. In Connecticut, mockingbirds have shown an affinity for a wide variety of nesting locations, including golf courses, city parks, landfills, and suburban yards. In rural areas they are partial to gardens, pastures with scattered trees, brushy meadows, and woodland edges. Males

BREEDING EVIDENCE

| | TOTAL | 562 | 94.3% (of all blocks) |
|---|---|---|---|
| ● | Confirmed | 433 | 77.0% (of total) |
| ● | Probable | 98 | 17.4% (of total) |
| ○ | Possible | 31 | 5.5% (of total) |

sing from a conspicuous perch atop a shrub or tree, telephone wires, or rooftop, with unmated individuals frequently singing at night in the spring.

**Atlas results**—During the survey period, the Northern Mockingbird was expanding its range; a vocal and easily identifiable bird with an affinity for human settlements, its presence in an atlas block would be hard to overlook. The highest incidence of confirmed breeding occurs in the western half of the state; probable and possible breeding is recorded most frequently in the east, particularly from inland locations. Lack of breeding evidence from several blocks in the northwest is probably due to the species' preference for lower elevations and warmer locales.

**Discussion**—Although there were isolated reports of nesting at Hartford in the middle of the last century, Sage et al. (1913) considered the Northern Mockingbird a very rare visitant to Connecticut. Its status remained the same for the next thirty years, as Cruickshank (1942) reported it as seldom seen anywhere in the New York City region. It was an uncommon nester in southern New England in the late 1940s (Bent 1948) but since then has become a prominent feature of our resident avifauna. First breeding records from Fairfield County date from 1958 in Westport and Weston (Bull 1964). Since then the species has increased in numbers and expanded its breeding range eastward and northward throughout the state.

The Northern Mockingbird is one of several species that have expanded their ranges into Connecticut from the south in recent decades. Like the Turkey Vulture, Red-bellied Woodpecker, Blue-gray Gnatcatcher, and Tufted Titmouse, it has successfully established a breeding population in an area in which it was previously only a rare visitor. Several factors may have

contributed in particular to the Northern Mockingbird's success in Connecticut. Increased suburban development with plantings providing food, cover, and suitable nest sites would favor an adaptable breeder and a trend to milder winters would also doubtless have assisted its spread. A major question to be considered is which species, if any, have suffered from the Northern Mockingbird's arrival on the scene. It is an aggressive defender of its nesting territory, little affected by parasitism from the Brown-headed Cowbird, and maintains a feeding territory in the winter. In what ways has its presence affected, for example, its close relative the Brown Thrasher, which is more restricted in its choice of nesting sites, requiring heavier vegetation and more extensive areas of bare ground on which to feed? Has the burgeoning population of suburban Northern Mockingbirds forced the Brown Thrasher to compete for the ever diminishing number of brushy fields and hedgerows in the Connecticut countryside?

*Frederick Purnell, Jr.*

## Brown Thrasher
*Toxostoma rufum*

The Brown Thrasher is a migratory breeder that is fairly common in suitable habitat. Small numbers winter in lowland areas of the state, particularly along the coast; most, however, winter in the southeastern United States. The eastern subspecies, *T. r. rufum*, breeds in Connecticut

**Habitat**—Brown Thrashers nest in suburban and rural areas, particularly in thickets, brushy hillsides, and woodland edges. The nests are made of twigs, dead leaves, and bark, lined with rootlets, and placed on the ground or in a low thicket or bush, usually 4 ft or less above ground. Bent (1948) found ground nesting much more frequent in New England than in southern or western populations, with up to 50% of nests on the ground, particularly in drier and warmer situations. New England birds were also found to be

less inclined to nest in close proximity to human habitations than elsewhere in the species' range (Bent 1948). The Brown Thrasher prefers open areas with patches of bare ground on which to feed. Males sing from a prominent perch in spring, though this species is generally far shier and less conspicuous than their close relative the Northern Mockingbird.

**Atlas results**—The comparatively low percentage of confirmed blocks is no doubt due in some degree to the species' reclusive habits. The incidence of confirmation was higher in the southern and western quadrants, with fewest records from the northeast and the higher elevations in the northwest. Areas of high urban development show little evidence of breeding.

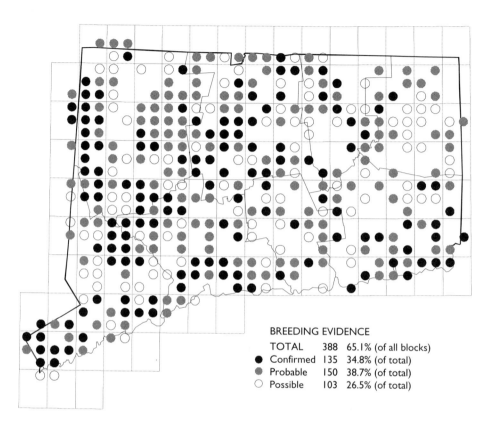

BREEDING EVIDENCE

| | TOTAL | 388 | 65.1% (of all blocks) |
|---|---|---|---|
| ● | Confirmed | 135 | 34.8% (of total) |
| ◉ | Probable | 150 | 38.7% (of total) |
| ○ | Possible | 103 | 26.5% (of total) |

**Discussion**—Considered common in Connecticut by Sage et al. (1913), the Brown Thrasher was still widely distributed throughout the New York City region fifty years ago (Cruickshank 1942), though by then it was slowly disappearing as a breeder within city limits. Long less numerous in Connecticut than its more adaptable relative the Gray Catbird, the Brown Thrasher has probably suffered from habitat destruction as suburban development has reduced the number of old fields and brushy pastures in the Connecticut countryside.

Survey results show how restricted the breeding range of the Brown Thrasher is in Connecticut in comparison to those of the Gray Catbird and the Northern Mockingbird. Both of the latter species have been able to utilize nesting locations in urban and suburban areas which the Brown Thrasher finds unsuitable. While ongoing development of farmland and "waste" areas for housing and commercial use has doubtless played a major role in defining the Brown Thrasher's nesting limits, a question arises as to the importance of interspecific competition. Has the successful invasion of the Northeast by the Northern Mockingbird restricted the number of potential nesting territories available to the Brown Thrasher?

In any event, it seems clear that the future of one of Connecticut's most engaging birds will be intimately tied to the fortunes of our rural landscape.

*Frederick Purnell, Jr.*

## Cedar Waxwing
### *Bombycilla cedrorum*

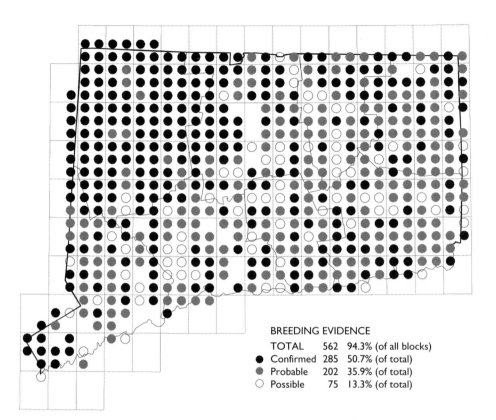

BREEDING EVIDENCE

| | TOTAL | 562 | 94.3% (of all blocks) |
|---|---|---|---|
| ● | Confirmed | 285 | 50.7% (of total) |
| ● | Probable | 202 | 35.9% (of total) |
| ○ | Possible | 75 | 13.3% (of total) |

This permanent resident may occur in almost any habitat at any time! From trees in the middle of a large city to the edges of a salt marsh, this species wanders to all with seemingly no rhyme or reason to its erratic behavior. Cedar Waxwings breed from southeastern Alaska and northern California east to Newfoundland and northern Georgia. In winter, the species is found in much of that area south to the Gulf Coast and south through the highlands of Mexico.

**Habitat**—Of all the habitats this species visits, second-growth situations seemed to be favored. Old fields, shrubby areas along river margins, and old orchards are the principal favored sites. Many fleshy fruits and berries are consumed by this species, and its erratic movements are probably tied to the availability of food. The nest is a well made cup of plant fibers and down, rootlets, fine twigs, and bark strips. This can be placed on a horizontal branch of either a deciduous or evergreen tree. Records show that they tend to be late nesters, with most nests being found in July and August (pers. obs.).

**Atlas results**—The species was reported from nearly all the blocks, showing that it is a regular breeder in the state.

**Discussion**—Due to the irregularity of occurrence and random wanderings of this species, details regarding actual status are not so clear cut as for many other species. In general, it appears that the status has not changed greatly over the years. Merriam (1877) listed it as a generally common resident and implied the sporadic nature of its occurrence at any one time. Sage et al. (1913) listed it

280

as common in the summer and sporadic in the winter. Although the state has gone from about 80% cleared land to a forested condition of about 75%, it appears to have had little effect on this species. More study is needed to understand fully the comings and going of this nomad.

Although a permanent resident, they show migratory movement that is especially obvious in the fall. During the cool mornings of September and October following cold fronts from the north, group after group can often be seen headed south. Other birds entering the state from the north replace those leaving and, thus, provide a year round presence of the species. They are also bimodal in their feeding habits. In the spring and summer, they can be seen hawking insects from perches, often near water. Fluttering out in twisting flight, they grab an insect in the air. When the berries of fall mature, they begin to eat fruit extensively, and flocks can often be seen descending on a tree, such as a cherry, and stripping it of its fruit. During these food binges the birds get into trouble and often become inebriated with the fermenting berries. At such times they can literally be picked up and held in the hand (Forbush 1929).

*Noble S. Proctor*

## European Starling
*Sturnus vulgaris*

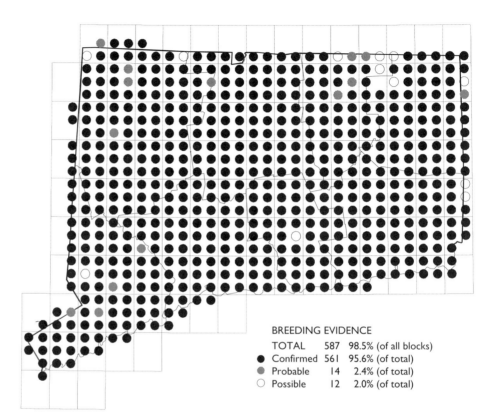

BREEDING EVIDENCE

| | TOTAL | 587 | 98.5% (of all blocks) |
|---|---|---|---|
| ● | Confirmed | 561 | 95.6% (of total) |
| ● | Probable | 14 | 2.4% (of total) |
| ○ | Possible | 12 | 2.0% (of total) |

An introduced species originally deliberately brought by people to North America, the European Starling has for many years been a common to abundant breeding species in Connecticut; it is now partially migratory (Dolbeer 1982), with huge numbers wintering in the state. It is not known to what extent the wintering birds are the same ones that breed in Connecticut, although banding evidence indicates that at least some individuals remain throughout the year (Bergstrom 1961).

**Habitat**—The European Starling nests exclusively in cavities including 1) natural holes in trees, 2) buildings, and 3) cavities in other human-built structures including bird houses. European Starlings commonly outcompete hole-nesting native species for the nest cavities, and among frequent losers in such competitions are Red-bellied Woodpeckers, Purple Martins, and Eastern Bluebirds. In addition, European Starlings require food sources that can be highly varied. In the warmer months of the year, including the breeding season, starlings can obtain arthropods by prying into the ground on open fields and lawns. In the fall and winter starlings often consume small fruits. Throughout the year these birds consume grain provided for livestock and find nourishment in garbage, both at landfills and elsewhere. Moreover, the relatively extensive foraging of the starling on crops gives it the distinction of being probably the worst agricultural pest among bird species in North America.

**Atlas results**—Confirmation of breeding from more than 90% of blocks indicates the continued success of this species throughout the state. Those few full blocks for which the species was not confirmed most likely represent unavoidable deficiencies of coverage rather than a genuine absence of breeding, though conceivably starlings might not be breeding if there were a block composed solely of mature forest.

**Discussion**—The species is not even mentioned in the nineteenth century writings on Connecticut birds. The European Starling was first introduced in New York City in 1890 and was first reported from Connecticut in June 1900 (Sage et al. 1913). Bishop (*in* Sage et al. 1913) prophetically wrote that the starling "is now so firmly settled along the coast as far east as New Haven that its distribution through the rest of the state seems only a matter of time." C. M. Jones (1931) reported that starlings reached the Woodstock area in 1914 and were nesting there by 1916.

Before the introduction of the species to the New World, European Starlings lived for many centuries in proximity to people and thus were well specialized to colonize North America when the opportunity arose. Because Connecticut is a relatively densely populated state, it is not surprising that this species finds suitable habitat statewide.

*George A. Clark, Jr.*

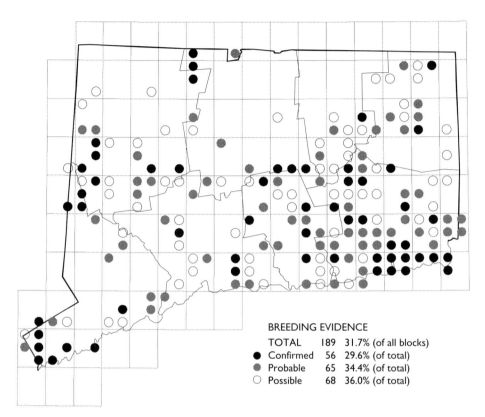

**BREEDING EVIDENCE**

| TOTAL | 189 | 31.7% (of all blocks) |
|---|---|---|
| ● Confirmed | 56 | 29.6% (of total) |
| ● Probable | 65 | 34.4% (of total) |
| ○ Possible | 68 | 36.0% (of total) |

## White-eyed Vireo
*Vireo griseus*

This species is a migratory breeder in the state. Its abundance as a breeder in Connecticut varies from plentiful to absent depending on location. The species as a whole winters in the south-eastern United States, the northern Caribbean islands, and northern Central America (AOU 1983, Barlow 1980).

**Habitat**—The White-eyed Vireo is typically found in shrubby growth with higher trees nearby as found along roadsides, streams, power line rights-of-way, or in brushy fields. The species is often found near plants having a somewhat southern distribution, for example, catbriers.

Relative to other vireos, the White-eyed has a very distinctive nest shape, being pointed or conical on the bottom in contrast to the rounded bottom of other Connecticut vireos. Moreover, the White-eyed nest is placed within a few feet of the ground and thus much lower than would be expected for other species of vireos.

**Atlas results**—Found in less than a third of all blocks, the White-eyed Vireo reaches its highest concentration of breeding in the southern part of the state and particularly in the southeast. An occurrence of the species predomi-nantly at low elevation and in river valleys goes along with a tendency to avoid higher elevations and more northern kinds of vegetation. The atlas findings do not show an extensive occurrence of the White-eyed Vireo in the northern part of the Connecticut River valley. Because birds can be found calling in summer in areas where no breeding is known, inferences as to

actual breeding locations are best based on confirmations of breeding.

**Discussion**—Linsley (1843) reported the species to be common at New Haven. Merriam (1877) stated that the White-eyed Vireo was common only in southern Connecticut and in the Connecticut River valley all the way north to the Massachusetts line. However, numerous records over many decades tabulated by Bagg and Eliot (1937) seem to show that the numbers of the White-eyed Vireo have undergone major fluctuations in the northern part of the Connecticut River valley, but that most of the time since 1850 the species has been uncommon to rare. Sage et al. (1913) considered it to be common in the southern part of the state and noted that it rarely bred in Litchfield County. In the northeastern highlands the species has been considered uncommon in recent decades (Manter 1975) and relatively local in summer distribution (pers. obs.). The first documentation of nesting in Mansfield came in 1975 (J. Suchecki; photograph in the files of the University of Connecticut Museum of Natural History). The roadside Breeding Bird Survey found a significant decrease in abundance of this species throughout its breeding range in the period 1978-1987.

The restricted distribution of the White-eyed Vireo in the state might be interpreted as showing a probable effect on range by some combination of factors involving climate, vegetation, and perhaps food. Because these factors are interacting it may prove difficult to find evidence that would distinguish their relative importance. Historic evidence from Connecticut and nearby (Griscom and Snyder 1955, Bull 1974, Meade *in* Andrle and Carroll 1988) indicates sharp fluctuations over periods of decades both in breeding range and in abundance towards the northern limits of range. This species might thus be a particularly interesting one for a closer analysis of the factors influencing distribution and abundance.

*George A. Clark, Jr.*

## Solitary Vireo
### *Vireo solitarius*

In Connecticut, the Solitary Vireo is an uncommon to locally fairly common migratory breeder in the limited areas of suitable habitat. The "Blue-headed Vireo" (*V. s. solitarius*) is the form found in Connecticut; this subspecies breeds from British Columbia east, except for the southern Appalachians, and winters from the southeastern United States south through Cuba and Central America to Nicaragua (AOU 1983, Barlow 1980).

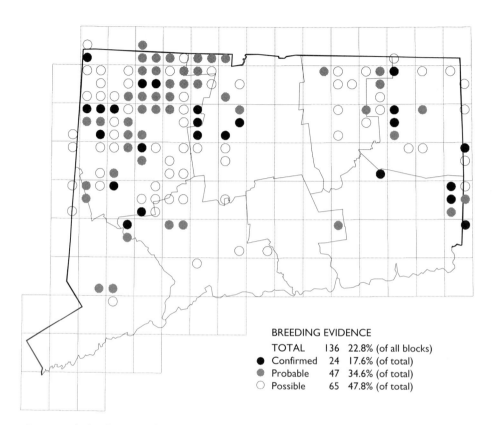

BREEDING EVIDENCE

| | TOTAL | 136 | 22.8% (of all blocks) |
|---|---|---|---|
| ● | Confirmed | 24 | 17.6% (of total) |
| ● | Probable | 47 | 34.6% (of total) |
| ○ | Possible | 65 | 47.8% (of total) |

**Habitat**—The species breeds in mixed coniferous-deciduous woodlands. Although the Solitary Vireo does nest in purely deciduous forest in part of Pennsylvania (James 1979), such a situation is unknown for Connecticut. Identification of nests of the different species of vireos can be difficult. A vireo nest in an area with conifers might be this species. Nests of Solitary Vireos

characteristically contain considerable birch bark though this trait is not diagnostic for identification of nests of this species (D. Rosgen, pers. comm.).

**Atlas results**—The Solitary Vireo breeds principally in the northern hills to the east and west, though nesting also occurs in suitable habitat at a few locations further south than the highlands.

**Discussion**—Merriam (1877) noted that "a few breed." He reported an 1875 nest in a chestnut at New Haven, but he provided no details on how that nest was identified. Because of the similarity of nests among the vireo species, apart from the distinctive one of the White-eyed Vireo, caution should be used in accepting reports based only on nests from areas outside

known breeding areas. Sage et al. (1913) did not mention the claimed New Haven nesting though they certainly must have been aware of Merriam's report. Sage et al. (1913) did list breeding records for the northwestern and northeastern hills, but breeding has been known also for localities further south (see Bull 1964). The roadside Breeding Bird Survey found that Solitary Vireos throughout their eastern breeding range underwent a significant decline from 1966 to 1978 but that from 1978 to 1987 there was only a possible trend towards a decrease in breeding numbers (Robbins et al. 1989b).

The distribution of this species appears to be closely tied to habitat which might in turn reflect local microclimatic conditions. This species is usually the first of the vireos to arrive in the spring and this tolerance of cool conditions may also be reflected in the relative coolness typically associated with its breeding sites. The Solitary Vireo differs from other vireo species in the state in having a strong association with conifers. Because the hemlock trees often used by breeding Solitary Vireos are now vulnerable to destruction by an insect pest, the woolly adelgid, that has recently invaded the southern part of the state, the future for breeding of the Solitary Vireo in Connecticut is thrown into question.

*George A. Clark, Jr.*

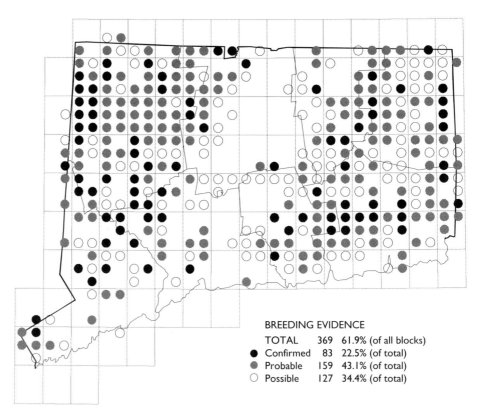

BREEDING EVIDENCE

| | TOTAL | 369 | 61.9% (of all blocks) |
|---|---|---|---|
| ● | Confirmed | 83 | 22.5% (of total) |
| ● | Probable | 159 | 43.1% (of total) |
| ○ | Possible | 127 | 34.4% (of total) |

## Yellow-throated Vireo
### *Vireo flavifrons*

This species is a fairly common migratory breeder. Probably because of its having relatively large territories, the species is nowhere numerous as a breeder in Connecticut. This species winters from southern Florida, south through certain of the Caribbean islands and Central America to northern South America (AOU 1983, Barlow 1980). Most authors who have studied the Yellow-throated Vireo closely have noted that it shows the greatest similarity with the Solitary Vireo among those vireos found in northeastern North America (e.g., James 1978, 1979).

**Habitat**—In Connecticut, the Yellow-throated Vireo is associated with deciduous forest with at least some very tall trees and a considerable contrast in height of the vegetation within the territory, so that territories may border or

include roads and even small open fields. Studies outside Connecticut have indicated a tendency for Yellow-throated Vireos to place their nests higher off the ground than is done by either Solitary or Red-eyed Vireos in the same locality (James 1979). In Connecticut, Yellow-throated Vireo nests were characterized by a very thick lip and upper parts, a

round shape relative to nests of other vireo species, and the presence of much birch bark (D. Rosgen, pers. comm.).

**Atlas results**—During the period of the atlas survey the Yellow-throated Vireo apparently bred throughout much of the state except in urban or highly developed suburban settings. It also appears

that the species was generally absent as a breeder in the area immediately adjacent to the Connecticut shoreline. It is somewhat surprising that the species was apparently absent through much of the Connecticut River valley. One possible explanation for the observed distribution is that deciduous trees of sufficient maturity and stature are lacking in many areas. Perhaps even more critical would be a lack of sufficiently large, contiguous, wooded areas to meet the territorial requirements.

**Discussion**—Merriam (1877) and Sage et al. (1913) considered the Yellow-throated Vireo to be "tolerably common" in summer. Reports from Connecticut alone do not clearly reveal long term upward or downward trends in the abundance of this species. Results from the roadside Breeding Bird Survey indicate the possibility of a decrease of this species as a breeder in eastern North America from 1966 to 1987 (Robbins et al. 1989b).

*George A. Clark, Jr.*

# Warbling Vireo
*Vireo gilvus*

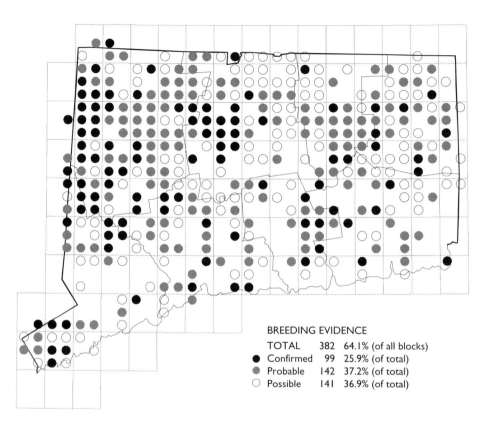

BREEDING EVIDENCE

| | | |
|---|---|---|
| TOTAL | 382 | 64.1% (of all blocks) |
| ● Confirmed | 99 | 25.9% (of total) |
| ● Probable | 142 | 37.2% (of total) |
| ○ Possible | 141 | 36.9% (of total) |

The Warbling Vireo is presently a fairly common breeder in Connecticut; the numbers of birds in the state appear to have fluctuated somewhat over recent decades at least. The subspecies in the state is the eastern *V. g. gilvus*, which breeds from central Alberta across southern Canada, including recently the Maritimes, and south to Texas and North Carolina. This subspecies winters from extreme southern Mexico, chiefly in the Pacific lowlands, to Nicaragua, whereas the smaller western races winter north of that to northwestern Mexico (Barlow 1980, Phillips 1991).

**Habitat**—The Warbling Vireo breeds in isolated groups of deciduous trees, typically with a lush growth of canopy and surrounded by more open country. Often these sites are along the shores of lakes, open marshes, streams, or rivers, but sometimes they are located in upland areas away from water. Of the vireos in Connecticut, this species is the one most commonly found in open settings with the fewest trees; also, its nests were said to show the distinctive trait of bearing substantial amounts of spider web silk on the outside, giving them a silvery, shiny appearance (D. Rosgen, pers. comm.).

The subtleties of habitat characteristics that can influence distribution are well illustrated by a study of the nest sites of the Warbling Vireo in Arizona (Walsberg 1981). Careful analysis showed that nests were exposed to the sky in the morning when warming could be advantageous and shaded in the afternoon when cooling would be advantageous. Whether similarly refined selection of nest sites occurs in other regions is unknown.

**Atlas results**—The Warbling Vireo was recorded in nearly two thirds of all blocks. The species tends to be less frequent nearer the coast and in relatively urbanized areas.

**Discussion**—Merriam (1877) termed it common and noted breeding in orchards. Sage et al. (1913) also considered it common but mentioned shade trees of villages and cities as habitat and said it was rare elsewhere in the state. At present the species occurs most frequently along the shores of bodies of water. Recent analyses of the roadside Breeding Bird Survey for eastern North America show a possible trend for a slight increase in numbers of this species over the period from 1966 to 1987 (Robbins et al. 1989b).

An apparent absence of reports of the Warbling and Red-eyed Vireos coexisting together in summer in the same trees, together with a few observations of initially Red-eyed Vireo and in later years Warbling Vireo in the summer in a particular set of trees in Coventry (pers. obs.), raises the question whether there might be some kind of exclusion or perhaps interspecific territoriality between these species.

*George A. Clark, Jr.*

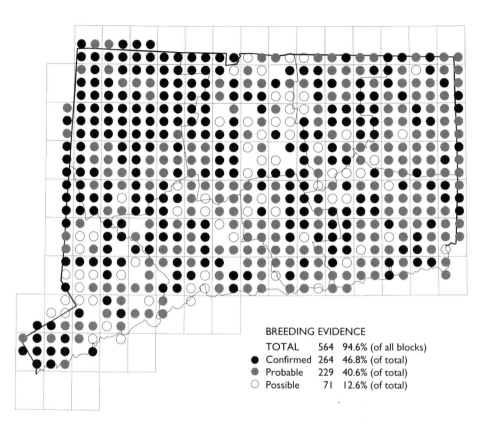

BREEDING EVIDENCE

| TOTAL | 564 | 94.6% (of all blocks) |
|---|---|---|
| ● Confirmed | 264 | 46.8% (of total) |
| ● Probable | 229 | 40.6% (of total) |
| ○ Possible | 71 | 12.6% (of total) |

## Red-eyed Vireo
### *Vireo olivaceus*

This is one of the most numerous forest birds in Connecticut and the most common of the vireo species in the state. It is a migratory breeder that winters in northern South America east of the Andes, chiefly in the Amazon Basin, and migrates through the Caribbean and Middle America (AOU 1983, Barlow 1980). The subspecies breeding in the state is nominate *V. o. olivaceus*.

**Habitat**—The Red-eyed Vireo is a characteristic bird of deciduous forests without apparent specialization for particular kinds of trees (Robinson and Holmes 1984). In Maryland, P. Williamson (1971) found that the Red-eyed Vireo territory was a cylinder reaching from the canopy to the low understory and covering less than two acres; also, Red-eyed Vireo territories were much smaller than those of Yellow-throated Vireos. Because of the small territories, often more than one territorial male can be heard singing from a single point. Nests of Red-eyed Vireos are typically placed below the canopy, and trees need not be particularly mature to attract these birds. Compared with other arboreal nesting vireos, the Red-eyed Vireo builds a very thin-walled nest which is usually small in size (D. Rosgen, pers. comm.).

**Atlas results**—The species was found in more than 90% of the blocks and is clearly one of the more widespread avian species in the state. It appears to be entirely absent only in heavily urban areas. Because the period of song in Connecticut extends from May through the summer to often late in September (pers. obs.), the species is relatively easily detected.

**Discussion**—Both Merriam (1877) and Sage et al. (1913) reported Red-eyed Vireos to be abundant in woodland. The primeval broadleaf deciduous forests, once covering a greater area of the state, may have supported more Red-eyed Vireos, but the species could hardly have been much more widespread than it is now. Breeding Bird Survey data for eastern North America indicate that the species increased significantly from 1966 to 1978 and then maintained a level population from 1978 to 1987 (Robbins et al. 1989b).

Although this species has undoubtedly declined in numbers around urban centers of the state, there appears to be no evidence for long term decline elsewhere in Connecticut. Indeed, the reforestation during the twentieth century has probably contributed to increased numbers in many parts of the state. In view of its generalized habitat requirements and the relatively small size of its territories, the Red-eyed Vireo would seem likely to continue to be the most common species of vireo in the state.

*George A. Clark, Jr.*

## Blue-winged Warbler
*Vermivora pinus*

A migratory breeder, the Blue-winged Warbler has expanded markedly in Connecticut since the mid-1800s. The species winters in Central America from southern Mexico, including the Yucatan Peninsula, to central Panama (AOU 1983). It migrates through the eastern United States and, rarely, through Cuba, Jamaica, Hispaniola, and the Bahama Islands (AOU 1983).

**Habitat**—In Connecticut, this species breeds in successional habitats with deciduous plants. Such habitats include: second-growth deciduous forests with understory saplings or shrubs; shrubby abandoned farm fields; open edges of streams, rivers, and marshes; and openings in mature deciduous forests. Blue-winged warblers nest on or very close to the ground, the nest typically being placed between plant stems or among exposed roots (Bent 1953).

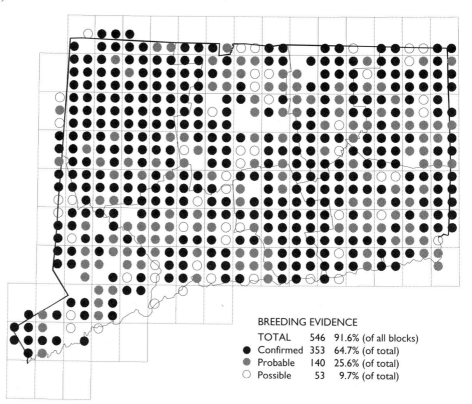

BREEDING EVIDENCE

| | TOTAL | 546 | 91.6% (of all blocks) |
|---|---|---|---|
| ● | Confirmed | 353 | 64.7% (of total) |
| ◉ | Probable | 140 | 25.6% (of total) |
| ○ | Possible | 53 | 9.7% (of total) |

**Atlas results**—During the atlas period, the Blue-winged Warbler was recorded virtually statewide. Confirmed or probable breeding occurred in over 80% of the blocks. The atlas map reveals a few blocks from which the Blue-winged Warbler was not recorded. In highly developed portions of the Stamford, Bridgeport-Milford, and South Hartford-Glastonbury areas, the absence of the species indicates that urban and suburban habitats can prove unsuitable for its nesting, even though these areas may contain planted trees and shrubs. Other small gaps on the atlas map probably reflect incomplete coverage rather than the absence of nesting Blue-winged Warblers.

**Discussion**—The historical status of this species in Connecticut is reviewed in papers by Gill (1980) and Bledsoe (1985). The first Connecticut populations of Blue-winged Warbler were found in the mid-1800s at the mouth of the Connecticut River. During the next several decades, the species spread along the shoreline and inland along the Connecticut and Naugatuck rivers. By 1900, the Blue-winged Warbler was common in lowland areas near Long Island Sound and had extended upriver to Portland and Seymour. From these areas, the species expanded north along river valleys and into the upland regions of the state. By 1960, the species had colonized nearly all of Connecticut. During their expansion, Blue-winged Warblers hybridized regularly with Golden-winged Warblers. (See the account of Blue-winged × Golden-winged Warblers for details about the hybridization of these species in Connecticut.)

After the demise of its agricultural sector in the early 1800s, Connecticut experienced an extensive regrowth of deciduous forests. This transition provided Blue-winged Warblers with suitable successional habitats for breeding. Although it is not clear whether Blue-winged Warblers inhabited the state before its deforestation in the 1700s, the subsequent habitat changes associated with the regrowth of natural habitats paved the way for the expansion of Blue-winged Warblers between 1850 and 1960.

*Anthony H. Bledsoe*

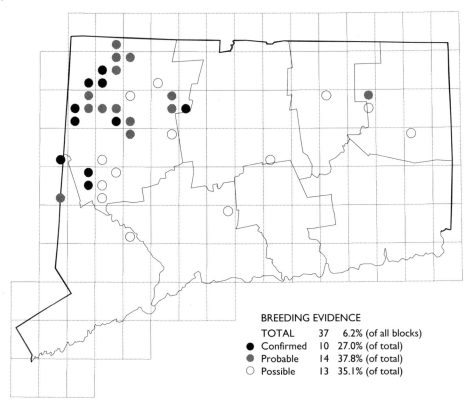

BREEDING EVIDENCE

| | | |
|---|---|---|
| TOTAL | 37 | 6.2% (of all blocks) |
| ● Confirmed | 10 | 27.0% (of total) |
| ◉ Probable | 14 | 37.8% (of total) |
| ○ Possible | 13 | 35.1% (of total) |

## Golden-winged Warbler
### *Vermivora chrysoptera*

A migratory breeder, this species currently nests in Connecticut only locally in the northwest sector. It has historically occurred in small, local populations in the state, but such populations were formerly more widely distributed. Thus, it is listed as a Species of Special Concern in the state. The Golden-winged Warbler winters in Central America from Guatemala and the Yucatan Peninsula south to northernmost South America (AOU 1983). It migrates through eastern North America east of the Rocky Mountains (AOU 1983).

**Habitat**—Golden-winged Warblers typically breed in ephemeral, early successional habitats that support sparsely distributed deciduous plants. In Connecticut, such habitats consist primarily of abandoned farmlands that have scattered trees and shrubs and are bordered by second-growth deciduous forests.

The Golden-winged Warbler is a "fugitive species" that breeds in ephemeral habitats, quickly establishes populations, and equally as quickly declines as succession renders areas unsuitable for its breeding. This pattern of local colonization, expansion, and subsequent extirpation pertains well to Golden-winged Warblers breeding in Connecticut.

The exact habitat requirements of this species and the specific nature of the changes that make formerly appropriate habitat unsuitable are not clear. In Connecticut, Golden-winged Warblers typically breed in open, grassy areas with comparatively few trees and typical early successional plants, such as birches. This kind of habitat develops within 10 years of the abandonment of agricultural lands and was more widespread formerly, as agricultural lands returned to deciduous forest. Suitable habitat usually lasts for only a few years, after which trees and shrubs become more dense and second-growth deciduous forest develops. When succession is slowed or reset by events such as flooding or fire, suitable habitat for Golden-winged Warblers may remain for longer periods of time.

**Atlas results**—During the atlas period, Golden-winged Warblers were recorded in barely 6% of the blocks. Over three-quarters of the blocks from which this species was recorded are in northwestern Connecticut, and the only confirmed breeding records were from northwestern blocks. The most records came from the Sharon, Kent, New Milford, and Torrington areas.

**Discussion**—The historical status of this species in Connecticut is reviewed by Gill (1980) and Bledsoe (1985). Before the mid-1800s, the Golden-winged Warbler was considered a rare migrant in Connecticut. The first recorded breeding, at Suffield in 1876 (Merriam 1877), was followed in the

late 1800s by observations of scattered, localized populations in both northern and southern Connecticut. Many of these populations expanded rapidly and subsequently contracted, a pattern typical of this species throughout its breeding distribution. From roughly 1920 to 1970, Golden-winged Warblers bred only in the northern two-thirds of the state. Since 1970, nesting in Connecticut has been recorded regularly only in the northwest sector. (See the account of Blue-winged × Golden-winged Warblers for details about the hybridization of these species.) Elsewhere, fewer than 10 blocks have supported this species. Nearly all of these observations pertained to birds that were considered only as possible breeders. In the northeast sector of the state, where small populations existed during the mid-1900s, Golden-winged Warblers were observed in only three blocks. The atlas results indicate that the localized populations which existed

away from the northwest sector in the 1960s and early 1970s have contracted since then and may no longer be extant.

*Anthony H. Bledsoe*

297

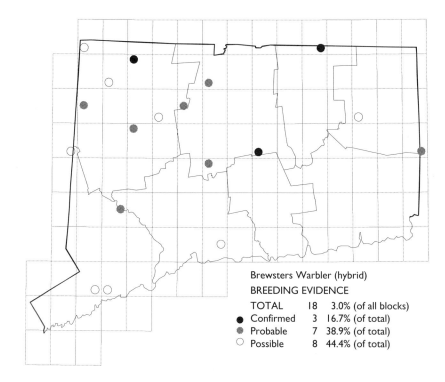

Brewsters Warbler (hybrid)
BREEDING EVIDENCE

| | TOTAL | 18 | 3.0% (of all blocks) |
|---|---|---|---|
| ● Confirmed | | 3 | 16.7% (of total) |
| ◍ Probable | | 7 | 38.9% (of total) |
| ○ Possible | | 8 | 44.4% (of total) |

## Blue-winged Warbler and Golden-winged Warbler hybrids
*Vermivora pinus* × *Vermivora chrysoptera*

Hybrids between Blue-winged and Golden-winged Warblers are migratory breeders in Connecticut. The hybrids occur in populations of the parental species and are usually rare, although they may be frequent in populations where both parental species are common. Most hybrids fall into one of two categories—"Brewster's" Warbler or "Lawrence's" Warbler. See the accounts of Blue-winged Warbler and Golden-winged Warbler for details about the status, distribution, and habitat of the parental species in Connecticut.

*Hybrid genetics*—Many Brewster's Warblers are first-generation hybrids between a Blue-winged Warbler and a Golden-winged Warbler. Such hybrids typically have yellow on the underparts (Parkes 1951). Both Lawrence's Warblers

and Brewster's Warblers without yellow on the underparts are products of subsequent matings. Extensive and prolonged interbreeding leads to the appearance of a variety of hybrids that may differ from typical hybrids in face pattern and the colors of the back, underparts, and wing bars. Hybridization of Blue-winged and Golden-winged Warblers has led to introgression, the flow of genetic information between the parental species over time.

Gill (1980) studied the history of

interaction in Connecticut and described 5 stages: stage 1) mostly Golden-wings with a few Blue-wings; stage 2) equal numbers of the parental forms and the appearance of a few hybrids (mostly Brewster's); stage 3) many Blue-wings, few Golden-wings, a range of hybrids, and the appearance of the Lawrence's type; stage 4) introgressed Blue-wings, no Golden-wings, and a few hybrids; and stage 5) Blue-wings with some variability in wing-bar color. The full

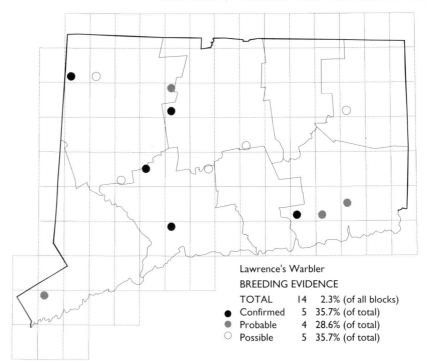

Lawrence's Warbler
BREEDING EVIDENCE

|  | TOTAL | 14 | 2.3% (of all blocks) |
|---|---|---|---|
| ● | Confirmed | 5 | 35.7% (of total) |
| ◉ | Probable | 4 | 28.6% (of total) |
| ○ | Possible | 5 | 35.7% (of total) |

sequence has occurred at several Connecticut localities, including Saybrook, Bridgeport, and Thomaston (Gill 1980).

**Habitat**—Hybrids nest in habitats occupied by the parental forms.

**Atlas results**—Hybrids were observed in 32 blocks scattered across the state. Slightly over half of the observations were from blocks in the northwest sector or immediately adjacent to it. Because all of the Connecticut populations except those in the northwestern sector are at or near stage 5 (see below), most of the hybrids outside of the northwestern sector probably represent birds raised away from the areas in which they were recorded during the atlas. Northwestern populations—The atlas results and other observations suggest that the northwestern populations are at stage 2 or 3. Lowland populations in the northwest will probably progress through stages 4 and 5 in the next few decades. In some areas out-

side of Connecticut, elevation and local habitat conditions may affect the course of hybridization (F. B. Gill, pers. comm.), and it is possible that upland groups of Golden-winged Warblers in the northwest may not engage in extensive hybridization with Blue-winged Warblers.

**Discussion**—As Blue-winged Warblers expanded in Connecticut in the late 1800s, they encountered populations of

Golden-winged Warblers. During this process hybridization occurred, and hybrids were frequently observed near Long Island Sound and along the Connecticut River Valley. In subsequent years, hybrids were recorded more widely as Blue-winged Warblers expanded further into Connecticut and continued to hybridize with local groups of Golden-winged Warblers.

*Anthony H. Bledsoe*

## Nashville Warbler
*Vermivora ruficapilla*

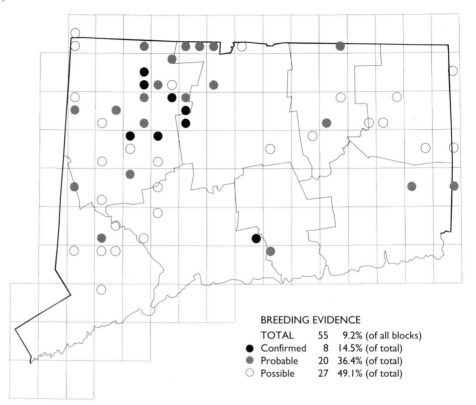

BREEDING EVIDENCE

| | TOTAL | 55 | 9.2% (of all blocks) |
|---|---|---|---|
| ● | Confirmed | 8 | 14.5% (of total) |
| ● | Probable | 20 | 36.4% (of total) |
| ○ | Possible | 27 | 49.1% (of total) |

The Nashville Warbler is an uncommon and local migratory breeder. It can be fairly common at times during migration, especially in the spring. The subspecies occurring is the eastern *V. r. ruficapilla*, which winters primarily from northern Mexico to Guatemala and casually in parts of the southern United States and northern Caribbean (AOU 1983). A rather distinctive subspecies breeds from British Columbia to California but has a similar winter range.

**Habitat**—In Connecticut the species is known to breed in overgrown fields and pastures with mixed species of trees often 10 to 15 feet high (C. M. Jones 1931). Nests are placed on the ground. Nashville Warblers often nest in wet habitats and open conifer woodland in northern New England (Bent 1953), but we do not know to what extent such sites might be used in Connecticut.

**Atlas results**—Seven confirmations of breeding were obtained in the northwestern hills, and one from the lower Connecticut River valley. Elsewhere, isolated birds were found; in many cases these likely were unpaired males. Further studies are needed to determine whether or not Nashville Warblers presently breed in the southwestern part of the state and in the northeastern hills.

**Discussion**—Merriam (1877) reported that the Nashville Warbler bred sparingly throughout the state. Sage et al. (1913) were somewhat more specific saying that it bred "in small numbers throughout the state, but more frequently in the northern part." Kuerzi and Kuerzi (1934) found the Nashville Warbler in summer in western Litchfield County. In Massachusetts,

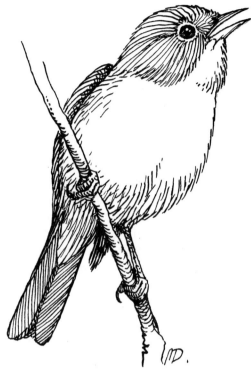

the species was said to have invaded as a breeder during the early 1800s, becoming common by 1842 (Griscom and Snyder 1955). Those authors cite the clearing of forests as the chief reasons Nashville Warblers spread into New England; as those forests have grown, the species has declined. The species has become rarer as a breeder in Connecticut (Zeranski and Baptist 1990). In part because the species has never been a common nester in Connecticut, it is not possible to trace in detail the fluctuation of its numbers in the state as a whole. Searches in Rhode Island in recent years have revealed the presence of a larger summer population than would have been anticipated from the published literature (R. Ferren, pers. comm.).

Relative to the situation in Connecticut, the Nashville Warbler is more frequent as a breeding bird at higher elevations in New England and New York (Kibbe *in* Laughlin and Kibbe 1985, Peterson *in* Andrle and Carroll 1988). In Connecticut the species appears to be reaching a limit of its range. The limit might be associated with either 1) temperature or 2) distribution of northern forms of vegetation. These two factors are linked, and hence it might be difficult to ascertain whether one or the other is of primary importance.

*George A. Clark, Jr.*

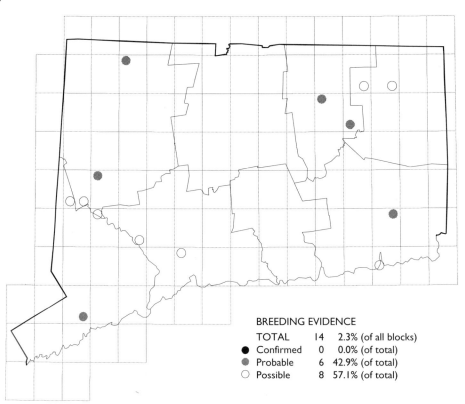

BREEDING EVIDENCE

| TOTAL | 14 | 2.3% (of all blocks) |
|---|---|---|
| ● Confirmed | 0 | 0.0% (of total) |
| ● Probable | 6 | 42.9% (of total) |
| ○ Possible | 8 | 57.1% (of total) |

## Northern Parula
### *Parula americana*

This migratory species formerly bred extensively in Connecticut. Although large numbers of Northern Parulas pass through the state as migrants and a few may remain through the summer, there has been no confirmation of breeding in the state in recent decades. It is, however, designated a Species of Special Concern in the state. The species continues to breed both north and south of Connecticut (Adamus 1987, Kibbe *in* Laughlin and Kibbe 1985, Hall 1983, Parmalee 1973). The Northern Parula winters principally in northern Central America and on the northern islands of the Caribbean region (AOU 1983, Bond 1961).

**Habitat**—Sage et al. (1913) reported for Connecticut that nests were constructed of *Usnea* lichens growing on cedars or a variety of other kinds of trees and placed from 3 to 20 feet off the ground. The birds often nested in wooded swamps. Although this species in southern New England constructed its nests from lichens, other plant materials have been used in other parts of its range (Bent 1953, Hall 1983).

**Atlas results**—The species was reported from a total of 14 blocks. In this case of a species for which no breeding has been confirmed in Connecticut for decades, the conservative interpretation is that the birds recorded during the atlas survey were nonbreeders.

**Discussion**—The species was a regular and widespread breeder in Connecticut in the 1870s. A catalogue of specimens in the National Museum of Natural History in Washington, D. C., lists two

clutches of Northern Parula from Eastford in 1873 (R. Clapp, pers. comm.). Merriam (1877) reported records of nesting in Portland and New Haven. Sage et al. (1913) summarized information on numerous nestings in the state towards the end the nineteenth century (see also Bent 1953). Writing about the Eastford area in 1897, C. M. Jones (1931) commented that the species seemed to be locally extirpated. Sage et al. (1913) noted the disappearance of the Northern Parula as a breeder in New Haven during the period from 1893 to 1913. Although the species was found in Litchfield County in the summer of 1936 (Mayr et al. 1937), it was very much on the decline as a breeder in that area by that time (Kuerzi and Kuerzi 1934). Craig (1978) was unable to locate any confirmed breeding records for recent decades.

The sharp decrease in the Northern Parula as a breeder in Connecticut was well underway by the end of the nineteenth century and is associated with the elimination of the *Usnea* lichens (Sage et al. 1913). In Connecticut the birds did not make an adjustment to the use of other kinds of nest materials. The cause of elimination of the *Usnea* is unknown, but there have been several suggested factors including drainage of wetlands, disease (Bull 1974), and air pollution (Craig 1978).

*George A. Clark, Jr.*

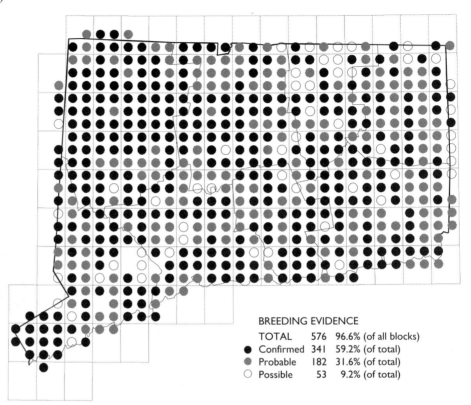

BREEDING EVIDENCE

| | TOTAL | 576 | 96.6% (of all blocks) |
|---|---|---|---|
| ● | Confirmed | 341 | 59.2% (of total) |
| ● | Probable | 182 | 31.6% (of total) |
| ○ | Possible | 53 | 9.2% (of total) |

## Yellow Warbler
### *Dendroica petechia*

The Yellow Warbler is a common migratory breeder in Connecticut and is certainly among those species of warblers most commonly encountered in the state. The northern populations of this species have a widespread breeding range throughout much of North America and winter widely through Central America, the West Indies, and northern South America to Amazonian parts of Brazil (AOU 1983). The subspecies breeding in Connecticut is nominate *aestiva*. Birds from populations in Newfoundland and the prairie provinces occur in the state during migration; these are known as the subspecies *amnicola*, which may actually involve more than one subspecies (Ramos and Warner 1980).

**Habitat**—In Connecticut the Yellow Warbler breeds in 1) brushy swamps or in brush along waterways and 2) some-what open upland areas with trees and shrubs, often with a low herbaceous ground cover as may be found in spacious yards of rural areas. As noted by Griscom (1949), many of the upland sites that seem appropriate for Yellow Warblers actually lack the species. The Yellow Warbler is primarily associated with deciduous rather than coniferous vegetation. Nests are commonly less than 6 ft above the ground or water but occasionally higher (Sage et al. 1913).

**Atlas results**—The Yellow Warbler was found statewide. Only extensive urban areas or tracts of mature upland forest might be expected to lack this species, but, in Connecticut, wetlands suitable for Yellow Warblers are widely available in both urban and forest settings.

**Discussion**—Merriam (1877) and Sage et al. (1913) characterized the species as common, a status maintained to the present. The numbers of Yellow Warblers probably increased following European settlement as have other species that use human altered, open, and disturbed habitats. Breeding Bird Survey data do not reveal a significant change in numbers along roadsides during the atlas survey period.

Yellow Warblers are susceptible to a number of potential threats in suburban settings. Since they nest low in vegetation, disturbances from lawn mowers, household pets, and pesticides (reducing available food) could limit breeding. Perceived declines in the Yellow Warbler due to increased parasitism by the Brown-headed Cowbird has been suggested, but the actual rate of brood parasitism and its effect on Yellow Warbler numbers is unknown. Judging from the present and past abundance of the species, these factors appear not to pose a serious threat, and are unlikely to alter the status of the species in Connecticut.

At present in rural areas of the state beavers are a major factor promoting development of additional wetlands suitable for Yellow Warblers. As noted by Kibbe (*in* Laughlin and Kibbe 1985), the Yellow Warbler as a species has one of the widest breeding ranges of any North American passerine.

Brushy deciduous habitat along streams or rivers such as often used by Yellow Warblers in Connecticut is extremely widespread geographically, occurring in areas of arctic taiga and even along those western desert waterways that retain water through the year. Closer study of this species in Connecticut might reveal why certain upland sites that appear suitable for breeding are not used by the birds.

*George A. Clark, Jr.*

## Chestnut-sided Warbler
*Dendroica pensylvanica*

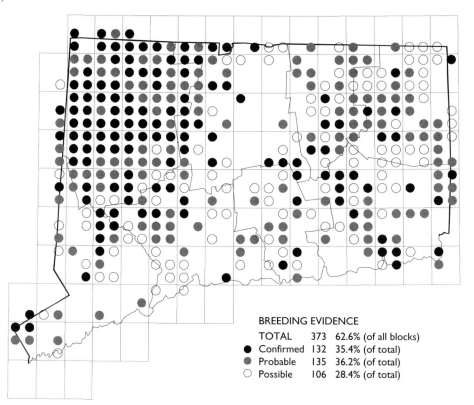

BREEDING EVIDENCE

| | TOTAL | 373 | 62.6% (of all blocks) |
|---|---|---|---|
| ● Confirmed | 132 | 35.4% (of total) |
| ● Probable | 135 | 36.2% (of total) |
| ○ Possible | 106 | 28.4% (of total) |

A migratory breeder which winters primarily in Central America (AOU 1983). The abundance of this species as a breeder varies considerably in different parts of the state, ranging from entirely absent to regular in occurrence.

**Habitat**—The Chestnut-sided Warbler commonly breeds in edge situations with hardwood trees and underbrush; sites are often rather dry but a stream runs through some breeding areas. On occasion the bird nests in woods, though typically not in dense or mature unbroken woodland.

**Atlas results**—The Chestnut-sided Warbler does not breed in many of the more urbanized areas of the state. The northwestern hills are clearly the area of heaviest concentration of blocks with confirmation of breeding. Part of the sparseness of records in eastern Connecticut might be attributable to a limitation of block busting in locating species that are regular but not so widespread as to be readily found or confirmed as breeding during a short visit.

**Discussion**—Although this species was rare in the northeastern United States in the early part of the nineteenth century (Bent 1953), the records from Connecticut in that period are too few to trace an increase in its numbers within the state. The species was known to breed in Connecticut by the time of Merriam (1877). Sage et al. (1913) added that it bred more abundantly in the northern part of the state.

The Chestnut-sided Warbler has been reported as generally absent or

rare as a breeder in the northeastern coastal plain as opposed to interior areas where the species is more widespread (Stone 1937, Bull 1974, Easton *in* Andrle and Carroll 1988, Griscom and Snyder 1955). Two factors may be suggested as contributing to a relative lack of Chestnut-sided Warblers in the coastal plain: 1) a prevalence of apparently unsuitable pine woodlands over much of the area, and 2) historically an extensive use of land for agriculture with associated elimination of vegetation that might be suited for Chestnut-sided Warblers.

A comparison with interior areas in which the species is uncommon may be informative. Eaton (*in* Andrle and Carroll 1988) noted that this species was uncommon along the Great Lakes Plain of New York state and interpreted this as a consequence of extensive agriculture in that area. In analyzing the situation in Vermont, Kibbe (*in* Laughlin and Kibbe 1985) noted that the species was common statewide except in the northwestern corner. As shown by maps for the Vermont atlas, the area least frequented by Chestnut-sided Warblers are lowlands adjacent to Lake Champlain and again much used for agriculture.

*George A. Clark, Jr.*

## Magnolia Warbler
*Dendroica magnolia*

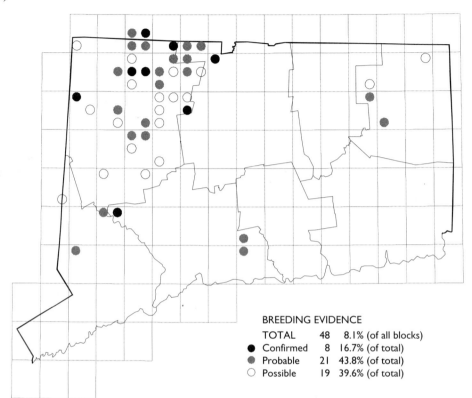

BREEDING EVIDENCE

| | TOTAL | 48 | 8.1% (of all blocks) |
|---|---|---|---|
| ● | Confirmed | 8 | 16.7% (of total) |
| ◉ | Probable | 21 | 43.8% (of total) |
| ○ | Possible | 19 | 39.6% (of total) |

This colorful species is a migratory breeder. The Magnolia Warbler winters primarily in Central America, the Greater Antilles, and the Bahamas (AOU 1983, Keast 1980). In Connecticut, the species is generally a rare and local breeder, principally in the northwestern hills.

**Habitat**—Craig (1978) characterized the species as nesting in open coniferous and mixed conifer-hardwood forests, particularly young second growth. More specifically for Connecticut, he listed 1) pine groves, 2) black spruce bogs, and 3) young open spruce plantations in which oak, birch, and aspen have invaded. Christmas tree plantations at higher elevations are a frequently used in the state. This conifer-associated species is not to be expected as a breeder within continuous stands of mature forest.

**Atlas results**—The eight confirmations were obtained in the northwestern hills where the number of localities was higher than might have been predicted on the basis of the more limited previous field work. The evidence for these confirmations and the probable breeding records was poorly recorded. An attempt should be made to better document breeding in the state.

**Discussion**—Sage et al. (1913) reported two summer records from Litchfield County and suggested that the species might breed there. Kuerzi and Kuerzi (1934) first found direct evidence of breeding in their observation of the feeding of young in that county. A number of later observers have confirmed nesting there (Craig 1978, Zeranski and Baptist 1990). No conclu-

sive evidence has been found for breeding of the Magnolia Warbler in eastern Connecticut, although isolated males have occasionally been found in summer, and nesting has been "suspected" (Craig 1978).

The center of abundance for breeding of this species lies at a latitude north of Connecticut, and in northern New England is at a generally higher elevation than occurs in most of Connecticut. This species is perhaps at a disadvantage as a potential breeder in Connecticut in that continuing matura-

tion of the forests has tended to eliminate the second growth favored for nesting by Magnolia Warblers. It would be of interest to have more details on the occurrence of apparently unpaired males that apparently spend at least part of the summer outside the ordinary breeding range of the species. Among features that would be of interest are their arrival dates, how long they stay in a

local area, and how the pattern of their singing compares with that of mated males within the usual breeding range.

*George A. Clark, Jr.*

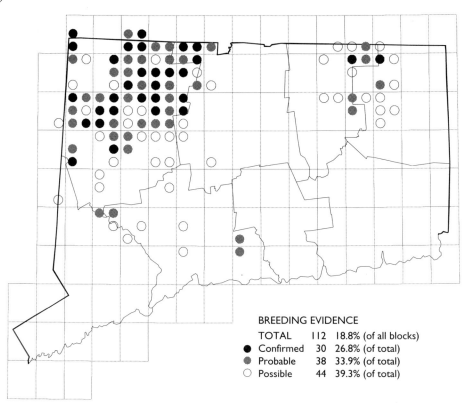

BREEDING EVIDENCE

| | TOTAL | 112 | 18.8% (of all blocks) |
|---|---|---|---|
| ● | Confirmed | 30 | 26.8% (of total) |
| ● | Probable | 38 | 33.9% (of total) |
| ○ | Possible | 44 | 39.3% (of total) |

## Black-throated Blue Warbler
### *Dendroica caerulescens*

This is an uncommon to fairly common breeding species in Connecticut. Northern Connecticut represents the southernmost edge of the breeding range of this beautiful Neotropical migrant in New England, although the species breeds southward in the Appalachian Mountains, where represented by the weakly differentiated race, *cairnsi* (AOU 1957). The Black-throated Blue Warbler migrates through the state in May, during which time it is an uncommon to locally common migrant. Highest breeding densities occur north of the state in western Massachusetts, Vermont, New Hampshire, Maine, and southern Canada. Fall migration lasts from late August into early October, peaking in the second week of September. The Black-throated Blue Warbler winters primarily in the West Indies, although some individuals may reach Central America and northern South America (AOU 1983).

**Habitat**—During migration, Black-throated Blue Warblers occupy a variety of habitats, including mature and secondary growth forests, parks, gardens, and residential neighborhoods. Breeding takes place within large tracts of unbroken, mature deciduous or mixed forests containing a dense undergrowth of saplings and shrubs. These habitats are often found within hilly or rough terrain. The well-concealed nests are usually placed less than 1 m above-ground within the shrub layer, and first nests of the season are frequently placed in small conifers. Three to five eggs are laid during mid to late May, but wet or cold weather may delay initiation of clutches (pers. obs.). In New Hampshire, males may be polygynous and some pairs double-brooded (K. E. Petit et al. 1988). Birds breeding in Connecticut may exhibit similar traits.

**Atlas results**—The Black-throated Blue Warbler was listed as probable or confirmed in approximately 11% of blocks surveyed during the atlas period. Nearly all observations were from the northeastern and, especially, the northwestern highland areas of the state. These physiographic regions contain extensive, unbroken tracts of forest—ideal breeding habitat for the Black-throated Blue Warbler. Most confirmed records of breeding originate from the Cornwall, Winsted, Torrington, and adjacent quadrangles. A few individuals may breed to coastal Connecticut in areas where suitable habitat exists.

Although reported as confirmed in only 5% of the atlas blocks, the secretive nature of female Black-throated Blue Warblers, their reluctance to flush from nests even when closely approached, and the high degree of concealment of nests, may contribute to this low percentage. Conversely, adults may feed fledged young for more than 30 days, which should increase detectability by atlasers. In addition, males frequently remain vocal and maintain territories until early August (pers. obs.).

**Discussion**—Coues noted in 1868 that the Black-throated Blue Warbler bred throughout New England but was most common in northern portions of the region. Baird et al. (1874) described the Black-throated Blue Warbler as a rare summer resident in the western portion of Connecticut, but suggested that it may breed as far south as the Connecticut coastline; the species was commonly observed in Connecticut until June (Stearns and Coues 1881). The earliest published breeding record in the state is of two nests at Eastford, Windham County, found 8 June 1874 (C. M. Jones 1876). Early published breeding localities also include Kent and Litchfield in 1905, Gales Ferry in 1918 (Graves 1919), and North Cornwall in 1931 (Scoville 1934). Throughout the twentieth century, the Black-throated Blue Warbler has apparently increased its breeding population, especially in the northwest portion of the state (Zeranski and Baptist 1990).

With the decline of agriculture in Connecticut, much second-growth forest now occupies former pastures and fields. As that habitat reverts to mature

forest and becomes suitable for breeding, the Black-throated Blue Warbler may expand its range and breeding densities within the state. That scenario, however, is dependent on those forests remaining contiguous and unfragmented. It is doubtful that the Black-throated Blue Warbler will ever become a common breeding species in densely populated portions of southern Connecticut. However, populations in northern areas of the state may remain stable or expand as more agricultural lands become forested again.

*Kenneth E. Petit*

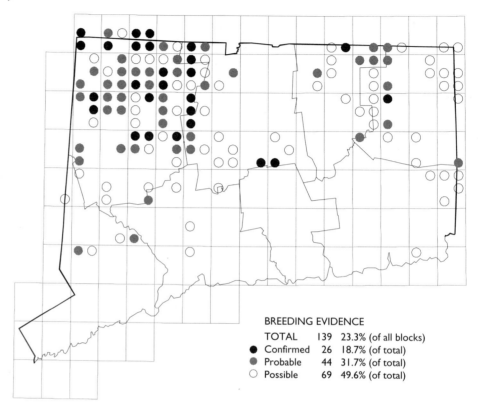

BREEDING EVIDENCE
TOTAL        139   23.3% (of all blocks)
● Confirmed    26   18.7% (of total)
● Probable     44   31.7% (of total)
○ Possible     69   49.6% (of total)

## Yellow-rumped Warbler
*Dendroica coronata*

An uncommon and local migratory breeder. The eastern North American subspecies known as the Myrtle Warbler (*D. c. coronata*) winters from coastal New England south through the southeastern United States, Central America, and over many of the Caribbean islands (AOU 1983, Keast 1980). Along the Connecticut coast, the species is uncommon in winter (Zeranski and Baptist 1990), and occasional individuals are found in the interior during that season. Wintering birds feed to a great extent on small fruits, especially bayberries, that are found along the coast (Bent 1953); in contrast, breeding birds are believed to be largely insectivorous. The wintering areas for those birds breeding in Connecticut has not been determined.

**Habitat**—The species is strongly associated with relatively mature conifers,

particularly white pine and hemlock. Nesting is apparently often in an edge situation (Craig 1978) such as by an opening in a grove of conifers.

**Atlas results**—Most of the 26 blocks for which confirmations were obtained were in the northwestern hills. For the northeastern highlands, two blocks with confirmations together with observa-

tions of possible or probable breeders from numerous other blocks indicate the local occurrence of breeding birds in that area.

**Discussion**—Sage et al. (1913) did not mention summer occurrence. Mayr et al. (1937), who observed this species on 31 May and 1 June in different localities in Litchfield County, were

apparently the first to record observations of Yellow-rumped Warblers during the breeding season in Connecticut. The first report of nesting in the state came from New Hartford in 1946, and subsequently there have been a small number of additional breeding records from the northwestern hills (Craig 1978, Zeranski and Baptist 1990). Although presence in summer had been indicated for the northeastern hills (Manter 1975, Craig 1978), no specific documentation of breeding had been recorded before the atlas survey.

The fairly widespread occurrence of breeding Yellow-rumped Warblers in Connecticut appears to be a result of a broad expansion of the breeding range of this species (Peterson *in* Andrle and Carroll 1988). Bull (1974) linked this widened range to the maturation of plantings of blocks of spruce and red pine, though many birds in this expansion have used other tree species such as hemlock and white pine. Presumably the increasing maturity of southern New England forests in recent decades has facilitated this range expansion.

*George A. Clark, Jr.*

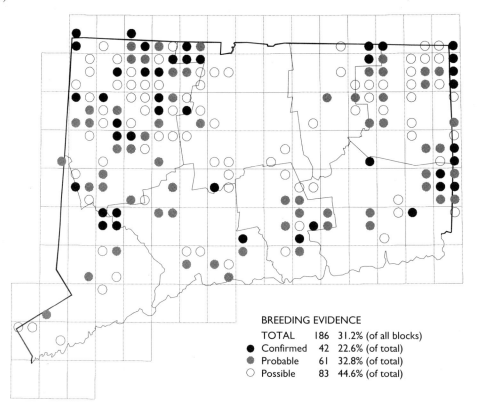

BREEDING EVIDENCE

| | | | |
|---|---|---|---|
| | TOTAL | 186 | 31.2% (of all blocks) |
| ● | Confirmed | 42 | 22.6% (of total) |
| ◉ | Probable | 61 | 32.8% (of total) |
| ○ | Possible | 83 | 44.6% (of total) |

## Black-throated Green Warbler
### *Dendroica virens*

This elegant warbler is a migratory breeder in Connecticut wintering in Middle America, northwestern South America, the Bahamas, and the western Greater Antilles. It is locally common in northeastern and northwestern Connecticut and scarcer southward to the coastal plain.

**Habitat**—Black-throated Green Warblers inhabit mature forests, usually mixed, especially hemlock–northern hardwoods. In southern Connecticut, they are generally restricted to cool ravines where hemlock prevails. They also may occur in white pine-northern hardwoods (Griscom 1949). At extremes of its range, the Black-throated Green Warbler may occur in nearly pure coniferous forest, primarily balsam fir, or pure deciduous forest, as in West Virginia (Brooks 1947, Collins 1983b, Hall 1983). Interestingly, a disjunct population breeds along the coastal lowlands from Virginia to South Carolina in bald cypress swamps.

In northern New England it feeds preferentially in yellow birch and conifers (Holmes and Robinson 1981). Population densities measured on Connecticut Breeding Bird Census plots include 63 per 100 ha in old growth hemlock–white pine–northern hardwoods in Litchfield (Cavanaugh & Magee 1967a, Magee 1968-1984a), 35 per 100 ha in similar habitat in Ashford (Suchecki 1974b), and 25 per 100 ha in oak-maple forest with scattered hemlock in Ashford (Suchecki 1974a). Craig (1987b) used a transect method to obtain an estimate of 27.5 per 100 ha in the Yale Forest in Ashford and Union.

**Atlas results**—Over half of atlas project reports of Black-throated Green Warblers were from Litchfield and Windham Counties. The species was more sparsely distributed in other counties with the lowest reporting frequencies in Fairfield and Tolland counties. Concentrations of reports occurred in Pachaug State Forest, Voluntown/ Sterling, and around Devils Hopyard State Park, East Haddam. Factors contributing to this pattern probably include topography, local climate, and extent of forest. Coniferous and mixed forests are more frequent in areas of high topographic relief. The Black-throated Green Warbler's sensitivity to habitat fragmentation also contributes to the sparseness of reports in Hartford County and along the coastal plain.

**Discussion**—The Black-throated Green Warbler was apparently more common and widespread in the late nineteenth and early twentieth centuries (Zeranski and Baptist 1990); however, this is based on a few subjective statements in the literature. Urbanization and subsequent suburban development in southwestern Connecticut and the central Connecticut River valley probably caused the removal of much habitable forest. Concurrent reforestation of farms in rural northern Connecticut may have offset this until fairly recently. This warbler is apparently sensitive to habitat fragmentation and isolation; Butcher et al. (1981) documented its disappearance from hemlock forest at the Connecticut Arboretum, New London, during the 1960s. Continued housing development in forested areas may further reduce this warbler's range. The recent arrival of hemlock pests in Connecticut may also cause deterioration of the Black-throated Green Warbler's habitat. A significant annual decline of 3.1% has been found on Breeding Bird Survey routes from 1978 to 1987 (Robbins et al. 1989b); the authors attribute this to loss of wintering habitat.

*Walter G. Ellison*

315

## Blackburnian Warbler
*Dendroica fusca*

The Blackburnian Warbler is an uncommon and local migratory breeder. It winters principally in highlands from Costa Rica to northern South America, chiefly in the Andes of Colombia, but also in Venezuela, Peru, and Bolivia (AOU 1983, Keast 1980).

**Habitat**—The species when breeding in Connecticut is strongly associated with conifers, particularly tall ones. Males commonly sing in the interior of the tops of the trees, far off the ground, and are thus often difficult to see. Kuerzi and Kuerzi (1934) reported that this species in Litchfield County used chiefly pines and hemlocks, and their generalization probably applies also to other parts of the state. The Blackburnian Warbler provides a dramatic example of geographic variation in habitats used. In the hills of West Virginia the species breeds not only in habitats with conifers but also in deciduous woodlands at lower elevations (Hall 1983).

**Atlas results**—The species was confirmed in 19 blocks, a good total for a species that is often difficult to observe. Breeding has been principally in the northwestern and northeastern highlands. The finding of the species in more than 15% of all blocks indicates that its occurrence has been more widespread during the breeding season than was indicated by the earlier literature.

**Discussion**—Sage et al. (1913) listed a number of summer records and indicated that the species undoubtedly nested in northern Litchfield County, although no direct evidence of breeding was

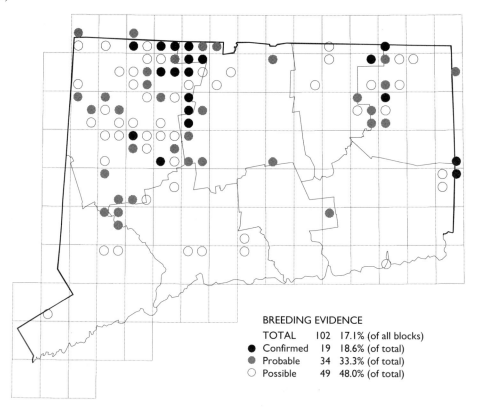

BREEDING EVIDENCE

| | TOTAL | 102 | 17.1% (of all blocks) |
|---|---|---|---|
| ● | Confirmed | 19 | 18.6% (of total) |
| ◐ | Probable | 34 | 33.3% (of total) |
| ○ | Possible | 49 | 48.0% (of total) |

apparently available at that time. Kuerzi and Kuerzi (1934) were the first to report definite evidence for breeding in that county. For the northeastern highlands, Taber (1951) reported a number of summer records, and Manter (1975) recorded a confirmation of breeding in 1968.

Like the Yellow-rumped Warbler, the Blackburnian Warbler has expanded its range in the northeastern states in the twentieth century (Levine *in* Andrle and Carroll 1988). The planting of conifers and the overall growth of natu-ral forest to greater maturity have facil-itated this expansion of breeding range. It would be of interest to have informa-tion on the heights of the trees used by the Blackburnian Warblers breeding in the state, because this information might aid in predicting whether exist-ing less mature forest stands are even-tually likely to be occupied by this species.

As in the case of other bird species that are extensively associated with hemlocks, there is at present a question about the eventual effects of the acci-dentally introduced Asian woolly adel-gid insect, which during the 1980s invaded southern Connecticut and caused substantial mortality of hem-locks. If this insect continues its north-ward expansion of range and numbers, the quantity of hemlock trees in the state could be greatly reduced, and this in turn might lower the numbers of such species as the Blackburnian Warbler.

*George A. Clark, Jr.*

## Pine Warbler
*Dendroica pinus*

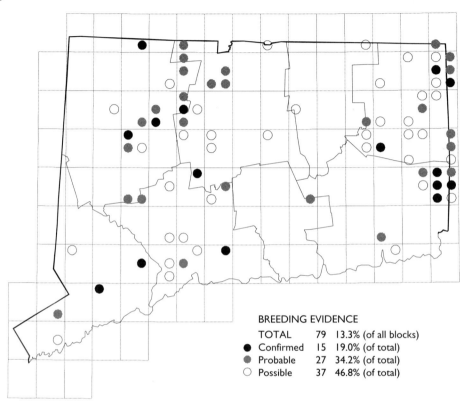

BREEDING EVIDENCE

| | | | |
|---|---|---|---|
| | TOTAL | 79 | 13.3% (of all blocks) |
| ● | Confirmed | 15 | 19.0% (of total) |
| ● | Probable | 27 | 34.2% (of total) |
| ○ | Possible | 37 | 46.8% (of total) |

This migratory breeder winters principally from the southern Atlantic and Gulf Coast states south into certain of the islands of the northern Caribbean and barely into northern Mexico (AOU 1983). The Pine Warbler appears to have a greater tolerance of cool conditions than do most warblers (Root 1988) and is occasionally found in winter in Connecticut. In accord with its temperature tolerance this is one of the earlier warblers to arrive in the breeding areas in the spring. As a nester in the state it is regular in restricted areas of suitable habitat.

**Habitat**—The common and scientific names for this warbler are highly appropriate to designate its breeding habitat. The species breeds typically in stands of tall pine trees with relatively few or no tall hardwoods interspersed among the pines. Commonly the underlying soils

are well drained (Craig 1978). Other warbler species that also breed in Connecticut habitats with tall pines include the Black-throated Green, Blackburnian, and Yellow-rumped, but these latter species appear to be more tolerant of interspersed hardwoods. Nevertheless, in some cases a juxtaposition of habitats is apparently suitable for Pine Warbler to breed in the vicinity of

Black-throated Green and Yellow-rumped Warblers; in such cases songs of males of all three species can be heard by a listener standing in one place.

**Atlas results**—Likely or known sites of breeding are predominantly very localized in the eastern and western highlands. Although the habitats of this species in the eastern United States are

widely present in the coastal plain, this distribution is not obvious in the pattern from Connecticut, perhaps reflecting the elimination by human development of most areas of the original pine barren habitat within the state.

**Discussion**—Linsley (1843) called the Pine Warbler common, but did not specify the time of year so it is not clear whether he was referring to breeding status. Merriam (1877) indicated that the species bred but did not indicate its abundance. However, Sage et al. (1913) considered it rather rare as a breeder. Craig (1978) also considered the species to be rare as a breeder in most parts of the state and listed seven areas across the state where Pine Warblers were suspected or known to have bred since 1950.

The Pine Warbler as a breeder in Connecticut shows a scattered distribution, a situation apparently equivalent to that in other parts of the Northeast away from the coast (Peterson *in* Andrle and Carroll 1988, Ellison *in* Laughlin and Kibbe 1985). This species is most numerous as a breeder in the southeastern United States, and it arrives as a migrant in Connecticut relatively early in spring. This timing of migration, appropriate for southern or relatively warm localities, might not be compatible with occupation of breeding sites in regions that do not become sufficiently warm until several weeks later in the spring. In contrast, warbler species that come north several weeks later, such as the Black-throated Green and Blackburnian Warblers, can move directly into those cooler sites at a time when the weather has become, on average, substantially warmer than at the time of northward migration of the Pine Warbler.

*George A. Clark, Jr.*

## Prairie Warbler
### *Dendroica discolor*

This migratory breeder winters principally in the West Indies (AOU 1983). It is regularly found as a breeder in Connecticut. Among North American species of nongame birds this has been one of the most extensively studied (Nolan 1978).

**Habitat**—In Connecticut this species breeds in brushy areas with mixed vegetation including scattered conifers that are generally less than 10 ft high. Typically the underlying soil is well drained. This species can apparently successfully breed even in relatively small patches of appropriate habitat. The margins of roadsides and the brush along power line or gas line rights-of-way often provide suitable sites. Occasionally the species has been found in summer in Connecticut within rather large blocks of second growth woodland, but it is unclear whether any breeding occurs in such situations. In other parts of its range this species uses drastically different breeding habitats, e.g., mangroves in Florida (Nolan 1978).

**Atlas results**—The species bred widely across the state, but tended to be absent in urban and densely settled suburban areas and also was lacking in heavily wooded areas.

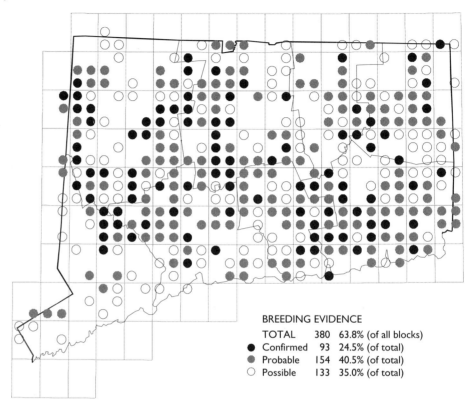

BREEDING EVIDENCE

| | TOTAL | 380 | 63.8% (of all blocks) |
|---|---|---|---|
| ● | Confirmed | 93 | 24.5% (of total) |
| ◉ | Probable | 154 | 40.5% (of total) |
| ○ | Possible | 133 | 35.0% (of total) |

**Discussion**—Linsley (1843) rated the Prairie Warbler as rare. However, Merriam's (1877) evidence indicated that the species was at least regular around Enfield and Saybrook, though uncommon at best around New Haven and Portland. Sage et al. (1913) rated the species as a common breeder in the southern part of the state, but less common in the northern sections. Since

then the species has apparently become more common in the northern counties. Nolan (1978) reported that the species bred in all counties of Connecticut.

The Prairie Warbler has its center of breeding distribution in the southeastern United States and approaches its northern limits in southern New England. In many areas of its range the species is associated with early successional stages that may be promoted particularly by fires such as historically occurred fairly regularly in the coastal pine barrens of the eastern United States. The deforestation starting in colonial times followed by subsequent modification of the landscape has presumably facilitated the recent increase in the numbers of birds breeding in Connecticut. The distribution of the Prairie Warbler shows some possible parallels with that of the Pine Warbler, with the latter being associated with more mature coniferous forest.

*George A. Clark, Jr.*

## Cerulean Warbler
### *Dendroica cerulea*

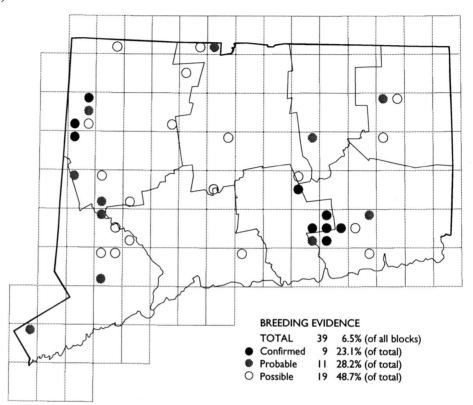

BREEDING EVIDENCE

| | | TOTAL | 39 | 6.5% (of all blocks) |
|---|---|---|---|---|
| ● | Confirmed | 9 | 23.1% (of total) |
| ◉ | Probable | 11 | 28.2% (of total) |
| ○ | Possible | 19 | 48.7% (of total) |

The Cerulean Warbler is a rare and local migratory breeder in Connecticut, first confirmed nesting in 1972. The species winters on the east slope of the Andes from Colombia to Peru and Bolivia. The range and population of this small, canopy inhabiting warbler continue to increase in Connecticut and New England at large (Petersen 1989).

**Habitat**—Cerulean Warblers occur in deciduous forest, generally tall, relatively open forest near a stream, river, or lake. Two primary forest types used in the Northeast include: tall, floodplain forest of major river systems dominated by cottonwood or silver maple (these sites are often the first occupied in a region) and, as populations spread, mesic oak-hickory-black birch forest. Highest population densities recorded in West Virginia are in mature oak-hickory forest (Hall 1983).

**Atlas results**—The atlas map shows the two populations established in the 1970s in the Housatonic Valley and East Haddam. All but one case of confirmed breeding were from these areas. Records of probable breeding seem to show population spread in the Housatonic Valley and east of the lower Connecticut River. Interesting reports came from Greenwich, Suffield,

Andover, and Hampton. A nesting population now appears established in western Windham County (G. A. Clark, Jr., pers. comm.). Connecticut currently has New England's largest population of this warbler but the species' foothold in the region may be tenuous due to its sensitivity to habitat fragmentation (Ambuel and Temple 1983).

**Discussion**—The Cerulean Warbler was originally a vagrant in Connecticut and New England; the first New England record was from Stratford, Connecticut, in 1841 (Sage et al. 1913). Reports were sparse through the 1950s but increased in the late 1960s and early 1970s (Zeranski and Baptist 1990). The species was found nesting in neighboring Dutchess County, New York, in 1922 and it spread to several locations in that county over the ensuing decade (Griscom 1923, Bagg and Eliot 1937); however, it took a half century to spread into Connecticut. A nest was found in Canton in 1972 (Finch 1972). Subsequently, populations were found in the Housatonic Valley at Kent and Sharon, and east of the Connecticut River in the hills of East Haddam. Spreading in new areas is usually modest, and dispersal often happens suddenly after years of consolidation of new populations. Dispersal is often from neighboring populations, for example from Dutchess County to the Housatonic Valley, and to Quabbin Reservoir, Massachusetts, apparently from northeastern Connecticut, but also may cover hundreds of miles with no apparent intervening population as in southwestern Quebec (Ouellet 1967), and Dutchess County (Bull 1974). Recent population trends have been declines including a significant 3.9% per year from 1966 to 1978, and a nonsignificant 0.9% per year from 1978 to 1987 (Robbins et al. 1989b). The combination of range expansion with population decline is paradoxical.

*Walter G. Ellison*

## Black-and-white Warbler
*Mniotilta varia*

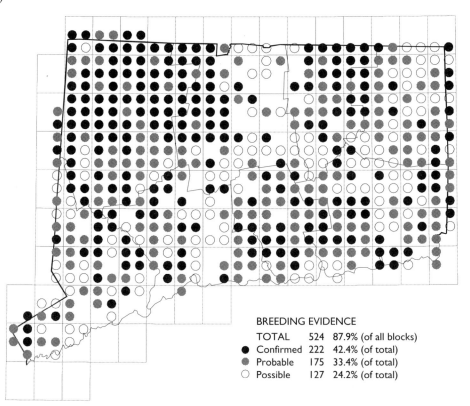

BREEDING EVIDENCE

| | TOTAL | 524 | 87.9% (of all blocks) |
|---|---|---|---|
| ● | Confirmed | 222 | 42.4% (of total) |
| ● | Probable | 175 | 33.4% (of total) |
| ○ | Possible | 127 | 24.2% (of total) |

This migratory breeder winters from Florida and the Bahama Islands south through the Caribbean islands and much of Central America to northern South America (AOU 1983). The species is common as a breeder in Connecticut. It is exceptional among the warblers of North America in being specialized for foraging on tree trunks and large branches, the surfaces of which are also commonly searched for food by woodpeckers, nuthatches, and the Brown Creeper.

**Habitat**—The species nests in deciduous or mixed deciduous-coniferous woodlands. The nest is hidden on the ground, commonly at the base of a tree trunk. During the breeding season the species does not ordinarily venture into habitats in which the trees are widely separated.

**Atlas results**—The Black-and-white Warbler was confirmed as a breeder in more than a third of all blocks. It is lacking as a breeder in some of the more highly developed urban areas of the state. The "possible" status in a number of blocks, such as in eastern Connecticut, might be a consequence of the limitations of block busting in those areas; a few hours in a block often may be insufficient to confirm breeding by this species.

**Discussion**—Merriam (1877) reported breeding for the southern part of the state, and Sage et al. (1913) termed the species a common summer resident, a status still applicable at present. With the increase in forests in the twentieth century it seems reasonable to assume

that the numbers of this species breeding in Connecticut have increased (Zeranski and Baptist 1990), though numbers have decreased in the more urban parts of New England (Griscom 1949).

Because of its close association with forests over a wide geographic range, the Black-and-white Warbler might be a species particularly worth monitoring in attempting to assess the effects of deforestation now underway in both the tropics and, to a lesser extent, the temperate zone breeding areas. It is therefore surprising that among 13 species that migrate to the Neotropics and both winter and breed in forest habitat, the Black-and-white Warbler was the only one showing a significant increase on the roadside Breeding Bird Survey in eastern North America over the period 1978-1987 (Robbins et al. 1989b). The factors underlying this increase are unknown and worthy of further investigation.

*George A. Clark, Jr.*

325

## American Redstart
### *Setophaga ruticilla*

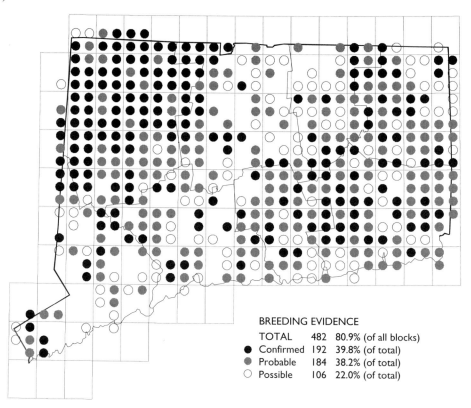

BREEDING EVIDENCE

| | | |
|---|---|---|
| TOTAL | 482 | 80.9% (of all blocks) |
| ● Confirmed | 192 | 39.8% (of total) |
| ◉ Probable | 184 | 38.2% (of total) |
| ○ Possible | 106 | 22.0% (of total) |

This delicate and hyperactive wood warbler is a migratory breeder in Connecticut and occupies a large wintering range including the Antilles, Middle America, and northern South America. Redstarts are common in eastern and northwestern Connecticut and uncommon in southwestern Connecticut and central Hartford County.

**Habitat**—The American Redstart inhabits a wide array of forested and shrubby habitats including alder and willow swamps, reforesting pastures, mature deciduous and mixed forests, and second growth deciduous woodlands. Redstarts are probably most common in deciduous forest with a thick midstory of saplings. Redstarts generally avoid predominantly coniferous forest but may occur in it, usually feeding in the few deciduous trees and shrubs (Sabo 1980). Population densi-

ties recorded in Connecticut include 43 per 100 ha in second growth deciduous forest (Cavanaugh & Magee 1967b, Magee 1968-1984a), 38 per 100 ha in young hardwoods released by removal of red pine (Magee 1979-1987), 30 per 100 ha in an abandoned pasture (Magee & Cavanaugh 1967, Magee 1968-1984b), and 14 per 100 ha in hemlock-northern hardwoods (Craig 1987).

**Atlas results**—The American Redstart shows a distributional pattern similar to many other forest birds. It is widespread but shows obvious gaps in its range in Connecticut's three most populous counties, Fairfield, New Haven, and Hartford. By contrast the species was recorded in over 90% of atlas blocks in Litchfield, Windham, Middlesex, and New London counties.

These gaps suggest that urbanization and suburban development has reduced available habitat. Redstarts may not be affected by woodlot size when forest habitat is fragmented (Robbins et al. 1989a), but they may be affected by isolation of blocks of suitable habitat (Askins and Philbrick 1987). Habitat use by the American Redstart is also affected by interactions with the Least Flycatcher. These aggressive birds harass redstarts and compete with them for food, causing redstarts to avoid areas where they are common (Sherry and Holmes 1988). In spite of this, the American Redstart occurred in 94% of the 293 blocks where Least Flycatchers were reported in Connecticut. Apparently the flycatchers cannot influence American Redstart distribution at the scale of an atlas block.

**Discussion**—Although many historical references called the American Redstart common (e.g., Sage et al. 1913), the species must have been less common in the nineteenth century than in the latter twentieth century due to extensive clearing of land in the 1800s. Griscom (1949) gave evidence of this from the Sudbury River valley in Massachusetts where the species increased from 1868–1945; by the latter date Griscom found the redstart "one of the most abundant woodland birds in eastern Massachusetts." In Connecticut, C. M. Jones (1931) considered the American Redstart very scarce in Eastford and Ashford during the 1890s. Since the 1950s local population declines have occurred in New England, especially in urban and suburban communities. The species is now rare in the Sudbury River valley (Walton 1984). Recent population trends based on Breeding Bird Survey routes are not significant but include a recent trend

reversal. American Redstart populations rose by 1.3% per year from 1966–1978, and fell by 1.2% per year from 1978–1987 (Robbins et al. 1989b). The recent declining trend may reflect habitat loss in wintering areas as redstarts are primarily forest birds in winter as well as summer (Robbins et al. 1989b).

*Walter G. Ellison*

## Prothonotary Warbler
### *Protonotaria citrea*

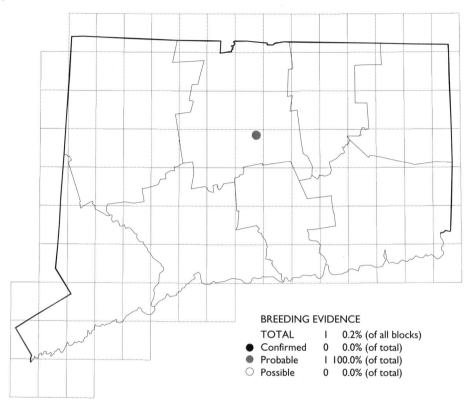

BREEDING EVIDENCE

| | | |
|---|---|---|
| TOTAL | 1 | 0.2% (of all blocks) |
| ● Confirmed | 0 | 0.0% (of total) |
| ◉ Probable | 1 | 100.0% (of total) |
| ○ Possible | 0 | 0.0% (of total) |

After departing wintering grounds in Central and South America (AOU 1983), the Prothonotary Warbler is usually observed in Connecticut during the last two weeks of April or the first two weeks of May, as a rare migrant. Most birds probably enter the state as a consequence of overshooting more southerly locations, where the species is a common summer resident. The Prothonotary Warbler is an accidental breeding species within the state.

**Habitat**—The Prothonotary Warbler favors swamps or forested margins of rivers or lakes that contain an abundance of live trees, shrubs, and dead snags. The few nesting attempts in Connecticut have been in such habitat. Cavities in snags are used as nesting sites. When available, Prothonotary Warblers will readily accept nest boxes (L. J. Petit et al. 1987).

**Atlas results**—During the atlas, the Prothonotary Warbler was recorded in just one atlas block. A male sang in a rich grove of cottonwoods along the Connecticut River just south of Brainard airport, Hartford, 17–24 June 1984 (Varza 1985). Although female Prothonotary Warblers are typically silent and inconspicuous during the breeding season, males are extremely vocal and easily detected. Therefore, it is unlikely that many breeding warblers went undetected by atlas participants.

**Discussion**—The Prothonotary Warbler has never been a common migratory or breeding species in Connecticut. Stearns and Coues (1881) called the warbler a "rare straggler to New England from the southern states." To

date, only one nesting record exists for the state. On 30 May 1946, a pair was observed feeding young at Fairfield (Bull 1964). The first published record of this species in Connecticut came from Glastonbury, 14 May 1910 (Sage et al. 1913).

In the past century, the status of the Prothonotary Warbler has not changed markedly; it is still a rare spring migrant and accidental breeding species. In recent years, however, reports of Prothonotary Warblers have increased within the state, and indeed from New England in general. At least one individual is sighted in Connecticut during spring in most years. These reports are probably a reflection of the greater numbers, coverage, and expertise of birders in the state, and not any northern range expansion by the Prothonotary Warbler. Throughout this century, nearly all reports of the species have been of single individuals, primarily from the southern or southwestern portions of the state. Individual singing males have occurred at East Rock Park, New Haven/Hamden, several years in spring. Spring occurrences have ranged between the following dates: 7 April 1974 at Redding (Kane and Buckley 1974) to 23 June 1971 at Westport (singing bird present from 1 June, R. Dewire et al.; see Boyajian 1971). This species is accidental in autumn, there being only three records falling between the dates 17 August and 27 November (Clark and Bevier 1993).

*Kenneth E. Petit*

## Worm-eating Warbler
### *Helmitheros vermivorus*

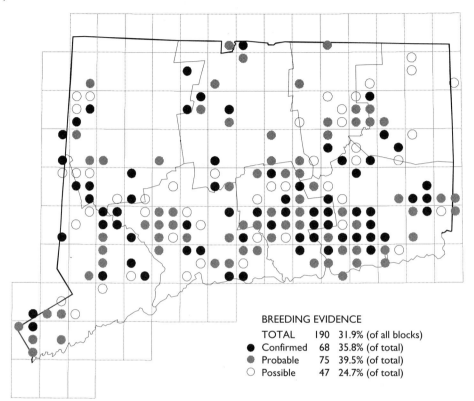

BREEDING EVIDENCE

| | TOTAL | 190 | 31.9% (of all blocks) |
|---|---|---|---|
| ● | Confirmed | 68 | 35.8% (of total) |
| ◉ | Probable | 75 | 39.5% (of total) |
| ○ | Possible | 47 | 24.7% (of total) |

The Worm-eating Warbler is a fairly common migratory breeder in Connecticut, where the species is near the northeastern limit of its range, which extends west south of the Great Lakes to the Ozarks. Most Worm-eating Warblers spend the winter along the Caribbean slope of Central America from southern Mexico to Panama and the northern West Indies.

**Habitat**—Worm-eating Warblers breed in deciduous forest or mixed deciduous and hemlock forest, usually on comparatively steep, well-drained hillsides or ravines with dense undergrowth but occasionally where the ground is quite open (Bent 1953, Mengel 1965). Bent (1953) suggested that an appropriate name for this species would be "hillside warbler" because of its preference for wooded hillsides. In Maryland, Greenberg (1987) found that it foraged primarily in oaks in spring but shifted to the understory during June and July. In both levels of vegetation, it fed primarily by gleaning insects from leaves. During winter, the Worm-eating Warbler is concentrated in tropical broadleaf forests, where it specializes on feeding on insects living in clusters of hanging, dead leaves (Greenberg 1987).

**Atlas results**—The Worm-eating Warbler is widely distributed in Connecticut. It was recorded in all major regions of the state but sparingly from some of the most heavily developed areas—the coast in southwestern Connecticut and the vicinity of Hartford. Worm-eating Warblers may have been absent in these areas because it is generally restricted to large tracts of forest.

**Discussion**—From the early literature, this species was known in New England chiefly from Connecticut, where it was found most frequently in the south but with occasional records to Massachusetts. Although apparently rare in Connecticut during the 1800s (Merriam 1877), several instances of breeding were reported late in that century (Sage et al. 1913). Its numbers have steadily increased since then, probably as a result of the growth of forest on abandoned farmland. Early records are from coastal areas, but it has spread progressively northward and is now found in most parts of the state (Zeranski and Baptist 1990). As late as the 1960s, it was considered a rare summer resident in northeastern Connecticut (Manter 1975), where it is now local but fairly common.

In a survey of 46 forest tracts in southeastern Connecticut, Askins et al. (1987) did not record Worm-eating Warbler in any forest smaller than 38 acres. Similarly, the smallest forest in Maryland in which Robbins et al. (1989a) found this species was 34 acres, and its probability of occurrence was less than 50% for forests smaller than 240 acres. Robbins (1979) reported that Worm-eating Warblers had declined or disappeared in areas of Maryland that had undergone rapid development since the 1950s. Only small, remnant patches of forest remain in these areas. Breeding bird atlas results from Montgomery and Howard counties, Maryland, show that this species is only found in areas that still have extensive tracts of forest (Robbins 1979). The absence of Worm-eating Warbler records in some parts of Fairfield and Hartford counties may be due to the absence of extensive forests in these areas. Although the Breeding Bird Survey results for Connecticut indicate that the Worm-eating Warbler increased significantly between 1966 and 1989, there has been no significant change between 1980 and 1989. Continued fragmentation of

Connecticut forests resulting from suburban development may cause this species to decline in the future.

*Robert A. Askins*

# Ovenbird
## *Seiurus aurocapillus*

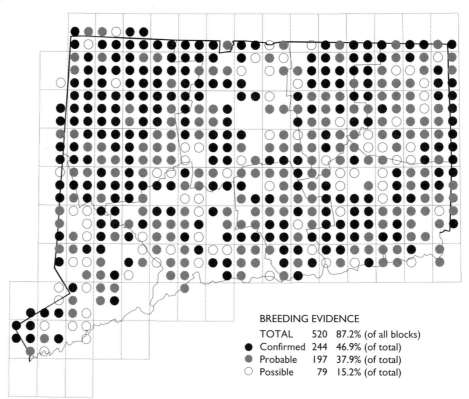

**BREEDING EVIDENCE**

| | TOTAL | 520 | 87.2% (of all blocks) |
|---|---|---|---|
| ● | Confirmed | 244 | 46.9% (of total) |
| ● | Probable | 197 | 37.9% (of total) |
| ○ | Possible | 79 | 15.2% (of total) |

Ovenbirds are common migratory breeders in Connecticut. Among the New World wood-warblers breeding in the state, it is the one that forages most extensively on the forest floor. The species as a whole spends the winter chiefly in Mexico, Central America, and the West Indies and sparingly in the southern United States and extreme northern South America (AOU 1983). Where in this winter range Connecticut breeders occur is unknown; the subspecies *S. a. aurocapillus* breeds here.

**Habitat**—This species nests on the ground in deciduous or mixed deciduous-coniferous forests growing on well drained soils.

**Atlas results**—The Ovenbird was confirmed or considered probable as a breeder in more than 70% of the blocks. The species was lacking in the more urban parts of the state. Detected in more blocks than any other breeding warbler typically found in forest habitat, the presence of the Ovenbird appears to be a good indicator of the presence of mature woodlands in a block.

**Discussion**—Linsley (1843) termed the species common. Merriam (1877) commented that it bred abundantly, and this evaluation was shared by Sage et al. (1913). In the North American roadside Breeding Bird Survey, the Ovenbird showed a statistically significant decrease in the period 1978–1987 (Robbins et al. 1989b). Such a change might have been anticipated in view of extensive deforestation on the wintering grounds and lesser amounts on the breeding grounds.

In view of recent concerns about the effects of Brown-headed Cowbirds on populations of warblers, it is of interest to note that many decades ago in Connecticut, Bishop found cowbird eggs in 11 out of 30 Ovenbird nests examined (Sage et al. 1913). Thus, at least this species of warbler has been able to sustain a large population in the state for over 70 years despite apparently substantial brood parasitism, at least at times.

Zach and Falls (1979) in a study in Canada found that Ovenbirds foraged extensively outside their song territories and that such foraging areas were also used by birds coming from other song territories. Their findings do not fit the common expectation for many noncolonial songbirds that the territory within which song is given should be a reasonable indication of the area within which feeding occurs. If their findings apply throughout the range of this species, then measurements of territorial size determined from the song perches of males might give overestimates of the number of birds that can breed in forest tracts.

*George A. Clark, Jr.*

## Northern Waterthrush
### *Seiurus noveboracensis*

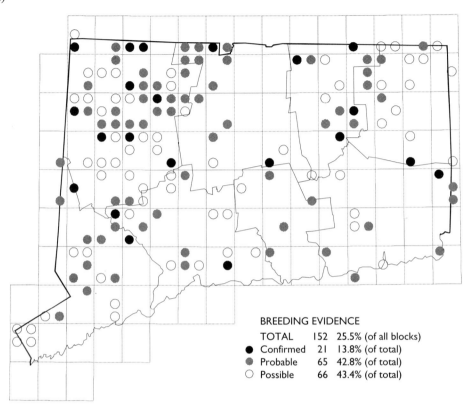

BREEDING EVIDENCE
TOTAL          152   25.5% (of all blocks)
● Confirmed     21   13.8% (of total)
● Probable      65   42.8% (of total)
○ Possible      66   43.4% (of total)

A migratory breeder, the Northern Waterthrush nests principally in the western and northeastern highlands. They are never abundant as breeding birds in Connecticut but small numbers occur in favorable habitat. This species winters in the Caribbean islands, Central America, and parts of northern South America (AOU 1983).

**Habitat**—This species breeds in wooded swamps, typically containing standing water with emergent tussocks of grass and the presence of hemlock trees (Craig 1985). Nests are typically placed in earthen banks or root systems exposed by the toppling of trees. In parts of its breeding range, this species may occupy sites away from standing water, such as spruce forest where the vegetation is wet (Vassallo and Rice 1982, Hall 1983). Although preferring sites with standing water, the Northern Waterthrush may occur along flowing streams. In contrast, the closely related Louisiana Waterthrush breeds in more open habitats along flowing streams and is apparently restricted to such sites (Craig 1985). Where appropriate habitats come together, the two species of waterthrushes can breed in the same area as in northern Connecticut (Craig 1985), Rhode Island, Massachusetts, Pennsylvania (Bent 1953), and West Virginia (Hall 1983). When breeding at such localities in Connecticut, the Louisiana uses the smaller, faster flowing streams, and the two species show no interspecific territoriality—one species is aggressive towards the other only rarely, when the young appear to be at risk due to the nearness of the opposite species (Craig 1985).

**Atlas results**—This species is secretive and often relatively quiet after mid-June and hence difficult to locate and relatively easily missed. Nevertheless, the atlas survey indicates the presence of the species over much of the state, though clearly the species is less frequent along the shore, through the Connecticut River valley, and in the southeastern part of the state. The adjective "Northern" seems appropriate for the distribution of the species in Connecticut. In the breeding season the Northern Waterthrush is much less widespread in the state than is the Louisiana Waterthrush.

**Discussion**—Merriam (1877) was uncertain whether Northern Waterthrushes bred in Connecticut, and Sage et al. (1913) knew of no breeding records for the state. Breeding in Connecticut was first reported from the northwestern hills in the early 1930s (summary in Zeranski and Baptist 1990), but records are too incomplete to trace satisfactorily the history of this species in the state. Presumably the substantial maturation of forests during the twentieth century has been favorable for the spread of this species.

Although habitat data are not available for most of the specific sites where this species was found during the atlas survey, occurrence of the species appears to match fairly closely the occurrence of extensive forest stands containing wooded swamps with hemlock. Summer temperatures are likely to be lower in such stands, and the effects of vegetation might not be readily separable from those of temperature.

*George A. Clark, Jr*

335

# Louisiana Waterthrush
*Seiurus motacilla*

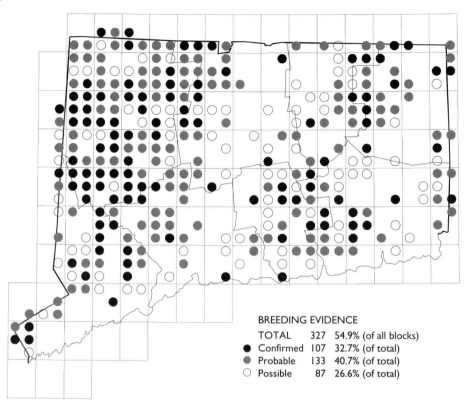

BREEDING EVIDENCE

| | TOTAL | 327 | 54.9% (of all blocks) |
|---|---|---|---|
| ● | Confirmed | 107 | 32.7% (of total) |
| ◉ | Probable | 133 | 40.7% (of total) |
| ○ | Possible | 87 | 26.6% (of total) |

The Louisiana Waterthrush is an uncommon to locally fairly common migratory breeder along streams away from the coast, particularly in the eastern and western highlands. The species winters primarily in the West Indies and Central America with small numbers going south to northeastern Colombia and northern Venezuela (AOU 1983).

**Habitat**—Louisiana Waterthrushes in Connecticut are associated with flowing streams (Craig 1985) with nests placed nearby in earthen banks or along the upraised root systems of fallen trees.

**Atlas results**—The scarcity of records in the central part of the state may be attributable to a combination of urban and suburban areas together with an open countryside along the streams or in rural areas. The absence of records through much of the eastern highlands

suggests a need for further study. This highland area had relatively few observers, and many of the blocks were covered by block busting. Because these birds are most easily detected by their song and become relatively quiet after early June, they are relatively easy to miss unless observers make a special effort to walk along streams in the woods.

**Discussion**—Merriam (1877) reported that this species bred regularly in southern Connecticut. Subsequently Sage et al. (1913) reported breeding throughout the state but that the species was rare in Litchfield County. For the Connecticut River valley just to the north of Connecticut, the evidence points clearly to a range expansion in the latter part of the nineteenth century (Griscom and

Snyder 1955). Maturation of forests along streams in many parts of Connecticut in the twentieth century has presumably favored an increase in this species. The specialized requirement for streams together with the intraspecific territoriality of this species would seemingly prevent establishment of a dense breeding population in any area.

The species seems likely to occur almost anywhere in the state where freshwater streams occur within a woodland or even with a bordering fringe of forest. Relative to the closely related Northern Waterthrush, the Louisiana differs not only in habitat but also in arriving substantially earlier in spring, in April commonly ten or more days before the Northerns return. The Louisiana Waterthrush habitats become ice free earlier than do those of Northern Waterthrushes, and thus productivity of invertebrates which serve as food can be higher earlier in the year. Furthermore, stream levels in many years drop substantially through the summer, and earlier breeding of the Louisiana Waterthrushes enables them to move away from the nesting area before production of their invertebrate prey falls off. Louisiana Waterthrushes characteristically feed on larger prey than do the Northerns, and this fits with the larger body size of the Louisianas and their presumably more productive habitat (Craig 1984, Craig 1987a).

*George A. Clark, Jr.*

# Kentucky Warbler
*Oporornis formosus*

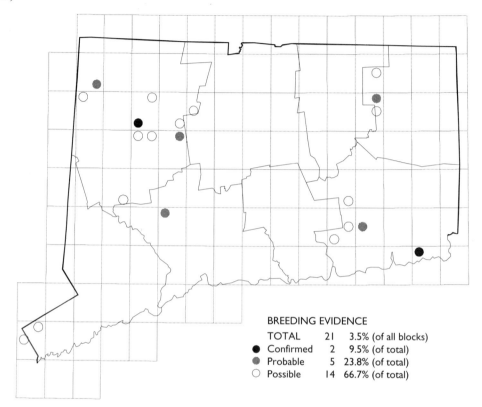

BREEDING EVIDENCE

| | | |
|---|---|---|
| TOTAL | 21 | 3.5% (of all blocks) |
| ● Confirmed | 2 | 9.5% (of total) |
| ◔ Probable | 5 | 23.8% (of total) |
| ○ Possible | 14 | 66.7% (of total) |

A migratory breeder that winters primarily from southern Mexico south through Central America into extreme northern South America (AOU 1983). This species breeds in Connecticut only very rarely and irregularly.

**Habitat**—Only incomplete information is available on the habitats in which Kentucky Warblers have been reported to breed in Connecticut. Voorhees (1893) found a fledgling in the underbrush near a path through a swampy woods, but, because the bird was well beyond the state of fledging, there is no assurance that this site was representative of the breeding area. During the atlas survey, an unpaired singing male that remained in Ashford for a number of days (E. Clark, pers. comm.) occupied a scrubby area of deciduous vegetation on relatively well drained soil on a hillside (G. Clark, pers. obs.).

Descriptions of breeding habitats to the south of Connecticut indicate use of a considerable variety of sites (Bent 1953, Craig 1978). Nesting may occur in both dry and wet sites and be in woodlands, forest edge, or scrubby areas; apparently a favored feature is a dense cover of broad-leaved vegetation. The nest is placed on or near the ground (Bent 1953).

**Atlas results**—For the 21 blocks from which Kentucky Warblers were reported during the atlas project, reports with details were submitted in several cases. In 1982, a male appeared for a second consecutive year in Litchfield, but no evidence of breeding was found (A. Magee). In 1983 a singing bird was present for more than a week in Harwinton (A. Szczesniak), but breeding could not be confirmed. In Litchfield, one bird of a pair was seen carrying a green caterpillar in the beak for a prolonged period (V. Peterson), thus indicating breeding. In a similar case, an adult was reported carrying food in Mystic in the summer of 1985 (Rosgen 1986), but no written documentation was filed. Reports in the seasonal notes of the *Connecticut Warbler* of a male returning to a site in Salem for up to six consecutive years to 1985 were likewise never further documented.

**Discussion**—Merriam (1877) knew of no breeding records for this species but reported past occurrence of the species at Suffield and Lyme. The first breeding record came from Greenwich in July 1892 when Voorhees (1893) saw a female feeding a fledgling; he returned later the same day and, as was the practice of many collectors of that time, shot a male a few hundred feet from that site. He was unable to relocate the female or juvenile. The next nesting report comes almost one-hundred years

later, also in Greenwich (*fide* T. Burke, 1988). A territorial male has been found at the same locality through the early 1990s. Craig (1978) mentioned three areas in central Connecticut where breeding was suspected after 1950, but conclusive evidence was lacking. In southern New York state, the Kentucky Warbler apparently peaked in abundance in the 1870s, subsequently declined, and is now again expanding its range (Sibley *in* Andrle and Carroll 1988). One, highly speculative, interpretation is that shifts in the breeding range of this species might have been related to the history of deforestation and reforestation in the Northeast over this same period of time.

The Kentucky Warbler reaches the northern limits of its breeding distribu-

tion in southern New England, and the species remains extremely rare as a breeder in Connecticut. If, as may be anticipated, future cases of breeding are found, an effort should be made to record the details as completely as possible.

*George A. Clark, Jr.*

## Common Yellowthroat
### *Geothlypis trichas*

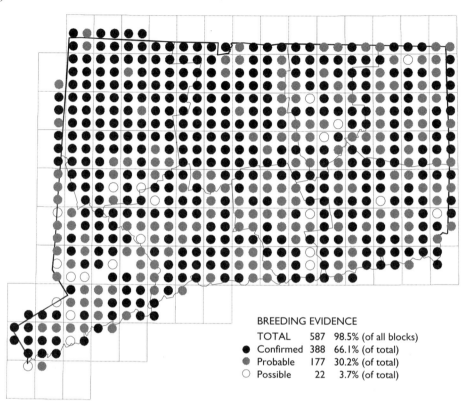

BREEDING EVIDENCE

| | TOTAL | 587 | 98.5% (of all blocks) |
|---|---|---|---|
| ● | Confirmed | 388 | 66.1% (of total) |
| ◉ | Probable | 177 | 30.2% (of total) |
| ○ | Possible | 22 | 3.7% (of total) |

Common Yellowthroat is an appropriate name to designate the abundance of this species as a breeder in Connecticut. Connecticut populations are migratory; only rarely is the species found into early winter. Eastern populations of yellowthroats winter in the southeastern United States, the Bahamas, the Greater Antilles, and eastern Mexico south to Costa Rica (AOU 1983).

Northeastern breeders have been named *G. t. brachidactylus*, or "Northern Yellowthroat" (AOU 1957), but may also be found combined under the nominate subspecies, *trichas*, or "Maryland Yellowthroat." Eastern races as a whole differ from western races by having predominantly grayish rather than whitish postocular lines on the adult male; our northern populations (*brachidactylus*) show extensive yellow below similar to western races (Ridgway 1902).

**Habitat**—This species breeds in dense deciduous brushy and scrubby tangles often with herbaceous vegetation interspersed. The ground beneath may be wet or dry. An area of suitable habitat apparently need not be large relative to the requirements of many other passerine species. Nests are placed on or near the ground (Bent 1953).

**Atlas results**—With breeding evidence found in nearly 99% of all blocks, the Common Yellowthroat occurred in a higher percentage of blocks than any other warbler. Clearly, the Common Yellowthroat is a strong contender for recognition as the most conspicuous and widespread warbler in the state.

**Discussion**—Linsley (1843) termed the species common, and this rating of abundance was continued by Merriam (1877) and Sage et al. (1913). There is no indication of a change in the status of this species in Connecticut within the time of historic records (Zeranski and Baptist 1990).

Among warblers breeding in North America, the Common Yellowthroat and the Yellow Warbler have the most extensive breeding ranges (Robbins et al. 1966). Furthermore, where their breeding ranges overlap the two species often occur together in the same habitat, particularly near water. Thus these species show a specialized association with what are some of the most widespread habitats in North America. Small areas of brushy tangles in wet areas can persist even in urban areas and thus enable the Common Yellowthroat to occur in nearly all blocks in Connecticut.

Spending much time in dense vegetation, the Common Yellowthroat shows a readiness to emerge from cover in response to a variety of squeaking or other soft noises made by people. Perhaps because the volume of cover available or used by Common Yellowthroats is often relatively small, and their ability to see through the cover is relatively slight, it might be important for this species to check out nearby disturbances for possible presence of potential predators. In contrast, species with more extensive and less densely vegetated territories in which to hide might frequently find it more advantageous to sneak away so as to minimize the chance of coming close to a possible predator. If these conjectures are correct, they might explain why it is often much easier to detect the presence of a silent Common Yellowthroat as opposed to, for example, a nonvocalizing Northern Waterthrush.

*George A. Clark, Jr.*

# Hooded Warbler
## *Wilsonia citrina*

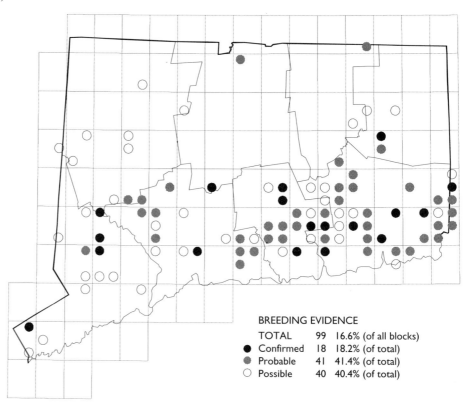

BREEDING EVIDENCE

| | | TOTAL | 99 | 16.6% (of all blocks) |
|---|---|---|---|---|
| ● | Confirmed | | 18 | 18.2% (of total) |
| ● | Probable | | 41 | 41.4% (of total) |
| ○ | Possible | | 40 | 40.4% (of total) |

The Hooded Warbler is a rare migrant and a rare to locally uncommon nesting species in Connecticut. The winter range of the Hooded Warbler extends from southern Tamaulipas, Veracruz, and the Yucatan peninsula south to southern Guatemala and Costa Rica. Rarely, it reaches to central Panama (Bent 1953). Generally, the Hooded Warbler numbers seem constant on the continent, though there is evidence of a slight increase in the eastern portion of its range (Robbins et al. 1986).

**Habitat**—In the literature, the Hooded Warbler in the more southerly heart of its breeding range is stated to be a bird of the lowlands, preferring well-watered woodlands and swampy land overgrown with bushes (Bent 1953, Forbush 1927). In Connecticut, the Hooded Warbler is a bird of mixed deciduous woodland and forest. This hearty songster inhabits thickly wooded areas that have dense thickets and sporadic sunny openings, often the result of lumbering, fire, or other circumstances. These woodlands consist typically of an upper canopy in the 25–40 ft range and a dense, shrubby ground cover, reaching to approximately 15 ft. The Hooded Warbler shows a decided preference for such sites on a slope or hillside (Bent 1953, Sage et al. 1913, Forbush 1927). In the eastern part of the state, and in some central and southern locations, the understory is often made up of dense growths of mountain laurel. The Hooded Warbler's proclivity for swampy environs in the South is not seen in this state, though small streams and wet areas, typical of a Connecticut woodland, are usually not far from known summering locations.

**Atlas results**—The Hooded Warbler is a bird of the southern half of the state. The blocks of probable and confirmed nesting are centered along the Housatonic, Naugatuck, and Connecticut River valleys. Results show the southeastern portion of the state to the Rhode Island border to be the area of highest concentration. Surveys of suitable habitat in northern portions of the state have failed to turn up Hooded Warblers consistently.

The Hooded Warbler is a loud and lively vocalist, and though locating the source of this merry song can be done with a fair amount of time and patience, locating the nest or observing evidence of nesting is quite difficult due to the dense underbrush that these birds usually inhabit. It is quite likely that far more Hooded Warblers nest in Connecticut than have been confirmed.

**Discussion**—The Hooded Warbler breeding population in Connecticut seems to have been stable for the past few decades. Apparently, this species has decreased since the late 1800s and early 1900s, when it was considered a common nester in coastal Connecticut

(Merriam 1877). From this coastal concentration, Hooded Warblers have spread up into the Housatonic, Naugatuck, and Connecticut River valleys; in the 1930s it was considered locally common along these waterways (Bagg and Eliot 1937). Approaching its northeastern breeding limits in our state, the population seems stable, varying little from year to year except where human-related habitat change or natural habitat progression excludes them.

Today, possibly due to the maturation of Connecticut's woodlands and an increase of urban-suburban sprawl, Hooded Warbler numbers have decreased to a stable level, best described as rare to locally uncommon. Yearly summer totals vary only slightly and the disappearance of birds from known locations due to habitat loss is usually compensated for by their appearance elsewhere. In the eastern part of the state, the Hooded Warbler is slightly on the increase. This can possibly be attributed to habitat changes following major defoliation by gypsy moths, which open up the canopy and allow the understory growth necessary for this species.

*Mark S. Szantyr*

## Canada Warbler
*Wilsonia canadensis*

The Canada Warbler is generally an uncommon breeder in Connecticut. This migratory breeder winters chiefly in northern South America from Venezuela and Colombia to southern Peru; it migrates through Middle America (AOU 1983).

**Habitat**—This species breeds in dense vegetation, often including mountain laurel, along the banks of small streams or other wet areas within woodlands. An overhead canopy typically shades the dense waterside cover frequented by the Canada Warbler. The soil below tends to retain moisture so that the ground is often damp. The nest is situated on or near the ground (Bent 1953). Outside Connecticut, nests have been found in very different habitats such as dry wooded situations away from wet areas (e.g., in northern Michigan; Krause 1965).

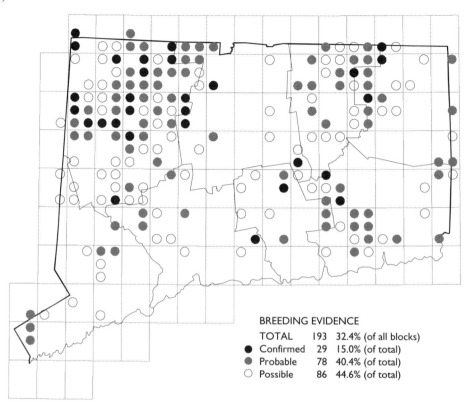

BREEDING EVIDENCE

| | | |
|---|---|---|
| TOTAL | 193 | 32.4% (of all blocks) |
| ● Confirmed | 29 | 15.0% (of total) |
| ◉ Probable | 78 | 40.4% (of total) |
| ○ Possible | 86 | 44.6% (of total) |

**Atlas results**—Evidence of breeding was impressively widespread but centered in the northwestern and northeastern hills. Pockets of habitat further south were also used, particularly in the central portions of the state. Observers confirmed nesting in a low percentage of blocks due to the dense and often inaccessible habitat used by this species.

**Discussion**—Linsley (1843) reported the Canada Warbler to be very rare in Stratford and New Haven. Citing W. W. Coe, Merriam (1877) reported that it undoubtedly bred in the area of Portland. Sage et al. (1913) stated that the species "undoubtedly breeds more or less regularly in the northwestern part of the state, although few nests

have been taken." They cite one specific nest with five eggs from Northford, where the nest was reportedly placed in a highly atypical site, a bush in a pasture. Kuerzi and Kuerzi (1934) reported a Canada Warbler nest from Litchfield County in 1933; they thus claimed the second state record of nesting for the species. However, C. M. Jones (1931) had previously reported collecting a

Canada Warbler nest with five eggs in the northeastern hills in June of 1895. Taber (1951) reported further summer occurrences of Canada Warblers in the northeastern highlands.

The Canada Warbler approaches its southern limit of distribution in Connecticut and further south in the Appalachian mountain range. Although the coastal plain does have wet areas

with adjacent dense stands of seemingly appropriate broad leaf vegetation, the underlying soils tend to be sandy and hence drier than the areas typically used by breeding Canada Warblers in Connecticut.

*George A. Clark, Jr.*

## Yellow-breasted Chat
*Icteria virens*

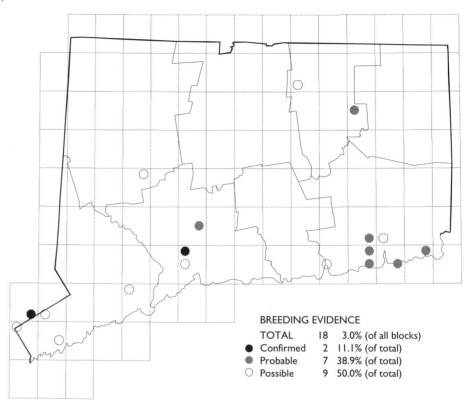

BREEDING EVIDENCE

| | TOTAL | 18 | 3.0% (of all blocks) |
|---|---|---|---|
| ● | Confirmed | 2 | 11.1% (of total) |
| ◉ | Probable | 7 | 38.9% (of total) |
| ○ | Possible | 9 | 50.0% (of total) |

The Yellow-breasted Chat is a localized habitat specialist that was once common in Connecticut but is now included on the state's Endangered Species list. It is a migratory breeder that is quite unobtrusive and sedulous about skulking deep in vegetation. The song is an extravagant series of whistles and harsh, grating noises, and despite its secretive nature, territorial birds frequently sing in flight, rising into the air and then sinking slowly with wings raised over the back and feet dangling.

The breeding subspecies is the eastern *I. v. virens*, which is smaller, greener above (not grayish), and shows less white in the malar than western birds; *virens* winters from northern Mexico to western Panama, whereas western *auricollis* winters south only to Guatemala. A few may remain in the breeding range, especially along the Gulf and southern Atlantic coasts.

**Habitat**—This species favors shrubby land and dense second-growth thickets. It is commonly found in dense tangles of blackberry, poison ivy, and Japanese honeysuckle in Virginia (Dennis 1958) and in dense stands of low trees and shrubs in abandoned agricultural fields in Indiana (Thompson and Nolan 1973). Thomas Ford (pers. comm.) found that the vegetation on a Yellow-breasted Chat territory near Haley Farm State Park, Groton, was dominated by Asiatic bittersweet, arrow-wood, and multiflora rose, and that the average height of the vegetation was 1.3 m. Yellow-breasted Chat disappeared from a site in the Connecticut College Arboretum, New London, as the low thicket was replaced with tall thicket and young forest (Butcher et al. 1981).

Although the species is frequently associated with streamside thickets or low wet areas, the primary factors appear to be low, dense vegetation without a closed tree canopy. During the winter, the Yellow-breasted Chat is found primarily in scrub habitats in Mexico and Central America (Rappole et al. 1983).

**Atlas results**—Of the 18 records, 15 are from the southern half of the state, the region where this species was historically a regular breeder (Sage et al. 1913, Forbush 1929). The decline of Yellow-breasted Chat is probably associated with the decline of farming and the reduction in the number and size of abandoned fields in Connecticut. The low thicket required by this species typically remains suitable for only a few years before it becomes high thicket or young forest. Moreover, small, isolated patches of thicket (< 3 acres) are not generally used for nesting by chats (Dennis 1958). Preservation of this species in the state will probably require management of some sites to maintain low thicket.

**Discussion**—The Yellow-breasted Chat was once a common breeding bird in

Connecticut, where it is near the northeastern limit of its range. Merriam (1877) described it as a common summer resident, breeding in dense undergrowth, and Sage et al. (1913) described it as a common summer resident breeding in brush lots throughout the state, but most abundantly in the southern portion. The species showed a persistent decline in the state after the 1920s (Zeranski and Baptist 1990) and is now a rare nester. BBS results suggest that this decline continued in Connecticut from 1966 to 1989, although the species occurred on so few survey routes that the results could not be analyzed statistically. The chat has also declined in New York (Eaton *in* Andrle and Carroll 1988), and BBS results indicate a significant general decline in the eastern United States since 1966. Territorial males were present in shrubby fields on the northern boundary of Haley Farm State Park, Groton, from 1984 to 1990 (R. Askins, unpubl. obs.) and intermittently at Barn Island Wildlife Management Area, Stonington, from 1980 to 1986 (Robert Dewire, pers. comm.). In 1990 and 1991, territorial males were reported from scrubby fields at two sites

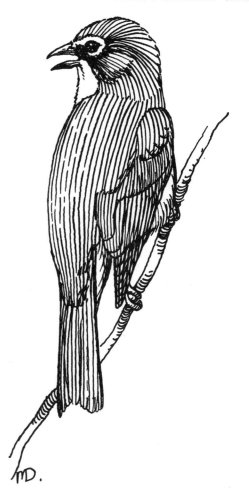

in Old Mystic and Stonington (Margaret Philbrick, pers. comm.) and along a power line right-of-way in Niantic (Andrew Dasinger, pers. comm.).

*Robert A. Askins*

# Scarlet Tanager
## *Piranga olivacea*

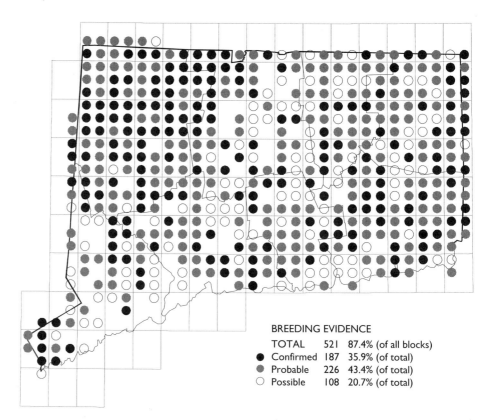

**BREEDING EVIDENCE**

| | TOTAL | 521 | 87.4% (of all blocks) |
|---|---|---|---|
| ● | Confirmed | 187 | 35.9% (of total) |
| ◐ | Probable | 226 | 43.4% (of total) |
| ○ | Possible | 108 | 20.7% (of total) |

Among the most colorful of Connecticut birds, the Scarlet Tanager is a fairly common migratory breeder throughout the Nutmeg State. This tanager winters mainly on the east slope of the Andes from Colombia to Peru and Bolivia.

**Habitat**—Scarlet Tanagers breed in a wide variety of forest types in Connecticut ranging from pine–oak woodland and hemlock–northern hardwoods forest to dry oak–hickory woodland. It may occur in relatively young successional woodland but apparently prefers mature forest. Shy (1984) observed that Scarlet Tanagers in sympatry with Summer Tanagers used denser forests with larger trees than the latter species; this broke down somewhat in allopatry. Scarlet Tanagers use conifers more than other birds of deciduous forest; typically, nests are placed in conifers (Bull 1974, Prescott 1965, pers. obs.),

and females fed in conifers as often as Black-throated Green Warblers in New Hampshire (Holmes 1986). Foods and feeding behavior are similar to the Rose-breasted Grosbeak; however, tanagers flycatch more often and tend to seek prey at greater distances (Holmes 1986, Robinson and Holmes 1982). Population densities of Scarlet Tanager in Connecticut include 42 per 100 ha in

mature hemlock–white pine–northern hardwoods (Cavanaugh & Magee 1967a, Magee 1968–1984a), 30 per 100 ha in similar habitat in Ashford and Union (Craig 1987b), 22 per 100 ha in second growth hardwoods (Cavanaugh & Magee 1967b, Magee 1968–1987), and 20 per 100 ha in mixed habitat including oak–hickory woodland and red maple swamp (Moseley et al. 1968–1984).

**Atlas results**—The Scarlet Tanager was found in the majority of blocks in all eight counties. Gaps are nonetheless evident in populous Hartford, New Haven, and Fairfield counties. The Scarlet Tanager is sensitive to forest fragmentation; it seldom occurs in forests of less than 30 acres (Robbins et al. 1989a). The gaps in the species' range in Connecticut's most urban counties seem to reflect its need for extensive mature forest unfragmented by suburban development.

**Discussion**—The scarce mature forest of Connecticut from the late eighteenth to early twentieth centuries probably supported fewer Scarlet Tanagers than the regenerated forests of the 1980s (Zeranski and Baptist 1990). The loss of mature forest reduces Scarlet Tanager populations. This was well documented by Griscom (1949) in eastern Massachusetts. The Scarlet Tanager is also susceptible to cool, damp weather in late May; many may starve during such conditions (Zumeta and Holmes 1978). Breeding Bird Survey data show that the Scarlet Tanager increased at a rate of 2.6% per year from 1966 to 1978 but declined by 1.2% per year from 1978 to 1987 (Robbins et al. 1989b). Reasons for this reversal of fortune may include fragmentation of mature forest in the breeding range and loss of wintering habitat in South America.

*Walter G. Ellison*

# Northern Cardinal
## *Cardinalis cardinalis*

The Northern Cardinal is a widely distributed resident breeder and is one of Connecticut's brightest and most vigorous songsters in spring. They are a common and familiar bird at feeders during winter months. This species has increased dramatically in abundance throughout Connecticut and much of the Northeast during this century. The Northern Cardinal occurs throughout the eastern United to southern Canada and from the desert southwest in California, Arizona, and Texas south to Guatemala.

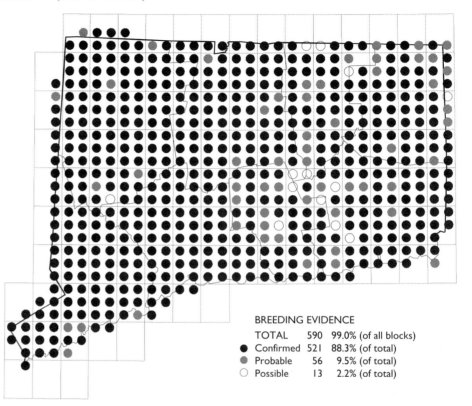

BREEDING EVIDENCE

| | | |
|---|---|---|
| TOTAL | 590 | 99.0% (of all blocks) |
| ● Confirmed | 521 | 88.3% (of total) |
| ◕ Probable | 56 | 9.5% (of total) |
| ○ Possible | 13 | 2.2% (of total) |

**Habitat**—The Northern Cardinal nests and forages in dense thickets bordering fields, woodlands, gardens, parks, and, less commonly, in scrub–shrub swamps along streams. Cardinals typically nest from March through August, with two or more broods per year. The female builds a cup-shaped nest of grass stems, leaves, twigs, and roots; the nest is lined with fine grasses or hair. Nests usually are placed 1–15 feet high in dense foliage of trees, brush, or vine tangles. Northern Cardinals forage on the ground for insects, fruit, and seeds.

**Atlas results**—The Northern Cardinal was one of the most widespread breeding birds in the state during atlas survey. Evidence of breeding was reported in nearly all blocks. The species seems to be absent only from areas of dense forest.

**Discussion**—Prior to 1900, the Northern Cardinal was considered rare and accidental in the state (Merriam 1877, Sage et al. 1913). To the west, the species had nested as far north as southern Ontario by 1901 (Erskine 1992) but was still rarely seen in Connecticut until the 1940s, when its range spread northeastward on the Atlantic seaboard. Nesting was first recorded in Connecticut at Greenwich in 1942 (Bull 1964) and two years later at Stratford. By the 1950s it was a regular wintering species, and by the early 1960s it ranged throughout the state (Bent et al.1968). To the north, cardinals first nested in Massachusetts in 1961, Maine in 1969, and Nova Scotia, the present limit of its range, in 1975 (Adamus 1987, Erskine 1992, Veit and Petersen 1993). Provision of food at bird feeders during winter probably enhances the survival of birds during winter and is thought to have been a major factor contributing to the cardinal's dramatic range expansion (Beddall 1963, Bent et al. 1968). Breeding Bird Survey results show that the cardinal population has consistently increased in southern New England (Robbins et al. 1986).

*Dwight Smith and Arnold Devine*

351

## Rose-breasted Grosbeak
### *Pheucticus ludovicianus*

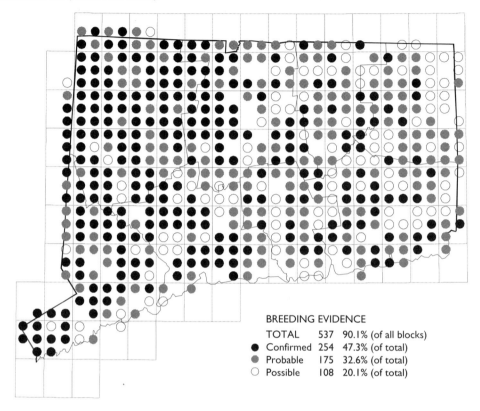

BREEDING EVIDENCE

| | TOTAL | 537 | 90.1% (of all blocks) |
|---|---|---|---|
| ● | Confirmed | 254 | 47.3% (of total) |
| ◐ | Probable | 175 | 32.6% (of total) |
| ○ | Possible | 108 | 20.1% (of total) |

The robust and mellow-voiced Rose-breasted Grosbeak is a migratory breeder in Connecticut wintering from central Mexico to eastern Peru. It is widespread and fairly common in Connecticut from May to early October.

**Habitat**—The Rose-breasted Grosbeak occurs in a wide range of wooded habitats from young successional woodlands, groves of mature trees such as hedgerows and suburban shade trees, to mature forest. They seem to avoid forests dominated by conifers in contrast to the otherwise similar Scarlet Tanager. The highest populations are in successional and mixed habitats, e.g., young hardwoods on abandoned pastureland 29 per 100 ha (Magee 1968–1984b), hardwoods released after cutting of a red pine plantation 43.5 per 100 ha (Magee 1979–1987), and mixed upland habitats including oak–hickory woodland and red maple swamp 31 per 100 ha (Moseley et al. 1968–1984). Lower densities recorded in mature forest including 16 per 100 ha in mature upland forest in Greenwich (Baptist 1981), and 2 per 100 ha in hemlock-northern hardwoods in Ashford and Union (Craig 1987b). In northern New England, grosbeaks show little preference for feeding in specific trees but often use yellow birch and sugar maple (Holmes and Robinson 1981). Grosbeaks capture prey by gleaning and hovering in deciduous foliage (Robinson and Holmes 1982).

**Atlas results**—The Rose-breasted Grosbeak was among the most widespread birds recorded during the

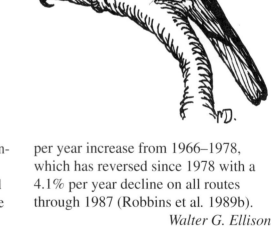

atlas. Absence from many blocks was probably as much due to chance as actual lack of grosbeaks. Some blocks lacking grosbeaks were in urban or intensively developed areas such as Hartford, Westport, and Bradley International Airport, Windsor Locks. Grosbeaks were also rather sparsely distributed along the coast. Nonetheless, Rose-breasted Grosbeaks were much better reported in heavily populated Fairfield, New Haven, and Hartford counties than other forest birds, e.g., American Redstart and Scarlet Tanager. This implies that the Rose-breasted Grosbeak may be less sensitive to habitat fragmentation than other forest birds.

**Discussion**—During the early to mid-1900s the Rose-breasted Grosbeak was rare in southern New England (Nuttall 1832, Sage et al. 1913, Bent et al. 1968). It increased substantially from 1880 onward (Griscom 1949, Bent et al. 1968). Three reasons for this may be a shift by the bird into successional and suburban habitats from mature forest (Forbush 1929), the abandonment of marginal farms after the Civil War leading to reforestation, and the decline of the native cagebird trade in the northeastern United States. Recent population trends revealed by BBS data include a significant 6.1%

per year increase from 1966–1978, which has reversed since 1978 with a 4.1% per year decline on all routes through 1987 (Robbins et al. 1989b).

*Walter G. Ellison*

## Indigo Bunting
*Passerina cyanea*

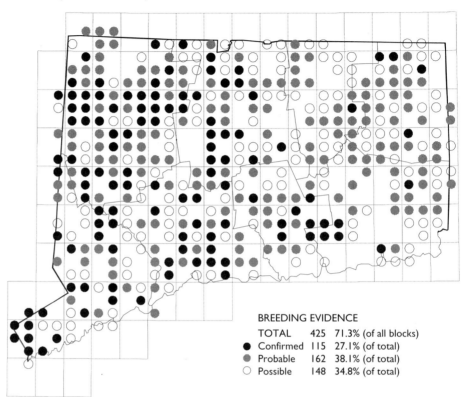

BREEDING EVIDENCE

| | TOTAL | 425 | 71.3% (of all blocks) |
|---|---|---|---|
| ● | Confirmed | 115 | 27.1% (of total) |
| ● | Probable | 162 | 38.1% (of total) |
| ○ | Possible | 148 | 34.8% (of total) |

A fairly common migrant in spring and fall and during the breeding season. This species has a preference for old field edges and cleared corridors for power lines.

**Habitat**—This is one species that has benefited from the extensive power line clearings that crisscross the state. These lines are kept in a state of growth that duplicates an old field situation, and the low shrubby growth is ideal for nesting. Old orchards are also favored spots, and it is difficult to travel far in rural Connecticut without hearing the sharp, choppy song of this species. When cleared farm lands revert back to scrub field conditions, the Indigo Bunting population increases.

**Atlas results**—The map shows that this species is fairly evenly distributed throughout the state. One must consider the difficulty in finding this species' nest. The well made nest of bark strips, rootlets, small twigs, and leaves is placed in the densest part of shrubby growth or tangles and can be most difficult to find. This undoubtedly accounts for the high number of possible and probable sightings compared to a relatively low quantity of confirmations of nesting. The drab female seems to disappear when returning to the nest and is suspected to be the only parent that tends the young (C. Harrison 1978). This also would present difficulty in confirmation of nesting by observing feeding of young birds. The male has been seen feeding fledged young (Proctor pers. records), but this may only happen when the female is renesting for the second brood.

**Discussion**—This species has had its ups and downs in the state. At the end of the 1800s when Connecticut was mostly cleared, the field margins undoubtedly provided fine habitat, and Merriam (1877) termed it a very common species. Sage et al. (1913) also considered it to be common. As the state slowly reverted back to a woodland condition, nesting areas had to be reduced and this may account for several reports that the population was declining. However, Mackenzie (1961) noted an increase in the Guilford area. As gas line rights-of-way and power lines opened up new lanes through forested areas the populations in such areas boomed (Proctor pers. records). At present the population seems to show no signs of decline. With the continued fragmentation of forest areas for building of homes, some nesting areas might appear at the edges of such sites. Extensive projects, such as shopping mall expansion, certainly will affect potential nesting sites. Examples of this can be seen by the development of the open field areas of the Quinnipiac marshes, which have fallen to such development and from which the Indigo Buntings have gone!

*Noble S. Proctor*

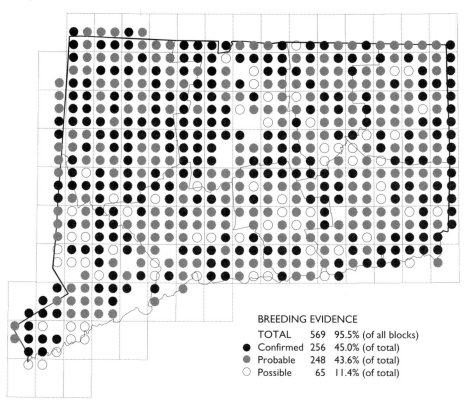

## Rufous-sided Towhee
*Pipilo erythrophthalmus*

BREEDING EVIDENCE

| | | |
|---|---|---|
| TOTAL | 569 | 95.5% (of all blocks) |
| ● Confirmed | 256 | 45.0% (of total) |
| ● Probable | 248 | 43.6% (of total) |
| ○ Possible | 65 | 11.4% (of total) |

This is a common summer breeder throughout the state. Within the past thirty years the number of wintering birds has increased with the expansion of increasingly popular bird feeding as a possible assisting factor. Most of the breeding population is migratory, however, spending the winter south to Florida, the Gulf Coast and possibly southern Texas. This is the winter range of our "Red-eyed" Towhee, subspecies *P. e. erythrophthalmus*; other races of the Rufous-sided Towhee in the West, the "Spotted" Towhees, breed and winter south to Guatemala.

**Habitat**—During migration this species appears in a wide variety of habitats from field edges and thickets to deep woods and swamplands. During the breeding season, it prefers the dense undergrowth of upland woodlands, often in dry locations with a low cover of blueberry and huckleberry. The nest is a cup of grasses, rootlets, and, often, grapevine strips placed on the ground. Wintering birds are most regular in dense coastal thickets where visits to bird feeders help to supplement their diet. During warm winters they often can be found well inland in the same situations. With increasingly mild winters in recent years, the number of over-wintering birds has increased, as indicated on Christmas Bird Counts.

**Atlas results**—As might be expected for such an adaptable species, records came from over 95% of all blocks. Of these, 45% were confirmed nesting, and over 40% were probable. Finding the nest of a ground nesting species such as this is always challenging.

Birds disappear in one area and often move considerable distances to reach the nest, making it difficult to locate the nesting site. One can safely presume, then, that most of the probable records are likely strong indications of breeding. When searching for any ground nesting species great care must be taken that the nest is not trampled in the process. Also, human scents are often followed by nest predators, placing the nest at risk of destruction. Always use the greatest care and proper techniques when hunting for ground nests. The species usually has numerous natural predators and adding a well-marked scout trail can destroy many nests.

**Discussion**—This species apparently has remained unchanged in status over the years. Both Merriam (1877) and Sage et al. (1913) considered it a common summer breeder. Wintering birds, however, were not present so regularly. Bull (1964) points out the upswing in wintering reports starting as long ago as the mid-1940s. He attributes this to the popularity in feeding of birds during the winter months. It would seem that the combination of milder winters and available food has made the wintering situation for this species much more advantageous.

*Noble S. Proctor*

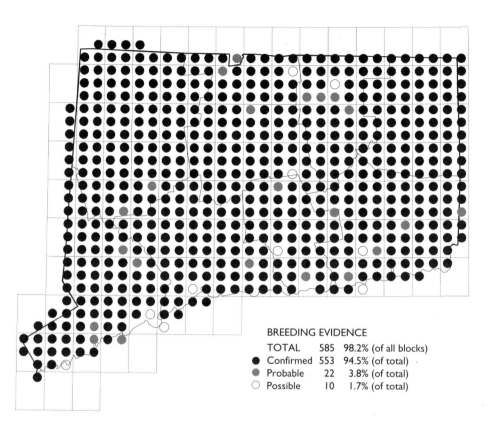

BREEDING EVIDENCE

| | TOTAL | 585 | 98.2% (of all blocks) |
|---|---|---|---|
| ● | Confirmed | 553 | 94.5% (of total) |
| ● | Probable | 22 | 3.8% (of total) |
| ○ | Possible | 10 | 1.7% (of total) |

## Chipping Sparrow
### *Spizella passerina*

A migratory breeder; occasional individuals may winter in Connecticut. For the species as a whole, the eastern part of the principal wintering range includes the southeastern United States and much of eastern Mexico (AOU 1983). Chipping Sparrows are common as breeders in Connecticut.

Although song is usually diagnostic for distinguishing the Chipping Sparrow from the closely related Field Sparrow, on 6 May 1971 in Mansfield a Field Sparrow was heard singing a full trill indistinguishable by ear from the song of a Chipping Sparrow (G. A. Clark, Jr., pers. obs.); Short (1966) reported from Nebraska a similar case of a Field Sparrow singing like a Chipping Sparrow.

**Habitat**—The species breeds in areas having short grass, lawns, or bare areas in close proximity to trees, often conifers. Even roads passing through woodland may provide adequate open area for the species. The species tends to be in areas of relatively well drained soils, often sandy, and avoids marshy areas.

**Atlas results**—The extremely widespread distribution of the Chipping Sparrow is indicated by its confirmation as a breeder in more than 90% of the blocks. Further searching probably would have raised the confirmation rate even higher.

**Discussion**—Linsley (1843) termed this species as common, and, later, Merriam (1877) and Sage et al. (1913) called it abundant. Thus, the species appears to have been regular and

numerous in the state for more than 150 years. Although there is evidence from Massachusetts for a decline in Chipping Sparrow populations in towns and cities during the peak of House Sparrow numbers from 1880 to 1915 (Griscom 1949), publications from Connecticut for that period do not report such a decline (Sage et al. 1913).

Among sparrows breeding in Connecticut, the Chipping and Field Sparrows are the smallest in size. Furthermore, they are the only native species of sparrows in Connecticut that do not use a backward jump with dragging by both feet to scratch for food items concealed in litter of dead leaves or other materials lying on the ground (Greenlaw 1976). Conceivably, the small size of these birds makes such scratching with the feet for food inefficient, but there is no direct evidence supporting this idea. Where breeding habitats of these two species abut, they overlap in home range and feed in the same vicinity without apparent conflict as observed in Coventry (G. A. Clark, Jr., pers. obs.). The Chipping Sparrow nests higher off the ground in association with the typically greater height of some trees in its habitat.

The Chipping Sparrow breeding range extends further north than does that of the Field Sparrow, but in winter the Chipping Sparrows tend to be further south than do the Field Sparrows (Root 1988). Although over the years the range of timing of the spring return by both these species to their respective breeding grounds is spread over a period of weeks, the two arrive in Connecticut during the same period in March and April so that the potential difference in cold tolerance exhibited in their wintering ranges is not apparent in the timing of their migrations.

*George A. Clark, Jr.*

# Field Sparrow
*Spizella puṣilla*

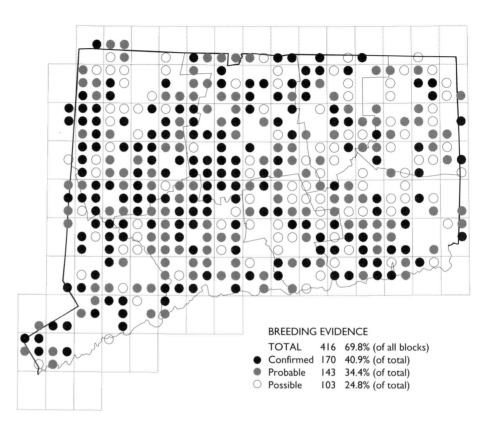

BREEDING EVIDENCE

| | TOTAL | 416 | 69.8% (of all blocks) |
|---|---|---|---|
| ● | Confirmed | 170 | 40.9% (of total) |
| ● | Probable | 143 | 34.4% (of total) |
| ○ | Possible | 103 | 24.8% (of total) |

Mainly a migratory breeder, but a small number of birds winter in the state. The Field Sparrow is a regularly encountered breeder in Connecticut but is substantially less common than the Chipping Sparrow. For the species as a whole, the main wintering areas are from the middle Atlantic and south central states south into Florida, the Gulf states, and northeastern Mexico (AOU 1983, Root 1988). The eastern subspecies *S. p. pusilla* occurs in Connecticut; these are quite distinct from the paler and grayer Great Plains populations, subspecies *arenacea*.

**Habitat**—The Field Sparrow uses abandoned fields or equivalent sites that include a substantial amount of relatively short woody trees together with bunch grasses. The soil is commonly sandy and well drained, although there can be standing water nearby. Many of the sites used by Field Sparrows have been subjected to human disturbance such as along power line rights-of-way. Compared with the Chipping Sparrow, the Field Sparrow often has shorter trees and higher grass in its habitat.

Field Sparrow nests are placed on or near the ground in contrast to Chipping Sparrow nests which are higher off the ground (Bull 1974, Buech 1982).

**Atlas results**—Recorded from nearly 70% of the blocks, this species is widely distributed across the state but

absent from extensively developed urban and suburban areas and also from mature forests.

**Discussion**—Merriam (1877) and Sage et al. (1913) termed this species "abundant," which might perhaps be interpreted as indicating numbers equivalent to those of the Chipping Sparrow in that period. In Connecticut the trend of recent decades for increasing suburbanization together with the development of relatively more mature woodlands has apparently tended to reduce the amount of habitat well suited for Field Sparrows; nevertheless the species remains widespread as a breeder in the state. In contrast to the relatively closely related Chipping Sparrow, which is generally favored by a suburban landscape of neatly mowed lawns with ornamental shrubs and trees, the Field Sparrow occupies a habitat which is often less tidy as considered by the criteria of traditional landscaping. Often found breeding in the vicinity of Field Sparrows is the Blue-winged Warbler, which frequently uses a similar habitat.

*George A. Clark, Jr.*

# Vesper Sparrow
*Pooecetes gramineus*

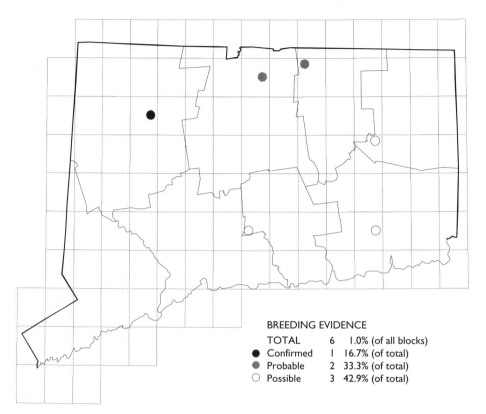

BREEDING EVIDENCE

| | TOTAL | 6 | 1.0% (of all blocks) |
|---|---|---|---|
| ● | Confirmed | 1 | 16.7% (of total) |
| ● | Probable | 2 | 33.3% (of total) |
| ○ | Possible | 3 | 42.9% (of total) |

This species is primarily an uncommon transient usually found in agricultural fields of interior Connecticut. Spring migrants occur from early April to late May and are frequently heard singing. Fall passage occurs from late September through October. The breeding population in the Northeast winters primarily in the southeastern United States. The Vesper Sparrow is only known to have nested once in the past decade in Connecticut and thus is included on the state's Endangered Species list.

**Habitat**—In southern New England, Vesper Sparrows nest in drier upland portions of pastureland, sandy fields, hayfields, brushy fencerows of smaller farm fields and extensive openings in pine woodland, seldom using areas near water. Sparsely scattered bush tops, sapling trees, or other high points are frequently employed as song posts and may be a partial requirement in some localities; otherwise activity is on the ground. In Connecticut, recent nesting attempts have included the grassland surrounding airports and noncultivated open fields. In contrast to the traditional farmland nest sites used in Pennsylvania, New York, and Vermont, this species has not been found breeding in such places in Connecticut, although agricultural areas are used regularly in migration.

**Atlas results**—The only confirmed nesting during the atlas, and in the past decade, occurred at the Torrington Fish and Game Club in 1984 when an adult with at least two fledglings was observed. Territorial birds were noted through June at two localities: in 1982 at Bradley International Airport, Windsor Locks, and in 1983 near Somersville, Somers. (Reports of breeding in 1985 appear to be in error.)

**Discussion**—Vesper Sparrows have declined significantly in the Northeast over the past several decades corresponding to changes in cutting practices of hayfields and regrowth of woodland in formerly cleared farmland (Robbins et al. 1986). Although many of these changes are more recent, the Vesper Sparrow appears to have remained scarce in Connecticut since the early 1900s (Sage et al. 1913), even though Merriam (1877) described the species as abundant in the late 1800s. Nesting or suspected nesting has been noted at only eight localities since 1943, primarily in the upper Connecticut River valley and the northwest uplands (Craig 1980).

This species undoubtedly benefited from land-clearing and opening of marginal agricultural land in eastern North America during the colonial period. Whether it advanced from core areas to the west is unknown.

Vesper Sparrows in western parts of the continent inhabit the vast stretches of open, dry grassland and sagebrush, where they are still fairly common. The species as a whole breeds from British Columbia and the Great Basin states east across the prairies to southern Ontario, sparingly to the Maritimes, and south to West Virginia. Breeders in the East are the darker, browner, and more coarsely streaked nominate subspecies *P. g. gramineus*.

Although suitable habitat for breeding exists in Connecticut, few localities are large enough to hold more than one or two pairs—a single pair may require two acres (Wiens 1969). In addition, Vesper Sparrows habitually avoid nesting near human habitation, further limiting potential breeding sites. Relative to the Savannah Sparrow, the Vesper Sparrow has fared rather poorly in the Northeast. This likely is due to the abandonment of poorer, marginal farmland on rocky and sandy soils, the habitat most suited to the Vesper Sparrow.

*Louis R. Bevier*

## Savannah Sparrow
*Passerculus sandwichensis*

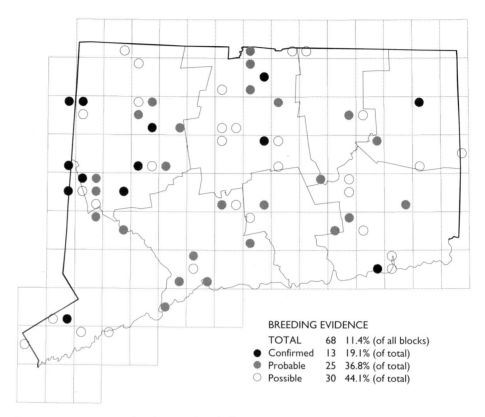

BREEDING EVIDENCE

| | TOTAL | 68 | 11.4% (of all blocks) |
|---|---|---|---|
| ● | Confirmed | 13 | 19.1% (of total) |
| ● | Probable | 25 | 36.8% (of total) |
| ○ | Possible | 30 | 44.1% (of total) |

The Savannah Sparrow is a widespread but now uncommon breeder currently listed as a Species of Special Concern. The wintering area for Connecticut breeding birds is unknown but presumably lies within those parts of the wintering range for the populations breeding in the Northeast designated as the subspecies *P. s. savanna*—in the southeastern and southcentral United States, the northern islands of the Caribbean, and southern Mexico.

**Habitat**—The Savannah Sparrow prefers grassy fields with damp soils, and among species of grassland sparrows in Connecticut this species occurs in the wettest sites. Sites with continual standing water in the grass would be unsuited for any grassland sparrow as all of these species place their nests on or very near the ground. Savannah Sparrows are known to nest on upland areas bordering salt marshes (Sage et al. 1913).

**Atlas results**—The Savannah Sparrow breeds in pockets of field habitat that remain around the state. Relative to the Grasshopper Sparrow, the Savannah Sparrow remains more widespread. The Savannah Sparrow can use not only airports but also pastures used to some extent for grazing or hay production. Occurrence of the species during summer does not necessarily indicate successful breeding, and like other grassland species, Savannah Sparrows may be vulnerable to effects of mowing relatively early in the summer (Crossman 1989).

**Discussion**—This species might have been rather scarce in the precolonial period, and might have undergone a considerable increase with the reduction of forests after the arrival of the Europeans. Merriam (1877) termed this an abundant summer resident, whereas Sage et al. (1913) only stated that a few bred at the borders of the larger salt marshes and on inland meadows, suggesting a much less common breeding status than that indicated by Merriam; Sage et al. added, however, that L. B. Woodruff considered the species to be a common summer resident in Litchfield. Overall, there has been a long term trend of decrease in abundance of this species during the twentieth century as grasslands have been replaced by forests, suburbs, or urban centers.

The greater success of the Savannah Sparrow relative to other species of grassland sparrows—e.g., Vesper, Grasshopper, and Henslow's sparrows—seems at least partly attributable to the habitat of the Savannah being particularly favorable for agriculture such as hay production or grazing, activities that have contributed to the maintenance of usable habitat for the birds. Nevertheless, there are pressures to make full use of available agricultural lands and thus to mow grasslands so as to maximize hay yield. Consequently, the Savannah Sparrow remains somewhat vulnerable as a breeding bird in the state. Crossman (1989) has made recommendations for mowing schedules, particularly for airport management, to help to assure maximal production of small birds nesting in grassy areas.

*George A. Clark, Jr.*

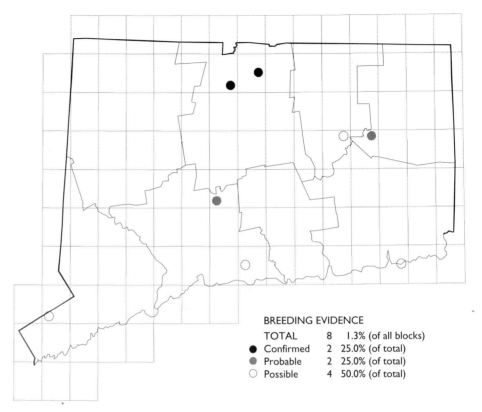

BREEDING EVIDENCE

| TOTAL | 8 | 1.3% (of all blocks) |
|---|---|---|
| ● Confirmed | 2 | 25.0% (of total) |
| ◉ Probable | 2 | 25.0% (of total) |
| ○ Possible | 4 | 50.0% (of total) |

## Grasshopper Sparrow
### *Ammodramus savannarum*

The Grasshopper Sparrow is a rare migratory breeder, currently designated Endangered in Connecticut. Migrants are encountered in open areas such as weedy fields; it is generally more scarce in spring than in fall. Migratory populations of this species breed in grassland throughout most of North America from southern Canada to northern Mexico; the subspecies occurring in Connecticut is *A. s. pratensis*, which winters in the southeastern and south-central states south to Costa Rica and the northern West Indies (AOU 1957); resident forms are found southward locally from Mexico to Ecuador and the West Indies.

**Habitat**—This species favors moderately dry grasslands, typically with bunch grasses and areas of open ground present (Crossman 1989). When the birds return in the spring the appearance of the habitat can be markedly dif-ferent from that later in the summer when the grass may have grown to several feet high (Whitmore 1979). In contrast to the Grasshopper Sparrow, the Savannah Sparrow typically favors a more continuous cover of sod grasses with more moist soils (Crossman 1989). Where both Grasshopper and Savannah Sparrows nest in the same area, as at Bradley International Airport in Windsor Locks, they overlap in territories with each species showing its particular habitat preference and with no special aggression toward the opposite species (Crossman 1989). Grasshopper Sparrows appear to prefer areas having elevated song perches (Crossman 1989), and provision of such perches might aid in attracting birds into new sites (Crossman 1989).

**Atlas results**—The species was found during the atlas project in only eight blocks. The best known sites are at airports which presently provide the only known localities used for breeding.

The requirement of this species for extensive field areas of suitable habitat is directly reflected in the atlas results. The kinds of soils and vegetation favorable for Grasshopper Sparrows would presumably not be particularly favorable for agriculture, and consequently such areas might be more likely allowed to grow into brushland or be converted to other uses. Although the Grasshopper Sparrow is smaller in size than the Savannah Sparrow and should therefore require less food, the Grasshopper Sparrow defends a larger territory, perhaps because there is less concentration of arthropod food than in the smaller, but presumably more productive, territories of Savannah Sparrows.

**Discussion**—Although information is not available on the status of this species before 1800, it seems possible that this was a midcontinental species which invaded Connecticut only after the countryside was opened up during the colonial period (Bent et al. 1968).

The Grasshopper Sparrow was much more common in the state during the late nineteenth century than at present, and the species has declined sharply through the twentieth century. Craig (1978) listed fourteen towns in the state where this species was either suspected or confirmed breeding before 1978; there are no indications of breeding since 1980 in these towns. With the gradual abandonment of farming as a predominant activity in the state, the gradual loss of extensive open fields has led to a sharp reduction in this species.

The Grasshopper Sparrow breeds in so few remaining localities that its extirpation as a breeder in the state is readily conceivable. In a detailed study of the habitat preference of the species, Crossman (1989) proposed management recommendations to assist in the conservation of the species at the few remaining breeding sites. One of his recommendations is the postponement of mowing of the airport grasslands in the summer until after the young are capable of flight so as to

reduce the chances of loss of birds by mowing. Longer grass has an advantage for aircraft safety in discouraging the presence of most bird species of larger size that constitute the greatest threat to planes landing or taking off.

*George A. Clark, Jr.*

## Sharp-tailed Sparrow
*Ammodramus caudacutus*

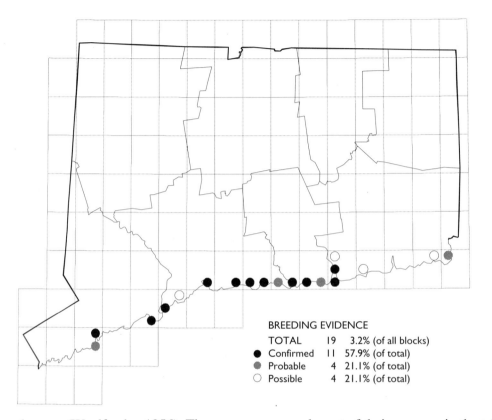

BREEDING EVIDENCE

| | TOTAL | 19 | 3.2% (of all blocks) |
|---|---|---|---|
| ● | Confirmed | 11 | 57.9% (of total) |
| ◍ | Probable | 4 | 21.1% (of total) |
| ○ | Possible | 4 | 21.1% (of total) |

This species is an uncommon to fairly common, but local, breeder in coastal salt marshes of the state. They are rarely seen away from breeding localities during migration along interior river systems and in overgrown weedy fields. Most winter south of Connecticut. This species is designated as a Species of Special Concern in Connecticut.

**Habitat**—The preferred habitat is the drier portion of the salt marsh, especially in areas of salt-meadow cord-grass. Although the birds move to edges of water channels while foraging in the marsh, the favored areas are the wispy, upturned areas of the cordgrass (Woolfenden 1956). Within this habitat, the Sharp-tailed Sparrow is a skulker, but it sings from the tops of grass clumps. This species is unusual in that the males do not actively defend a territory in the marsh but wander throughout

the area (Woolfenden 1956). The female, however, is defensive of the nesting sites. In Connecticut, this territory of defense is roughly 200 sq ft (Proctor 1972). The nest is made of grasses and is placed within the upturned sweeps of cord-grass at a level high enough to avoid flooding by the tide. There is no direct conflict with the closely related Seaside Sparrows that

spend most of their summer in the taller salt-marsh cord-grass, edges of ditches, and main water courses of the marsh (Woolfenden 1956). Seaside Sparrows need four times as much area for foraging, and comparisons of the total number of individuals in an area have revealed that the Sharp-tailed Sparrow is usually four times as common as the Seaside Sparrow (Proctor 1972).

**Atlas results**—The species shows a major dependence on the coastal marshes in the state. Some are found a short distance up the Connecticut River, on islands with cord-grass along the river's edge.

**Discussion**—The fate of this sparrow has always been based on the condition of the coastal salt marsh habitat. No alternate habitat is used for nesting in the state. Merriam (1877) and Sage et al. (1913) considered it an abundant summer resident in the coastal marshes. In areas such as Fairfield County where much of the seacoast has been developed and marshes destroyed, this sparrow has disappeared. But in the extensive marshes such as those of Milford Point and Great Island, the populations can still be termed at least common.

The Sharp-tailed Sparrows that breed in Connecticut are part of the southern Atlantic coast populations, in our case the subspecies *A. c. caudacutus*, which, on adults, show distinct dark streaks below and a dark, brownish-olive back color. Recent studies on Long Island have shown that the songs and displays of these birds differ markedly from the northern and interior populations sometimes referred to as the "Nelson's" Sparrow, which includes three disjunct populations of the subspecies *nelsoni*, *alterus*, and *subvirgatus* (Greenlaw 1993). Although no careful analysis of Connecticut specimens has been made, these forms are said to occur as migrants (Sage et al. 1913, Montagna 1942). The breeders in the Maritimes south to central Maine (*subvirgatus*) are the dullest and grayest and have the faintest streaking below, while the interior Canadian breeders (*nelsoni*) are the richest buff below. The "Nelson's" types all give loud primary songs and perform song flight displays, whereas the southern forms give "whisper songs" and do not have a song flight display (Greenlaw 1993). It would be of interest if these behaviors were studied for both migrants and breeding birds in Connecticut. There is a substantial series of Sharp-tailed Sparrow specimens, part of the John Sage collection, at the University of Connecticut; these could prove valuable for further study.

*Noble S. Proctor*

## Seaside Sparrow
### *Ammodramus maritimus*

This species is a fairly common summer breeder in coastal salt marshes. It is even more restricted in its occurrence to these marshes than the co-occurring Sharp-tailed Sparrow. Inland records for Seaside Sparrow are lacking. Overwintering birds are also much rarer than for the Sharp-tailed Sparrow. The species is currently designated as a Species of Special Concern in Connecticut.

**Habitat**—This is a bird of the wettest parts of the salt marsh where the tall salt-marsh cord-grass grows (Woolfenden 1956). Locating this species can be more difficult than finding Sharp-tailed Sparrows because the Seaside Sparrow frequents the ditch edges farther out in a marsh and the wettest edge regions of the larger waterways throughout the marsh. The nest is made of grasses and is placed very near the ground yet high enough to avoid flooding by ordinary tides. Like the Sharp-tailed Sparrow, the male does not defend the nest site and instead wanders in the marsh. There is no hostile interaction with the Sharp-tailed Sparrows resident in the same marshlands (Woolfenden 1956). The female defends the nest site. Because of the limited foraging area along any one ditch she must cover a rather extensive area of the marsh. This affects the total number of birds of this species that can live in one marsh and accounts for the four-to-one ratio by which the Sharp-tailed exceeds the Seaside (Proctor 1972).

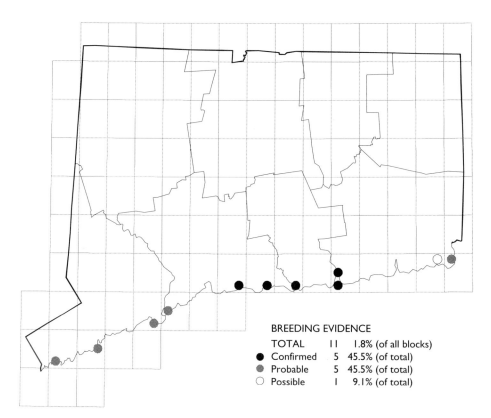

BREEDING EVIDENCE

| TOTAL | 11 | 1.8% (of all blocks) |
|---|---|---|
| ● Confirmed | 5 | 45.5% (of total) |
| ● Probable | 5 | 45.5% (of total) |
| ○ Possible | 1 | 9.1% (of total) |

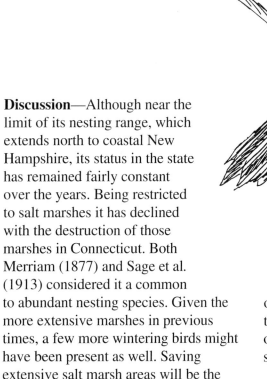

**Atlas results**—The map shows critically placed nesting marshes for this species. Confirmation of breeding occurred only in the more extensive marshes, where there is sufficient salt-marsh cord-grass growth, such as in Milford, Branford, Guilford, and Old Saybrook. The high incidence of breeding confirmation may be attributed to the open habitat, which facilitates observations of adults feeding fledglings in a species for which nests are so difficult to find. Additional comparison with the Sharp-tailed Sparrow is provided in the account for that species.

**Discussion**—Although near the limit of its nesting range, which extends north to coastal New Hampshire, its status in the state has remained fairly constant over the years. Being restricted to salt marshes it has declined with the destruction of those marshes in Connecticut. Both Merriam (1877) and Sage et al. (1913) considered it a common to abundant nesting species. Given the more extensive marshes in previous times, a few more wintering birds might have been present as well. Saving extensive salt marsh areas will be the only hope for continued occurrence of this species in the state. Small pockets of marsh simply do not attract this species as a nesting bird.

*Noble S. Proctor*

# Song Sparrow
## *Melospiza melodia*

The Song Sparrow is a very common nesting species throughout Connecticut. Many also winter in the state, with more along the coast than inland. The number of wintering birds varies from year to year depending on the weather and food availability. Migrant birds leave the state by late November and winter to the south and west of New England. In 1988, a Song Sparrow banded in Connecticut was found in Arkansas (Burkett banding data). The majority return in early March, and males start singing immediately; one of the earliest singing records for the state is 21 February 1900 (Sage et al. 1913).

**Habitat**—Song Sparrows can be found in almost any shrubby open location—hedge rows, abandoned fields, wetland edges, second growth woods, rural and suburban yards. Almost all early nests are on the ground under thick shrubs; later nests may be built 2–4 ft off the ground in trees, shrubs, or thick, tall grass (Nice 1964).

**Atlas results**—Song Sparrows were found in the most blocks of all species recorded during the atlas and are clearly one of the state's most common birds.

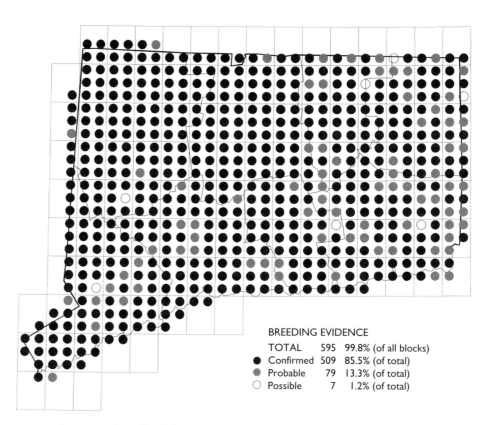

BREEDING EVIDENCE

| | TOTAL | 595 | 99.8% (of all blocks) |
|---|---|---|---|
| ● | Confirmed | 509 | 85.5% (of total) |
| ● | Probable | 79 | 13.3% (of total) |
| ○ | Possible | 7 | 1.2% (of total) |

**Discussion**—Undoubtedly this is a bird that has profited from human presence in the state, as there was much less appropriate habitat available before colonization and clearing for agriculture. In all historical literature the Song Sparrow is referred to as a common bird (Merriam 1877, Sage et al. 1913). In the late 1800s, the population was said to have declined due to competition with the House Sparrow but had recovered by 1920 (Bagg and Eliot, 1937). Song Sparrow nests are frequently parasitized by Brown-headed Cowbirds; Margaret Nice (1964) found 43.9% of the Song Sparrow nests she observed held cowbird eggs. Nevertheless, cowbird parasitism does not appear to have adversely affected Connecticut's Song Sparrow population. Adequate habitat appears to be available for feeding and nesting throughout the state.

Breeding Bird Survey data show that among the New England states, Connecticut had the second highest mean number of Song Sparrows per route (30.4) from 1965–1979; Vermont averaged only about three more birds per route (Robbins et al. 1986). Although this indicates there are many Song Sparrows in Connecticut, analysis of population trends from these same data reveals a highly significant decline of 3.2% per year during the 1980s (see Appendix 2). This decline was noted for the East as a whole from 1965 to 1979 (Robbins et al. 1986). It is difficult to imagine that this species would disappear from the state due to changes in land practices, but this decline appears to reflect a similar decline seen in other species of birds that use farmland in the state. In contrast, the Song Sparrow has extended its breeding range in the southeast United States in Kentucky and Georgia, since about the turn of the century, and more recently, in South Carolina (Mengel 1963). This expansion involves another subspecies, however, and perhaps it is only the northeastern breeders, subspecies *melodia*, that are declining. The geographic variation in eastern populations of the Song Sparrow is, however, much less well-defined compared to the that seen in the West; the various named forms in the East are based on rather subtle distinctions.

*Winifred B. Burkett*

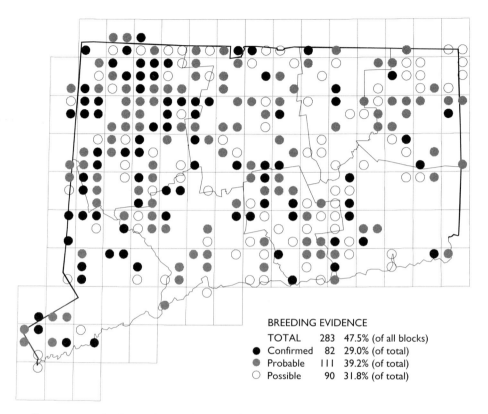

## Swamp Sparrow
*Melospiza georgiana*

Swamp Sparrows regularly nest in Connecticut wherever appropriate wetland habitats occur. They are a common migrant throughout the state during September and October, most leaving the state to winter in the southeastern United States. Some do spend the winter in Connecticut in marshes along the coast, and a few turn up on inland Christmas Counts during milder winters. Migrants arrive back at inland sites in April and May.

BREEDING EVIDENCE

| | TOTAL | 283 | 47.5% (of all blocks) |
|---|---|---|---|
| ● | Confirmed | 82 | 29.0% (of total) |
| ● | Probable | 111 | 39.2% (of total) |
| ○ | Possible | 90 | 31.8% (of total) |

**Habitat**—Swamp Sparrows nest in freshwater marshes, swamps, bogs, wet meadows, on the shores of lakes and slow moving streams (Wetherbee *in* Bent et al. 1968), and occasionally in brackish and freshwater tidal marshes (Greenberg and Droege 1990). Nests are always over or very close to the water and are frequently built between cattail or grass stalks or upon the bent-down clumps of stalks and leaves. After the nesting season they may also be found in weedy fields and hedge rows with other sparrows (Wetherbee *in* Bent et al. 1968).

**Atlas results**—The distribution of breeding Swamp Sparrows is directly affected by availability of appropriate wetland habitat. This is seen in the absence of reports from higher dry parts of the state and urban areas. The habit of male Swamp Sparrows singing from fairly conspicuous perches makes them easy to detect, but the species' secretive nature and use of wet habitats for nesting undoubtedly made confirmation of nesting difficult.

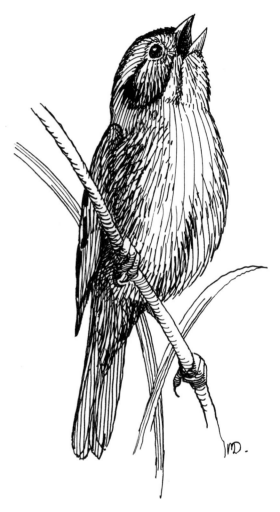

**Discussion**—Bagg and Eliot (1937) state that the Swamp Sparrow's breeding range expanded south into Massachusetts and northern Connecticut in the mid-1800s. No similar range expansion was noted in New York State, where Swamp Sparrows have always been considered a common breeding bird (Zeranski and Baptist 1990). Sage et al. (1913) found the Swamp Sparrow to be common during the summer in the northern part of the state but absent from the southern part of the state, except at the Quinnipiac Marshes, where it was common, and near Bridgeport. It is interesting to note that Swamp Sparrows were found breeding in coastal marshes at Norwalk and Hammonasset State Park and in brackish tidal marshes along the Connecticut River; there are no historical data on their occurrence in these areas (Sage et al. 1913). This may indicate a continuing range expansion of the "Coastal Plain" Swamp Sparrow (*M. g. nigrescens*), a subspecies of the mid-Atlantic coastal marshes that recently has colonized tidal habitats north to Cape Cod (Greenberg and Droege 1990). As this subspecies potentially could be a rare breeder in the state, more study is needed to establish the extent of its breeding in Connecticut; the nominate subspecies, *georgiana*, is the form known breeding in other parts of the state.

*Winifred B. Burkett*

375

## White-throated Sparrow
### *Zonotrichia albicollis*

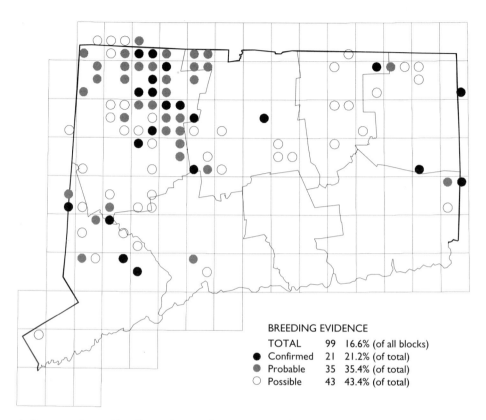

BREEDING EVIDENCE

| | TOTAL | 99 | 16.6% (of all blocks) |
|---|---|---|---|
| ● | Confirmed | 21 | 21.2% (of total) |
| ● | Probable | 35 | 35.4% (of total) |
| ○ | Possible | 43 | 43.4% (of total) |

A common spring and fall migrant with marked fluctuations in numbers at times. Wintering populations seemed to be scattered in pockets along the coast and less concentrated inland. A small summer resident population nests in scattered localities.

**Habitat**—This species is a bird of the underbrush and thicket, more often heard by chip note or song before being seen. It can be a common feeder bird in the winter but during mild winters seems to prefer foraging for food afield. During migration, the White-throated Sparrow can appear in any habitat. There is a marked preference for bog areas and swamp edges for nesting. The nest is a cup of grasses and rootlets tucked deep into a grass clump often under overhanging branches of low growing shrubs.

**Atlas results**—Confirmed nest sites point out the concentration of nesting in the northwestern hills with its many scattered bogs. The species also bred down the Housatonic River valley to some extent, whereas the Connecticut River was devoid of nesting.

Although the species was not confirmed breeding in Bethany, the probable sites there are at bogs that often have birds throughout the summer. The damage that would be done to the plant life within these fragile bogs outweighs the need for confirmation of nesting sites by finding the actual nest.

**Discussion**—Bagg and Eliot (1937) reported the expansion of this species into Connecticut during the first decade of the 1900s and listed it as a rare breeder as far south as Massachusetts prior to 1900. It appears always to have been a fairly common migrant throughout the state. Surprisingly, it was not confirmed as a nesting species in the state until 1963 (Carleton 1963b), although territorial birds had been reported as early as 1908 by Job. In 1965, it nested as close as ten miles from the coast at Bethany Bog (Proctor pers. obs.). Since the 1960s, the species has increased as a nesting species in scattered localities statewide but concentrated in the north-western portion of the state.

*Noble S. Proctor*

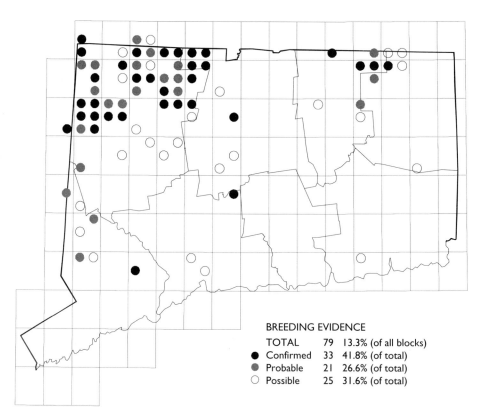

BREEDING EVIDENCE

| | TOTAL | 79 | 13.3% (of all blocks) |
|---|---|---|---|
| ● | Confirmed | 33 | 41.8% (of total) |
| ● | Probable | 21 | 26.6% (of total) |
| ○ | Possible | 25 | 31.6% (of total) |

## Dark-eyed Junco
### *Junco hyemalis*

The race of Dark-eyed Junco breeding in Connecticut is the Slate-colored Junco, the *hyemalis* group of sub-species. The Dark-eyed Junco is generally migratory and winters in the central and eastern states from New England and Illinois south to the Gulf of Mexico (Root 1988). Males predominate in the more northern wintering populations, and females predominate to the south as summarized by Root (1988). The Dark-eyed Junco tends to be uncommon and local as a breeder in Connecticut.

**Habitat**—As breeders, juncos in Connecticut are typically associated with mature conifers such as hemlock, often on slopes, with scattered rocks on the surface and a relatively sparse undergrowth of vegetation.

**Atlas results**—The species is clearly rather well established as a breeder in both the northwestern and northeastern hills. Scattered confirmations and other reports to the south indicate that breeding can occur elsewhere in the state, presumably in pockets of habitat resembling those found in the northern hills.

**Discussion**—This species has apparently extended its breeding range into Connecticut from the north during the twentieth century. Sage et al. (1913) did not mention breeding within the state, although they noted a juvenile collected in July in New Haven. In apparently the earliest report of nesting juncos in the state, Brockway (1923) found four

young in a nest at Hadlyme. Kuerzi and Kuerzi (1934) reported the occurrence of the Dark-eyed Junco in summer in Litchfield County, but apparently knew of no direct evidence of breeding. In a fairly detailed report on summer birds at Union in the northeastern highlands, Taber (1951) did not mention the Dark-eyed Junco; however, the fifth edition of the AOU Check-list listed Union,

and, more rarely, Hadlyme as the then known eastern and southern limits for breeding in the state (AOU 1957).

Because in the latter part of the nineteenth and early twentieth centuries coverage of much of the state, particularly the more northern parts, was apparently sparse, relatively little is known about the timing and sequence of establishment of the junco as a breeder in the

state. Presumably the invasion of this species was related to the regrowth of forests. This idea leads to the speculation that the species might have been present as a breeder in colonial times and then eliminated by deforestation on favorable sites, but there is presently no obvious way of testing this speculation.

*George A. Clark, Jr.*

## Bobolink
*Dolichonyx oryzivorus*

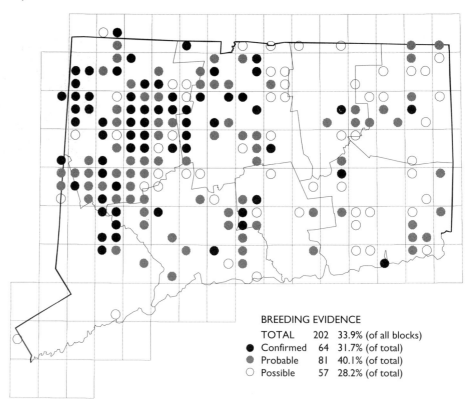

BREEDING EVIDENCE

| | TOTAL | 202 | 33.9% (of all blocks) |
|---|---|---|---|
| ● | Confirmed | 64 | 31.7% (of total) |
| ◉ | Probable | 81 | 40.1% (of total) |
| ○ | Possible | 57 | 28.2% (of total) |

The Bobolink is a transequatorial migrant that navigates by using a magnetic compass and visual cues such as stars (Beason 1987, 1989). It is an uncommon breeder in Connecticut, although it can be locally common (Zeranski and Baptist 1990). Bobolinks have been increasing in Ontario and the Maritimes (Robbins et al. 1986), and the bulk of fall migrants in Connecticut may be from such areas. They winter primarily in northern Argentina and migrate mainly east of the Andes (AOU 1983).

The Bobolink is one of only a few species shown to lay a clutch of multiple paternity, the female copulating with more than one male (Gavin and Bollinger 1985). At the same time, the species is polygynous, a male mating with more than one female (Bent 1958). Females occasionally have helpers at the nest (Beason and Trout 1984).

**Habitat**—Bobolinks generally require wet or luxuriant, as opposed to dry, meadows for breeding. The nest is usually placed on the ground in a dense clump of thin leafed grass (Bent 1958; Wiens 1969). Several pairs may nest in the same field. In fall, Bobolinks frequent fields with ripening corn and weedy fields with grasses, amaranths, pigweed, and goosefoot.

**Atlas results**—Nearly all the confirmed breeding reports are from the northwestern region of the state. The Bobolink does breed in the northeastern hills more heavily than is suggested by the block counts, which reflect, in part, the greater coverage given western Connecticut during the atlas. Compared to the distribution of the Eastern Meadowlark, another grassland icterine, one sees a similar pattern; however, the atlas results for the Bobolink show a stronger prevalence of confirmations in the western half of the state. There is also a notable lack of records from Fairfield County, which is probably correlated with human development in that region.

**Discussion**—The Bobolink was abundant in New England until the first half of the 1900s, when its numbers declined and it disappeared as a breeder in many areas. However, during the 1800s the species also spread westward with the cultivation of cereal crops across the Great Plains and into the Great Basin (Bent 1958). In Connecticut, the Bobolink was a common breeder through the late 1800s (Merriam 1877), but decreasing by the turn of the century, when it was still common in the northern part of the state but only nested around large salt marshes in the southern part, particular-

ly at Stratford and at Hammonasset Point (Sage et al. 1913). The species is no longer found as a regular breeder along the coast of Connecticut.

The decline of Bobolinks was due in part to the slaughter of thousands that descended on rice crops in the South and, in New England, its value for market as the delicious morsel called "Reed-bird" (Bent 1958). Locally, most of the decline as a breeder can probably be attributed to the steady reduction in agriculture and changes in haying practices. Hay was formerly harvested manually during July when most young had fledged; presently, hay is mechanically cut in June when chicks are not developed enough to have left the nest (Bent 1958). Abandoned agricultural land was transformed either by successional growth or human development.

Bobolinks express a high degree of breeding site fidelity, particularly if the

area is of high quality (Bollinger and Gavin 1989). This may facilitate conservation efforts if such habitat can be identified and managed to prevent succession as well as human development.

*George Gale*

381

## Red-winged Blackbird
*Agelaius phoeniceus*

Connecticut populations of this migratory breeder presumably winter primarily in the southeastern United States (Root 1988). The species is common as a breeding bird in Connecticut and is usually colonial in its nesting.

In recent decades this has been one of the most intensively studied passerine species in North America. It has been of interest to biologists studying basic questions in ecology and reproductive biology because the species is widespread and common, has relatively easily accessible nest sites, and is colonial in its breeding. Thus, relative to most other species breeding in Connecticut, it is possible to find large numbers of nests so samples of observations can be large enough to be evaluated statistically. Furthermore, because the species is at times an agricultural pest in feeding on crops, there is also an economic interest in this species (Dolbeer 1980).

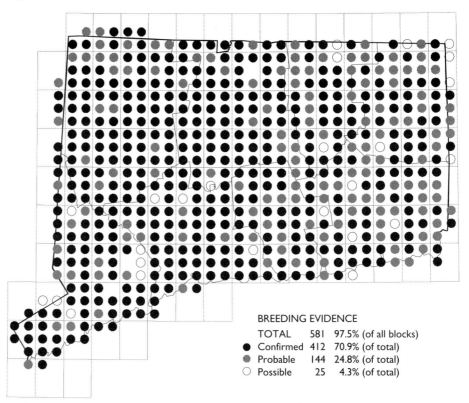

BREEDING EVIDENCE

| | | | |
|---|---|---|---|
| TOTAL | | 581 | 97.5% (of all blocks) |
| ● Confirmed | 412 | 70.9% (of total) |
| ● Probable | 144 | 24.8% (of total) |
| ○ Possible | 25 | 4.3% (of total) |

**Habitat**—Although open marshes with bushes or herbaceous vegetation, often including cattail, constitute the primary breeding habitat, the birds often nest in open grassy fields, usually near marshes. In a marsh, the nests are suspended a few feet up in the vegetation, whereas in fields, the nests are virtually at ground level. The birds generally do not nest in highly saline salt marshes.

Studies indicate that breeding Red-winged Blackbirds generally prefer marsh habitats over upland sites (Albers 1978, R. G. Clark and Weatherhead 1987).

**Atlas results**—The species was found in about 97% of blocks and confirmed in nearly 70%. The species was absent in few areas of the state, and that find-

ing might be due to minor deficiencies in coverage. The species tends to avoid breeding in heavily urbanized areas except where marshes are present.

**Discussion**—Linsley (1843), Merriam (1877), Sage et al. (1913), and Craig (1990) all indicated a common to abundant status for the species; the species status is unchanged today.

The variation of breeding habits for this species contrasts with a relative inflexibility of nesting habitat as exemplified by, for example, the Eastern Meadowlark, which nests only in fields. Relative to the meadowlark, the Red-winged Blackbird feeds in a greater variety of habitats. The meadowlark has specialization in its head muscles and beak shape especially favorable for foraging in fields (Beecher 1951). Thus for the Red-winged Blackbird, versatility in potential selection of sites for feeding appears to be one factor associated with the variety of sites in which Red-wings can nest.

*George A. Clark, Jr.*

## Eastern Meadowlark
### *Sturnella magna*

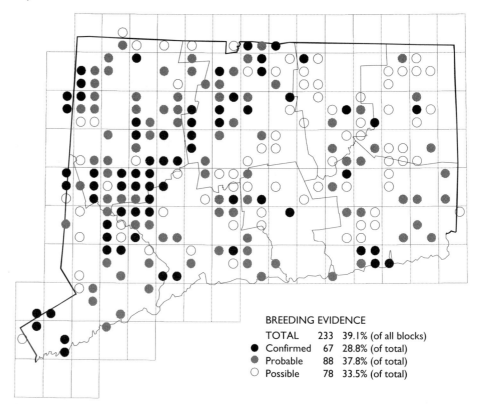

BREEDING EVIDENCE

| | TOTAL | 233 | 39.1% (of all blocks) |
|---|---|---|---|
| ● | Confirmed | 67 | 28.8% (of total) |
| ◐ | Probable | 88 | 37.8% (of total) |
| ○ | Possible | 78 | 33.5% (of total) |

The Eastern Meadowlark is a grassland specialist that was once an abundant breeding bird in Connecticut, but is now restricted to widely scattered sites with suitable habitat (Zeranski and Baptist 1990). Breeding Bird Surveys indicate that the Eastern Meadowlark population decreased at a rate of 10% per year between 1966 and 1989. Given this extremely rapid rate of decline, this species should receive special attention. In winter, the Eastern Meadowlark withdraws, for the most part, to the south of Connecticut. Depending on the severity of the winter, it can be uncommon in the state, especially in salt marshes and other open habitats along the coast (Zeranski and Baptist 1990). Of about six recognized subspecies, *S. m. magna* breeds in Connecticut (AOU 1957).

**Habitat**—The Eastern Meadowlark is typically found in large, grassy fields with elevated singing perches, such as fence posts or isolated trees (Wiens 1969). Compared to other species of grassland birds, the Eastern Meadowlark nests in a wider range of grass cover and vegetation density (Wiens 1969, Whitmore and Hall 1978). In Illinois and Michigan, the Eastern Meadowlark was most abundant and frequent in grass-dominated habitats such as hayfields and pastures, and it was less common in habitats dominated by broad-leaved forbs, such as old fields (Roseberry and Klimstra 1970, Granlund *in* Brewer et al. 1991); the species shows a similar preference in Connecticut. Nesting occurred in grassland with a dense mat of dead grass on the ground and little woody vegetation. Herkert (1991) detected

Eastern Meadowlarks in small, isolated patches of grassland (< 25 acres) during the breeding season, so apparently the Eastern Meadowlark does not require large tracts of habitat.

**Atlas results**—Even though the Eastern Meadowlark has become less common, it is still widely but somewhat thinly distributed in Connecticut in suitable habitat. The prevalence of confirmations in the western half of the state may reflect the greater concentration of observer effort in that region rather than the actual distribution of abundance of Eastern Meadowlarks in the state.

**Discussion**—This species thrived when much of Connecticut was farmland and pasture, but it declined as farming was abandoned in most areas in the state. Also, mowing of hayfields during the nesting season can cause heavy mortality of the eggs and young (Roseberry and Klimstra 1970), so the shift to earlier mowing during the summer has proba-

bly contributed to the decline of this species (Zeranski and Baptist 1990). Interestingly, at the northeastern extreme of the Eastern Meadowlark's range, the species has increased slightly and expanded its range. For example, meadowlarks were rarely recorded in Nova Scotia in the nineteenth century but are found regularly now, both in summer and winter (Tufts 1986). Extensive meadows remain in the low-lying coastal areas of this province.

The very similar appearing Western Meadowlark (*S. neglecta*) has bred within twenty miles of Connecticut in Dutchess County, New York (male Western mated to female Eastern; Bull 1974), and yet has never definitely been recorded in our state.

*Robert A. Askins*

## Common Grackle
*Quiscalus quiscula*

Common Grackles are fairly common as breeders in Connecticut. The species as a whole winters principally from the mid-Atlantic states south into Florida, and, to the west, in the south central and Gulf Coast states (AOU 1983, Root 1988). Relatively small numbers winter in Connecticut, particularly along the coast. Evidence from banding indicates that the grackles from one breeding area disperse widely during the winter months and that the birds often change their wintering locations from year to year (Dolbeer 1982). Connecticut lies in a zone where a varied array of intermediate individuals between rather distinctive end forms of the Common Grackle exists (see *Discussion*).

**Habitat**—This species frequently breeds in small colonies of a few pairs nesting well off the ground in conifers situated near water. In the breeding sea-

son, grackles commonly forage along the edges of streams, ponds, and lakes as well as on open fields and lawns. Nesting is most prevalent in agricultural, residential, and park-like areas. Grackles are fairly versatile in selection of nest sites, even cavities being used occasionally (Bent 1958). After breeding, in late summer and fall, the birds gather in flocks often numbering in the

hundreds or thousands, and these aggregations frequent farm fields, feed lots, woodlands, and other areas.

**Atlas results**—The species was detected in more than 98% of the blocks and confirmed as breeding in more than 87%. The Common Grackle thus ranks among the group of species having the most widespread distribution in the state.

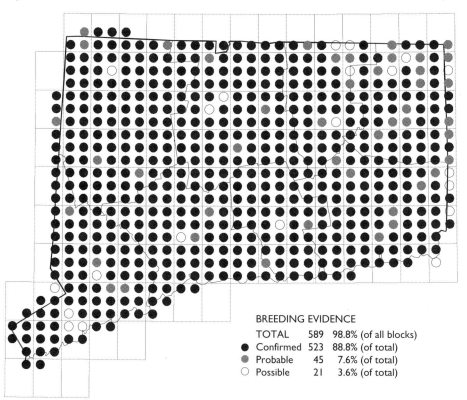

BREEDING EVIDENCE

| | TOTAL | 589 | 98.8% (of all blocks) |
|---|---|---|---|
| ● | Confirmed | 523 | 88.8% (of total) |
| ● | Probable | 45 | 7.6% (of total) |
| ○ | Possible | 21 | 3.6% (of total) |

**Discussion**—Linsley (1843), Merriam (1877), and Sage et al. (1913) considered the Common Grackle a common breeder. This species is highly favored by human activities and often nests in planted conifers. The widespread creation of artificial small ponds by people provides foraging sites for these birds along shorelines. Breeding grackles do not require large plots of lawn for foraging and can thus use many residential areas that are avoided by species such as meadowlarks. Grackles often visit concentrated sources of food at farms and feed lots.

The Common Grackle was regarded as two species until the 1950s—the Bronzed Grackle and the Florida Grackle, which included a subspecies called the Purple Grackle. The Bronzed Grackle, *Q. q. versicolor*, is the northern, highly migratory form with a uniformly brassy-bronze back and belly that breeds over most of the East. The Florida Grackle, *Q. q. quiscula*, breeds in the southeastern United States and has a bottle-green back and purple-blue belly. A continuous range of intermediate forms occurs along the line of contact from southern New England to southwestern Louisiana, including a broad region of the mid-Atlantic states

east of the Appalachians, where the truly purple grackles occur without the parent forms (Chapman 1892, Huntington 1952). Chapman named a series of intermediates occurring from Louisiana to Connecticut the subspecies *stonei*; however, this and the form *ridgwayi* have been shown to include a broad range of forms without defined limits (Huntington 1952). Huntington studied a colony of grackles in Hamden composed of interbreeding Bronzed and intermediate grackles. This appears to be the situation throughout the state, although a greater proportion of true Bronzed types apparently occurs in northern parts of the state (Sage et al. 1913). The "purple" grackles are usually seen in southern Connecticut.

It would be good to have a thorough study of the breeding ecology and behavior of this species. Its conspicuous displays, tendencies for colonial breeding, and apparent ranging over wide areas to obtain food while breeding, all make this a species of considerable interest. However, the difficulty of visiting nests on a regular basis and the usually small size of the breeding colonies pose potential problems for such a study.

*George A. Clark, Jr.*

## Brown-headed Cowbird
*Molothrus ater*

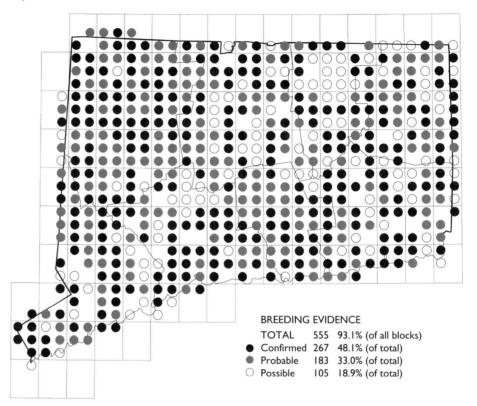

BREEDING EVIDENCE

| | TOTAL | 555 | 93.1% (of all blocks) |
|---|---|---|---|
| ● | Confirmed | 267 | 48.1% (of total) |
| ● | Probable | 183 | 33.0% (of total) |
| ○ | Possible | 105 | 18.9% (of total) |

This brood parasite is primarily a migratory breeder that arrives in early March and generally begins to withdraw southward from late September onward. Brown-headed Cowbirds wintering in Connecticut are typically localized around dairy farms and feedlots in mixed flocks with other blackbirds, and are generally more common in the southern part of the state. The Brown-headed Cowbird is not so specialized in its use of host species as some other well-known brood parasites, such as the Common Cuckoo (*Cuculus canorus*) in the Old World.

**Habitat**—The Brown-headed Cowbird occurs in woodland, forest edge, secondary growth, and grassland. Its broad range of habitat use is primarily a consequence of its reproductive habits as a brood parasite. In searching for the nests of appropriate host species in which to lay their eggs, cowbirds frequent habitats that are quite different from their normal feeding habitat of open fields and grasslands. Female cowbirds may penetrate many miles into forested areas to lay their eggs, and increasing fragmentation of solid blocks of forested habitats has allowed the cowbird greater access to forest interior species as hosts. Strips of forest created to connect larger woodlots may actually have allowed increased predation and parasitism of forest birds (Wilcove 1985, Ambuel and Temple 1983).

**Atlas results**—The results show that the cowbird is widespread in the state and is found in virtually all types of habitat.

**Discussion**—The status of the Brown-headed Cowbird in eastern North America before European colonization may never be known, but it was reported as common by Bartram as early as 1791 (Wilson 1808). It was probably most abundant, however, in the Great Plains where it was known to follow the Bison, hence its early name of "Buffalo Bird." Cowbirds were known from eastern North America early in the settlement of this continent, the type specimen being taken in South Carolina in the 1700s, but its status may not have been well understood because it was overlooked in the flocks of blackbirds with which it associated. Cowbirds are essentially a South American group, and the Brown-headed Cowbird probably invaded North America from that continent in prehistoric times (Friedmann 1929). The Brown-headed Cowbird flourished with the clearing of forests for agriculture and the introduction of livestock, both actions providing increased access to new host species and ample foraging habitat (Brittingham and Temple 1983, Mayfield 1965). Its range expansion appears to have been chiefly northward during this period (Phillips 1991). Although still numerous, its abundance has declined over recent decades in the Northeast, probably as a result of reforestation; in the central portions of the continent, however, the cowbird population continues to increase tremendously (Robbins et al. 1986).

The Brown-headed Cowbird has received renewed research interest

because brood parasitism is suggested to be among the causes for recent population declines of many North American migrant songbirds (Terborgh 1989, Brittingham and Temple 1983). As forests become increasingly fragmented, more forest edge and openings are created, allowing greatly increased parasitism of forest interior species. In addition, the overall increase in abundance coupled with forest fragmentation has brought cowbirds into contact with many species that are thought to have few, if any, behavioral defenses against brood parasitism. One study, however, showed no difference in rates of parasitism or abandonment of nests due to cowbirds between one species thought to have evolved in contact with cowbirds, the Blue-winged Warbler, and another that had not, the Golden-winged Warbler (Coker and Confer 1990). Research in a number of midwestern and mid-Atlantic states suggest intense levels of parasitism, with some populations of host species raising more cowbird young than young of their own. Whether this level of parasitism adversely affects those populations is still uncertain. In isolated instances, cowbirds have severely depressed the numbers of some species, especially where habitat is limited. The intensity and severity of brood parasitism among Connecticut songbirds needs additional study.

*Phillip F. Elliott*

389

## Orchard Oriole
*Icterus spurius*

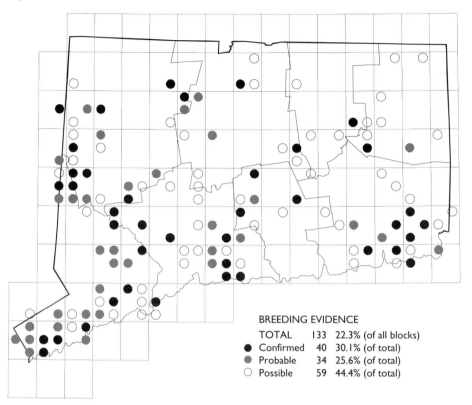

BREEDING EVIDENCE

| | TOTAL | 133 | 22.3% (of all blocks) |
|---|---|---|---|
| ● | Confirmed | 40 | 30.1% (of total) |
| ● | Probable | 34 | 25.6% (of total) |
| ○ | Possible | 59 | 44.4% (of total) |

The Orchard Oriole is an uncommon and local migratory breeder in Connecticut. The species as a whole winters mainly from Mexico south through Central America to northern South America. Orchard Orioles are reported to be far more numerous in winter in Guatemala and Honduras than in Costa Rica or Panama (Bent 1958).

**Habitat**—The species ordinarily nests in relatively mature deciduous trees with open areas, such as fields or lawns, and often ponds or other open water nearby. Habitats used by the Orchard Oriole appear to overlap those of the Northern Oriole (Bull 1974). However, the Northern Oriole often nests in sites where the density of trees is greater than in the areas ordinarily used by breeding Orchard Orioles.

**Atlas results**—Although the species was observed in more than 20% of the blocks, confirmation of breeding was obtained in less than 7% of all blocks. Breeding was more prevalent in the southern part of the state. The species tended to be absent as a breeder in the western and eastern highlands.

**Discussion**—Through the nineteenth century and into the early twentieth century the species was a common breeder along the Connecticut coast but was infrequent as a breeder in the interior of the state (Sage et al. 1913). Reports from coastline areas indicate that the species became less common there starting in the 1950s (Bull 1964, Mackenzie 1961). More recently in the

1970s and 1980s, there has been an increase in the numbers of birds breeding along the Connecticut coast (Askins 1990, Zeranski and Baptist 1990).

The Orchard Oriole is a species whose breeding population is mainly south of Connecticut. This oriole approaches the northern boundary of its range in the interior parts of the state. The maturation of Connecticut's forests and loss of agricultural lands during the twentieth century have probably worked against expansion of the numbers of this species. The time from the decrease in numbers reported in the 1950s to the rebound of the population in the 1970s corresponds roughly to the period of extensive use of pesticides in Connecticut and elsewhere in North America, but much study would be required to determine whether this correspondence in timing was anything more than a coincidence.

A detailed comparative study of the seemingly very similar habitats and behavior of the Orchard and Northern Orioles might help in clarifying our understanding of the ways in which similar species share the environment. Bent (1958) has commented on differences in nest structure, and the Northern Oriole tends to place its nest higher off the ground (Sage et al. 1913, Bent 1958).

*George A. Clark, Jr.*

391

## Northern Oriole
*Icterus galbula*

This striking bird and its familiar whistled calls are well-known to many people; it is a common migratory breeder in Connecticut. The Baltimore Oriole, subspecies *galbula*, breeding in eastern North America winters principally from Mexico south through Central America to northern South America and in the Greater Antilles east to the Virgin Islands (AOU 1983). Individual birds occasionally winter in Connecticut, but it is unknown whether these individuals also breed in the state.

**Habitat**—In Connecticut the species uses mature, typically deciduous, trees for nesting; there is ordinarily at least some open area such as roadway, lawn, or field near the nest tree. The species avoids the interior of continuous woodlands.

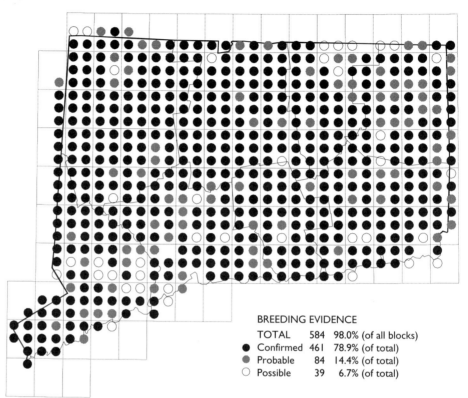

BREEDING EVIDENCE

| | TOTAL | 584 | 98.0% (of all blocks) |
|---|---|---|---|
| ● | Confirmed | 461 | 78.9% (of total) |
| ● | Probable | 84 | 14.4% (of total) |
| ○ | Possible | 39 | 6.7% (of total) |

**Atlas results**—The Northern Oriole was found in 98% of the blocks and confirmed as breeding in more than three-quarters of those blocks. It is indeed a well represented species statewide. Once the leaves drop in fall, oriole nests become much more conspicuous and provide a ready means of obtaining confirmations of breeding (Ellison *in* Laughlin and Kibbe 1985).

**Discussion**—Sage et al. (1913) considered the species to be an abundant breeder although they did note a decrease in the period 1900–1901 near New Haven. In subsequent decades the species has been less numerous, but nevertheless is regular in suitable habitat (Zeranski and Baptist 1990). During the twentieth century, transformation of much the Connecticut landscape from agricultural use to relatively mature woodlands may well have contributed to a decrease in this species. Also, elimination of many shade trees from towns and frequently a denser clustering of buildings in towns and cities has eliminated potential habitat for Northern Orioles. Because use of pesticides and high levels of air pollution can potentially affect arthropod populations, less food might be available for orioles in heavily urban settings, though the birds appear to be persisting in some suitably large parks surrounded by urban areas. In contrast to those human changes that would tend to reduce oriole populations, forest fragmentation in Connecticut has probably created additional habitat for this species.

Among insectivorous forest songbirds that breed in Connecticut and migrate to the New World tropics for winter, the largest body sizes are found in three species of woodland thrushes, the Scarlet Tanager, Rose-breasted Grosbeak, and the two species of orioles. All of these species show some variety in the habitats in which they forage and nest. Nevertheless, although quantitative comparisons have not been made in a single study, all these species, when in Connecticut and foraging on arthropods and nesting, appear to differ in their typical habitats. The forest thrushes tend to feed primarily on the ground or in the understory, often in the forest interior (Dilger 1956). The Rose-breasted Grosbeaks feed and nest off the ground but below the canopy in edge situations, whereas the Scarlet Tanagers feed and nest within the forest interior. The orioles, like the grosbeaks, use edge situations but differ in tending to feed and nest relatively higher in the trees. Differences between the two oriole species are discussed in the account for the Orchard Oriole. Thus these songbirds, sharing the features of relatively large size and the property of wintering in the tropics, appear to differ in foraging areas and nest sites while in Connecticut.

*George A. Clark, Jr.*

# Purple Finch
*Carpodacus purpureus*

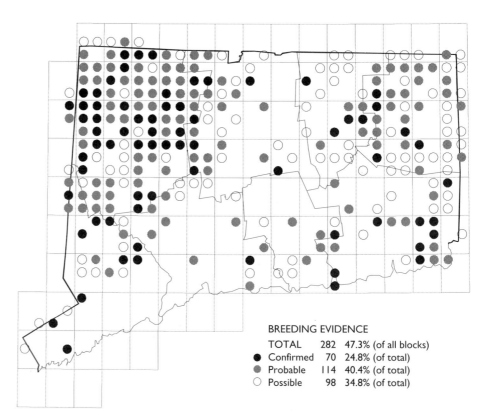

BREEDING EVIDENCE

| | TOTAL | 282 | 47.3% (of all blocks) |
|---|---|---|---|
| ● | Confirmed | 70 | 24.8% (of total) |
| ◉ | Probable | 114 | 40.4% (of total) |
| ○ | Possible | 98 | 34.8% (of total) |

A migratory breeder. In the eastern part of its range the species winters from southern Canada south into Florida and the Gulf Coast states (AOU 1983); this includes the subspecies *C. p. purpureus* which breeds in our state. The species is relatively erratic as a migrant, with the magnitude of the southward movement in the colder months presumed to be related to the quantity of the cone crop in the northern areas (Root 1988). The extent to which particular birds both breed and winter in Connecticut is unknown. As a breeder the species is generally uncommon and declining in the state (see Appendix 2).

**Habitat**—The Purple Finch ordinarily nests in mature conifers, either in woodlands or more open settings (Bent 1968). The nest is usually over 12 feet off the ground (Bent et al. 1968).

**Atlas results**—The Purple Finch was confirmed as a breeder over a surprisingly great portion of the state with the western highlands being the primary area. The species was evidently largely absent as a breeder in the more urbanized areas of the state. It is also notable that breeding tends to be more concentrated in the interior of the state rather than along the coast. The relative lack

of breeding in the coastal localities might be associated with a relative lack of conifers in those areas, but this idea needs testing with observations from the field.

**Discussion**—Sage et al. (1913) noted that the species was more common in summer around Litchfield than along the coast. Nevertheless, birds have

often been present in summer in locations near the coast (Mackenzie 1961) and at times breeding (Askins 1990).

Although in Massachusetts a decline in Purple Finch populations has been associated with the increase of the introduced House Sparrow (Bent et al. 1968), it does not seem to be clear that these changes were due to competition between the species. About a century later, the introduced House Finch, which is similar to the Purple Finch in size and general appearance, invaded Connecticut, and again the impacts, if any, on the Purple Finch are unclear. Purple and House Finches coexist in many parts of western North America, and it is difficult to assess the possible extent of competition. The nesting sites are different for the two species, and this would minimize one conceivably important aspect of any potential competition.

*George A. Clark, Jr.*

395

## House Finch
### *Carpodacus mexicanus*

This species, originally from western North America, was introduced into the eastern United States initially in the New York City area in the early 1940s (Bull 1964) and has now spread to cover much of eastern North America. The species can be found throughout the year in Connecticut, but banding evidence indicates at least a partial migration of birds in the eastern United States (Belthoff and Gauthreaux 1991). As a breeder in Connecticut the species is now common to abundant.

**Habitat**—In Connecticut the species commonly nests in the vicinity of buildings, such as in climbing vines on outer walls, in structural indentations, and in ornamental conifers planted as shrubs or hedges alongside buildings. For feeding the birds may travel many yards from the nesting areas and may

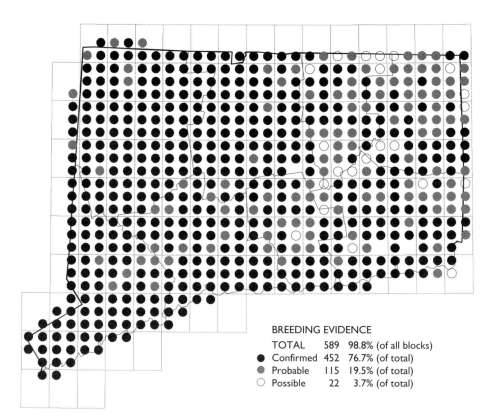

BREEDING EVIDENCE

TOTAL       589   98.8% (of all blocks)
● Confirmed  452   76.7% (of total)
● Probable   115   19.5% (of total)
○ Possible    22    3.7% (of total)

then be found in residential yards and agricultural fields at a distance from the buildings. The species generally avoids entering extensive stands of continuous woodland. With a preference for edge situations the species does well in both urban and suburban settings as well as many rural locations.

**Atlas results**—Located in more than 98% of all blocks, this species was confirmed as breeding in more than three-quarters. The species is clearly solidly established throughout the state. An exceptional nest location of House Finches found during the atlas survey was inside a suit of metal armor standing in front of a gift shop at a rural

intersection in northeastern Connecticut; the birds entered through the opening for the face in the helmet (pers. obs.).

**Discussion**—The first report of this species in Connecticut came from Fairfield County in 1951. The species gradually spread across the state (Zeranski and Baptist 1990) with the earliest record from the northeastern corner of the state coming in 1965 (Manter 1975). By the end of the 1970s the species was strongly established statewide (Zeranski and Baptist 1990).

In less than 30 years this species went from an unrecorded status to being one of the most frequently seen species statewide. This provides a dramatic illustration of the rapidity with which an introduced species with appropriate characteristics can spread. The increase in House Finches has been linked to a decrease in House Sparrows (Kricher 1983) with a competitive superiority of House Finches for obtaining nest sites in vines apparently being one aspect of the association between these two species.

*George A. Clark, Jr.*

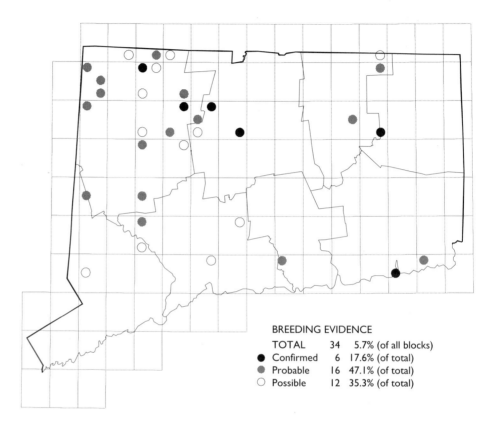

BREEDING EVIDENCE

| | TOTAL | 34 | 5.7% (of all blocks) |
|---|---|---|---|
| ● | Confirmed | 6 | 17.6% (of total) |
| ◉ | Probable | 16 | 47.1% (of total) |
| ○ | Possible | 12 | 35.3% (of total) |

# Pine Siskin
## *Carduelis pinus*

A breeder that is sporadically migratory. In the eastern part of its wintering range the species extends primarily from southern Canada south to Florida and the Gulf Coast (AOU 1983); the distribution of the wintering population varies greatly from year to year in this erratic migrant. Wintering flights are believed to occur as a consequence of a limited cone crop which would provide an insufficient food supply for the birds if they attempted to winter in the breeding area. As a breeder in Connecticut the species is rare.

**Habitat**—The species usually breeds in conifers and generally at a middle height (Palmer *in* Bent et al. 1968). Breeding may occur in woodlands or more open areas such as in parks or rural residential settings. An apparently typical nest found in a West Hartford park was located about 20 feet off the ground in a spruce.

**Atlas results**—During the field survey, confirmations of breeding were obtained from six widely scattered blocks, and birds were at least present in an additional 28 blocks. The northwestern and northeastern highlands appear to be the principal areas of occurrence of Pine Siskins in summer. The relatively early timing in spring of nesting by this species, before most major survey effort was underway for the atlas, might have made this species less likely to be confirmed as a breeder.

**Discussion**—Sage et al. (1913) did not mention any summer records from Connecticut, but records of breeding have subsequently been obtained from numerous localities, mainly in the more northern parts of the state (Zeranski and Baptist 1990).

The atlas findings indicate that the breeding activity and summer presence of the species have, at least in some years, been much more widespread than previously thought. Breeding may be particularly likely to follow a major flight in the preceding winter, but may also be facilitated by the increased maturity of stands of conifers in the latter part of the twentieth century (Peterson *in* Andrle and Carroll 1988). In New York state, 1985 was a year with marked breeding activity on the part of wintering birds (Peterson, loc. cit.), and thus the period of years sampled in the Connecticut atlas might also be unrepresentative for longer periods. It would be of interest to attempt to determine to what extent the breeding of the Pine Siskin continues at present and in the future in the state.

*George A. Clark, Jr.*

## American Goldfinch
### *Carduelis tristis*

An erratically migratory breeder. In the eastern North American part of its range, this species winters from southern Canada south to Florida and the Gulf states (AOU 1983). In Connecticut the numbers of wintering birds are quite variable from year to year. As a breeder the species is common in Connecticut. Unlike most other passerines that breed in Connecticut, the American Goldfinch feeds seeds to the young in the nest. These seeds do not mature until well into the summer, and the American Goldfinch nests later in the summer than do most species in the state; nests with eggs have been found in Connecticut from the beginning of July to the end of August (Sage et al. 1913).

**Habitat**—Nests are typically placed from 5 to 30 feet above the ground in shrubs or trees located in or near weedy

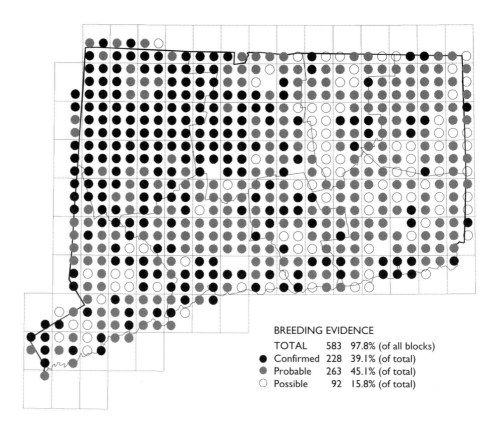

BREEDING EVIDENCE

| | TOTAL | 583 | 97.8% (of all blocks) |
|---|---|---|---|
| ● | Confirmed | 228 | 39.1% (of total) |
| ● | Probable | 263 | 45.1% (of total) |
| ○ | Possible | 92 | 15.8% (of total) |

fields, marshes, and residential areas (Middleton 1979, Sage et al. 1913, Tyler in Bent et al. 1968).

**Atlas results**—Although detected in over 97% of the blocks, the American Goldfinch was confirmed as breeding in only 38% of all blocks. Two factors might particularly influence this result. The American Goldfinch is a highly

distinctive species readily found by its distinctive and frequently given notes and thus is easily detected as present in an area. However, because American Goldfinches often nest so late in the summer, partly after the end of the period of intensive surveying for the atlas, there was an increased chance of missing breeding in blocks that were otherwise relatively well covered.

**Discussion**—Linsley (1843), Merriam (1877), and Sage et al. (1913) considered the species to be common to abundant in Connecticut.

A number of studies have found that in many areas the presence of thistles is important for the nesting of this species. Material from these plants is used in nest construction, and seeds are fed to the young (Tyler *in* Bent et al. 1968, Miller 1978). During the breeding season the need of these birds to move about widely to find food precludes territoriality of a usual kind, while the need to avoid nest predation precludes the placing of nests close together as in a colony (Miller 1978).

The erratic movements of nonbreeding American Goldfinches are presumably related to local and regional changes in the natural availability of the seeds that constitute the diet. At present we generally do not have enough information on the status of the seed crops to predict the direction and magnitude of the movements of the nonbreeding birds.

*George A. Clark, Jr.*

401

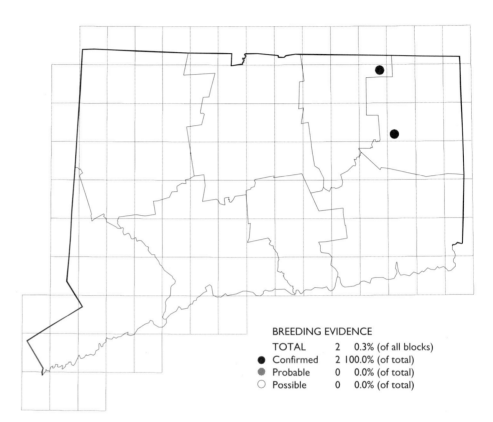

BREEDING EVIDENCE

| | | |
|---|---|---|
| TOTAL | 2 | 0.3% (of all blocks) |
| ● Confirmed | 2 | 100.0% (of total) |
| ◉ Probable | 0 | 0.0% (of total) |
| ○ Possible | 0 | 0.0% (of total) |

## Evening Grosbeak
### *Coccothraustes vespertinus*

An erratic migrant and wintering species in Connecticut, first found breeding in the state during the atlas survey. Like many other cardueline finches, this species is erratic in its movements which in winter may extend as far south as the Gulf Coast (AOU 1983, Root 1988). As a breeder in Connecticut the species is rare and local. The common name is somewhat a misnomer for, in the winter months, this species commonly goes to roost in midday and can be difficult to locate during the afternoon hours (Speirs *in* Bent et al. 1968).

**Habitat**—Little has been recorded about the habitat of Evening Grosbeaks breeding in Connecticut. Records compiled by Speirs *in* Bent et al. (1968) indicate that nests may be placed from 12 to 55 feet off the ground in either deciduous or coniferous trees.

**Atlas results**—The first record of breeding in the state came from Chaplin in late May and early June of 1983 when a pair built a nest in an oak tree (D. Rosgen in *Audubon Afield*, summer 1983). The second record came in 1986 from Ashford (Varza and Rosgen 1987).

**Discussion**—The species began to invade the northeastern states from the midwest in the latter half of the nineteenth century; this invasion of the east has been attributed to human planting of box elders, a favored source of food for these grosbeaks (Speirs in Bent et al. 1968). The earliest recorded occurrence of the Evening Grosbeak in Connecticut came in 1890 (Sage et al.

1913). A major increase in records in Connecticut and nearby states came after 1940 (Griscom and Snyder 1955, Bull 1964).

Breeding of Evening Grosbeaks occurred in central Vermont as early as 1926 (Oatman *in* Laughlin and Kibbe 1985), but breeding was not confirmed for New York state until 1946 (Beehler 1978). As in the case of a number of other cardueline finch species, the erratic movements of the Evening Grosbeak are attributed to the seeking of adequate food sources. Probably the maturation of Connecticut trees during the twentieth century has been one factor facilitating the occasional breeding of the species in the state.

*George A. Clark, Jr.*

## House Sparrow
*Passer domesticus*

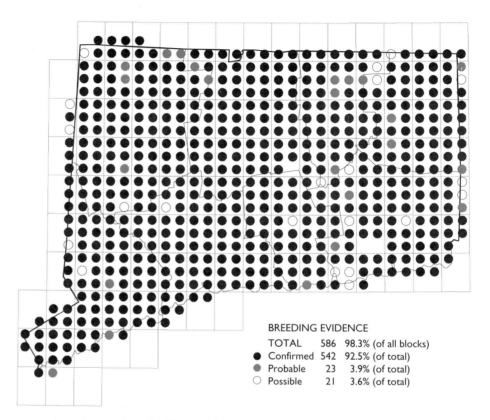

BREEDING EVIDENCE

| | TOTAL | 586 | 98.3% (of all blocks) |
|---|---|---|---|
| ● | Confirmed | 542 | 92.5% (of total) |
| ● | Probable | 23 | 3.9% (of total) |
| ○ | Possible | 21 | 3.6% (of total) |

An introduced and generally nonmigratory breeder, although migrating individuals have been reported from New Jersey (Broun 1972).

**Habitat**—In Connecticut this species is generally found in the vicinity of buildings and thus closely linked with human activities. The species is prevalent where food is available in cities and on farms, especially those with livestock. The species is often lacking in Connecticut suburban areas where there may be an insufficient supply of grain, seeds, or other foods. Nest sites are typically in cavities or other shelters, particularly inside buildings, in nest boxes, or vines on the sides of buildings. House Sparrows commonly outcompete species such as Tree Swallows or Eastern Bluebirds for control of nest boxes in cases in which the boxes are placed near buildings. On exceptional occasions in Connecticut, House Sparrows nest in a tree where they build a relatively large enclosed domed nest with a side entrance; such nests were observed in dense conifers at a now defunct game farm in the town of Willington (pers. obs.). Outdoor nests of a similar kind are also known from other parts of the range of this species (Summers-Smith 1963).

**Atlas results**—The House Sparrow was confirmed as breeding in more than 90% of all blocks and was present in nearly all blocks. However, as pointed out by Mackenzie (1961), House Sparrows are often highly local in their occurrence so that by a deliberate plan "it is entirely possible to spend a day in the field without seeing a single House Sparrow."

**Discussion**—Zeranski and Baptist (1990) have listed numerous introductions of this originally European species into the northeastern United States between 1853 and 1867. By the 1870s the species was widespread in cities and most smaller towns throughout Connecticut. In the early part of the twentieth century as horses were replaced by motor vehicles for transport and farming, House Sparrow populations declined generally in the eastern United States. More recently, an increase in the numbers of the introduced House Finches has been accompanied by a decrease in the populations of House Sparrows as determined from Christmas Counts (Kricher 1983).

Although House Sparrows tend to be regularly found at certain favored sites, it is clear that they readily disperse even over a number of miles to new sites. This potential for dispersal is well demonstrated by their successful colonization of remote sites such as isolated ranches in the western United States or in Australia. Thus it can be predicted that removal of House Sparrows from a site favorable for their nesting will be effective for only a relatively short time until replacements arrive.

*George A. Clark, Jr.*

405

# Possible Breeders

## and Miscellaneous Species

## Northern Pintail
*Anas acuta*

The Northern Pintail breeds throughout the Northern Hemisphere but is principally a migratory species in Connecticut. In the eastern portion of the wintering range in North America, the species occurs along the Atlantic coast from Massachusetts south as far as northern South America (AOU 1983; see also Root 1988). Some birds winter in Connecticut but the species is generally considered uncommon or rare in that season (Zeranski and Baptist 1990), and the numbers of wintering birds did not change appreciably between 1955 and 1989 (Merola and Chasko 1989).

No description of breeding habitat is available from Connecticut. R. S. Palmer (1976) reported that the species typically breeds in open country with scattered small bodies of water surrounded by grasslands or other open areas. Relative to other species of dabbling ducks in the genus *Anas*, this

species may nest far from water, even over a mile away in prairies of central North America (Duncan 1987).

The only evidence for breeding by this species in Connecticut originated during the atlas survey. Male Northern Pintails were observed apparently mated to hybrid female ducks (Mallard cross with unknown species, not American Black Duck) in 1983 and 1986 at West Hartford and Litchfield respectively. In the second case, the female was seen accompanied by seven young (Varza and Rosgen 1987). These reports do not constitute unambiguous evidence for breeding in the state. In

neither case were the males known to have bred with the hybrid female ducks.

Because in both cases the descriptive evidence suggested hybrid female ducks were possibly mated with male Northern Pintail, it would be highly desirable for observers to publish or place on file extensive documentation of additional cases of breeding by this species. The Northern Pintail seems likely to continue to be at most a sporadic breeder in the state because suitable habitat is very limited.

*George A. Clark, Jr.*

## Northern Shoveler
### *Anas clypeata*

This is one of several spatulate-billed species called shovelers, so named because of their peculiarly shaped bill. The Northern Shoveler is the only species of these ducks found in the Northern Hemisphere, where it breeds from Europe across Asia to interior central and western North America. It is only a sporadic breeder in eastern North America and is primarily a migrant in Connecticut, where it is also a rare winter and summer visitor. Most migrants are found along the coast, e.g., at Milford Point.

The Northern Shoveler is quite gregarious outside of the nesting season, and in areas where it is common, densely congregated flocks may form when the birds are feeding, these tightly grouped flocks moving as a whole over shallow ponds. The species is quite local in the Northeast with Plum Island, Massachusetts, and Jamaica Bay NWR, New York, being the nearest localities with significant numbers of migrants.

The Northern Shoveler is an abundant nester in the prairie pothole country of the northern Great Plains and west. Nests typically are built on the ground in grassy meadows near water (Palmer 1976).

During the atlas survey, a male and female of this species were observed together in Hamden from 30 April to 19 May 1983, and the male was observed alone as late as 24 June, but no evidence of breeding was obtained. Another summering bird was found in the Lordship marshes, Stratford. Despite such occasional sightings of birds in summer or late spring, no direct evidence of breeding has ever been obtained for this species in Connecticut (Merola and Chasko 1989). Breeding has occurred at least once in Vermont in the past and several times in New York, usually at wildlife refuges.

*Louis R. Bevier*

## Red-breasted Merganser
### *Mergus serrator*

This is a common migratory and predacious duck that is found around the Northern Hemisphere, mainly nesting in boreal areas. The Red-breasted Merganser occurs in large flocks on Long Island Sound in winter; it is otherwise a common migrant along the Connecticut coast and rare inland. It has never been known to nest in Connecticut.

Unlike the other mergansers that nest in Connecticut, this species is a ground nester. It is an irregular and rare nesting species at sandy estuaries and small islands around Long Island. Bull (1974) enumerates these breeding reports, including one from nearby Fisher's Island. Although a ground-nester, the species appears to require extensive cover at the nest site (Palmer 1976).

The atlas survey revealed two summering Red-breasted Mergansers along the coast, but there is no evidence for breeding. The occasional occurrence of individual birds during the summer is known in the coastal area of Connecticut (Zeranski and Baptist 1990). Although breeding was not found, it should be noted that Connecticut lies within the known breeding range for this species. In addition to those reports listed by Bull (1974), the species was found breeding during other atlas surveys—on Long Island, New York, Lake Champlain, and even a smaller lake in interior Vermont (Sibley *in* Andrle and Carroll 1988, Fichtel *in* Laughlin and Kibbe 1985). Comparison of abundance and distribution of this species with the older literature should be done with caution; this species was frequently confused with the Common Merganser, and many older statements completely reverse the actual status of the two species.

*Louis R. Bevier*

410

## Black Rail
### *Laterallus jamaicensis*

This is a secretive and locally occurring rarity of coastal salt marshes. At present, the Black Rail breeds regularly on the Atlantic coast as far north as southern coastal New Jersey, but at least formerly, it nested as far north as Connecticut. Apparently, the species has undergone a recent rapid decline over much of its range (Kerlinger and Wiedner 1991).

The Black Rail primarily occurs in the higher portions of coastal salt marsh with low mats of salt-meadow cord-grass, often in the vicinity of reeds, into which the rails may forage. There are at least two reports of this species from freshwater marshes dominated by river bulrush inland along the Connecticut River. South of the state, Black Rails are only known to nest in areas of *Spartina* (cord-grass) within coastal salt marsh.

The only report during the atlas was of a single bird heard calling at Barn Island, Stonington, in June 1985; this individual called for one week and then fell silent (J. Lee *fide* D. Rosgen).

The only credible reports of nesting in the state were made by J. N. Clark, who found six nests over a period of years beginning in July 1876 near the mouth of the Connecticut River (Clark 1897). One nest contained ten eggs on 13 July 1876 in "Saybrook," and another nest held nine eggs on 13 June 1884 at Great Island (Clark 1884). Merriam (1877) describes the eggs he examined from the first nest but gives the date of that nest as 10 July, apparently in error. Apart from Clark's finds, there are about twenty other reports spanning the years 1893 to 1991 and falling between the dates 18 May and 6 October. About eight of these reports, from late spring into summer or autumn, are concentrated

## Black Rail, *continued*

in the complex of marshes at the mouth of the Housatonic River, both the Great Meadows marshes in Stratford and the Milford Point/Nell's Island marshes in Milford. Continued investigation in this area might provide evidence of nesting, especially in light of the occurrences there in 1990 and 1991. Other coastal marshes where the Black Rail has been found include: Quinnipiac, Guilford, Hammonasset Beach State Park, and Barn Island. Some birds reportedly were collected at the sites above, but to date, the whereabouts of the specimens and eggs are unknown and presumed lost with the private collections in which they were held.

The two interior records come from the town of Cromwell at Dead Man's Swamp (captured and photographed, 25 June–July 1980; Proctor 1981) and Cromwell Meadows (summer 1987; Craig 1990). Kerlinger and Wiedner (1991) have suggested that the Black Rail is a somewhat nomadic breeder, at least on the mid-Atlantic coast; hence, these interior reports from Connecticut may have involved prospecting individuals that had wandered away from coastal marshes. There are only two other reports from interior freshwater marshes in the Northeast—both during migration at Troy Meadows and at Assunpink Wildlife Management Area in north-

ern New Jersey (Leck 1984). The species regularly occupies such habitats in western North America. Interestingly, the first report of the species in New England (a questionable record) was from an inland, freshwater marsh at Hazardville, Enfield, Connecticut (Baird et al. 1884). Those authors credit J. H. Batty as having shot two birds with young in June "several years ago." Merriam (1877) apparently misspelled the locality as "Hazenville." The validity of this report is suspect and has been questioned by Bull (1964).

*Noble S. Proctor*

## Monk Parakeet
*Myiopsitta monachus*

Although not reported by atlas participants or entered into the atlas database, this species almost certainly nested throughout the atlas period. This resident of temperate eastern South America was introduced into the United States through escapes and releases in the late 1960s. By 1972, the Monk Parakeet was established in New York, southern New England, and at scattered localities in the middle Atlantic states (Long 1981). Because this small parrot was considered an agricultural pest, an eradication program was initiated in Connecticut and continued until at least 1976; however, through conversations with residents at one nest site in Bridgeport, it was determined that the Monk Parakeet had continued to breed in the state over this period to the present (Olivieri and Pearson 1992).

The Monk Parakeet is a highly gregarious species. It is unusual among the parrots because it builds stick nests and may form colonies. Colonial nest may become quite large and house several pairs, each with its own nest compartment within the larger structure. The nest masses may be used for several years. In Connecticut, these nests have been constructed primarily in conifers, but other trees and even telephone poles may be used (Olivieri and Pearson 1992). Between ten and fifteen nest sites exist in Connecticut from Norwalk to Branford. Although current localities are all near the coast, the species at one time nested inland as far as Vernon. Outside Connecticut, at least two current nesting localities are known in Rhode Island at Warwick and Providence (Olivieri and Pearson 1992).

The Connecticut birds have been observed feeding on a variety of foods including: crab apples, wild cherries, bird seed mixes, grass, and leaf buds of birch, ash, and maple. The species is partly sustained in the state by supplementary food sources, such as bird feeders. Although this species is known to damage cereal crops in South America (Long 1981), no instances of crop damage are documented in Connecticut, in part due to the small area remaining in cultivation in the state. Predators of this species appear to be few in Connecticut. In one instance, a pair of Great Horned Owls nested on top of the large Monk Parakeet nest! The effect on native birds and vegetation requires further study in Connecticut.

*Louis R. Bevier*

413

## Chuck-will's-widow
*Caprimulgus carolinus*

This is a migratory breeder in the southeast United States, wintering along the Gulf Coast south through Middle America rarely to northern South America. Its breeding range has been spreading gradually northward over the past several decades, and since the mid-1970s it has bred in small numbers with some regularity on Long Island, New York (Meade *in* Andrle and Carroll 1988). Likewise, it has occurred regularly in West Virginia only since 1974 (Hall 1983), but has been fairly common but local in southern New Jersey since the 1930s (Bull 1974, Leck 1984). Occurrences in Connecticut have increased since the mid-1960s, most being found in late spring and early summer primarily near the coast (Zeranski and Baptist 1990).

Birds on Long Island nest in dune shrubland or pine barrens (Meade *in* Andrle and Carroll 1988). Over most of its breeding range, the species nests on the ground in oak and pine woodland. It prefers areas of drier woodland adjacent to openings or fields.

During the atlas, this species was detected at three localities along the Connecticut coast. These were calling birds found in appropriate habitat where they remained for a week or more in early summer. Although the spread of this species appears to have stalled with its establishment on Long Island, the Chuck-will's-widow might eventually breed in Connecticut if the northward range expansion continues. Besides its distinctive, loud calls, this species is distinguished from the Whip-poor-will by its larger size, warmer buff underparts and chin, and, in males, white only on the inner webs of the outer tail feathers. In the hand, lateral filaments on the bristles surrounding the mouth are diagnostic for both sexes of this species from all other North and Middle American goatsuckers. Reports of this species in Connecticut still require careful documentation.

*Louis R. Bevier*

414

## White-winged Crossbill
### *Loxia leucoptera*

*This species is not included in the final totals, and the the record is not accepted.* An intriguing but unconfirmed single observer report exists for the atlas. The descriptive evidence (not submitted in writing) for this sight report is intriguing, however, and mentioned in this section for the sake of completeness.

This slender billed relative of the Red Crossbill (*L. curvirostra*) has a circumpolar distribution in boreal conifers except for an isolated population in the mountains on the Caribbean island of Hispaniola in the countries of Haiti and the Dominican Republic. Among North American breeding species, the situation provides an extreme example of a north-south disjunction in breeding range. An occasional irruptive migratory species, the usual breeding range is far to the north of Connecticut, where these crossbills typically occur as erratic migrants or wintering birds (AOU

1983, Root 1988). Not only are the movements of this species erratic, but it may breed at virtually any season including winter (Taber *in* Bent 1968). Both migrations and breeding appear to be determined by the size of the cone crop in an area, with birds moving into areas with relatively good cone crops.

In Connecticut, a pair and their three fledged young were reported by Jim Lafley in Pachaug Forest, Voluntown, 19 June 1986 (Varza and Rosgen 1987).

The Voluntown area contains substantial tracts of conifers and thus provides the kind of conditions that would likely facilitate the breeding of White-winged Crossbills. However, this would represent an extraordinary extralimital breeding record for the species and thus has been treated with extreme scrutiny.

The species is typically associated with spruce, larch, or fir trees, and nests are placed anywhere from a few feet to 70 feet off the ground (Taber *in* Bent

415

## White-winged Crossbill, *continued*

1968). The weaker bill structure of this species is adapted to the softer and more brittle cones of these conifers.

There are no other reports of this species breeding in the state. Prior to this report, there was a major movement of White-winged Crossbills into New York state during winter of 1984–1985, and the first confirmation of breeding outside of the Adirondacks came in April 1985 (Peterson *in* Andrle and Carroll 1988). These birds apparently made use of planted European larch and Norway spruce. Also intriguing in association with the Connecticut report is a record of three adults seen in a West Bridgewater, Massachusetts, 8 June 1986 (Veit and Petersen 1993). The nearest breeding records to Connecticut are otherwise in northern Vermont. In the winter of 1985–1986, White-winged Crossbills were reported only in small numbers from Connecticut (Varza 1986), and the likelihood of birds remaining to nest seems low. In the future, observers who find these crossbills remaining for a period of weeks in one area in Connecticut should be on the lookout for the possibility of breeding.

*Louis R. Bevier*

# About the Contributing Authors

**Robert A. Askins** has conducted extensive research on birds in Connecticut and is on the faculty at Connecticut College where he currently chairs the Department of Zoology. His research on forest bird communities and population changes have resulted in major contributions to ornithology.

**Robert I. Bertin** is on the faculty at the College of the Holy Cross in Worcester, Massachusetts. As a part of his program for the M.S. degree at the University of Connecticut, he studied the habitats of the Wood Thrush and Veery in the state.

**Louis R. Bevier** is Secretary of the Connecticut Ornithological Association's Rare Records Committee.

**Anthony H. Bledsoe**, now at the University of Pittsburgh, studied Connecticut birds extensively while completing his doctoral studies at Yale University and subsequently while teaching at Wesleyan University.

**Winifred B. Burkett**, now in Texas, is a past Secretary of the Connecticut Ornithological Association and was for a number of years one of the most active bird banders in Connecticut.

**Elizabeth Bushnell**, now a graduate student at the University of Rhode Island, studied Mute Swans as a part of her undergraduate honors program at the University of Connecticut.

**Marshal T. Case** has watched birds in Connecticut for a number of years and is a past Vice President of the National Audubon Society.

**George A. Clark, Jr.** is on the faculty of the University of Connecticut and is a past President of the Northeastern Bird Banding Association.

**Robert K. Colwell**, on the faculty at the University of Connecticut, has conducted field research on numerous species of hummingbirds as a part of ecological investigations throughout the Americas.

**Michael R. Conover**, now on the faculty at Utah State University, was for a number of years a wildlife biologist at the Connecticut Agricultural Experiment Station in New Haven.

**Arnold Devine** has studied birds, especially owls, in Connecticut for a number of years and has been a member of the Connecticut Rare Records Committee. He received his M.S. in biology at Southern Connecticut State University and currently works for the Connecticut Department of Environmental Protection. He and Dwight Smith have written a bird finding guide to Connecticut (in preparation).

**Michael DiGiorgio** is a graphic design artist for a major publishing firm in Connecticut. His paintings and drawings of birds are based on extensive notes and sketches made while watching birds in the field. His illustrations have appeared in numerous magazines and journals; he was also an artist for *The Audubon Society Master Guide to Birding*.

**Phillip F. Elliott** of the faculty at Eastern Connecticut State University conducted extensive research on Brown-headed Cowbirds as a part of his Ph.D. program at Kansas State University and has subsequently been involved in ornithological research in Connecticut.

**Walter G. Ellison**, author of *A Guide to Bird Finding in Vermont*, studied the ecology and behavior of the Blue-gray Gnatcatcher as a part of his M.S. program at the University of Connecticut and currently is pursuing a Ph.D. at New York State University with the focus of his research on the "Bicknell's" Gray-cheeked Thrush.

**George Gale** studied prehistoric human exploitation of birds in the Aleutian Islands as a part of his M.S. program at the University of Connecticut, where he is now studying the Worm-eating Warbler as a part of his Ph.D. program. He has studied birds in Connecticut for a number of years.

**Donald A. Hopkins** has been a leader in organizing and conducting detailed investigations of Bald Eagles in Connecticut.

**Gordon Loery**, of the White Memorial Foundation in Litchfield, has been one of the most active bird banders in Connecticut and a leader in the study of the demographics of chickadee populations.

**Donald E. McIvor** is a student at Utah State University working with Michael Conover.

**Leslie J. Mehrhoff** of the Connecticut Department of Environmental Protection has been heavily involved in the establishment of the Natural Diversity Data Base, which provides a means of determining the location of critical habitats.

**Paul R. Merola** is a waterfowl biologist with the Connecticut Department of Environmental Protection and has been a leader in the program to track the movements of Canada Geese in the state.

**Kenneth E. Petit** has studied birds as an assistant in the Hubbard Brook research project in New Hampshire and is now a graduate student at Southern Connecticut State University.

**Alan F. Poole** is now based at the Philadelphia Academy of Natural Sciences where he is editing the most extensive compilation yet undertaken on the biology of the birds of North America; he has conducted major studies of Ospreys in New England and has published a book on that species.

**Noble S. Proctor** is on the faculty of Southern Connecticut State University; among the books he has published on birds is one on bird finding in Connecticut.

**Frederick Purnell, Jr.**, has studied birds in Connecticut for a number of years and is a past Vice Chairman of the Connecticut Rare Records Committee. He is chairman of the philosophy department at Queens College in New York City.

**Fred C. Sibley** is in the ornithology section at the Peabody Museum of Natural History of Yale University and has been a leader in bird banding in Connecticut and a long-term member of the Connecticut Rare Records Committee.

**Dwight G. Smith** is on the faculty of Southern Connecticut State University. He has spent many years studying hawks and owls in Connecticut and has authored numerous papers based on that research. He and Arnold Devine have written a bird finding guide to Connecticut (in preparation).

**Jeffrey A. Spendelow** is a biologist with the U.S. Fish and Wildlife Service at their Patuxent center in Laurel, Maryland. He has studied birds in Connecticut for many years, having received his doctorate for ornithological studies completed while at Yale University. He has been the leader for the Falkner Island Tern Project.

**Mark S. Szantyr** has participated extensively in bird banding in Connecticut. He is an avid photographer and an accomplished artist whose paintings, drawings, and prints are predominantly of birds. Mark is a past Secretary of the Connecticut Rare Records Committee.

**Christopher S. Wood** has studied birds in Connecticut for over twenty years and received his M.S. in biology at Southern Connecticut State University. He is director of the Nature Conservancy's Sunny Valley Preserve in New Milford and Bridgewater.

**George W. Zepko** has watched birds in Connecticut since 1955, studied the Barn Owl in the Middletown area since 1980, and is a founding member of Connecticut Ornithological Association. He is Manager of User Services at the Computing Center of Wesleyan University and has worked with computers since 1959.

# Appendices

# Appendix 1

## BLOCK TOTALS FOR BIRD SPECIES

This appendix lists the species reported during the atlas. The number of blocks for each category of breeding status and the total number of blocks for each species is listed. Designations under the Connecticut Endangered Species Act (Chapter 495 of the General Statutes) as listed in 1992 are indicated as follows: Endangered (E), Threatened (T), and Species of Special Concern (SC). The names and sequence of species follow the AOU Check-list (AOU 1983).

| Species | Possible | Probable | Confirmed | Total | Species | Possible | Probable | Confirmed | Total |
|---|---|---|---|---|---|---|---|---|---|
| Common Loon (SC) | 7 | 3 | 0 | 10 | Mallard | 53 | 109 | 265 | 427 |
| Pied-billed Grebe (E) | 17 | 5 | 2 | 24 | Northern Pintail | 4 | 0 | 0 | 4 |
| Double-crested Cormorant | 29 | 5 | 6 | 40 | Blue-winged Teal | 6 | 4 | 3 | 13 |
| American Bittern (E) | 20 | 13 | 1 | 34 | Northern Shoveler | 1 | 1 | 0 | 2 |
| Least Bittern (T) | 9 | 4 | 6 | 19 | Gadwall | 4 | 7 | 6 | 17 |
| Great Blue Heron (SC) | 98 | 37 | 19 | 154 | Hooded Merganser | 15 | 12 | 16 | 43 |
| Great Egret (T) | 8 | 0 | 3 | 11 | Common Merganser | 7 | 11 | 15 | 33 |
| Snowy Egret (T) | 15 | 6 | 3 | 24 | Red-breasted Merganser | 2 | 0 | 0 | 2 |
| Little Blue Heron (SC) | 2 | 1 | 2 | 5 | Turkey Vulture | 176 | 110 | 15 | 301 |
| Tricolored Heron (SC) | 0 | 1 | 0 | 1 | Osprey (SC) | 13 | 3 | 14 | 30 |
| Cattle Egret (SC) | 1 | 0 | 1 | 2 | Bald Eagle (E) | 1 | 1 | 0 | 2 |
| Green Heron | 157 | 100 | 77 | 334 | Northern Harrier (E) | 9 | 5 | 0 | 14 |
| Black-crowned Night-Heron (SC) | 23 | 19 | 14 | 56 | Sharp-shinned Hawk (T) | 26 | 7 | 5 | 38 |
| Yellow-crowned Night-Heron (SC) | 5 | 1 | 3 | 9 | Cooper's Hawk (T) | 21 | 5 | 8 | 34 |
| Glossy Ibis (SC) | 5 | 0 | 2 | 7 | Northern Goshawk | 29 | 15 | 38 | 82 |
| Mute Swan | 12 | 15 | 98 | 125 | Red-shouldered Hawk (SC) | 69 | 49 | 51 | 169 |
| Canada Goose | 44 | 51 | 282 | 377 | Broad-winged Hawk | 123 | 87 | 123 | 333 |
| Wood Duck | 24 | 42 | 258 | 324 | Red-tailed Hawk | 132 | 152 | 155 | 439 |
| Green-winged Teal | 2 | 2 | 0 | 4 | American Kestrel | 106 | 101 | 78 | 285 |
| American Black Duck | 47 | 59 | 65 | 171 | Ring-necked Pheasant | 66 | 44 | 63 | 173 |

| Species | Possible | Probable | Confirmed | Total |
|---|---|---|---|---|
| Ruffed Grouse | 76 | 79 | 185 | 340 |
| Wild Turkey | 93 | 30 | 147 | 270 |
| Northern Bobwhite | 86 | 56 | 24 | 166 |
| Black Rail (T) | 1 | 0 | 0 | 1 |
| Clapper Rail | 0 | 6 | 8 | 14 |
| King Rail (T) | 2 | 1 | 1 | 4 |
| Virginia Rail | 22 | 36 | 12 | 70 |
| Sora | 5 | 13 | 2 | 20 |
| Common Moorhen (T) | 2 | 4 | 4 | 10 |
| Piping Plover (T) | 1 | 1 | 11 | 13 |
| Killdeer | 73 | 97 | 197 | 367 |
| American Oystercatcher (SC) | 2 | 2 | 5 | 9 |
| Willet (T) | 1 | 1 | 7 | 9 |
| Spotted Sandpiper | 84 | 78 | 40 | 202 |
| Upland Sandpiper (E) | 2 | 1 | 2 | 5 |
| Common Snipe | 8 | 4 | 0 | 12 |
| American Woodcock | 74 | 101 | 43 | 218 |
| Laughing Gull | 0 | 2 | 0 | 2 |
| Herring Gull | 19 | 3 | 12 | 34 |
| Great Black-backed Gull | 15 | 4 | 10 | 29 |
| Roseate Tern (E) | 1 | 1 | 3 | 5 |
| Common Tern (SC) | 8 | 0 | 18 | 26 |
| Least Tern (T) | 5 | 6 | 10 | 21 |
| Black Skimmer | 1 | 2 | 1 | 4 |
| Rock Dove | 86 | 120 | 237 | 443 |
| Mourning Dove | 21 | 180 | 390 | 591 |
| Black-billed Cuckoo | 117 | 59 | 31 | 207 |
| Yellow-billed Cuckoo | 107 | 60 | 20 | 187 |
| Barn Owl (T) | 5 | 6 | 6 | 17 |
| Eastern Screech-Owl | 57 | 76 | 65 | 198 |

| Species | Possible | Probable | Confirmed | Total |
|---|---|---|---|---|
| Great Horned Owl | 76 | 90 | 104 | 270 |
| Barred Owl | 69 | 82 | 56 | 207 |
| Long-eared Owl (E) | 1 | 0 | 1 | 2 |
| Northern Saw-whet Owl (SC) | 7 | 8 | 3 | 18 |
| Common Nighthawk (SC) | 40 | 18 | 7 | 65 |
| Chuck-will's-widow | 3 | 0 | 0 | 3 |
| Whip-poor-will (SC) | 32 | 62 | 5 | 99 |
| Chimney Swift | 116 | 254 | 137 | 507 |
| Ruby-throated Hummingbird | 130 | 72 | 50 | 252 |
| Belted Kingfisher | 123 | 100 | 159 | 382 |
| Red-headed Woodpecker (E) | 13 | 4 | 2 | 19 |
| Red-bellied Woodpecker | 70 | 47 | 58 | 175 |
| Yellow-bellied Sapsucker | 31 | 22 | 38 | 91 |
| Downy Woodpecker | 106 | 197 | 280 | 583 |
| Hairy Woodpecker | 116 | 170 | 171 | 457 |
| Northern Flicker | 58 | 203 | 329 | 590 |
| Pileated Woodpecker | 88 | 105 | 45 | 238 |
| Olive-sided Flycatcher (SC) | 4 | 0 | 1 | 5 |
| Eastern Wood-Pewee | 144 | 231 | 132 | 507 |
| Acadian Flycatcher | 29 | 13 | 19 | 61 |
| Alder Flycatcher | 27 | 22 | 12 | 61 |
| Willow Flycatcher | 52 | 53 | 33 | 138 |
| Least Flycatcher | 108 | 126 | 59 | 293 |
| Eastern Phoebe | 69 | 59 | 419 | 547 |
| Great Crested Flycatcher | 154 | 199 | 128 | 481 |
| Eastern Kingbird | 33 | 78 | 468 | 579 |
| Horned Lark (T) | 4 | 2 | 5 | 11 |
| Purple Martin (SC) | 14 | 6 | 39 | 59 |
| Tree Swallow | 126 | 88 | 292 | 506 |
| Northern Rough-winged Swallow | 56 | 61 | 114 | 231 |

| Species | Possible | Probable | Confirmed | Total | Species | Possible | Probable | Confirmed | Total |
|---|---|---|---|---|---|---|---|---|---|
| Bank Swallow | 59 | 40 | 121 | 220 | Solitary Vireo | 65 | 47 | 24 | 136 |
| Cliff Swallow | 7 | 6 | 34 | 47 | Yellow-throated Vireo | 127 | 159 | 83 | 369 |
| Barn Swallow | 29 | 60 | 492 | 581 | Warbling Vireo | 141 | 142 | 99 | 382 |
| Blue Jay | 13 | 102 | 475 | 590 | Red-eyed Vireo | 71 | 229 | 264 | 564 |
| American Crow | 26 | 100 | 465 | 591 | Blue-winged Warbler | 53 | 140 | 353 | 546 |
| Fish Crow | 23 | 9 | 19 | 51 | Golden-winged Warbler (SC) | 13 | 14 | 10 | 37 |
| Common Raven (SC) | 3 | 6 | 0 | 9 | *Brewster's Warbler* (hybrid) | 8 | 7 | 3 | 18 |
| Black-capped Chickadee | 9 | 80 | 502 | 591 | *Lawrence's Warbler* (hybrid) | 5 | 4 | 5 | 14 |
| Tufted Titmouse | 25 | 76 | 484 | 585 | Nashville Warbler | 27 | 20 | 8 | 55 |
| Red-breasted Nuthatch | 50 | 30 | 19 | 99 | Northern Parula (SC) | 8 | 6 | 0 | 14 |
| White-breasted Nuthatch | 121 | 202 | 216 | 539 | Yellow Warbler | 53 | 182 | 341 | 576 |
| Brown Creeper | 124 | 114 | 66 | 304 | Chestnut-sided Warbler | 106 | 135 | 132 | 373 |
| Carolina Wren | 57 | 69 | 57 | 183 | Magnolia Warbler | 19 | 21 | 8 | 48 |
| House Wren | 62 | 144 | 375 | 581 | Black-throated Blue Warbler | 44 | 38 | 30 | 112 |
| Winter Wren | 21 | 22 | 10 | 53 | Yellow-rumped Warbler | 69 | 44 | 26 | 139 |
| Marsh Wren | 16 | 24 | 15 | 55 | Black-throated Green Warbler | 83 | 61 | 42 | 186 |
| Golden-crowned Kinglet | 5 | 4 | 2 | 11 | Blackburnian Warbler | 49 | 34 | 19 | 102 |
| Blue-gray Gnatcatcher | 108 | 101 | 97 | 306 | Pine Warbler | 37 | 27 | 15 | 79 |
| Eastern Bluebird | 66 | 36 | 232 | 334 | Prairie Warbler | 133 | 154 | 93 | 380 |
| Veery | 118 | 231 | 168 | 517 | Cerulean Warbler | 19 | 11 | 9 | 39 |
| Swainson's Thrush | 6 | 3 | 0 | 9 | Black-and-white Warbler | 127 | 175 | 222 | 524 |
| Hermit Thrush | 42 | 102 | 36 | 180 | American Redstart | 106 | 184 | 192 | 482 |
| Wood Thrush | 75 | 246 | 245 | 566 | Prothonotary Warbler | 0 | 1 | 0 | 1 |
| American Robin | 0 | 1 | 592 | 593 | Worm-eating Warbler | 47 | 75 | 68 | 190 |
| Gray Catbird | 0 | 22 | 571 | 593 | Ovenbird | 79 | 197 | 244 | 520 |
| Northern Mockingbird | 31 | 98 | 433 | 562 | Northern Waterthrush | 66 | 65 | 21 | 152 |
| Brown Thrasher | 103 | 150 | 135 | 388 | Louisiana Waterthrush | 87 | 133 | 107 | 327 |
| Cedar Waxwing | 75 | 202 | 285 | 562 | Kentucky Warbler | 14 | 5 | 2 | 21 |
| European Starling | 12 | 14 | 561 | 587 | Common Yellowthroat | 22 | 177 | 388 | 587 |
| White-eyed Vireo | 68 | 65 | 56 | 189 | Hooded Warbler | 40 | 41 | 18 | 99 |

| Species | Possible | Probable | Confirmed | Total | Species | Possible | Probable | Confirmed | Total |
|---|---|---|---|---|---|---|---|---|---|
| Canada Warbler | 86 | 78 | 29 | 193 | White-throated Sparrow | 43 | 35 | 21 | 99 |
| Yellow-breasted Chat (E) | 9 | 7 | 2 | 18 | Dark-eyed Junco | 25 | 21 | 33 | 79 |
| Scarlet Tanager | 108 | 226 | 187 | 521 | Bobolink | 57 | 81 | 64 | 202 |
| Northern Cardinal | 13 | 56 | 521 | 590 | Red-winged Blackbird | 25 | 144 | 412 | 581 |
| Rose-breasted Grosbeak | 108 | 175 | 254 | 537 | Eastern Meadowlark | 78 | 88 | 67 | 233 |
| Indigo Bunting | 148 | 162 | 115 | 425 | Common Grackle | 21 | 45 | 523 | 589 |
| Rufous-sided Towhee | 65 | 248 | 256 | 569 | Brown-headed Cowbird | 105 | 183 | 267 | 555 |
| Chipping Sparrow | 10 | 22 | 553 | 585 | Orchard Oriole | 59 | 34 | 40 | 133 |
| Field Sparrow | 103 | 143 | 170 | 416 | Northern Oriole | 39 | 84 | 461 | 584 |
| Vesper Sparrow (E) | 3 | 2 | 1 | 6 | Purple Finch | 98 | 114 | 70 | 282 |
| Savannah Sparrow (SC) | 30 | 25 | 13 | 68 | House Finch | 22 | 115 | 452 | 589 |
| Grasshopper Sparrow (E) | 4 | 2 | 2 | 8 | Pine Siskin | 12 | 16 | 6 | 34 |
| Sharp-tailed Sparrow (SC) | 4 | 4 | 11 | 19 | American Goldfinch | 92 | 263 | 228 | 583 |
| Seaside Sparrow (SC) | 1 | 5 | 5 | 11 | Evening Grosbeak | 0 | 0 | 2 | 2 |
| Song Sparrow | 7 | 79 | 509 | 595 | House Sparrow | 21 | 23 | 542 | 586 |
| Swamp Sparrow | 90 | 111 | 82 | 283 | | | | | |

# *Appendix 2*

## Breeding Bird Survey Population Trends

The following table lists the estimated population trends for selected species based on data collected from Breeding Bird Survey routes in Connecticut and southern New England between 1980 and 1989, the period of years encompassing the time of this atlas. The Southern New England region corresponds to stratum 12 on BBS maps. Although these strata maps have changed over the years, this region is the same as published in Robbins et al. (1986). It includes southeastern New York, Connecticut, Rhode Island, central and eastern Massachusetts, coastal New Hampshire, and southern coastal Maine. Excluded are Long Island, Cape Cod, and extreme northwestern Connecticut.

Values for **trends** are expressed as percent annual change. For example, the American Kestrel has declined at an annual rate of −6.1%.[†] The statistical significance of the trend is shown by asterisks, which indicate the degree of assurance, or probability, that the value differs from zero, or no change in population (*=p<.10, **=p<.05, ***=p<.01). The **average relative abundance** is the average number of birds detected on *all* routes used in the analysis period for each region. The **number of routes** sampled in each region is listed in the third column.

[†] formula for *overall* decline 1980–1989 is: $([(\%\text{trend}/100)+1]^9-1)(100)$

*These data should not be over-interpreted.* Estimates based on fewer than 10 routes are based on too few routes to estimate the variance of the trend. They should not be used. Also, while the Breeding Bird Surveys are an important index of bird populations, those using these data should be aware of several considerations. In addition to the biases listed by Robbins et al. (1986), one should be aware that the routes follow roads, which means that the sampling points lie along routes more likely to change over time, usually in the direction of development. Furthermore, there is a strong bias toward sampling easily detected and widespread species; rare and local, nocturnal, colonial nesting birds, and waterfowl are poorly sampled. Last, the statistical methods used to calculate the population trends have some limitations (*see* Geissler and Sauer 1990, James et al. 1990). These values are presented as one gauge of bird populations in Connecticut during the atlas.

This information was furnished by Sam Droege at the USFWS Office of Migratory Bird Management. I thank Robert Askins for providing the files from which these data were summarized. In addition, my gratitude is extended to all the volunteer participants who run Breeding Bird Surveys.

| Species | SOUTHERN NEW ENGLAND | | | CONNECTICUT | | |
|---|---|---|---|---|---|---|
| | trend | avg. relative abundance | no. of routes | trend | avg. relative abundance | no. of routes |
| Common Loon | +2.1*** | 0.08 | 3 | — | — | — |
| Double-crested Cormorant | +12.0** | 1.08 | 12 | +9.8 | 0.61 | 5 |
| American Bittern | +5.6*** | 0.03 | 6 | — | — | — |
| Great Blue Heron | +7.4*** | 0.33 | 21 | +6.5 | 0.15 | 7 |
| Green Heron | +1.4 | 0.40 | 29 | +0.7 | 0.31 | 13 |
| Black-cr. Night-Heron | −4.7** | 0.11 | 8 | −3.0 | 0.03 | 3 |
| Mute Swan | +3.6 | 0.81 | 8 | −9.9* | 0.15 | 5 |
| Canada Goose | +1.8 | 6.54 | 30 | −1.9 | 5.19 | 14 |
| Wood Duck | +7.3 | 0.32 | 19 | +7.9 | 0.40 | 7 |
| American Black Duck | −0.5 | 0.20 | 11 | −4.0 | 0.14 | 4 |
| Mallard | −0.3 | 2.30 | 35 | +1.8 | 2.36 | 16 |
| Turkey Vulture | +2.3 | 0.34 | 20 | +0.9 | 0.56 | 12 |
| Osprey | −1.6 | 0.04 | 5 | −1.5 | 0.02 | 3 |
| Cooper's Hawk | −0.6 | 0.04 | 6 | −1.0 | 0.04 | 5 |
| Northern Goshawk | +0.4 | 0.01 | 3 | +3.7*** | 0.01 | 2 |
| Red-shouldered Hawk | −1.5 | 0.03 | 8 | −1.4 | 0.04 | 7 |
| Broad-winged Hawk | −0.4 | 0.17 | 24 | −0.7 | 0.21 | 11 |
| Red-tailed Hawk | +1.9 | 0.31 | 25 | −0.5 | 0.40 | 13 |
| American Kestrel | −6.1*** | 0.33 | 24 | −4.3 | 0.21 | 9 |
| Ring-necked Pheasant | −5.4*** | 1.54 | 30 | −2.9* | 0.68 | 12 |
| Ruffed Grouse | −3.0* | 0.05 | 10 | −3.5* | 0.04 | 5 |
| Wild Turkey | +11.6*** | 0.09 | 4 | +11.7*** | 0.08 | 3 |
| Northern Bobwhite | −6.6 | 1.42 | 15 | −6.6 | 1.42 | 7 |
| Killdeer | +3.0 | 1.05 | 34 | +0.7 | 0.62 | 13 |
| Spotted Sandpiper | +2.9** | 0.11 | 12 | +2.1 | 0.15 | 8 |
| American Woodcock | −4.6*** | 0.07 | 6 | +5.9 | 0.08 | 4 |
| Ring-billed Gull | −4.1 | 0.24 | 10 | +2.7 | 0.07 | 4 |

| Species | SOUTHERN NEW ENGLAND | | | CONNECTICUT | | |
| | trend | avg. relative abundance | no. of routes | trend | avg. relative abundance | no. of routes |
|---|---|---|---|---|---|---|
| Herring Gull | −5.1 | 12.09 | 26 | −5.8 | 3.10 | 9 |
| Great Black-backed Gull | −3.5 | 0.82 | 10 | +5.7 | 0.09 | 2 |
| Rock Dove | +6.7* | 8.58 | 38 | +9.8* | 4.95 | 17 |
| Mourning Dove | +1.2 | 24.48 | 39 | −0.4 | 24.57 | 17 |
| Black-billed Cuckoo | −15.2*** | 0.87 | 34 | −15.7*** | 1.04 | 15 |
| Yellow-billed Cuckoo | −14.0*** | 0.66 | 31 | −14.8*** | 0.74 | 15 |
| Eastern Screech-Owl | −5.4*** | 0.07 | 4 | −2.2** | 0.02 | 3 |
| Great Horned Owl | +0.3 | 0.05 | 7 | −1.6 | 0.07 | 6 |
| Whip-poor-will | −8.6*** | 0.16 | 11 | −6.4* | 0.11 | 2 |
| Chimney Swift | +2.2 | 8.69 | 39 | +0.1 | 7.90 | 17 |
| Ruby-throated Hummingbird | −1.0 | 0.07 | 17 | −1.0 | 0.10 | 9 |
| Belted Kingfisher | −1.5 | 0.31 | 28 | −3.3 | 0.55 | 15 |
| Red-bellied Woodpecker | +12.1*** | 0.82 | 18 | +11.4*** | 0.78 | 14 |
| Yellow-bellied Flycatcher | −0.2 | 0.22 | 8 | 0.0 | 0.25 | 7 |
| Downy Woodpecker | +2.5 | 3.71 | 39 | +1.6 | 4.00 | 17 |
| Hairy Woodpecker | −4.3 | 0.91 | 37 | −4.6** | 0.79 | 17 |
| Northern Flicker | +2.3 | 5.23 | 39 | +0.4 | 5.76 | 17 |
| Pileated Woodpecker | +2.9 | 0.20 | 18 | +6.1 | 0.23 | 10 |
| Eastern Wood-Pewee | −1.0 | 3.95 | 39 | +0.7 | 3.73 | 17 |
| Acadian Flycatcher | +6.0 | 0.16 | 3 | +6.0 | 0.16 | 3 |
| Least Flycatcher | −3.3 | 1.35 | 29 | −3.6 | 1.83 | 15 |
| Eastern Phoebe | +5.5*** | 5.97 | 38 | +3.7 | 5.26 | 17 |
| Great Crested Flycatcher | −7.6*** | 2.68 | 39 | −8.6*** | 3.26 | 17 |
| Eastern Kingbird | −4.8*** | 6.68 | 39 | −4.5* | 4.13 | 17 |
| Purple Martin | +47.7*** | 0.49 | 5 | — | — | — |
| Tree Swallow | −1.4 | 5.01 | 36 | +6.1** | 3.15 | 15 |
| N. Rough-winged Swallow | +6.7 | 0.38 | 23 | +7.6 | 0.55 | 13 |

| Species | SOUTHERN NEW ENGLAND | | | CONNECTICUT | | |
|---|---|---|---|---|---|---|
| | trend | avg. relative abundance | no. of routes | trend | avg. relative abundance | no. of routes |
| Bank Swallow | −7.4 | 1.48 | 23 | −10.3 | 2.08 | 11 |
| Cliff Swallow | +2.7 | 0.33 | 8 | +9.8 | 0.34 | 2 |
| Barn Swallow | −0.7 | 10.04 | 39 | +1.3 | 9.48 | 17 |
| Blue Jay | −4.3*** | 24.83 | 39 | −5.8*** | 17.81 | 17 |
| American Crow | +3.8*** | 38.47 | 39 | +3.6*** | 36.73 | 17 |
| Fish Crow | −9.1 | 0.11 | 6 | −10.6 | 0.12 | 4 |
| Common Raven | −3.7*** | 0.09 | 2 | — | — | — |
| Black-capped Chickadee | −1.8 | 20.74 | 39 | −3.8* | 12.53 | 17 |
| Tufted Titmouse | +2.5** | 11.47 | 38 | +1.1 | 11.76 | 17 |
| Red-breasted Nuthatch | −5.6** | 0.32 | 21 | −5.0 | 0.16 | 6 |
| White-breasted Nuthatch | −1.5 | 3.86 | 38 | +0.1 | 3.36 | 17 |
| Brown Creeper | −7.0*** | 0.52 | 29 | −8.6** | 0.26 | 12 |
| Carolina Wren | +26.1*** | 1.01 | 13 | 27.6*** | 0.89 | 6 |
| House Wren | −1.8 | 11.59 | 39 | −3.2* | 12.26 | 17 |
| Winter Wren | +5.8 | 0.06 | 9 | +6.4 | 0.10 | 5 |
| Marsh Wren | +21.6*** | 0.44 | 7 | +17.3 | 0.76 | 3 |
| Blue-gray Gnatcatcher | +7.6** | 0.30 | 23 | +10.2*** | 0.68 | 15 |
| Eastern Bluebird | +6.8** | 0.30 | 22 | +7.7** | 0.55 | 15 |
| Veery | −4.3*** | 5.71 | 37 | −4.3*** | 8.06 | 17 |
| Hermit Thrush | +5.5*** | 0.47 | 20 | +4.0 | 0.23 | 7 |
| Wood Thrush | −2.5** | 13.50 | 39 | −2.3* | 15.07 | 17 |
| American Robin | +1.5** | 53.89 | 39 | +2.4** | 49.31 | 17 |
| Gray Catbird | −0.3 | 22.86 | 39 | 0.0 | 26.87 | 17 |
| Northern Mockingbird | +0.9 | 10.72 | 39 | +0.2 | 10.68 | 17 |
| Brown Thrasher | −11.2*** | 0.83 | 35 | −12.4*** | 0.79 | 15 |
| Cedar Waxwing | −2.5 | 7.94 | 36 | −3.0 | 4.11 | 15 |
| European Starling | −1.4 | 71.68 | 39 | −1.1 | 62.24 | 17 |

| Species | SOUTHERN NEW ENGLAND | | | CONNECTICUT | | |
|---|---|---|---|---|---|---|
| | trend | avg. relative abundance | no. of routes | trend | avg. relative abundance | no. of routes |
| White-eyed Vireo | +4.3 | 0.28 | 14 | +5.1 | 0.44 | 11 |
| Solitary Vireo | +0.9 | 0.30 | 20 | +7.1*** | 0.22 | 7 |
| Yellow-throated Vireo | −4.9 | 1.02 | 28 | −5.2 | 2.14 | 16 |
| Warbling Vireo | 0.0 | 1.79 | 32 | −2.9 | 2.28 | 14 |
| Red-eyed Vireo | −4.8*** | 16.47 | 39 | −2.2* | 14.55 | 17 |
| Blue-winged Warbler | −5.7*** | 3.20 | 33 | −8.2*** | 4.54 | 17 |
| Nashville Warbler | −4.4 | 0.27 | 14 | −1.1 | 0.02 | 3 |
| Northern Parula | +5.2 | 0.03 | 5 | 6.7 | 0.03 | 2 |
| Yellow Warbler | −1.9 | 9.96 | 39 | −3.3 | 11.79 | 17 |
| Chestnut-sided Warbler | −6.7** | 3.49 | 38 | −8.3** | 4.63 | 17 |
| Magnolia Warbler | −6.7*** | 0.08 | 7 | −8.0* | 0.08 | 3 |
| Black-thr. Blue Warbler | −1.0 | 0.12 | 12 | −0.8 | 0.25 | 8 |
| Yellow-rumped Warbler | +0.6 | 0.57 | 17 | −4.5 | 0.27 | 5 |
| Black-thr. Green Warbler | −1.4 | 0.52 | 25 | +0.8 | 0.25 | 9 |
| Blackburnian Warbler | −1.1 | 0.15 | 15 | +0.6 | 0.16 | 6 |
| Pine Warbler | +5.5 | 1.70 | 24 | +0.9 | 0.11 | 7 |
| Prairie Warbler | −1.8 | 1.57 | 34 | −4.8*** | 2.26 | 16 |
| Cerulean Warbler | +5.3*** | 0.02 | 3 | +8.0*** | 0.01 | 2 |
| Black-and-white Warbler | −3.4* | 3.21 | 38 | −4.0 | 3.34 | 17 |
| American Redstart | +0.5 | 3.21 | 38 | +1.1 | 5.17 | 17 |
| Worm-eating Warbler | +2.2 | 0.38 | 15 | +1.2 | 0.47 | 11 |
| Ovenbird | −1.2 | 11.07 | 38 | −1.6 | 10.49 | 17 |
| Northern Waterthrush | +7.0*** | 0.11 | 14 | +7.5*** | 0.17 | 7 |
| Louisiana Waterthrush | −1.8 | 0.56 | 22 | −5.4* | 0.77 | 14 |
| Common Yellowthroat | −3.5*** | 18.35 | 39 | −4.7*** | 14.97 | 17 |
| Hooded Warbler | +9.1** | 0.13 | 9 | +8.9* | 0.16 | 4 |
| Canada Warbler | −9.9** | 0.32 | 16 | −13.5 | 0.37 | 8 |

| Species | SOUTHERN NEW ENGLAND | | | CONNECTICUT | | |
|---|---|---|---|---|---|---|
| | trend | avg. relative abundance | no. of routes | trend | avg. relative abundance | no. of routes |
| Scarlet Tanager | −5.7*** | 4.48 | 38 | −7.4*** | 4.42 | 17 |
| Northern Cardinal | −1.4 | 13.54 | 39 | −2.9*** | 15.83 | 17 |
| Rose-breasted Grosbeak | −6.6*** | 3.71 | 38 | −6.4 | 4.45 | 17 |
| Indigo Bunting | −5.7** | 2.57 | 36 | −3.0 | 1.68 | 16 |
| Rufous-sided Towhee | −7.8*** | 7.51 | 39 | −8.1*** | 5.93 | 17 |
| Chipping Sparrow | +1.3 | 17.39 | 39 | +0.9 | 15.74 | 17 |
| Field Sparrow | −5.1** | 1.78 | 37 | −6.9** | 1.93 | 16 |
| Savannah Sparrow | −6.4 | 0.18 | 9 | −6.7*** | 0.02 | 3 |
| Song Sparrow | −2.5*** | 24.85 | 39 | −3.2*** | 26.35 | 17 |
| Swamp Sparrow | −1.7 | 1.10 | 29 | −1.1 | 1.03 | 13 |
| White-throated Sparrow | −6.0*** | 0.65 | 14 | −7.1 | 0.05 | 3 |
| Dark-eyed Junco | +9.8 | 0.04 | 3 | +10.7 | 0.04 | 2 |
| Bobolink | −5.5 | 3.32 | 27 | −7.2 | 1.42 | 12 |
| Red-winged Blackbird | −6.6*** | 29.69 | 39 | −7.3*** | 28.62 | 17 |
| Eastern Meadowlark | −11.4*** | 1.74 | 33 | −12.8*** | 1.25 | 15 |
| Common Grackle | +0.2 | 34.52 | 39 | −0.4 | 32.41 | 17 |
| Brown-headed Cowbird | −2.0 | 5.82 | 39 | −1.8 | 5.96 | 17 |
| Orchard Oriole | +4.5 | 0.12 | 14 | +4.8 | 0.12 | 8 |
| Baltimore Oriole | −4.9*** | 12.94 | 39 | −6.1*** | 13.02 | 17 |
| Purple Finch | −6.1*** | 0.90 | 32 | −6.6*** | 1.00 | 13 |
| House Finch | +15.1*** | 18.79 | 39 | +15.0*** | 18.94 | 17 |
| American Goldfinch | +5.0** | 6.23 | 39 | +6.3* | 5.34 | 17 |
| House Sparrow | +1.3 | 29.01 | 39 | +1.8 | 26.82 | 17 |

# Appendix 3

## Plants

English vernacular names and scientific names follow
*Preliminary Checklist of the Vascular Flora of Connecticut*
by Joseph J. Dowhan (1979).

*Acer*—maples
alder—*Alnus* spp.
algae, green—*Vaucheria* spp.
amaranth—*Amaranthus* spp.
arrow-wood—*Viburnum* spp.
Asiatic bittersweet—*Celastrus orbiculatus*
aspen, quaking—*Populus tremuloides*
bayberry—*Myrica pensylvanica*
beech, American—*Fagus grandifolia*
birch—*Betula* spp.
birch, black—*Betula lenta*
birch, gray—*Betula populifolia*
birch, white—*Betula papyrifera*
birch, yellow—*Betula lutea*
bittersweet, Asiatic—*Celastris orbiculatus*
blackberry—*Rubus* spp.
blueberry—*Vaccinium* spp.
box elder—*Acer negundo*
bulrush—*Scirpus* spp.
bulrush, river—*Scirpus fluviatilis*
buttonwood—(see sycamore)
canary-grass, reed—*Phalaris arundinacea*
*Carya*—hickories

*Castanea*—chestnuts
catbrier—*Smilax* spp.
cattail—*Typha* spp.
cattail, narrow-leaved—*Typha angustifolia*
cedar, red—*Juniperus virginiana*
chestnut, American—*Castanea dentata*
cord-grass—*Spartina* spp.
cord-grass, fresh-water—*Spartina pectinata*
cord-grass, salt-marsh—*Spartina alterniflora*
cord-grass, salt-meadow—*Spartina patens*
corn—*Zea mays*
cottonwood—*Populus deltoides*
eelgrass—*Zostera marina*
elm, American—*Ulmus* spp.
goosefoot—*Chenopodium* spp.
ground-pine—*Lycopodium* spp.
hemlock, eastern—*Tsuga canadensis*
hickory—*Carya* spp.
hickory, pignut—*Carya glabra*
honeysuckle—*Lonicera* spp.
honeysuckle, Japanese—*Lonicera japonica*
huckleberry—*Gaylussacia* spp.
ivy, poison—*Toxicodendron radicans*
larch—*Larix* spp.
larch, European—*Larix decidua*
laurel, mountain—*Kalmia latifolia*
lichens—*Usnea* spp.

maple—*Acer* spp.
maple, red—*Acer rubrum*
maple, silver—*Acer saccharinum*
maple, sugar—*Acer saccharum*
oak—*Quercus* spp.
oak, red—*Quercus rubra*
pigweed—*Chenopodium* spp.
pine, red—*Pinus resinosa*
pine, white—*Pinus strobus*
pondweed—*Potamogeton* spp.
poplar, balsam—*Populus balsamifera*
*Populus*—poplars, aspens, and cottonwoods
*Quercus*—oaks
reed, common—*Phragmites australis*
rice, wild—*Zizania aquatica*
rose, multiflora—*Rosa multiflora*
*Salix*—willows
sea lettuce—*Ulva* spp.
smartweeds—*Polygonum* spp.
*Spartina* spp.—cord-grass

spruce, black—*Picea mariana*
spruce, Norway—*Picea abies*
spruce—*Picea* spp.
sumac—*Rhus* spp.
sycamore, American—*Platanus occidentalis*
*Typha*—cattails
willow—*Salix* spp.

## Animal species (other than birds)

adelgid, woolly—*Adelges tsugae*
bluefish—*Pomatomus saltatrix*
crab, fiddler—*Uca* spp.
deer, white-tailed—*Odocoileus virginianus*
microtine rodent—voles and muskrats
    subfamily Microtinae, family Crecetidae
moth, gypsy—*Lymantria dispar*
muskrat—*Ondatra zibethica*
raccoon—*Procyon lotor*
silk moths—primarily large nocturnal moths of
    the family Saturniidae

# Literature Cited

(see also Annotated Bibliography on pp. 19–22)

Adamus, P. R. [1987]. *Atlas of breeding birds in Maine, 1978–1983*. Maine Department of Inland Fisheries and Wildlife, Augusta, Maine.

Albers, P. H. 1978. Habitat selection by breeding Red-winged Blackbirds. *Wilson Bulletin* 90:619–634.

Aldrich, J. W., and H. Friedmann. 1943. A revision of the Ruffed Grouse. *Condor* 45:85–103.

Aldrich, J. W., and A. J. Duvall. 1958. Distribution and migration of races of the Mourning Dove. *Condor* 60:108–128.

Allen, J. A. 1864. Catalogue of the birds found at Springfield, Massachusetts. *Proceedings of the Essex Institute* 4:48–80.

Allin, C. C., G. G. Chasko, and T. P. Husband. 1987. Mute Swans in the Atlantic flyway: a review of the history, population growth and management needs. *Transactions of the Northeast Section of the Wildlife Society* 44:32–47.

Ambuel, B., and S. A. Temple. 1983. Area-dependent changes in the bird communities and vegetation of southern Wisconsin forests. *Ecology* 64:1057–1068.

Amadon, D. 1938. Hooded Merganser nesting in Connecticut. *Auk* 55:123.

American Ornithologists' Union. 1957. *Check-list of North American birds*. 5th ed. American Ornithologists' Union, Lawrence, Kansas.

American Ornithologists' Union. 1983. *Check-list of North American birds*. 6th ed. American Ornithologists' Union, Lawrence, Kansas.

Ames, P. L. 1966. DDT residues in the eggs of the Osprey in the northeastern USA and their relation to nest success. *Journal of Applied Ecology* 3 (Supplement): 87–97.

Ames, P. L., and G. S. Mersereau. 1964. Some factors in the decline of the Osprey in Connecticut. *Auk* 81:173–185.

Andrle, R. F., and J. R. Carroll. 1988. *The atlas of breeding birds in New York state*. Cornell University Press, Ithaca, New York.

Ankney, C. D., D. D. Dennis, L. N. Wishard, and J. E. Seeb. 1986. Low genic variation between Black Ducks and Mallards. *Auk* 103:701–709.

Ankney, C. D., and J. Hopkins. 1985. Habitat selection by roof-nesting Killdeer. *Journal of Field Ornithology* 56:284–286.

AOU. *See* American Ornithologists' Union.

Armstrong, J. T. 1965. Breeding home range in the nighthawk and other birds: its evolutionary and ecological significance. *Ecology* 46:619–629.

Ashenden, J. E. 1988. The Ontario Lakes loon survey—status report. In *Papers from the 1987 Conference on Loon Research and Management*, ed. P. I. V. Strong, 185–195. North American Loon Fund, Meredith, New Hampshire.

Askins, R. A. 1990. *Birds of the Connecticut College Arboretum*. Connecticut College Arboretum Bulletin no. 31. New London.

Askins, R. A., J. F. Lynch, and R. Greenberg. 1990. Population declines in migratory birds in eastern North America. In *Current ornithology*, Vol. 7, ed. D. M. Power, 1–57. Plenum Press, New York.

Askins, R. A., and M. J. Philbrick. 1987. Effects of changes in regional forest abundance on the decline and recovery of a forest bird community. *Wilson Bulletin* 99:7–21.

Askins, R. A., M. J. Philbrick, and D. S. Sugeno. 1987. Relationship between the regional abundance of forest and the composition of forest bird communities. *Biological Conservation* 39:129–152.

Atwater, S., and J. Schnell, eds. 1989. *Ruffed Grouse*. Stackpoll Books, Harrisburg, Pennsylvania.

Audubon, J. J. 1831. Ornithological biography, Vol. 1. Adam Black, Edinburgh.

Austin, O. L. 1953. The migration of the Common Tern (*Sterna hirundo*) in the western hemisphere. *Bird-Banding* 24:39–55.

Bagg, A. C., and S. A. Eliot, Jr. 1937. *Birds of the Connecticut Valley in Massachusetts*. Hampshire Bookshop, Northampton, Mass.

Bagg, A. M., and H. M. Parker. 1951. The Turkey Vulture in New England and eastern Canada up to 1950. *Auk* 68:315–333.

Baird, S. F., T. M. Brewer, and R. Ridgway. 1874. *A history of North American birds: land birds*, 3 vols. Reprint 1905. Little, Brown and Co., Boston.

Baird, S. F., T. M. Brewer, and R. Ridgway. 1884. *The water birds of North America*, Vol. 1. Memoirs of the Mus. of Comp. Zool. no. 12. Little, Brown and Co., Boston.

Balgooyen, T. G. 1976. *Behavior and ecology of the American Kestrel* (Falco sparverius L.) *in the Sierra Nevada of California*. University of California Publications in Zoology, vol. 103.

Baptist, T. R. 1981. Mature mixed upland forest. *American Birds* 35:50.

Baptist, T. R. 1982. First state breeding record of Black Skimmers. *Connecticut Warbler* 2:47–48.

Baptist, T. R. 1991. Common Raven in Connecticut. *Connecticut Warbler* 11:73–76.

Barlow, J. C. 1980. Patterns of ecological interactions among migrant and resident vireos on the wintering grounds. In *Migrant birds in the neotropics*, eds. A. Keast and E. S. Morton, 79–107. Smithsonian Institution Press, Washington, D.C.

Barlow, J. C., and W. B. McGillivray. 1983. Foraging and habitat relationships of the sibling species Willow Flycatcher (*Empidonax traillii* ) and Alder Flycatcher (*E. alnorum*) in southern Ontario. *Canadian Journal of Zoology* 61:1510–1516.

Bart, J., and S. P. Klosiewski. 1989. Use of presence-absence to measure changes in avian density. *Journal of Wildlife Management* 53:847–852.

Beal, F. E. L. 1912. *Food of the woodpeckers of the United States*. U.S. Department of Agriculture, Biological Survey Bulletin no. 37:1–64. Washington, D.C.

Beal, F. E. L., and W. L. McAtee. 1922. *Food of some well-known birds of forest, farm, and garden*. U.S. Department of Agriculture, Farmer's Bulletin no. 506:1–33. Washington, D.C.

Beason, R. C. 1987. Interaction of visual and non-visual cues during migratory orientation by the Bobolink (*Dolichonyx oryzivorus*). *Journal für Ornithologie* 128:317–324.

Beason, R. C. 1989. Use of an inclination compass during migratory orientation by the Bobolink (*Dolichonyx oryzivorus*). *Ethology* 81:291–299.

Beason, R. C., and L. L. Trout. 1984. Cooperative breeding in the Bobolink. *Wilson Bulletin* 96:709–710.

Beckley, O. E. 1963. *Wood Duck nesting box program: ten year summary 1953–1962*. Connecticut State Board of Fisheries and Game, Hartford, Connecticut.

Beddall, B. G. 1963. Range expansion of the cardinal and other birds in the northeastern states. *Wilson Bulletin* 75: 140–158.

Beecher, W. J. 1951. Adaptations for food-getting in the American blackbirds. *Auk* 68:411–440.

Beehler, B. M. 1978. *Birdlife of the Adirondack Park*. Adirondack Mountain Club, Glenns Falls, New York.

Bell, M. 1985. *The Face of Connecticut*. Connecticut Geological and Natural History Survey Bulletin no. 110.

Belles-Isles, J. C., and J. Picman. 1986a. House Wren nest destroying behavior. *Condor* 88: 190–193.

Belles-Isles, J. C., and J. Picman. 1986b. Nesting boxes and nest site preferences in House Wrens. *Condor* 88: 483–486.

Bellrose, F. C. 1990. The history of Wood Duck management. In *Proceedings of the 1988 North American Wood Duck symposium*, eds. L. H. Fredrickson, G. R. Burger, S. P. Havera, D. A. Graber, R. E. Kirby, and T. S. Taylor, 13–20. St. Louis, Missouri.

Belthoff, J. R., and S. A. Gauthreaux, Jr. 1991. Partial migration and differential winter distribution of House Finches in the eastern United States. *Condor* 93:374–382.

Bendire, C. 1895. Life histories of North American birds. *U.S. National Museum Special Bulletin* no. 3. Washington, D.C.

Bent, A. C. 1919. Life histories of North American diving birds. *U.S. National Museum Bulletin* no. 107. Washington, D.C.

Bent, A. C. 1926. Life histories of North American marsh birds. *U.S. National Museum Bulletin* no. 135. Washington, D.C.

Bent, A. C. 1929. Life histories of North American shore birds. *U.S. National Museum Bulletin* no. 146. Washington, D.C.

Bent, A. C. 1932. Life histories of North American gallinaceous birds. *U.S. National Museum Bulletin* no. 162. Washington, D.C.

Bent, A. C. 1937. Life histories of North American birds of prey. Part 1. *U.S. National Museum Bulletin* no. 167. Washington, D.C.

Bent, A. C. 1938. Life histories of North American birds of prey. Part 2. *U.S. National Museum Bulletin* no. 170. Washington, D.C.

Bent, A. C. 1939. Life histories of North American woodpeckers. *U.S. National Museum Bulletin* no. 174. Washington, D.C.

Bent, A. C. 1940. Life histories of North American cuckoos, goatsuckers, hummingbirds, and their allies. *U.S. National Museum Bulletin* no. 176. Washington, D.C.

Bent, A. C. 1942. Life histories of North American flycatchers, larks, swallows, and their allies. *U.S. National Museum Bulletin* no. 179. Washington, D.C.

Bent, A. C. 1946. Life histories of North American jays, crows and titmice. *U.S. National Museum Bulletin* no. 191. Washington, D.C.

Bent, A. C. 1948. Life histories of North American nuthatches, wrens, thrashers and their allies. *U.S. National Museum Bulletin* no. 195. Washington, D.C.

Bent, A. C. 1953. Life histories of North American wood warblers. *U.S. National Museum Bulletin* no. 203. Washington, D.C.

Bent, A. C. 1958. Life histories of North American blackbirds, orioles, tanagers, and allies. *U.S. National Museum Bulletin* no. 211. Washington, D.C.

Bent, A. C., and collaborators, ed. O. L. Austin, Jr. 1968. Life histories of North American cardinals, grosbeaks, buntings, towhees, finches, sparrows, and allies. *U.S. National Museum Bulletin* no. 237, parts 1–3. Washington, D.C.

Bergstrom, E. A. [ca. 1960]. Incomplete annotated list of Connecticut bird records. Connecticut State Museum of Natural History, Storrs, Connecticut. Photocopy.

Bergstrom, E. A. 1961. Some Starlings resident in Connecticut. *Bird Banding* 32:57–58.

Bertin, R. I. 1975. Factors influencing the distribution of the Wood Thrush and Veery in western Connecticut woodland. Master's thesis. University of Connecticut, Storrs, Connecticut.

Bertin, R. I. 1977. Breeding habitats of the Wood Thrush and Veery. *Condor* 79:303–311.

Billard, R. S. 1948. An ecological study of the Virginia Rail and the Sora in some Connecticut swamps, 1947. Master's thesis, Iowa State University, Ames.

Bledsoe, A. H. 1985. Connecticut birds: Blue-winged and Golden-winged Warblers. *Connecticut Warbler* 5:23–26.

Bledsoe, A. H. 1988. Status and hybridization of Clapper and King Rails in Connecticut. *Connecticut Warbler* 8(1): 61–65.

Blodgett, B. G., and P. J. Lyons. 1988. The recolonization of Massachusetts by the Common Loon (*Gavia immer*). In *Papers from the 1987 Conference on Loon Research and Management*, ed. P. I. V. Strong, 177–184. North American Loon Fund, Meredith, New Hampshire.

Bock, C. E., and L. W. Lepthien. 1972. Winter eruptions of Red-breasted Nuthatches in North America, 1950–1970. *American Birds* 26:558–560.

Bollinger, E. K., and T. A. Gavin 1989. The effects of site quality on breeding-site fidelity in Bobolinks. *Auk* 106:584–594.

Bond, J. 1961. *Birds of the West Indies*. Houghton Mifflin Company, Boston.

Boyajian, N. R. 1971. The nesting season, Hudson-St. Lawrence Region. *American Birds* 25:836–840.

Brewer, R., G. A. McPeek, and R. J. Adams, Jr. 1991. *The atlas of breeding birds of Michigan*. Michigan State University Press, East Lansing.

Brittingham, M. C., and S. A. Temple. 1983. Have cowbirds caused forest songbirds to decline? *BioScience* 33:31–35.

Brockway, A. W. 1923. Nesting of the junco (*Junco hyemalis hyemalis*) in southern Connecticut. *Auk* 40:330.

Brooks, M. 1942. Birds at the extremities of their ranges. *Wilson Bulletin* 54:12–16.

Brooks, M. 1947. Breeding habitats of certain wood warblers in the unglaciated Appalachian region. *Auk* 64:291–295.

Broun, M. 1972. Apparent migratory behavior in the House Sparrow. *Auk* 89:187–189.

Browning, M. R. 1992. Geographic variation in *Hirundo pyrrhonota* (Cliff Swallow) from northern North America. *Western Birds* 23:21–29.

Browning, M. R. 1993. Comments on the taxonomy of *Empidonax traillii* (Willow Flycatcher). *Western Birds* 24:241–257.

Brumbach, J. J. 1965. *The Climate of Connecticut*. Connecticut Geological and Natural History Survey Bulletin no. 99.

Buckley, F. G., and P. A. Buckley. 1982. Microenvironmental determinants of survival in salt marsh-nesting Common Terns. *Colonial Waterbirds* 5:39–48.

Buech, R. R. 1982. Nesting ecology and cowbird parasitism of Clay-colored, Chipping, and Field Sparrows in a Christmas tree plantation. *Journal of Field Ornithology* 53:363–369.

Bull, J. 1964. *Birds of the New York area*. Harper and Row, New York.

Bull, J. 1974. *Birds of New York state*. Doubleday/Natural History Press, Garden City, New York. Reprint, 1985 (with *Supplement*, Federation of New York Bird Clubs, 1976). Cornell University Press, Ithaca, New York.

Bull, J. 1981. Double-crested Cormorant breeding at Fisher's Island. *Kingbird* 32:83.

Burger, J. 1978. Competition between Cattle Egrets and native North American herons, egrets, and ibises. *Condor* 80:15–23.

Burger, J. 1979. Competition and predation: Herring Gulls versus Laughing Gulls. *Condor* 81:269–277.

Burger, J., and M. Gochfeld. 1988. Nest-site selection and temporal patterns in habitat use of Roseate and Common Terns. *Auk* 105:433–438.

Burger, J., and M. Gochfeld. 1990. *The Black Skimmer, social dynamics of a colonial species*. Columbia University Press, New York.

Burger, J., and J. Shister. 1978. Nest site competition and competitive interactions of Herring and Laughing Gulls in New Jersey. *Auk* 95:252–266.

Butcher, G. S., W. A. Niering, W. J. Barry, and R. H. Goodwin. 1981. Equilibrium biogeography and the size of nature preserves: An avian case study. *Oecologia* 49:29–37.

Cannings, R. J. 1987. The breeding biology of Northern Saw-whet Owls in southern British Columbia. In *Biology and conservation of northern forest owls*, eds. R. W. Nero, R. J. Clark, R. J. Knapton, and R. H. Hamre, 193–198. U.S. Forest Service, General Technical Report RM-142.

Carleton, G. 1963a. The spring migration, Hudson-St. Lawrence region. *Audubon Field Notes* 17:392–394.

Carleton, G. 1963b. The nesting season, Hudson-St. Lawrence region. *Audubon Field Notes* 17:449–452.

Carleton, G. 1965. The nesting season, Hudson-St. Lawrence region. *Audubon Field Notes* 19:528–530.

Caughley, G., D. Grice, R. Barker, and B. Brown. 1988. The edge of the range. *Journal of Animal Ecology* 57:771–786.

Cavanaugh, J., and A. Magee. 1967a. Climax hemlock-white pine forest, with transition hardwoods. *Audubon Field Notes* 21:626–627.

Cavanaugh, J., and A. Magee. 1967b. Second-growth hardwood forest. *Audubon Field Notes* 21:614.

Chamberlain-Auger, J. A., P. J. Auger, and E. G. Strauss. 1990. Breeding biology of American Crows. *Wilson Bulletin* 102:615–622.

Chapman, F. M. 1892. A preliminary study of the grackles of the sub-genus *Quiscalus*. *Bulletin of the American Museum of Natural History* 4:1–20.

Chasko, G. G. 1985. The impact of Mute Swans on waterfowl and waterfowl habitat. Connecticut Dept. of Environmental Protection, Wildlife Bureau. Federal Aid Project Report W-49-R-10.

Chasko, G. G., and M. R. Conover. 1988. Urban-suburban Canada geese: too much of a good thing? *Living Bird* 7:8–13.

Christiansen, D. A., Jr., and S. E. Reinert. 1990. Habitat use of the Northern Harrier in a coastal Massachusetts shrubland with notes on population trends in southeastern New England. *Journal of Raptor Research* 24:84–90.

Clark, G. A., Jr. 1968. An indoor Blue Jay nest. *Bird-Banding* 39:55–56.

Clark, G. A., Jr. 1979. Body weights of birds: a review. *Condor* 81:193–202.

Clark, G. A., Jr., and L. R. Bevier. 1993. Fifth report of the Connecticut Rare Records Committee. *Connecticut Warbler* 13:1–9.

Clark, J. N. 1884. Nesting of the Little Black Rail in Connecticut. *Auk* 1:393–394.

Clark, J. N. 1897. The Little Black Rail. *Nidologist* 4:86–88. [Not seen; summarized in an unpublished typescript on Connecticut birds by E. A. Bergstrom.]

Clark, R. G., and P. J. Weatherhead. 1987. Influence of population size on habitat use by territorial male Red-winged Blackbirds in agricultural landscapes. *Auk* 104:311–315.

Cody, M. L., ed. 1985. *Habitat selection in birds*. Academic Press, New York.

Coffin, C. C. 1940. Excavations of southwest Connecticut. *Bulletin Archaeological Society of Connecticut* 10:33–49.

Coker, D. R., and J. L. Confer. 1990. Brown-headed Cowbird para-sitism on Golden-winged and Blue-winged warblers. *Wilson Bulletin* 102:550–552.

Coleman, J. S., and J. D. Fraser. 1989. Habitat use and home ranges of Black and Turkey Vultures. *Journal of Wildlife Management* 53:782–792.

Collar, N. J., and P. Andrew. 1988. *Birds to watch*. International Council for Bird Preservation, Technical Publication no. 8. Cambridge.

Collins, S. L. 1983a. Geographic variation in habitat structure for the wood warblers in Maine and Minnesota. *Oecologia* 59:246–252.

Collins, S. L. 1983b. Geographic variation in habitat structure of the Black-throated Green Warbler (*Dendroica virens*). *Auk* 100:382–389.

Colwell, R. K. 1984. Community biology and sexual selection: lessons from hummingbird flower mites. In *Community Ecology*, eds. J. Diamond and T. J. Case, 406–424. Harper and Row, New York.

Converse, K. A. 1985. A study of resident nuisance Canada geese in Connecticut and New York. Ph.D. dissertation, University of Massachusetts, Amherst, Massachusetts.

Cooke, M. T., and P. Knappen. 1941. Some birds naturalized in North America. *Proceedings of the North American Wildlife Conference* 5:176–183.

Cooper, D., H. Hays, and C. Pessino. 1970. Breeding of the Common and Roseate Terns on Great Gull Island. *Proceedings of the Linnaean Society of New York* 71:83–104.

Cooper, R. J. 1981. Relative abundance of Georgia caprimulgids based on call-counts. *Wilson Bulletin* 93:363–371.

Coues, E. 1868. *Catalogue of the birds of North America*. Proceedings of the Essex Institute 5:249–314.

Craig, R. J. 1975. Distributional ecology of marsh birds of the Connecticut River. Master's thesis, University of Connecticut, Storrs, Connecticut.

Craig, R. J. 1978. The Rare Vertebrates of Connecticut. U.S. Department of Agriculture, Soil Conservation Service, Storrs, Connecticut.

Craig, R. J. [ca. 1980]. Notes and records on bird species listed in "The Rare Vertebrates of Connecticut." Photocopy. Connecticut State Museum of Natural History, Storrs, Connecticut.

Craig, R. J. 1984. Comparative foraging ecology of Louisiana and Northern Waterthrushes. *Wilson Bulletin* 96:173–183.

Craig, R. J. 1985. Comparative habitat use by Louisiana and Northern Waterthrushes. *Wilson Bulletin* 97:347–355.

Craig, R. J. 1987a. Divergent prey selection in two species of waterthrushes (*Seiurus*). *Auk* 104:180–187.

Craig, R. J. 1987b. Population densities of forest birds in northeastern Connecticut. *Connecticut Warbler* 7:27–31.

Craig, R. J. 1990. *Historic trends in the distribution and populations of estuarine marsh birds of the Connecticut River*. Connecticut Agricultural Experiment Station Research Bulletin no. 83. Storrs, Connecticut.

Cramp, S., and K. E. L. Simmons, eds. 1989. *The birds of the western Palearctic*, Vol. 5. Oxford University Press, Oxford.

Crossman, T. I. 1989. Habitat use by Grasshopper and Savannah Sparrows at Bradley International Airport and management recommendations. Master's thesis, University of Connecticut, Storrs, Connecticut.

Cruickshank, A. D. 1942. *Birds around New York City: where and when to find them*. American Museum of Natural History Handbook Series no. 13. New York.

Dambach, C. A. 1947. Grazed and ungrazed sugar maple woodland. *Audubon Field Notes* 1:199.

Davis, T. H. 1968. Willet nesting on Long Island, New York. *Wilson Bulletin* 80:330.

Davis, W. J. 1989. Raven. *Massachusetts Wildlife* 39:22–26.

DeGraaf, R. M., and W. M. Healy, eds. 1990. Is forest fragmentation a management issue in the northeast? U.S. Forest Service, Northeastern Forest Experiment Station, General Technical Report NE-140.

Dennis, J. V. 1958. Some aspects of the breeding ecology of the Yellow-breasted Chat (*Icteria virens*). *Bird-Banding* 29:169–183.

DEP (Connecticut Department of Environmental Protection). 1982. *Atlas of the public water supply sources & drainage basins of Connecticut*. Natural Resources Center, Bulletin no. 4. Hartford, Connecticut.

DEP. 1992. *Atlas of Connecticut Topographic Maps*. Natural Resources Center, Bulletin no. 17. Hartford, Connecticut.

de Smet, K., and M. P. Conrad. 1988. First documented nesting record and status of the Willow Flycatcher in Manitoba. *Blue Jay* 46:149–154.

Dewire, R. C. 1981. A new nesting species for Connecticut. *Connecticut Warbler* 1:52.

Dhondt, A. A. 1989. Ecological and evolutionary effects of interspecific competition in tits. *Wilson Bulletin* 101:198–216.

Dickson, D. R., and C. L. McAfee. 1988. *Forest statistics for Connecticut: 1972 and 1985*. U.S. Forest Service, Northeastern Forest Experiment Station, Resource Bulletin NE-105.

DiCostanzo, J. 1978. Occurrence of the Common Tern in the interior of South America. *Bird-Banding* 49:248–251.

Dilger, W. C. 1956. Adaptive modifications and ecological isolating mechanisms in the thrush genera *Catharus* and *Hylocichla*. *Wilson Bulletin* 68:171–199.

Dill, H. H., and F. B. Lee. 1970. *Home grown honkers*. U.S. Fish and Wildlife Service, Washington, D.C.

Dolbeer, R. A. 1980. *Blackbirds and corn in Ohio*. U. S. Department of the Interior Fish and Wildlife Service, Resource Publication no. 136. Washington, D.C.

Dolbeer, R. A. 1982. Migration patterns for age and sex classes of blackbirds and starlings. *Journal of Field Ornithology* 53:28–46.

Dolbeer, R. A. 1991. Migration patterns of Double-crested Cormorants east of the Rocky Mountains *Journal of Field Ornithology* 62:83–93.

Dowhan, J. J., and R. J. Craig. 1976. *Rare and endangered species of Connecticut and their habitats*. Connecticut Geological and Natural History Survey, Report of Investigations no. 6. Hartford, Connecticut.

Drury, W. H. 1973. Population changes in New England seabirds. *Bird-Banding* 44:267–313.

Duncan, D. C. 1987. Nest-site distribution and overland brood movements of Northern Pintails in Alberta. *Journal of Wildlife Management* 51:716–723.

Dwight, J., Jr. 1890. The Horned Lark in North America. *Auk* 7:138–158.

Eaton, E. H. 1914. *Birds of New York*, Part 2. New York State Museum Memoir no. 12.

Eddleman, W. R., F. L. Knopf, B. Meanley, F. A. Reid, and R. Zembal. 1988. Conservation of North American rallids. *Wilson Bulletin* 100:458–475.

Ehrlich, P. R., D. S. Dobkin, and D. Wheye. 1988. *The birder's handbook*. Simon and Schuster, New York.

Eiserer, L. 1980. Effects of grass length and mowing on foraging behavior of the American Robin (*Turdus migratorius*). *Auk* 97:576–580.

Eliot, S. A., Jr. 1934. Recent duck records in southwestern New England. *Auk* 51:511–513.

Ellison, W. G. 1993. Historical patterns of vagrancy by Blue-gray Gnatcatchers in New England. *Journal of Field Ornithology* 64:358–366.

Eltringham, S. K. 1963. The British population of the Mute Swan in 1961. *Bird Study* 10:10–28.

Emlen, J. T., Jr. 1954. Territory, nest building and pair formation in Cliff Swallows. *Auk* 77:16–35.

Enders, F., and A. Magee. 1965. Shrubby swamp and sedge hummocks. *Audubon Field Notes* 19:625–627.

Erskine, A. J. 1992. *Atlas of breeding birds of the maritime provinces*. Nova Scotia Museum and Nimbus Publishing Limited, Halifax, Nova Scotia.

Feinsinger, P., and R. K. Colwell. 1978. Community organization among neotropical nectar-feeding birds. *American Zoologist* 18:779–795.

Finch, D. W. 1971. The nesting season, Northeastern Maritime Region. *American Birds* 25:830–836.

Finch, D. W. 1972. The nesting season, Northeastern Maritime Region. *American Birds* 26:832–837.

Finch, D. W. 1973. The nesting season, Northeastern Maritime Region. *American Birds* 27:1020–1025.

Finch, D. W. 1975. The nesting season, Northeastern Maritime Region. *American Birds* 29:745–750.

Finch, D. W. 1976. The nesting season, Northeastern Maritime Region. *American Birds* 30:926–930.

Fitzpatrick, J. W. 1980. Wintering of North American tyrant flycatchers in the tropics. In *Migrant birds in the neotropics*, eds. A. Keast and E. S. Morton, 67–78. Smithsonian Institution Press, Washington, D. C.

Fleischer, R. C., M. T. Murphy, and L. E. Hunt. 1985. Clutch size increase and intraspecific brood parasitism in the Yellow-billed Cuckoo. *Wilson Bulletin* 97:125–127.

Forbush, E. H. 1912. *A history of game birds, wildfowl and shorebirds of Massachusetts and adjacent states*. Massachusetts State Board of Agriculture, Boston.

Forbush, E. H. 1916. *A history of game birds, wildfowl and shorebirds of Massachusetts and adjacent states*. 2d ed. Massachusetts State Board of Agriculture, Boston.

Forbush, E. H. 1925–1929. *Birds of Massachusetts and other New England states*. 3 vols. Massachusetts Department of Agriculture, Boston.

Frakes, M. A., and R. E. Johnson. 1982. Niche convergence in *Empidonax* flycatchers. *Condor* 84:286–291.

Frank, W. J. 1948. Wood Duck nesting box usage in Connecticut. *Journal of Wildlife Management* 12:128–136.

Friedmann, H. 1929. *The Cowbirds: a study in the biology of social parasitism*. Charles C. Thomas, Springfield, Illinois.

Gavin, T. A., and E. K. Bollinger 1985. Multiple paternity in a territorial passerine: the Bobolink. *Auk* 102:550–555.

Geissler, P. H., and J. R. Sauer. 1990. Topics in route-regression analysis. In *Survey designs and statistical methods for the estimation of avian population trends*, eds. J. R. Sauer and S. Droege,

54–57. U. S. Fish and Wildlife Service Biological Report 90(1). Washington, D. C.

Gibbs, J. P., S. Woodward, M. L. Hunter, and A. E. Hutchinson. 1987. Determinants of Great Blue Heron colony distribution in coastal Maine. *Auk* 104:38–47.

Gill, F. B. 1980. Historical aspects of hybridization between Blue-winged and Golden-winged Warblers. *Auk* 97:1–18.

Gochfeld, M., and J. Burger. 1987. Nest-site selection: comparison of Roseate and Common Terns (*Sterna dougallii* and *S. hirundo*) in a Long Island, New York, colony. *Bird Behaviour* 7:58–66.

Gorski, L. J. 1969a. Systematics and ecology of sibling species of Traill's Flycatcher. Ph.D. dissertation, University of Connecticut, Storrs, Connecticut.

Gorski, L. J. 1969b. Traill's Flycatchers of the "fitz-bew" songform wintering in Panama. *Auk* 86:745–747.

Gorski, L. J. 1970a. Systematics and ecology of sibling species of Traill's Flycatcher. *Dissertation Abstracts International* 30B:3495.

Gorski, L. J. 1970b. Banding the two song forms of Traill's Flycatcher. *Bird-Banding* 41:204–206.

Gorski, L. J. 1971. Traill's Flycatchers of the "fee-bee-o" songform wintering in Peru. *Auk* 88:429–431.

Grant, P. J. 1983. The 'Marsh Hawk' problem. *British Birds* 76:373–376.

Graber, J. W., R. R. Graber, and E. L. Kirk. 1977. Illinois birds: Picidae. Illinois Natural History Survey, Biological Notes no. 102.

Graves, F. M. 1919. Notes from a Connecticut pine swamp. *Auk* 36:293–294.

Greenberg, R. 1987. Seasonal foraging specialization in the Worm-eating Warbler. *Condor* 89:158–168.

Greenberg, R., and S. Droege. 1990. Adaptations to tidal marshes in breeding populations of the Swamp Sparrow. *Condor* 92:393–404.

Greenlaw, J. S. 1976. Use of bilateral scratching behavior by emberizines and icterids. *Condor* 78:94–97.

Greenlaw, J. S. 1993. Behavioral and morphological diversification in Sharp-tailed Sparrows (*Ammodramus caudacutus*) of the Atlantic coast. *Auk* 110:286–303.

Grier, J. W., J. B. Elder, F. J. Gramlich, N. F. Green, J. V. Kussmar, and J. P. Mattson. 1983. Northern states Bald Eagle recovery plan. U.S. Fish and Wildlife Service, Washington, D.C.

Griscom, L. 1923. *Birds of the New York City region*. American Museum of Natural History Handbook Series, no. 9. New York.

Griscom, L. 1948. The present status of New England waterfowl. *Proceedings of the Northeast Wildlife Conference*, 79–85.

Griscom, L. 1949. *The birds of Concord*. Harvard University Press, Cambridge.

Griscom, L., and D. E. Snyder. 1955. *The Birds of Massachusetts: an annotated and revised check list*. Peabody Museum, Salem, Massachusetts.

Grünberger, S., and B. Leisler. 1990. Angeborne und erfahrungsbedingte Komponenten der Habitatwahl der Tannenmeise (*Parus ater*). [Innate and learned components in the habitat selection of Coal Tits.] *Journal für Ornithologie* 131:460–464.

Gwinner, E. 1988. The control of migration in European warblers. *Acta XIX Congressus Internationalis Ornithologici*, part I:215–249. Ottawa, Canada.

Hall, G. A. 1983. *West Virginia birds: distribution and ecology*. Carnegie Museum of Natural History Special Publication no. 7. Pittsburgh.

Hancock, J., and H. Elliott. 1978. The herons of the world. London Editions, London.

Hancock, J., and J. Kushlan. 1984. The herons handbook. Harper and Row, New York.

Hand, J., and J. Mockalis. 1982. Connecticut field notes, spring 1982. *Connecticut Warbler* 2:38–41.

Hand, J., and J. Mockalis. 1983. Connecticut field notes, summer 1983. *Connecticut Warbler* 3:41–43.

Hanson, H. C. 1965. *The Giant Canada Goose*. Southern Illinois University Press, Carbondale, Illinois.

Haramis, G. M. 1990. The breeding ecology of the Wood Duck: a review. In *Proceedings of the 1988 North American Wood Duck Symposium,* eds. L. H. Fredrickson, G. V. Burger, S. P. Havera, D. A. Graber, R. E. Kirby, and T. S. Taylor, 45–60. St. Louis, Missouri.

Harding, K. C. 1925. Semi-colonization of Veeries. Bulletin of the Northeastern Bird-banding Association 1:4–7.

Harrison, C. 1978. *A field guide to the nests, eggs and nestlings of North American birds*. William Collins Sons and Co. New York.

Harrison, H. H. 1975. *A field guide to birds' nests in the United States east of the Mississippi River*. Houghton Mifflin Company, Boston.

Hatch, D. 1988. Squabbling over swans. *Connecticut Audubon*, Spring:28–32.

Hayman, P., J. Marchant, and T. Prater. 1986. *Shorebirds*. Houghton Mifflin Co., Boston.

Hays, H. 1972. Polyandry in the Spotted Sandpiper. *Living Bird* 11:43–57.

Hays, H. 1975. Probable Common × Roseate Tern hybrids. *Auk* 92:219–234.

Heatwole, H. 1965. Some aspects of the association of Cattle Egrets with cattle. *Animal Behaviour* 13:79–83.

Heichel, G. H., and W. W. Washko. 1976. *Bird damage to Connecticut corn*. Connecticut Agricultural Experiment Station Bulletin no. 761. New Haven, Connecticut.

Herkert, J. R. 1991. *Prairie birds of Illinois: population response to two centuries of habitat change*. Illinois Natural History Survey Bulletin no. 34:393–399.

Hespenheide, H. A. 1971. Flycatcher habitat selection in the eastern deciduous forest. *Auk* 88:61–74.

Heusmann, H. W. 1979. Massachusetts waterfowl research program. Commonwealth of Massachusetts Division of Fisheries and Wildlife, Project W-42-R. Boston.

Heusmann, H. W. 1991. The history and status of the Mallard in the Atlantic Flyway. *Wildlife Society Bull*etin 19:14–22.

Hill, N. P. 1965. *The birds of Cape Cod, Massachusetts*. William Morrow, New York.

Hills, C. F. [ca. 1983]. Personal notes on birds seen in Connecticut and summary of other bird records. Unpublished. Connecticut State Museum of Natural History, Storrs, Connecticut.

Holmes, R. T. 1986. Foraging patterns of forest birds: male-female differences. *Wilson Bulletin* 98:196–213.

Holmes, R. T., and S. K. Robinson. 1981. Tree species preferences of foraging insectivorous birds in a northern hardwood forest. *Oecologia* 48:31–35.

Holmes, R. T., and T. W. Sherry. 1988. Assessing population trends of New Hampshire forest birds: local vs. regional patterns. *Auk* 105:756–768.

Honeywill, A. W., Jr., F. F. Burr, P. L. Buttrick, D. B. Pangburn, A. A. Saunders, and C. H. Pangburn. 1908. *List of birds of the New Haven region*. New Haven Bird Club Bulletin no. 1. New Haven, Connecticut.

Hopkins, D. A. 1990. Non-breeding Bald Eagles in northwest Connecticut during late spring and summer. *Connecticut Warbler* 10:10–14.

Hopkins, D. A. 1992. Bald Eagles successfully nest in Connecticut in 1992. *Connecticut Warbler* 12:121–124.

Hopkins, D. A., G. S. Mersereau, and L. Fischer. 1987. Nesting Sharp-shinned Hawks in Connecticut. *Connecticut Warbler* 7:18–19.

Hopkins, D. A., G. S. Mersereau, and M. J. O'Leary. 1993. A third adult Bald Eagle takes an active part in raising young eagles in Connecticut. *Connecticut Warbler* 13:114–116.

Howe, M. A. 1982. Social organization in a nesting population of eastern Willets (*Catoptrophorus semipalmatus*). *Auk* 99:88–102.

Howes, P. G. 1928. Notes on the birds of Stamford, Connecticut and vicinity. *Oologist* 45:70–96.

Hoyt, S. F. 1957. The ecology of the Pileated Woodpecker. *American Midland Naturalist* 38:246–256.

Hudgins, J. E., G. L. Storm, and J. S. Wakely. 1985. Local movements and diurnal habitat selection by male American Woodcock in Pennsylvania. *Journal of Wildlife Management* 49:614–619.

Huntington, C. E. 1952. Hybridization in the Purple Grackle, *Quiscalus quiscula*. *Systematic Zoology* 1:149–170.

Hurley, R. J., and E. C. Franks. 1976. Changes in the breeding ranges of two grassland birds. *Auk* 93:108–115.

Hutto, R. L. 1988. Is tropical deforestation responsible for the reported declines in neotropical migrant populations? *American Birds* 42:375–379.

Ingold, D. J. 1989. Nesting phenology and competition for nest sites among Red-headed and Red-bellied Woodpeckers and European Starlings. *Auk* 106:209–217.

Jackson, J. A. 1976. A comparison of some aspects of the breeding ecology of Red-headed and Red-bellied Woodpeckers in Kansas. *Condor* 78:67–76.

Jackson, S. N. 1985. *The Connecticut Wild Turkey program*. Revised by Brian Miller. Connecticut Department of Environmental Protection, Wildlife Division pamphlet. Hartford.

James, F. C., R. F. Johnston, N. O. Wamer, G. J. Niemi, and W. J. Boecklen. 1984. The Grinnellian niche of the Wood Thrush. *American Naturalist* 124:17–30.

James, F. C., C. E. McCulloch, and L. E. Wolfe. 1990. Methodological issues in the estimation of trends in bird populations with an example: the Pine Warbler. In *Survey designs and statistical methods for the estimation of avian population trends*, eds. J. R. Sauer and S. Droege, 84–97. U. S. Fish and Wildlife Service Biological Report 90(1). Washington, D. C.

James, R. D. 1978. Pairing and nest site selection in Solitary and Yellow-throated Vireos with a description of a ritualized nest building display. *Canadian Journal of Zoology* 56:1163–1169.

James, R. D. 1979. The comparative foraging behavior of Yellow-throated and Solitary Vireos: the effect of habitat and sympatry.

In *The role of insectivorous birds in forest ecosystems*, eds. J. G. Dickson, R. N. Conner, R. R. Fleet, J. C. Kroll, and J. A. Jackson, 137–163. Academic Press, New York.

Job, H. K. 1908. "A list of birds observed in Litchfield County, Connecticut." In *The Sport of Bird Study*. Litchfield County University [Winsted, Connecticut]; 1922 ed., Macmillan, New York.

Johnsgard, P. A. 1979. Order Anseriformes. In *Check-list of birds of the World*, eds. E. Mayr and G. W. Cottrell, 425–506. Vol. 1. 2d ed. Museum of Comparative Zoology, Cambridge, Massachusetts.

Johnsgard, P. A., and R. DiSilvestro. 1976. Seventy-five years of changes in Mallard-Black Duck ratios in eastern North America. *American Birds* 30:905–908.

Johnson, A. W., and J. D. Goodall. 1965–1967. *The birds of Chile*, 2 vols. Platt, Buenos Aires.

Johnson, R. R., and J. J. Dinsmore. 1986. Habitat use by breeding Virginia Rails and Soras. *Journal of Wildlife Management* 50:387–392.

Johnson, W. C., and T. Webb. 1989. The role of Blue Jays (*Cyanocitta cristata* ) in the postglacial dispersal of fagaceous trees in eastern North America. *Journal of Biogeography* 16:561–572.

Johnston, D. W. 1971. Niche relationships among some deciduous forest flycatchers. *Auk* 88:796–804.

Johnston, R. F. 1967. Seasonal variation in the food of the Purple Martin *Progne subis* in Kansas. *Ibis* 109:8–13.

Jones, C. M. 1876. Breeding of Black-throated Blue Warbler in Connecticut. *Bulletin of the Nuttall Ornithological Club* 1:11–13.

Jones, C. M. 1931. *Field notes on Connecticut birds*. University of Iowa Studies in Natural History 13:5–40.

Jones, J. 1987. Are starlings really responsible for the decline of the Red-headed Woodpecker? *Chat* 51:37–38.

Kalmbach, E. R. 1931. *The European Starling in the United States*. U.S. Department of Agriculture, Farmer's Bulletin no. 1571:1–26. Washington, D. C.

Kane, R., and P. A. Buckley. 1974. The spring migration, Hudson-St. Lawrence Region. *American Birds* 28:779–784.

Kania, G. S., and H. R. Smith. 1986. Observations of agonistic interactions between a pair of feral Mute Swans and nesting waterfowl. *Connecticut Warbler* 6:35–37.

Kaplan, J. 1990. Connecticut field notes, summer 1989. *Connecticut Warbler* 10:19–24.

Kaplan, J. 1991. Connecticut field notes, summer 1990. *Connecticut Warbler* 11:26–32.

Kaplan, J. 1992. Connecticut field notes, summer 1991. *Connecticut Warbler* 12:28–32.

Kaplan, J., and F. Mantlik. 1990. Connecticut field notes, spring 1990. *Connecticut Warbler* 10:98–106.

Keast, A. 1980. Spatial relationships between migratory parulid warblers and their ecological counterparts in the neotropics. In *Migrant birds in the neotropics*, eds. A. Keast and E. S. Morton, 109–130. Smithsonian Institution Press, Washington, D. C.

Kerlinger, P., and D. Wiedner. 1991. Vocal behavior and habitat use of Black Rails in southern New Jersey. *Records of New Jersey Birds* 16:58–62.

Kiff, L. F. 1989. Historic breeding records of the Common Merganser in southeastern United States. *Wilson Bulletin* 101:141–143.

Kilham, L. 1963. Food storing of Red-bellied Woodpeckers. *Wilson Bulletin* 75:227–234.

Kilham, L. 1983. *Life history studies of woodpeckers of eastern North America*. Publications of the Nuttall Ornithological Club, no. 20. Cambridge, Massachusetts.

Kilham, L. 1989. *The American Crow and the Common Raven*. Texas A & M University Press, College Station, Texas.

Knight, R. L., D. J. Grout, and S. A. Temple. 1987. Nest-defense behavior of the American Crow in urban and rural areas. *Condor* 89:175–177.

Krause, H. 1965. Nesting of a pair of Canada Warblers. *Living Bird* 4:5–11.

Kress, S. W., E. H. Weinstein, and I. C. T. Nisbet, eds. 1983. The status of tern populations in northeastern United States and adjacent Canada. *Colonial Waterbirds* 6:84–106.

Kricher, J. C. 1981. Range expansion of the Tufted Titmouse (*Parus bicolor*), in Massachusetts. *American Birds* 35:750–753.

Kricher, J. C. 1983. Correlation between House Finch increase and House Sparrow decline. *American Birds* 37:358–360.

Krieg, D. C. 1971. *The behavioral patterns of the Eastern Bluebird (Sialia sialis)*. New York State Museum and Science Service Bulletin no. 415. Albany, New York.

Kroodsma, D. E., and H. Momose. Songs of the Japanese population of the Winter Wren (*Troglodytes troglodytes*). *Condor* 93:424–432.

Kuerzi, J. F., and R. G. Kuerzi. 1934. Notes on the summer birds of western Litchfield County, Connecticut. *Proceedings of the Linnaean Society of New York* 43:1–13.

Kuerzi, R. G. 1941. Life history studies of the Tree Swallow. *Proceedings of the Linnaean Society of New York* 52:1–52.

Lack, D. 1971. *Ecological isolation in birds*. Harvard University Press, Cambridge.

Laughlin, S. B., ed. 1982. *Proceedings of the northeastern breeding bird atlas conference*. Vermont Institute of Natural Science. Woodstock, Vermont.

Laughlin, S. B., and D. P. Kibbe, eds. 1985. *The atlas of breeding birds of Vermont*. University Press of New England, Hanover, New Hampshire.

Lawrence, L. 1967. A comparative life history study of four species of woodpeckers. *Ornithological Monographs* no. 5.

Leck, C. F. 1984. *The status and distribution of New Jersey's birds*. Rutgers University Press, New Brunswick, New Jersey.

Linsley, J. H. 1843. A catalogue of the birds of Connecticut arranged according to their natural families. *American Journal of Science and Arts* 44:249–274.

Loery, G., and J. D. Nichols. 1985. Dynamics of a Black-capped Chickadee population, 1958–1983. *Ecology* 66:1195–1203.

Loery, G., K. H. Pollock, J. D. Nichols, and J. E. Hines. 1987. Age-specificity of Black-capped Chickadee survival rates: analysis of capture-recapture data. *Ecology* 68:1038–1044.

Long, J. L. 1981. *Introduced birds of the World*. Universe Books, New York.

Loranger, A. J. 1980. Fall foods of the Ring-necked Pheasant in Connecticut, 1963–1979. Master's thesis, University of Connecticut, Storrs, Connecticut.

Lougee, R. W. 1957. A Connecticut breeding record for the Blue-gray Gnatcatcher. *Auk* 75:352.

Lucas, W. H. 1891. Florida gallinule in Connecticut. *Ornithologist and Oologist* 16:149.

Lumsden, H. G., J. Robinson, and R. Hartford. 1986. Choice of nest boxes by cavity-nesting ducks. *Wilson Bulletin* 98:167–168.

Lunk, W. A. 1962. The Rough-winged Swallow *Stelgidopteryx ruficollis* (Vieillot): a study based on its breeding biology in Michigan. Publications of the Nuttall Ornithological Club, no. 4. Cambridge, Massachusetts.

Luppi, J. A. 1985. Connecticut birds: Red-bellied Woodpecker. *Connecticut Warbler* 5:35–38.

Lynch, P. J., and D. G. Smith. 1984. Census of Eastern Screech-Owls (*Otus asio*) in urban open-space areas using tape-recorded song. *American Birds* 38:388–391.

MacArthur, R. H. 1972. *Geographical ecology*. Harper and Row, New York.

Mackenzie, L. 1961. *The Birds of Guilford, Connecticut*. Peabody Museum of Natural History, Yale Univ., New Haven, Connecticut.

Magee, A. 1968–1984a. Climax hemlock-white pine forest, with transition hardwoods. *Audubon Field Notes* 22–23; *American Birds* 25, 27–38.

Magee, A. 1968–1984b. Upland brushy pasture. *Audubon Field Notes* 22–23, *American Birds* 25, 27–38.

Magee, A. 1968–1987. Second-growth hardwood forest. *Audubon Field Notes* 22–23, *American Birds* 25, 27–38. (1984–1987 unpublished, at Cornell Laboratory of Ornithology).

Magee, A. 1979–1987. Red pine plantation. *American Birds* 33–38. (1984–1987 unpublished, at Cornell Laboratory of Ornithology).

Magee, A., and J. Cavanaugh. 1967. Upland brushy pasture. *Audubon Field Notes* 21:656.

Manter, J. A. 1975. *Birds of Storrs, Connecticut, and vicinity*. 2d ed. Natchaug Ornithological Society, Storrs, Connecticut.

Marra, P., and M. Bull. 1986a. The Norwalk Island heron colonies: a history. *Connecticut Warbler* 6:23–26.

Marra, P., and M. Bull. 1986b. Dispersal of herons from Chimon Island. *Connecticut Warbler* 6:44–47.

Martin, T. E. 1988. On the advantage of being different. *Proceedings of the National Academy of Science* 85:2196–2199.

Mayfield, H. F. 1965. The Brown-headed Cowbird with old and new hosts. *Living Bird* 4:13–28.

Mayr, E., J. Kuerzi, and R. Kuerzi. 1937. Additional notes from Litchfield County, Connecticut. *Proceedings of the Linnaean Society of New York* 48:98.

McNair, D. B. 1985. An auxiliary with a mated pair and food-caching behavior in the Fish Crow. *Wilson Bulletin* 97:123–125.

Meanley, B., and D. K. Wetherbee. 1962. Ecological notes on mixed populations of King Rails and Clapper Rails in Delaware Bay marshes. *Auk* 79:453–457.

Mendall, H. L., and C. M. Aldous. 1943. *The ecology and management of the American Woodcock*. Maine Cooperative Wildlife Research Unit, Orono, Maine.

Mengel, R. 1965. The Birds of Kentucky. *Ornithological Monographs* no. 2.

Merola, P. R. 1991. Waterfowl population studies. Connecticut Department of Environmental Protection, Wildlife Bureau, Federal Aid Project Report W-49-R-16.

Merola, P. R. and G. G. Chasko. 1989. Waterfowl in Connecticut. Connecticut Department of Environmental Protection, Wildlife Bureau Publication no. WF-4.

Merola, P. R. and G. G. Chasko. 1990. Tidal marsh assessment. Connecticut Department of Environmental Protection, Wildlife Bureau, Federal Aid Project Report W-49-R-15.

Merriam, C. H. 1877. *A review of the birds of Connecticut with remarks on their habits*. Transactions of the Connecticut Academy, Vol. 4. New Haven, Connecticut.

Middleton, A. L. A. 1979. Influence of age and habitat on reproduction by the American Goldfinch. *Ecology* 60:418–432.

Miller, L. J. 1978. The spatial and temporal dispersions of nests as an adaptation to food exploitation and nest predation in the American Goldfinch. Dissertation Abstracts International B39:57–58.

Mills, A. M. 1986. The influence of moonlight on the behavior of goatsuckers (Caprimulgidae). *Auk* 103:370–378.

Minot, H. D. 1877. *The land-birds and game-birds of New England*. Naturalist's Agency, Salem, Massachusetts. 2d ed. 1895. Edited by W. Brewster. Houghton, Mifflin and Company, Boston.

Minser, W.G., and J. L. Byford. 1981. Developing quail habitat on farmland. *Journal of Soil and Water Conservation* 36:17–18.

Montagna, W. 1942. The Sharp-tailed Sparrows of the Atlantic coast. *Wilson Bulletin* 54:107–120.

Morris, R. O. 1901. *The birds of Springfield*. Henry R. Johnson, Springfield, Massachusetts.

Moseley, L. H., L. L. Barkman, and P. Brody. 1968–1984. Mixed upland habitat and swamp. *Audubon Field Notes* 22–24, *American Birds* 25–38.

Mosher, J. A., and C. J. Henny. 1976. Thermal adaptiveness of plumage color in screech owls. *Auk* 93:614–619.

Moss, W. W., and J. H. Camin. 1970. Nest parasitism, productivity and clutch size in the Purple Martin. *Science* 168:1000–1002.

Mulliken, E. H. 1938. Waterfowl, rail and shorebirds commonly hunted for sport in Connecticut. Mimeograph, Connecticut Fish and Game.

Nice, M. M. 1964. *Studies in the life history of the Song Sparrow*. Reprint. Dover, New York.

Nichols, C. K. 1953. The nesting season, Hudson-St. Lawrence region. *Audubon Field Notes* 7:298–302.

Nichols, C. K. 1956. The spring season, Hudson-St. Lawrence region. *Audubon Field Notes* 10:316–320.

Nichols, C. K. 1959. The nesting season, Hudson-St. Lawrence region. *Audubon Field Notes* 13:355–358.

Nisbet, I. C. T. 1971. The Laughing Gull in the northeast. *American Birds* 25:677–683.

Nisbet, I. C. T. 1973. Terns in Massachusetts: present numbers and historical changes. *Bird-Banding* 43:27–55.

Nisbet, I. C. T. 1980. Status and trends of the Roseate Tern, *Sterna dougallii*, in North America and the Caribbean. Unpublished report, U.S. Fish and Wildlife Service, Office of Endangered Species, Newton Corner, Massachusetts.

Nisbet, I. C. T. 1981. Biological characteristics of the Roseate Tern, *Sterna dougallii*. Unpublished report, U.S. Fish and Wildlife Service, Office of Endangered Species, Newton Corner, Massachusetts.

Nisbet, I. C. T. 1983. Territorial feeding by Common Terns. *Colonial Waterbirds* 6:64–70.

Nisbet, I. C. T. 1984. Migration and winter quarters of North American Roseate Terns as shown by banding recoveries. *Journal of Field Ornithology* 55:1–17.

Nisbet, I. C. T. 1989. Status and biology of the northeastern population of the Roseate Tern (*Sterna dougallii*)—a literature survey and update: 1981–1989. Unpublished report, U.S. Fish and Wildlife Service, Office of Endangered Species, Newton Corner, Massachusetts.

Nolan, V., Jr. 1978. The ecology and behavior of the Prairie Warbler *Dendroica discolor*. Ornithological Monographs no. 26.

Nuttall, T. 1832. *A manual of ornithology of the United States and Canada—The land birds*. 2nd edition with additions. 1840. Hilliard, Gray and Company, Boston.

O'Brien, M., and R. A. Askins. 1985. The effects of Mute Swans on native waterfowl. *Connecticut Warbler* 5:27–31.

Olivieri, A., and L. Pearson. 1992. Monk Parakeets in Bridgeport, Connecticut. *Connecticut Warbler* 12:104–111.

Oring, L. W. 1969. Summer biology of the Gadwall at Delta, Manitoba. *Wilson Bulletin* 81:44–54.

Oring, L. W., and M. L. Knudson. 1972. Monogamy and polyandry in the Spotted Sandpiper. *Living Bird Quarterly* 11:59–73.

Oring, L. W., and D. B. Lank. 1982. Sexual selection, arrival times, philopatry and site fidelity in the polyandrous Spotted Sandpiper. *Behavioral Ecology and Sociobiology* 10:185–191.

Oring, L. W., D. B. Lank, and S. J. Maxson. 1983. Population studies of the polyandrous Spotted Sandpiper. *Auk* 100:272–285.

Ouellet, H. 1967. The distribution of the Cerulean Warbler in the Province of Quebec, Canada. *Auk* 84:272–274.

Owen, R. B., Jr. 1977. American Woodcock. In *Management of migratory shore and upland game birds in North America*, ed. G. C. Sanderson, 149–186. Reprint 1980. University of Nebraska Press, Lincoln, Nebraska.

Palmer, G. E. 1972. Upland beech-maple forest. *American Birds* 26:942.

Palmer, R. S., ed. 1962. *Handbook of North American birds*, Vol. 1, loons through flamingos. Yale University Press, New Haven, Connecticut.

Palmer, R. S., ed. 1976. *Handbook of North American birds*, Vols. 2 and 3, waterfowl (pts. 1 and 2). Yale University Press, New Haven, Connecticut.

Palmer, R. S., ed. 1988. *Handbook of North American birds*, Vols. 4 and 5, diurnal raptors (pts. 1 and 2). Yale University Press, New Haven, Connecticut.

Parkes, K. C. 1951. The genetics of the Golden-winged × Blue-winged Warbler complex. *Wilson Bulletin* 63:4–15.

Parmalee, D. F. 1973. The nest of the Northern Parula. *Living Bird* 12:197–199.

Petersen, W. R. 1989. New England region. *American Birds* 43:1288–1291.

Peterson, R. T. 1980. *A field guide to the birds*. 4th ed. Houghton Mifflin Company, Boston.

Petit, K. E., M. D. Dixon, and R. T. Holmes. 1988. A case of polygyny in the Black-throated Blue Warbler. *Wilson Bulletin* 100:132–134.

Petit, L. J., W. J. Fleming, K. E. Petit, and D. R. Petit. 1987. Nest-box use by Prothonotary Warblers (*Protonotaria citrea*). *Wilson Bulletin* 100:132–134.

Phillips, A. R. 1986. *The known birds of North and Middle America*, Part 1. Allan R. Phillips, Denver, Colorado.

Phillips, A. R. 1991. *The known birds of North and Middle America*, Part 2. Allan R. Phillips, Denver, Colorado.

Pielou, E. C. 1991. *After the ice age: the return of life to glaciated North America*. University of Chicago Press, Chicago.

Pink, E., and O. Waterman. 1980. The birds of Dutchess County, 1964–1979. Ralph T. Waterman Bird Club, Dutchess County, New York.

Pinkowski, B. C. 1979a. Foraging ecology and habitat utilization in the genus *Sialia*. In *The role of insectivorous birds in forest ecosystems*, eds. J. G. Dickson, R. N. Conner, R. R. Fleet, J. C. Kroll, and J. A. Jackson, 165–190. Academic Press, New York.

Pinkowski, B. C. 1979b. Nest site selection in Eastern Bluebirds. *Condor* 81:435–436.

Poole, A. F. 1989. *Ospreys: a natural and unnatural history*. Cambridge University Press, Cambridge.

Post, W., and F. Enders. 1970. Notes on a salt marsh Virginia Rail population. *Kingbird* 20:61–67.

Potter, E. F. 1987. Are starlings really responsible for the decline of the Red-headed Woodpecker? *Chat* 51:38–39.

Poulson, T. C. 1969. Salt and water balance in Seaside and Sharp-tailed Sparrows. *Auk* 86:473–489.

Prescott, D. R. C. 1987. Territorial responses to song playback in allopatric and sympatric populations of Alder (*Empidonax alnorum*) and Willow (*E. traillii*) flycatchers. *Wilson Bulletin* 99:611–619.

Prescott, K. W. 1965. The Scarlet Tanager (*Piranga olivacea*). New Jersey State Museum Investigations, no. 2.

Proctor, N. S. 1972. Population and interaction studies of Seaside and Sharp-tailed Sparrows in a Connecticut salt marsh. Master's thesis, Southern Connecticut State College, New Haven.

Proctor, N. S. 1978. *Twenty-five birding areas in Connecticut*. Pequot Press, Chester, Connecticut.

Proctor, N. S. 1981. The Black Rail: mystery bird of the marsh. *Connecticut Warbler* 1:15–16.

Pulliam, H. R. 1988. Sources, sinks, and population regulation. *American Naturalist* 132:652–661.

Purdie, H. A. 1877. Notice of a few birds of rare or accidental occurrence in New England. *Bulletin of the Nuttall Ornithological Club* 2:20–22.

Pyle, P., S. N. G. Howell, R. P. Yunick, and D. F. DeSante. 1987. *Identification guide to North American passerines*. Slate Creek Press, Bolinas, CA.

Raach, A., and B. Leisler. 1989. Auswirkung der Jungenerfahrung auf die Wahl von Habitatstrukturen und auf das Erkundungsverhalten des Mariskensangers (*Acrocephalus melanopogon*). [The role of early experience in the selection of habitat structures and in exploratory behavior of the Moustached Warbler.] *Journal für Ornithologie* 130:256–259.

Ralph, C. J., and J. M. Scott, eds. 1981. Estimating numbers of terrestrial birds. *Studies in Avian Biology* no. 6.

Ramos, M. A., and D. W. Warner. 1980. Analysis of North American subspecies of migrant birds wintering in Los Tuxtlas, southern Veracruz, Mexico. In *Migrant birds in the neotropics*, eds. A. Keast and E. S. Morton, 173–180. Smithsonian Institution Press, Washington, D.C.

Rappole, J. H., E. S. Morton, T. E. Lovejoy, and J. L. Ruos. 1983. Nearctic avian migrants in the Neotropics. U.S. Fish and Wildlife Service, Washington, D.C.

Ricklefs, R. E. 1989. Nest predation and the species diversity of birds. *Trends in Ecology and Evolution* 4:184–186.

Ridgely, R. S., and J. A. Gwynne, Jr. 1989. *A guide to the birds of Panama*. 2d ed. Princeton University Press, Princeton, New Jersey.

Ridgway, R. 1902. The birds of North and Middle America. *U.S. National Museum Bulletin* no. 50, pt. 2. Washington, D.C.

Ridgway, R. 1904. The birds of North and Middle America. *U.S. National Museum Bulletin* no. 50, pt. 3. Washington, D.C.

Ridgway, R. 1914. The birds of North and Middle America. *U.S. National Museum Bulletin* no. 50, pt. 6. Washington, D.C.

Riegner, M. F. 1982. The diet of Yellow-crowned Night-Herons in the eastern and southern United States. *Colonial Waterbirds* 5:173–176.

Ripley, S. D. 1957. *A paddling of ducks*. Harcourt, Brace, and Co., New York.

Ripley, S. D. 1977. *Rails of the world*. M. F. Feheley, Toronto.

Ripley, S. D. 1988. On the occurrence of a pair of Red-bellied Woodpeckers in northwestern Connecticut. *Connecticut Warbler* 8 (4):88–89.

Robbins, C. S. 1979. Effect of forest fragmentation on bird populations. In *Management of north central forests for nongame birds*, ed. R. M. DeGraaf. U.S. Forest Service, General Technical Report NC-51.

Robbins, C. S. 1990. Use of breeding bird atlases to monitor population change. In *Survey design and statistical methods for the estimation of avian population trends*, eds. J. R. Sauer and S. Droege, 18–22. U.S. Fish and Wildlife Service, Biological Report 90(1).

Robbins, C. S., B. Bruun, and H. S. Zim. 1966. *Birds of North America*. Golden Press, New York.

Robbins, C. S., D. Bystrak, and P. H. Geissler. 1986. *The breeding bird survey: its first fifteen years, 1965–1979*. U.S. Fish and Wildlife Service, Resource Publication 157.

Robbins, C. S., D. K. Dawson, and B. A. Dowell. 1989a. Habitat area requirements of breeding forest birds in the Middle Atlantic States. *Wildlife Monographs* 103:1–34.

Robbins, C. S., J. R. Sauer, R. S. Greenberg, and S. Droege. 1989b. Population declines in North American birds that migrate to the neotropics. *Proceedings of the National Academy of Sciences* 86:7658–7662.

Robertson, R. J., and H. L. Gibbs. 1982. Superterritoriality in Tree Swallows: a re-examination. *Condor* 84:313–316.

Robinson, S. K., and R. T. Holmes. 1982. Foraging behavior of forest birds: the relationships among search tactics, diet, and habitat structure. *Ecology* 63:1918–1931.

Robinson, S. K., and R. T. Holmes. 1984. Effects of plant species and foliage structure on the foraging behavior of forest birds. *Auk* 101:672–684.

Rodgers, R. D. 1983. Reducing wildlife losses to tillage in fallow wheat fields. *Wildlife Society Bulletin* 11:31–38.

Root, T. 1988. *Atlas of wintering North American birds: An analysis of Christmas Bird Count data.* University of Chicago Press, Chicago.

Roseberry, J. L., and W. D. Klimstra. 1970. The nesting ecology and reproductive performance of the Eastern Meadowlark. *Wilson Bulletin* 82:243–267.

Roseberry, J. L., and W. D. Klimstra. 1984. *Population ecology of the Bobwhite.* Southern Illinois University Press, Carbondale, Illinois.

Rosgen, D. 1986. Connecticut field notes, summer 1985. *Connecticut Warbler* 6:11–13.

Rosgen, D. 1987. Connecticut field notes, summer 1986. *Connecticut Warbler* 7:9–12.

Rosgen, D., and J. M. Zingo. 1993. The Connecticut bluebird restoration project: successfully managing for the Eastern Bluebird and other native cavity-nesting birds. *Connecticut Warbler* 13:91–103.

Rusch, D. H., C. D. Ankney, H. Boyd, J. R. Longcore, F. Montalbano, J. K. Ringelman and V. D. Stotts. 1989. Population ecology and harvest of the American Black Duck: a review. *Wildlife Society Bulletin* 17:379–406.

Sabo, S. R. 1980. Niche and habitat relations in subalpine bird communities of the White Mountains of New Hampshire. *Ecological Monographs* 50:241–259.

Safina, C. 1990a. Foraging habitat partitioning in Roseate and Common Terns. *Auk* 107:351–358.

Safina, C. 1990b. Bluefish mediation of foraging competition between Roseate and Common Terns. *Ecology* 71:1804–1809.

Safina, C., J. Burger, M. Gochfeld, and R. H. Wagner. 1988. Evidence for prey limitation of Common and Roseate Tern reproduction. *Condor* 90:852–859.

Sage, J. H., L. B. Bishop, and W. P. Bliss. 1913. *The Birds of Connecticut.* Connecticut Geological and Natural History Survey Bulletin no. 20.

Samuel, D. E. 1969. House Sparrow occupancy of Cliff Swallow nests. *Wilson Bulletin* 81:103–104.

Samuels, E. A. 1867. *Ornithology and oology of New England.* Nichols and Noyes, Boston.

Samuels, E. A. 1883. *Our northern and eastern birds.* R. Worthington, New York.

Saunders, A. A. 1922. A question concerning the distribution of the Long-billed Marsh Wren. *Auk* 39:267–268.

Saunders, A. A. 1936. *Ecology of the birds of Quaker Run Valley, Allegheny State Park, New York.* New York State Museum Handbook no. 16.

Saunders, A. A. 1950. Changes in status of Connecticut birds. *Auk* 67:253–255.

Savard, J. P. L., and J. B. Falls. 1981. Influence of habitat structure in the nesting height of birds in urban areas. *Canadian Journal of Zoology* 59:924–932.

Schorger, A. W. 1952. Introduction of the domestic pigeon. *Auk* 69:462–463.

Schorger, A. W. 1966. *The Wild Turkey: its history and domestication.* University of Oklahoma Press, Norman, Oklahoma.

Schuchert, C. 1914. *Mammut americanum* in Connecticut. *The American Journal of Science* 187:321–330.

Scoville, S., Jr. 1934. The nesting of the Canada Warbler in Connecticut. *Auk* 51:526.

Sealey, S. G. 1985. Erect posture of the young Black-billed Cuckoo: an adaptation for early mobility in a nomadic species. *Auk* 102:889–892.

Serrentino, P., and M. England. 1989. Northern Harrier. In *Proceedings of the northeast raptor management symposium and workshop*. National Wildlife Federation, Washington, D. C.

Seutin, G. 1991. Morphometric identification of Traill's Flycatchers: an assessment of Stein's formula. *Journal of Field Ornithology* 62:308–313.

Sharrock, J. T. R., ed. 1976. *The atlas of breeding birds in Britain and Ireland*. British Trust for Ornithology, Tring, England.

Sherry, T. W., and R. T. Holmes. 1988. Habitat selection by breeding American Redstarts in response to a dominant competitor, the Least Flycatcher. *Auk* 105:350–364.

Shoemaker, V. H. 1972. Osmoregulation and excretion in birds. In *Avian biology*, Vol. 2, eds. D. S. Farner, J. R. King, and K. C. Parkes, 527–574. Academic Press, New York.

Short, L. L. 1966. Field Sparrow sings Chipping Sparrow song. *Auk* 83:665.

Shy, E. 1984. Habitat shift and geographical variation in North American tanagers (Thraupinae: *Piranga*). *Oecologia* 63:281–285.

Sibley, D. A. 1988. *Cape May bird report—1987*. Cape May Bird Observatory, Cape May, New Jersey.

Sibley, F. C., and M. G. Bull. 1990. Tabulation of survey results on Connecticut islands from 1977 to 1989. Unpublished report to Department of Environmental Protection, Wildlife Bureau.

Sibley, F. C., and R. Schwartz. 1985. The 1983 colonial seabird survey. *Connecticut Warbler* 5:40–43.

Skutch, A. F. 1987. Helpers at birds' nests. University of Iowa Press, Iowa City, Iowa.

Smith, C. C., and R. P. Balda. 1979. Competition among insects, birds and mammals for conifer seeds. *American Zoologist* 19:1065–1083.

Smith, C. F. 1978. Distributional ecology of Barred and Great Horned Owls in relation to human disturbance. Master's thesis, University of Connecticut, Storrs, Connecticut.

Smith, C. R., ed. 1990. *Handbook for atlasing American breeding birds*. Vermont Institute of Natural Science, Woodstock, Vermont.

Smith, D. G., and A. Devine. 1993. Winter ecology of the Long-eared Owl in Connecticut. *Connecticut Warbler* 13:44–53.

Smith, D. G., A. Devine, and R. Gilbert. 1987. Screech Owl roost site selection. *Birding* 19:6–15.

Smith, D. G., A. Devine, and D. Walsh. 1987. Censusing (Eastern) Screech-Owls in southern Connecticut. In *Biology and conservation of northern forest owls*, eds. R. W. Nero, R. J. Clark, R. J. Knapton, and R. H. Hamre, 255–267. U.S. Forest Service, General Technical Report RM-142.

Smith, K. G. 1986. Winter population dynamics of three species of mast-eating birds in the eastern United States. *Wilson Bulletin* 98:407–418.

Spendelow, J. A. 1982. An analysis of temporal variation in, and the effects of habitat modification on, the reproductive success of Roseate Terns. *Colonial Waterbirds* 5:19–31.

Spendelow, J.A. 1991a. Half-buried tires enhance Roseate Tern reproductive success. U.S. Fish and Wildlife Service, Research Information Bulletin 91–14.

Spendelow, J.A. 1991b. Postfledging survival and recruitment of known-origin Roseate Terns (*Sterna dougallii*) at Falkner Island, Connecticut. *Colonial Waterbirds* 14:108–115.

Spendelow, J. A., and S. R. Patton. 1988. National atlas of coastal waterbird colonies in the contiguous United States: 1976–1982. U.S. Fish and Wildlife Service, Biological Report 88(5).

Spitzer, P. R. 1978. Osprey egg and nestling transfers: their value as ecological experiments and as management procedures. In *Endangered birds: management techniques for preserving threatened species*, ed. S. A. Temple, 171–182. University of Wisconsin Press, Madison, Wisconsin.

Spitzer, P. R., A. F. Poole, and M. Scheibel. 1983. Initial population recovery of breeding Ospreys in the region between New York City and Boston. In *Biology and management of Bald Eagles and Ospreys*, ed. D. Bird, 231–241. Harpell Press, Ste. Anne de Bellevue, Quebec.

Spitzer, P. R., R. W. Risebrough, W. Walker, R. Hernandez, A. Poole, D. Puleston, and I. C. T. Nisbet. 1978. Productivity of Ospreys in Connecticut—Long Island increases as DDE residues decline. *Science* 202:333–335.

Stalmaster, M. U. 1987. *The Bald Eagle*. Universe Books, New York.

Stauffer, D. F., and L. B. Best. 1982. Nest-site selection by cavity nesting birds of riparian habitats in Iowa. *Wilson Bulletin* 94:329–337.

Steadman, D. W. 1988. Prehistoric birds of New York state. In *The atlas of breeding birds in New York state*, eds. R. F. Andrle and J. R. Carroll, 19–24. Cornell University Press, Ithaca, New York.

Stearns, W. A., and E. Coues. 1881. *New England bird life, part I: oscines*. Lee and Shepard, Boston.

Stearns, W. A., and E. Coues. 1883. *New England bird life, part II: non-oscine passeres, birds of prey, game and water birds*. Lee and Shepard, Boston.

Stedman, S. J. 1987. Nesting habitat of Willow Flycatchers in Tennessee. *Migrant* 58:49–50.

Stein, R. C. 1958. The behavioral, ecological and morphological characteristics of two populations of the Alder Flycatcher, *Empidonax traillii* (Audubon). New York State Museum and Science Service Bulletin 371:1–63.

Stein, R. C. 1963. Isolating mechanisms between populations of Traill's Flycatchers. *Proceedings of the American Philosophical Society* 107:21–50.

Stiles, E. W. 1982. Expansions of mockingbird and multiflora rose in the northeastern United States and Canada. *Am. Birds* 36:358–364.

Stiles, F. G., and A. F. Skutch. 1989. *A guide to the birds of Costa Rica*. Cornell University Press, Ithaca, New York.

Stone, W. 1937. *Bird studies at old Cape May*. 2 vols. Delaware Valley Ornithological Club, Philadelphia.

Suchecki, J. L. 1974a. Upland oak-maple forest. *American Birds* 28:990–991.

Suchecki, J. L. 1974b. Hemlock-white pine-hardwood. *American Birds* 28:1012–1013.

Summers-Smith, D. 1963. *The House Sparrow*. Collins, London

Taber, W. 1951. The northern element in the summer bird life of south-central New England. *Wilson Bulletin* 63:69–74.

Tate, J., Jr. 1981. The Blue List for 1981. *American Birds* 35:3–10.

Tate, J., Jr. 1986. The Blue List for 1986. *American Birds* 40:221–236.

Tate, J., Jr., and D. J. Tate. 1982. The Blue List for 1982. *American Birds* 36:126–135.

Taylor, C. 1989. Connecticut field notes, summer 1988. *Connecticut Warbler* 9:7–13.

Terborgh, J. 1989. *Where have all the birds gone?* Princeton University Press, Princeton, New Jersey.

Thompson, C. F., and V. Nolan, Jr. 1973. Population ecology of the Yellow-breasted Chat (*Icteria virens*) in southern Indiana. *Ecological Monographs* 43:145–171.

Todd, W. E. C. 1940. *Birds of western Pennsylvania*. University of Pittsburgh Press, Pittsburgh, Pennsylvania.

Tuck, L. M. 1972. *The snipes*. Canadian Wildlife Service Monograph Series no. 5.

Tufts, R. W. 1986. Birds of Nova Scotia. 3rd ed. (I. A. McLaren ed.). Nimbus and The Nova Scotia Museum, Halifax, Nova Scotia.

Turner, A., and C. Rose. 1989. *Swallows & martins*. Houghton Mifflin Company, Boston.

Turner, J. R. G., J. J. Lennon, and J. A. Lawrenson. 1988. British bird species distribution and the energy theory. *Nature* 335:539–541.

Tyrrell, R. A., and E. Q. Tyrrell. 1985. Hummingbirds: their life and behavior. Crown Publishers, New York.

USFWS (U.S. Fish and Wildlife Service). 1989. Roseate Tern recovery plan—northeastern population. U.S. Fish and Wildlife Service, Office of Endangered Species, Newton Corner, Massachusetts.

Varza, D. 1985. Connecticut field notes, summer 1984. *Connecticut Warbler* 5:9–11.

Varza, D., and D. Rosgen. 1987. Connecticut field notes, summer 1986. *Connecticut Warbler* 7:9–12.

LITERATURE CITED

Vassallo, M. I., and J. C. Rice. 1982. Ecological release and ecological flexibility in habitat use and foraging of an insular avifauna. *Wilson Bulletin* 94:139–155.

Verner, J., and G. H. Engelsen. 1970. Territories, multiple nest building and polygyny in the Long-billed Marsh Wren. *Auk* 87:557–567.

Veit, R. R., and W. R. Petersen. 1993. *Birds of Massachusetts*. Massachusetts Audubon Society, Lincoln, Massachusetts.

Vickery, P. D. 1977a. The spring migration, Northeastern Maritime Region. *American Birds* 31:972–977.

Vickery, P. D. 1977b. The nesting season, Northeastern Maritime Region. *American Birds* 31:1110–1114.

Vickery, P. D. 1978. The spring migration, Northeastern Maritime Region. *American Birds* 32:977–981.

Voorhees, C. G. 1893. Occurrence and breeding of the Kentucky Warbler in Connecticut. *Auk* 10:86.

Wackenhut, P. B., K. A. Strait, and R. C. Whitmore. 1983. Probable investigator-induced egg drop by a Horned Lark. *Wilson Bulletin* 95:489–490.

Walsberg, G. E. 1981. Nest-site selection and the radiative environment of the Warbling Vireo. *Condor* 83:86–88.

Walton, R. K. 1984. *Birds of the Sudbury River Valley: an historical perspective*. Massachusetts Audubon Society, Lincoln, Massachusetts.

Wheelwright, N. 1986. The diet of American Robins: an analysis of U.S. Biological Survey records. *Auk* 103:710–725.

White, R. P. 1988. Wintering grounds and migration patterns of the Upland Sandpiper. *American Birds* 42:1247–1253.

Whitmore, R. C. 1979. Temporal variation in the selected habitats of a guild of grassland sparrows. *Wilson Bulletin* 91:592–598.

Whitmore, R. C., and G. A. Hall. 1978. The response of passerine species to a new resource: reclaimed surface mines in West Virginia. *American Birds* 32:6–9.

Wiemeyer, S. N., P. I. Spitzer, W. C. Krantz, G. L. Lamont, and E. Cromartie. 1975. Effects of environmental pollutants on Connecticut and Maryland Ospreys. *Journal of Wildlife Management* 39:124–139.

Wiens, J. A. 1969. An approach to the study of ecological relationships among grassland birds. *Ornithological Monographs* no. 8.

Wiens, J. A. 1989. *The ecology of bird communities*. 2 vols. Cambridge University Press, Cambridge.

Wilcove, D. S. 1985. Nest predation in forest tracts and the decline of migratory songbirds. *Ecology* 66:1211–1214.

Willey, C. H. 1968. The ecological significance of the Mute Swan in Rhode Island. *Transactions of the Northeast Section of the Wildlife Society* 25:121–134.

Willey, C. H., and B. F. Halla. 1972. *Mute Swans of Rhode Island*. Rhode Island Department of Natural Resources, Wildlife Pamphlet no. 8.

Williams, J. B., and G. O. Batzli. 1979. Competition among bark-foraging birds in central Illinois: experimental evidence. *Condor* 81:122–132.

Williamson, K. 1975. Birds and climatic change. *Bird Study* 22:143–164.

Williamson, P. 1971. Feeding ecology of the Red-eyed Vireo (*Vireo olivaceus*) and associated foliage-gleaning birds. *Ecological Monographs* 41:129–152.

Wilson, A. 1808. *American ornithology; or, the natural history of the birds of the United States*, Vol 1. Bradford and Inskeep, Philadelphia.

Wolinski, R. A. 1988. Some bird population changes in Michigan: 1900 to 1965. *Jack-pine Warbler* 66:59–69.

Wood, D. S. 1992. Color and size variation in eastern White-breasted Nuthatches. *Wilson Bulletin* 104:599–611.

Woolfenden, G. E. 1956. *Comparative breeding behavior of* Ammospiza caudacuta *and* A. maritima. University of Kansas Publications, Museum of Natural History, 10:45–75.

Yahner, R. H., and D. P. Scott. 1988. Effects of forest fragmentation on depredation of artificial nests. *Journal of Wildlife Management* 52:158–161.

Zach, R., and J. B. Falls. 1979. Foraging and territoriality of male Ovenbirds (Aves: Parulidae) in a heterogeneous habitat. *Journal of Animal Ecology* 48:33–52.

Zeranski, J. D., and T. R. Baptist. 1990. *Connecticut birds*. University Press of New England, Hanover, New Hampshire.

Zink, R. M., and B. A. Fall. 1981. Breeding distribution, song and habitat of the Alder Flycatcher and Willow Flycatcher in Minnesota. *Loon* 53:208–214.

Zumeta, D. C., and R. T. Holmes. 1978. Habitat shift and roadside mortality of Scarlet Tanagers during a cold wet New England spring. *Wilson Bulletin* 90:575–586.

# Index

## Caveat lector
## IMPORTANT:  limitations of the data

Valid research inquiries regarding the data for the Connecticut breeding bird atlas may be directed to the Natural Resources Center of the Department of Environmental Protection. Those wishing to use the data should be aware of the following:

- The level of effort was not uniform throughout the state, and no measure of effort is possible with these data. In general, the northwestern corner of the state, chiefly Litchfield County, received greater coverage than elsewhere; the northeastern corner of the state, chiefly Tolland and Windham counties, received the least coverage overall but had good local coverage.

- Not all blocks are of equal area. Blocks at the margins of Connecticut's state boundary are portions of blocks within the state. Consult the USGS quadrangles for the area within Connecticut on these partial blocks.

- The islands off Guilford (Goose Is. and Falkner Is.) are included within the blocks at the bottom of the Guilford quadrangle (blocks 097E and 097F; see p. 9, Fig. 1).

- The presence or absence of a species in a *single* block alone usually has little biological significance. Rather, it is the *overall* pattern represented by *several clustered* blocks that suggests the range of the species.

- The list of species for each block is *not comprehensive*. Although people may wish to include the list for a block in an environmental assessment or analysis, it should be noted that:

  a) other bird species were likely present but not noted;

  b) do *not* infer presence or absence in a particular park, forest, preserve, development site, etc., based on the list of species for a given block (some listed species may not be present in the specific area of study although present elsewhere in the block);

  c) some listed species may no longer occur and other species may have moved into the block due to habitat changes since the atlas period.

- It should not be assumed that any block's habitat or bird community composition remained constant throughout the atlas period.

THE ATLAS OF BREEDING BIRDS OF CONNECTICUT

*Designed by Mary Crombie, Acorn Studio*

*Copyediting by Dr. Michael K. Oliver*

*Composed on a Macintosh IIcx,*

*Apple Computer, Inc.*

*using Times amd Gill Sans*

*Printed on recycled paper by*

*Sweet Printing Company*

*Glastonbury, Connecticut*